WAYS OF KNOWING

JEAN-GUY A. GOULET

Ways of Knowing
Experience, Knowledge, and Power among the Dene Tha

University of Nebraska Press

Lincoln & London

⊗ The paper in this book meets the minimum
requirements of American National Standard for
Information Sciences—Permanence of Paper for
Printed Library Materials, ANSI Z39.48-1984.

Library of Congress Cataloging in Publication Data
Goulet, Jean-Guy
Ways of knowing: experience, knowledge, and
power among the Dene Tha / Jean-Guy A. Goulet.
p.   cm. Includes bibliographical references and index.
ISBN 0-8032-2171-1 (cloth: alkaline paper) –
ISBN 0-8032-7074-7 (paperback: alkaline paper)
1. Dene Tha Indians – Social conditions 2. Dene
Tha Indians – Religion. 3. Dene Tha
philosophy. 4. Social change – Alberta –
Chateh. 5. Chateh (Alta.) –
Social life and customs. I. Title.
E99.D25G68 1998
305.897'2071232–dc21
98-20984 CIP

To Christine and Alexis

CONTENTS

Preface

I initiated fieldwork among the Dene Tha in July 1979, and in the course of the twelve following years I spent a total of thirty-six months among them, investigating the processes whereby they represent themselves—to themselves and to others—as an indigenous population with a distinctive world view, epistemology, and ethics. They have retained this distinctive culture despite more than a century of ever increasing participation in numerous Euro-Canadian institutions—economic, religious, educational, medical, political, and judicial.[1] Over the years, as I became more and more involved in Dene Tha lives and ritual activities, I gained a better appreciation of their view of "true knowledge" as personal knowledge. This has led me to investigate Dene Tha social life in the "experiential mode" that Frederick Barth, Michael Jackson, Barbara Tedlock, Unni Wikan, and others have referred to as "radical participation." Recent developments in contemporary anthropology, in particular the anthropology of experience (Bruner 1986a, 1986b, 1993; V. Turner 1985, 1986), narrative ethnography (B. Tedlock 1991a, 1992), and ethnomethodologically inspired analysis of Dene Tha verbatim records (G. Watson 1992, 1996), have come to inform my writing. I now see accounts of personal experience as an integral part of the ethnographic description.

This book is a narrative ethnography and an ethnomethodologically inspired analysis of accounts of experiences lived by both the Dene Tha and myself, as the anthropologist interacting with them. It makes use, with permission gratefully acknowledged, of material published in *Culture* (1989), the *Journal of Anthropological Research* (1994a), and the *Journal of the Royal Anthropological Institute* (1996b), as well as of material used in other publications for which I have retained use rights: parts of an article in the *Canadian Journal of Anthropology* (1982); parts of a chapter in *Amerindian Rebirth*, published by the University of Toronto Press (1994b); parts of a chapter in *Being Changed by Cross-Cultural Encounters*, published by Broadview Press (1994c); and parts of a chapter in *Shamanism and Northern Ecology*, published by Mouton de Gruyter (1996a). I also thank the University of Alberta Press for permission to use parts of an account of a vision by Willy Denechoan published in Steve Simon's *Healing Waters* (1995). Although parts of chapters in this book correspond to parts of previously published material, each thematically oriented chapter introduces extensive new data and novel analysis.

Over the years many friends and colleagues, as well as anonymous reviewers, have commented on various presentations or publications concerning aspects of Dene Tha culture. Their insightful questions, requests for additional information, references to relevant literature, as well as criticism, were very helpful in my efforts to formulate and reformulate findings. I therefore wish to thank here Kenelm Burridge, Harvey Feit, Stan Gibson, Marjorie Halprin, June Helm, Antonia Mills, Patrick Moore, Achiel Peelman, Robin Ridington, Benson Saler, Richard Slobodin, David Smith, Stephen Sharp, Cora Weber-Pillwax, and David Young. Christine Hanssens, Lorna Watson, and Graham Watson deserve a special mention for their attentive, critical reading of the manuscript of this book at various stages of its development and for their numerous helpful comments and suggestions.

A special note of gratitude goes to Patrick Moore, who in 1980 generously permitted access to the manuscript of his grammar of Dene Dháh and who with a Dene Tha in November 1996 went over every quotation in Dene Dháh to correct the spelling where required. I thank Peter Farqharson and Alexandra Bock for their assistance in verifying the accuracy of quotations from anthropological sources. I am grateful to Judy Price and Barbara Wilkes for careful proofreading of the manuscript. I also thank Camile Piché and Jean Marsan for the information provided from the archives of the Missionary Oblates of Mary Immaculate in McLennan, Alberta, concerning the history of the residential school in Chateh. To Robin Poitras, from the University of Calgary Department of Geography, my acknowledgment for the map included in this book. I thank the staff at the University of Nebraska Press for their enthusiastic support. Finally, to Kimberley C. Vivier my appreciation for her fine editorial skills that helped transform my manuscript into a more literate discourse. In the end, however, I alone remain responsible for the views expressed here. Financial support from the Social Sciences and Humanities Research Council of Canada and from the Canadian Research Centre for Anthropology of Saint Paul University, Ottawa, for my research among the Dene Tha, is gratefully acknowledged, as well as a Sabbatical Research Fellowship from the University of Calgary that gave me a full year, from July 1995 to June 1996, to devote to this book. And above all, my gratitude to the people of Chateh, who welcomed me into their lives and homes, taught me patiently over the years, and shared so much with me. *Wohteh setsin wáhjon.*

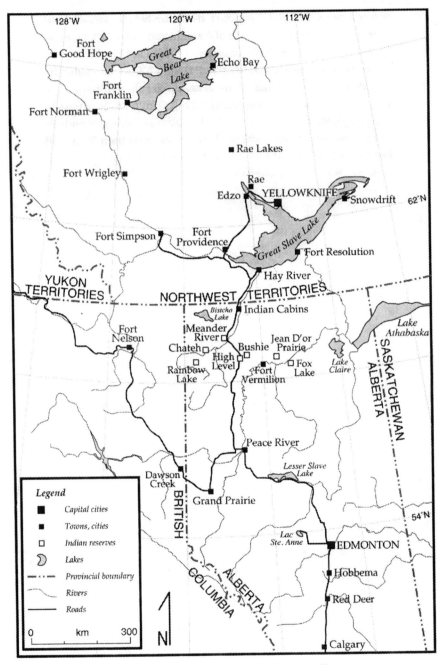

The Dene Tha Homeland and Surroundings

Introduction

*

If you're an Indian, you know what is going on. —Dene Tha speaker

A Dene Tha man and his wife are drinking tea with me at the kitchen table, glancing across the road toward the band office where a judge will soon hold court. Their teenage son will be charged with shooting and nearly killing a close relative. The parents have been telling me how the soul of the child they lost soon after birth was retrieved from heaven and brought back to them to reincarnate. This, they say, was done through the power of older men in the community. The man then shifts the conversation to the impending fate of his son in the hands of the justice. He says: "There are two ways, *chint'e* ['power'] and *yú* [medicine]. You do not say bad medicine. It is good; it is to help others. Some person knows something, his power, he has it. He doesn't like what you do to him. He could think of you one night, and your spirit would follow his power. He could take your spirit, and you get into an accident." The man pauses, looks at his wife, and picks up the conversation again, saying: "Like [that woman] wants to kill him [names a neighbor] through medicine or power, but his mother and dad protect him with their power too. It's like he is in a bottle; they can't get in to you. If you're Indian, you know what is going on; it is really powerful."[1]

When the man and his wife leave to go to court, I wonder about our conversation. A non-Indian judge will decide their son's fate. The parents know that the evidence that counts in the eyes of the Dene Tha is inadmissible in the court of justice. The judge would not accept that their son was the victim of someone who, out of anger, used his power to make their son lose his mind, causing him to shoot a close relative. The judge would not take into consideration the parents' unsuccessful attempt to use their power to protect their son.[2] "If you are an Indian, you know what is going on," concludes the man. Can I, a Euro-Canadian anthropologist, understand what is going on? The couple's mother tongue, life history, culture, and social circumstances differ dramatically from mine. The two nevertheless seek to communicate with me, in the belief that we can make sense of each other. The belief that communication between us is possible is *our* starting point. It is the precondition for our engagement with each other as fellow human beings. Without it "the entire anthropological enterprise would be impossible" (Ingold 1993, 230).

My objective as a sociocultural anthropologist is to comprehend the words, concerns, and behavior of people like this Dene Tha man and woman. My reasons for becoming an anthropologist in the first place lie, in part, in a personal interest going back to childhood. As a child, I often thought about what I might have become had I not been born where I happened to have been born (in Ottawa, Canada, to French Canadian parents), but somewhere else, among "Others." Years later, when I took my first course in anthropology, I recognized immediately the profession that would provide a way to pursue this matter. Here was an occupation that required one to be present in the world of others. The goals of this journey were not only to understand others or to test a particular theoretical proposition. The objective of the profession was also to educate oneself and others about the character of culture, the set of ideas and practices, however implicit, through which we human beings apprehend the world and ourselves in it.

My first experience of fieldwork was among the pastoralist Wayu (Guajiro) of Colombia in 1975 and 1976. I lived three months in a residential school for Guajiro children between five and twenty years of age. Older bilingual Guajiro students became my instructors in *Wayunaiki*, "the language of the Wayu." I studied the language for three months. Then, with the assistance of the family of one of my instructors, I moved to Aipiachi, in the heart of the Guajira peninsula, where I would never hear a word of Spanish. I was to live among people where there were none of the institutions, schools, police stations, missions, banks, markets, and so on that characterize Western and Westernized societies.

When I arrived in Aipiachi with my instructor and his family, we drove up to the household of Martina Püshaina. Martina and her brother, Serria, who lived nearby with three of his wives and three of his married sons, greeted us in the customary way: *ân-*

tüshi pia, "you have arrived," to which I answered, *âa ântüshi taya,* "yes, I have arrived." We followed this with a bit of conversation, and then I went to the nearby cooking area where Martina's daughter, America, was cooking a meal. America greeted me: *jama tawala,* "how are you, my brother." My kinship identity in the family and locality was thus decided. America's mother, brothers, and maternal uncles became mine too. America's mother then asked my instructor whether I knew how to dream. I answered in the affirmative, which, my instructor later told me, was a necessary condition for my acceptance in the family and locality. I was surprised at such a condition and at the time could not appreciate its significance. In due course I became aware of and participated in a complex system of dreaming and dream telling that is at the very core of the Guajiro way of life, a system in which animals dreamed-of represent human beings and vice versa (Goulet 1978, 1994c; Watson-Franke 1981; Perrin 1992).

In the days that followed my arrival in Martina's family, I was introduced to every household in Aipiachi. All the residents were pointed out to me, and their kinship and/or affinal relationship to me were specified. For the next ten months, I was greeted and I greeted others as kinsmen. In the event of a birth, of a marriage and the transfer of bride wealth to the woman's family, of a compensation sought for an injury or for a death, or of a funeral, I was expected to participate according to my kin relationship to those involved. So, as an adopted member of a polygamist extended family, I witnessed a way of life totally foreign to my own. It became my task to describe and analyze the social organization and religion of the Wayu and to demonstrate how they had recourse to complex mechanisms of ritual exchange and social control to constitute relatively stable and enduring clusters of populations in various locales across the Guajira peninsula (Goulet 1978, 1980, 1981).

My second experience of fieldwork has been among the Dene Tha of northwestern Alberta, Canada. In 1978 I was appointed part-time researcher at Saint Paul University's Canadian Research Centre for Anthropology. The Dene Tha of northwestern Alberta rapidly became the main focus of my research interest. Europeans and their descendants have encouraged, and at times coerced, the Dene to adopt Canadian forms of economic activity, political processes, health care, and religious life.[3] I wanted to study the interaction between "Others" and Euro-Canadians who attempt to use their institutions and values to shape the lives of those they seek to colonize and/or assimilate.

The resulting social change is there for everyone to see: the Dene hunt, trap, and engage in the fur trade, but they also participate marginally in the labor market; they draw on old-age pensions, unemployment insurance, and welfare to meet more and more of their daily needs; they elect representatives to their band councils and pass bylaws to regulate activities on the reserve; they experience periodically high levels of violence related to alcohol abuse; they visit the local health station to be cared for by local nurses and visiting doctors; they declare themselves Roman Catholics and engage in Christian rituals.

In such a context one might be tempted to join the chorus of earlier researchers who since the 1920s have characterized Native North American societies as suffering from "deculturation," "disorganization," and "disintegration." According to William Koolage (1975, 45–46), anthropologists who applied such constructs to their observations of Dene societies failed to consider the many ways in which the Dene were creatively adapting to their new socioeconomic circumstances. Why? Because anthropologists largely engaged in short periods of fieldwork and thus lacked the time to learn the language, to observe seldom-occurring events, and to come to an appreciation of the relationships between Dene concepts and practices (Koolage 1975, 52). Koolage hoped for a different kind of anthropological account of social life among the Dene of the subarctic. He invited anthropologists to abandon negative assessments of Dene communities and to engage constructively with the Dene themselves in their creative efforts to constitute a living culture.

If not disintegration of the old ways, what then was taking place in Chateh? I could not deny that at face value the Dene Tha were behaving more and more like the Euro-Canadians they were taught to emulate. I still wanted to find out if the Dene Tha had actually repudiated their own institutions and values to embrace the new. I wondered if they would, or could, live compartmentalized lives, indigenous in some contexts, Euro-Canadian in others. I knew the Dene Tha practiced a version of the Prophet

Introduction

Dance complex, through which an indigenous world view is expressed, transformed, and conveyed. Could I find among the Dene Tha evidence in support of Victor Turner's understanding of the "creative function" of ritual performance as a means of creating and re-creating "the categories through which men perceive reality" (1968, 7)? It was with these questions in mind that I approached the Dene Tha of Chateh.

Answers to such questions require sharing for a considerable time the daily life of the Dene Tha, to know them "not only as players of social roles, but as unique individuals, each with a style and a personality of his or her own" (V. Turner 1975, 29). According to Johannes Fabian (1991, 398), "shared time (not just in its almost abstract meaning, which puts the emphasis on shared, but also in its concrete meaning that stresses *time passed together*)" is a precondition to the production of ethnographic knowledge (emphasis in original). Passing time together is to engage jointly in social activities, to share a meal, to dance together, to participate in a healing ceremony, and so on, as described extensively in chapter 1. When people are known as individuals in their day-to-day activities, ethnographic data can be placed in the proper context.

Understanding Dene Tha individuals also depends on an ability on our part to listen to Dene Tha accounts of their lives as they are told in Dene Dháh, their native tongue. It is common knowledge among anthropologists that the complexity and richness of an indigenous apprehension and comprehension of the world is best conveyed in the indigenous language. My experience with the Wayu had taught me that bilingual Guajiro speakers simplified Guajiro reality when speaking in Spanish with anthropologists. In many instances I came to understand what the Dene Tha told me in English only after asking them to tell me the "same" in Dene Dháh and then asking them to translate this second account back into English. The final English account always differed in important aspects from the initial one. It was closer to the original Dene Tha concepts the speaker had in mind. Moreover, close association with the Dene Elders and prophets would have been impossible without a certain command of Dene Dháh. For instance, I was invited to the house of the head prophet for drumming lessons only when I was able to communicate with him in Dene Dháh and had demonstrated a willingness to interact with the Dene Tha on their terms.

This book, therefore, presents my understanding of Dene Tha social life in the form of a narrative ethnography. It is the result of an exercise in radical participation such as is advocated by proponents of "experience-near" anthropology. It encompasses fine-grained accounts of Dene Tha life experiences. These include the pursuit of knowledge based on personal experience and observation rather than on instruction; the vision quest and the gift from animals to humans of a power to heal and to harm; the tensions in a social life in which the professed regard for one another's autonomy goes hand in hand with overt or covert expressions of animosity; the interaction with the dead through dreams and/or visions; the birth of children seen as cases of reincarnation; and the ways of knowing and praying, expressed in daily lives as well as in the Prophet Dance, that enable the Dene Tha to incorporate and reinterpret, according to a distinctively Northern Athapaskan view, the Christian symbols and rituals introduced among them over more than a century of missionary activity.

THE DENE THA WORLD, YESTERDAY AND TODAY

In the anthropological literature the people of Chateh are referred to as Slavey (Asch 1981, 348; 1986), as "the Hay River, Albertan Beaver Indians" (Mills 1982, 67), as "the Dene Tha branch of the Beaver Indians" (J. Smith 1987, 444), or as the "Hay Lakes Alberta Dene" (Helm 1994, 15). Chateh, also known as Assumption (see map in Asch 1981, 338), is listed by the Department of Indian and Northern Affairs, Canada (1987, 91), as the reservation of Hay Lakes (the name officially given to the band in 1953 by the federal government), with a population of 809 in December 1986. In its 1991 census figures the government of Canada reports a total population with aboriginal rights of 750 residing in Hay Lakes and 115 residing in Bushie River, near High Level.

The three names, Hay Lakes, Assumption, and Chateh, reflect distinct phases in the history of the Dene Tha and in their relationship to state and church. Hay Lakes, some thirteen kilometers north from the present-day site of Chateh, was a seasonal place of gathering for the Dene Tha until the mid-1940s. The

DeneTha knew the site for its rich wildlife (fish, moose, deer, beaver, muskrat, ducks, and geese), its abundant pasture for their horses, and its proximity to their traplines extending westward and northward toward and into British Columbia. In spring and fall the Dene Tha would come from Meander River to Hay Lakes to hunt duck and geese.

In 1900 the Dene Tha signed Treaty 8. Unknowingly, they became subject to the Indian Act and to the Department of Indian Affairs. The department's mandate was to look after the welfare of the Dene Tha, to promote their assimilation into mainstream Canadian society, and to open the former territory of the Dene Tha to peaceful settlement and exploitation by Europeans and Euro-Canadians. A band membership list was therefore drawn naming all the individuals who could live on the land set aside for the Dene Tha. Adult members were called on to elect a chief and a council to act as the local indigenous counterpart to the Indian agent and other officials from the Department of Indian Affairs.

The Dene Tha understood the treaty as a means of establishing a kinship-like alliance between themselves and the Canadian government.[4] The treaty-signing ceremony was concluded with a gift of money from the federal government to each of the band members. This money, says a Dene Tha Elder, was "not to sell anything but to make us brothers and sisters. That is what my father, who saw them give money to the people, used to say. It [the treaty] will not be a lie for God as long as night follows night, and as long as the sun lasts, and as long as the water flows." Every year since, in midsummer, the federal government sends an agent, nowadays usually an officer of the Royal Canadian Mounted Police, to hand over the five-dollar bill it promised to give annually to each band member. In Dene Dháh, treaty day is appropriately called "the day they give money to people."

In the years that followed the signing of Treaty 8, the Dene Tha experienced minimal contact with Euro-Canadians. Although the Dene Tha hunting and gathering activities were by then well articulated with the wider capitalist system of mercantile exchange through the fur trade, contact was limited to the occasional visit to the Hudson Bay trading post in Fort Vermillion, on the banks of the Athapaska River, where the Dene Tha would sell their furs and purchase their supplies of flour, lard, tea, sugar, ammunition, and the like for a new round of hunting or trapping on the land. Throughout the subarctic, in the absence of economic developments designed to exploit intensively the region's natural resources, "the almost static conditions that prevailed until about 1950 were the result of deliberate policy . . . designed to preserve the early postcontact *status quo* as nearly as possible, in order to retain the fur trade and its resources" (Slobodin 1975, 285). In this way indigenous populations provided for all their needs at a minimal cost to the Canadian government.

After the fur traders, the missionaries became the most significant outsiders to the Dene Tha. Missionaries first sought to convert them to Roman Catholicism and later operated a residential school to instruct Dene Tha children in Euro-Canadian ways. In 1917 Father Joseph Habay, O.M.I., built a rudimentary log chapel on the shore of Hay Lakes, where he carried out his missionary work (the site was named after him in 1953). He was followed by Father Arbet, who built another chapel at Hay Lakes in 1927–28. Dene Tha Elders recall how Father Arbet would travel by dog team from Habay to visit the Dene Tha families dispersed throughout northwestern Alberta and British Columbia. The relationship between the Dene Tha and the missionary who ate with them and slept in their house, lying, like them, on the floor, was one of hospitality and puzzlement. In the words of one devout Catholic woman, "Before we go to mission [meaning the residential school], Father Arbet used to come to visit us in the bush. We get pictures of Mary and Jesus, but we do not know what they are. We laugh and say, 'This woman looks like this woman.' We learn to do the sign of the cross when we pray, and we laugh a lot then. It's funny to us. But when we got in mission, then we learned a lot."

A few Dene and Cree families established themselves at Habay near the church, with the missionaries. A larger settlement came into existence in the mid-1930s when four brothers from Meander River, along with their families and other relatives, established a base for their hunting and trapping activities in Hay Lakes. "Before we moved here, we were all people from Meander," said a Dene Tha in his fifties, "but here [in Hay Lakes] our parents died and were buried here, that is why we are from here."

In 1938 and again in 1948 the Dene Tha requested that a residential school and hospital be built in Hay Lakes. In a letter dated 17 July 1948 the band chief wrote to the Minister of Mines in Ottawa as follows: "We Hay Lakes Indians take the liberty of submitting to you some communications and asking you a few questions. We are Indians, poor, ignorant, and we start to realize our situation among white people. We are trappers part in Alberta and part in British Columbia. But trapping is getting so poor that some of us might have to find work amongst white people but only 6 of us have been at school at Fort Vermillion and can speak english [sic]." In this letter the chief expressed the widely shared notion among Native North American Indians that powerful and wealthy individuals have as an obligation to assist those who are less fortunate. The chief underlined the need for a local hospital, given the band's hardships and the seventeen deaths in the previous year, "3 of old age, 1 childbirth, 1 pneumonia, the other 12 were T.B. [tuberculosis]." The chief then added that the band wanted a local boarding school, "because it is impossible for us to send our children to a day school." This was so because band members traveled considerable distances from Hay Lakes to their traplines in northwestern Alberta or northeastern British Columbia. The chief noted that long journeys in the bush made it "very difficult, not to say impossible to carry with dogs enough supplies 80 miles away, for big families like we have."

Following this petition, construction of a boarding school soon began, not at Hay Lakes but at a site thirteen kilometers inland. Less liable to flooding, this location was deemed more appropriate for a residential school and an adjacent farm to support its staff and pupils. It is on this site, named Assumption, that in February 1951 the missionaries opened their residential school to 74 children (28 boys and 46 girls). They were joined by 16 other children in March. From 1951 to 1969 the number of students ranged from 72 to 125 (the peak year being 1960). Over these years more and more families built their log cabins closer to the mission site and residential school. A cemetery was created nearby, and the people of Hay Lakes became the people of Assumption. In the summers of 1966 and 1967, 120 Dene Tha were living in Habay and 575 were living in Assumption (Macaulay and Boag 1974, 16–17). Families, however, kept log cabins in the bush, where, to this day, men in their fifties and over, along with their sons or other relatives, spend extended periods of time trapping and hunting throughout the winter and spring.

In 1965 major discoveries of oil and natural gas around Assumption led to the construction of a road between High Level and what was to become the town of Rainbow Lake, approximately sixty kilometers west of Assumption. Band members soon marched onto the steps of the Alberta legislature in Edmonton asking for jobs and better living conditions. This action led to the construction by the federal government of new houses for the Dene Tha made of a simple wood frame and plywood. In 1969 the Department of Indian Affairs established a day school in Assumption. That same year missionaries closed their boarding school and the band decided on Chateh as the name of their settlement, in honor of the chief who had signed Treaty 8 on behalf of the Slavey Indians of Hay Lakes.

Today the residents of Chateh are all Dene Tha except for some Cree men and women who have married into the community and the non-Indians associated with Euro-Canadian institutions—the nursing station, store, police, and church—all located on Indian land with the approval of the band authorities. When I arrived in Chateh, people identified their place of residence within a number of discrete residential clusters: first, with the central townsite comprising the day school, the band-owned and-operated store, the police station, the nursing station, the nursing home, and the residences of non-Dene professionals living on the reserve; second, moving westward along the Gun River, farther and farther away from the townsite, with the First Prairie, the Second Prairie, and the Third Prairie, each associated with a cluster of related families; third, with the other families living along the road to Habay and those living close to the burial ground; and fourth, with the trailer park at the end of the airstrip where mostly younger couples live.

The Dene Tha contemporary lifestyle is, therefore, modern in more ways than one, and over the past two hundred years the Dene Tha have lived through all the changes experienced by other Northern Athapaskans.[5] The seminomadic hunters and gatherers of the past who traveled across the land with horse wagons, canoes, and dogsleds have now settled permanently on a reservation to live in government-built houses serviced with electricity but mostly without running water. Sources of household income are many: income generated from trapping, wages earned on and off the reservation through part-time work, as well as family allowance, old-age pension benefits, and social welfare provided by different levels of government. Cars, trucks, skidoos, and motorboats are the means of transportation to traplines or nearby towns. All families rely on store-bought food in addition to the substantial and sustained amounts of moose meat, fowl, and fish harvested by men and the small game, fish, and berries harvested by women. Over ten years, countless visits to Dene Tha households brought me face to face with the rich products of hunting, fishing, trapping, and gathering activities.

A household is most often constituted of three generations of family members living under one roof and addressing one another by kinship terms. The status achieved in parenthood is, therefore, immediately reflected in the change of a compound kinship term of reference. People refer to individuals according to their relationship to the firstborn child. When this child receives a name, for instance Dih, the parents and siblings become known as *Dihtá*, "the father of Dih"; *Dıhmo*, "the mother of Dih"; *Dihdéédzé*, "the sister of Dih"; *Dihchidle*, "the younger brother of Dih"; and so on.

It is common practice for the first-married daughter to give her first child to her own mother to raise. In the words of a Dene Tha mother who gave her firstborn son to her own mother: "Lots of people do that. First they [the boys] go with a girl; they have a kid; when they get married [that is, when they set their own household], they just let it [stay] with her grandmother or mother." When a child is given to grandparents to raise, they are told: "He/she will grow up and help you." A Dene Tha mother who said of her oldest child, a daughter, "I gave her to my mother," went on to explain: "It's just one of the things that has been going on in the band ever since I could remember. It has always been like that. In just every house there is a baby like that, given to the mother by the natural mother." In the 1970s Dene Tha band members who worked for the Voice of Alberta Native

Women Society had as one of their main objectives the legal transfer of guardianship rights from the natural mother to the grandparents. A member of this society said, "All I had to do was to get the natural mother's signature, and then the grandparents', and they got the [children's] allowance." When the transfer of a child occurs in this fashion, the grandparents are generally in their late thirties or early forties. They raise the young child in the company of their own unmarried children. These adopted children are raised knowing who their biological parents and siblings are. They often visit each other but live in different households.

Many other aspects of the Dene culture—ways of learning by observation, patterns of social interaction, healing practices, ritual activity—are also relatively strong. English, for instance, is seldom heard in Dene Tha homes, except for the omnipresent voice of the television. Most adults under forty are fluent in English, although they raise their children in their native tongue. Children eventually attend the local public school and learn to speak English, but they play in the schoolyard speaking Dene Dháh. The traditional forms of social control, of healing, and of praying, described and analyzed later in this book, endure alongside the parallel and complementary services offered by a detachment of the Royal Canadian Mounted Police, a nursing station, and a Roman Catholic church.

In brief, the Dene Tha have been the subject of sustained missionary and government interventions over the last century. As a result, like all other Native North Americans, the Dene Tha have experienced extensive socioeconomic changes, leading some to observe that "all Indians are in an important sense creatures of Euro-Canadian society, are to be understood primarily in terms of a massive adjustment to Euro-Canadian administrative structure, participation in a cash economy, and the pervasive influence of Euro-Canadian technology" (G. Watson 1981, 457). True, but in an equally important sense, all Indians are the creators of their own social life, reinterpreting and using for their own purposes the very institutions designed to assimilate them into Euro-Canadian society.

In this book I show that the Dene Tha shape their lives according to a distinctive indigenous tradition. Contemporary Dene

Introduction

Tha operate on the basis of epistemological and ethical values that are not shared by Euro-Canadians. Dreams are still lived as an essential part of one's ability to orient oneself in the world and to act responsibly within it. Ghosts of the dead still wander in the community to reincarnate or to steal the soul of a child. Animal helpers are one's lifetime companion and a source of power to heal and to harm. All these phenomena are real to the Dene Tha in the sense that they are confronted and cannot be wished away. These phenomena are part of a normal, ordinary life. This was the world of the Dene as recorded by explorers, traders, and missionaries in the eighteenth and nineteenth centuries, and it is largely still the world of the Dene Tha as I experienced it over twelve years, beginning in July 1979. This world needs to be understood primarily from the perspective of its creator, the Dene Tha.

ANTHROPOLOGISTS AND DENE RELIGION

Reviewers of the ethnographic literature on Northern Athapaskans, or Dene, identify religion, cosmology, and ideology as a domain whose investigation "seems quite inadequate" (Slobodin 1975, 284), "least satisfactory" (Krech 1980, 94), or "poorest" (Désveaux 1991, 122).[6] In a historical review of Northern Athapaskan research Edward Rogers (1981, 27) writes that, with the exception of the work of Robin Ridington (1968, 1971, 1978) and David Smith (1973), Dene "religion has been a topic of limited investigation, frequently without capturing the essence of the religious philosophy nor the integral part it played in the life of the people." The contributions of Smith to the comprehension "of the symbolic ordering of supernatural causality" among the Chipewyan, and of R. Ridington to the understanding of "the importance of learning through personal experience" among the Beaver, are also regarded as exceptional, by Henry Sharp (1986, 270) and Scott Rushforth (1992, 483), respectively.

Rushforth (1986, 252) suggests that religion is less well known than any other aspect of Dene culture because of "the general difficulty anthropologists have in translating the meaning of religious experience," as well as "the relative lack of formal religious institutions among Dene" and "the deeply personal nature of their [Dene] religious beliefs, which makes many people hesitant

Introduction

to discuss them in any detail." In an earlier publication (Goulet 1994a) I argued that these reasons did not account fully for the relative lack of progress in the ethnography of Dene religion. I suggested that significant progress in the study of Dene religion depends on investigators gaining experiential knowledge as they engage in Dene ritual processes in coactivity with their enactors. With hindsight I believe that the very use of the term "religion" is misplaced, for it misrepresents Dene Tha ways of knowing, thinking, and living.

Although this is not the place to enter into a debate on the definition of religion or about the use of the word "religion" as an adequate translation of non-Western terms, it is noteworthy that it is only with the Enlightenment "that the Other became a member of a non-Christian religion" and that dialectically "the Christian likewise became a member of the Christian religion" (McGrane 1989, 57). From early Christianity on, peoples have been divided between those who held the true faith and those who held the false ones. The opposition between peoples was not a racial or a religious one in the modern sense; it was a spiritual and theological one. To the Christian European, the Other was an unbeliever (Congar 1953, 51–52). As Bernard McGrane (1989, 16) reminds us, there is a long period in European history when "*there is Christianity but there is no 'religion.'* Religion is not yet the genus of which 'Christianity' will be a species" (emphasis in original). To seek religion among the Dene or among any other indigenous population is to pursue a Eurocentric agenda foreign to the very people whose way of life one seeks to understand.[7]

People everywhere are "active agents in the historical construction of their own world" (Bruner 1986a, 12). It follows that we ought to "leave the definition of the unit of investigation up to the people rather than imposing categories derived from our own ever-shifting theoretical frames" (Bruner 1986a, 9). James Faris's (1990, 241) report of a sharp exchange between an anthropological linguist and a (Southern Athapaskan) Navajo medicine man is instructive and relevant here. The anthropologist and Navajo argued "over whether the Navajo language contained a word which might be adequately translated as 'religion.'" The Navajo argued that it did not, whereas the anthropologist insisted that the term *nahaga* appropriately rendered the English

xxvi

term "religion." That term, the Navajo held, would be better rendered as "'the way, moving along in ceremony, or the practices by which Navajo life came to be as it is'" (Faris 1990, 241). These meanings closely parallel those found in the expressions *Dene Kéh*, "Kaska way" (Moore n.d.d) and *Dene Tha kínhín*, "Dene Tha way." Following Dene usage, I see no need to assign to a category, be it religious, mystical, or supernatural, the propositions and inclinations that define their productive and reproductive practices. In this book, therefore, I write about *Dene Tha kínhín*, "the Dene Tha way of living and doing things." I pay attention first to Dene epistemology, to their conception of knowledge, its acquisition and transmission, not only from person to person in our land but also from inhabitants of the other land to human beings living in our land.

The Dene Tha differentiate between *ndahdigeh*, "our land," and *echuhdigeh*, "the other land," and their respective inhabitants, but they do not do so in the way Euro–North Americans may oppose the natural and the supernatural, the field of science on the one hand and the field of mysticism, magic, and religion on the other. The other land, also referred to as *yake*, "heaven," is experienced firsthand in dreams or in visions when the soul journeys away from the body. It is in the other land that one meets relatives who have passed away as well as Christian figures such as Mary and Jesus. Dene Tha Elders easily follow an account of a trip to a nearby town with a story of a journey to the other land. To the nearby town in our land they traveled by car. To the other land they traveled with their souls. In both cases they visit actual places and meet real, living people.

Events in the other land and in our land are also intimately associated. For instance, atmospheric events in this land are an expression of someone's condition in the other land. When a violent storm with exceptionally strong winds swept over Chateh the day after a young man was shot to death, people said the storm was his feelings. When low clouds drizzled over Chateh for three days, a Dene Tha healer explained that it was his power feeling let down because patients of his had not brought the appropriate gifts as promised. When exceptionally bright red northern lights were seen in the sky, Dene Tha said they were because their leading prophet had lost much blood in the course of an operation undergone in the hospital at the time.

Dene Tha view both kinds of phenomena, those pertaining to our land and those pertaining to the other land, as amenable to true knowledge: that is to say, personal, firsthand knowledge. To know through dreams or visions is to know with one's mind. People say *sindí tah edahdîh*, "with my mind I know." To translate *sindi* as "my mind" is to follow Dene Tha practice, which is not to say that what the Dene Tha understand by such words is what English speakers do. The English concept 'mind' is "a concept specific to Anglo culture, which has no exact semantic equivalent in other European languages, let alone in other geographically and culturally more distant, languages of the world" (Wierzbicka 1989, 46). To the Dene Tha the mind is the seat of one's will, intellect, and memory. The mind is the potential recipient from animal helpers of a power to heal and to harm. The mind is an essential part of one's individuality and endures beyond one's particular incarnation. As such the mind resides more in "his or her soul," *mbeyuné*, than in "his or her body," *mbezí*. Soul and mind are constitutive of one's identity throughout one's life experiences in our land and in the other land.

D. Smith (1988) emphasizes that Chipewyan people consider dreams to be real and, therefore, not fundamentally different from other experiences. R. Ridington (1990, 95) writes that from the perspective of the Dene, their knowledge is "a means of production more fundamental than any set of artifacts." For that reason, he argues strongly that dreaming and acting with a power be included in accounts of Dene hunting technology. Julie Cruikshank also warns against the outsider's inclination to oppose spiritual knowledge derived from a vision quest and practical knowledge acquired through observation of masterful fellow Dene. "There is no evidence," she writes (1990, 344), "that an Athapaskan storyteller would distinguish between these two kinds of knowledge." On the contrary, a Dene narrator sees the successful vision quest as inherently practical because it results "in a mutually supportive relationship between hunter and game" (Cruikshank 1990, 344). Rushforth (1992, 495 n. 8) also reports that although Bearlakers differentiate states of dreaming from states of wakefulness, they "consider dreams to be

real"; in their view, "knowledge acquired through dreams is experiential, primary."[8] Such knowledge concerns real phenomena. It therefore enters decisions concerning social interaction
with fellow human beings and with animals conceived of as
"other-than-human persons." Both experiential knowledge
gained through dreams and/or visions and experiential knowledge gained in our land must pass practical tests. In both cases
success in relevant activities, for example, hunting, curing, foretelling the future, provide the Dene Tha with the crucial evidence that the acquired knowledge is valid. Therefore, as noted
by Ake Hultkrantz (1990, 181), in the case of the Dene I cannot
subscribe to the notion that there is "a clear break between two
experienced worlds, a natural world of daily experience and a
supernatural or metaphysical reality." Rather, I maintain that we
ought to describe how the Dene Tha constitute or make their
knowledge of our land and of the other land available to one another, and to the ethnographer, without recourse to terms such
as "religion," "mystical," or "supernatural."

LEARNING AMONG THE DENE

Two general propositions concerning Dene epistemology are
worth considering briefly here (I examine them in more detail in
following chapters). First, anthropologists observe that among
the Dene, religious institutions are informal and religious beliefs
are deeply personal and generally not spoken of. But of even
greater significance is the fact that among them, a person who
has undergone what Euro–North Americans would consider a
religious or mystical experience is described not as a believer but
as someone who "knows." This formulation is an expression of
the Dene belief that all true knowledge—both knowledge that
Euro–North Americans would consider mundane and that
which they would consider religious—is derived directly from
personal experience. As a consequence Dene informants are
firm in their conviction that individuals, including ethnographers, who have not directly experienced the reality of revelation or instruction through dreams and visions do not and cannot understand a crucial dimension of the Dene knowledge
system.

The argument can be made that the more willing the Dene

were to discuss their ways of knowing with the mind and their ways of interacting with inhabitants of the other land, the less genuine, and the more a dead thing of the past, their way would be.[9] Indeed, a Dene's verbal claim that she or he is knowledgeable and powerful would be seen by other Dene "as evidence that the speaker lacked knowledge and power" (Rushforth 1992, 486). Knowledge and power have to be manifest primarily through action, that is, nonverbally. Dene believe that to teach someone about such phenomena by means of explicit instruction, whether expressed in Dene Dháh or in English, displays a lack of faith in that person's ability to learn directly from personal experience, both in and out of ritual contexts. If "as a responsible academic" R. Ridington knows he "cannot dream up another culture that does not exist," he has also learned that "to understand the Dunne-za thoughtworld," he "must be willing to dream *into* it" (1988, 73). Marie-Françoise Guédon (1988) found the same among the Nabesna. To explore Nabesna shamanism, she had to do so partly through her own dreaming. Including in one's investigative repertoire a willingness to dream and to experience visions, and to offer accounts of one's dreams and visions to Dene, is a far cry from relying solely on observation and interviews to learn about the Dene way of life.

The second general proposition follows from the first: since learning through personal experience is the cornerstone of the Dene way of life, personal experience is also the necessary entry point for its anthropological investigation. "If, for one reason or another," a Dene cannot learn from personal experiences, he or she prefers to learn not by instruction "but by 'watching people who know how to do things.' Next, they prefer to learn informally by hearing mythical, historical, or personal narratives" (Rushforth 1992, 488). To a large extent Dene expect outsiders, anthropologists among them, to learn in a similar way. When pressed to explain Dene religious beliefs by the organizers of an international symposium on Native North American religion, Julian Hardisty, a Slavey from Fort Franklin, had nothing to reveal. He simply told his interviewers, "If you want to know anything, you have to figure it out yourself, that's what I think" (in Waugh and Prithipaul 1979, 64). Even when it comes to the Prophet Dance, the most public manifestation of their relationship to the other land and its inhabitants, the Dene expected me to observe and involve myself in the performance of the ritual without the benefit of prior instruction. Knowledge would be personal knowledge derived from experience.

The Dene view of knowledge and learning challenges our Western-based practices of teaching by instruction. The relative emphasis on verbal and nonverbal forms of communication in ritual performances varies from group to group, some groups exhibiting "an extreme concentration on non-verbal communicative forms in their sacred performances" (Barth 1987, 64). The concentration on nonverbal communication in ritual performances is certainly dominant among the Dene. Their notions of secrecy and power derived from animal helpers encountered in the vision quest inhibit public verbalization of experiences. These notions go hand in hand with the very individualized form of vision quest among the Dene Tha and with their highly developed sense of individual autonomy. As long as the Dene insist on the primacy of experience of phenomena pertaining to the other land over explicit teachings about them, personal experience on the part of the investigator becomes the cornerstone and the necessary entry point for the investigation of such phenomena.

This has profound implications for how Dene regard academics who come to them to collect data. It is generally true that the investigator is also observed. Her or "his questions, observations, indications, inclinations, attitudes and motives are discerned by respondents in the course of their continuing interaction with him" or her (Anderson and Lee 1982, 302–3). Among the Dene the investigator's willingness to learn experientially and to observe quietly people's nonverbal behavior are the prerequisites for progress in an ethnography of the Dene way of living and doing things. Investigators who hold to research methods that clearly separate observer and observed stand to lose, because, in the eyes of the Dene, they are too far removed from the authoritative source of true knowledge. In this respect, the situation among the Dene Tha is comparable to the one Jeanne Favret-Saada found in her investigation of witchcraft among the peasants of Le Bocage in contemporary France. In Le Bocage, as among the Dene, "there is no room for uninvolved observers" (Favret-Saada 1980, 12). Favret-Saada observed among French peasants what investigators have found among many other groups, namely that simply "'informing' an ethnographer, that is, someone who claims to know for the sake of knowing, is literally unthinkable" (1980, 9).

Although instructive conversations about a wide range of topics are a common feature of Dene social life, Dene actively engage in them "when the point of view of all participants is well known" and "where there is no threat to the speaker's view of himself or the world" (Scollon and Scollon 1983, 15–16). That is why Dene tend to restrict their discussion of experiences of dreams, visions and power to people they know well. Such discussions occur between those who are "in the know." Therefore, to live such experiences and to share them with other Dene of like experience is to provide evidence that one is not totally deaf or blind to events of the inner life that are intimately connected to developments in our land and in the other land.

Before communicating about knowledge obtained through dreams and visions, the Dene assess the investigator's personal experiences of such phenomena. Dene offer a degree of explanation to one who knows and understands, according to their estimation of his or her understanding. This estimation of the ethnographer's knowledge, as opposed to the investigator's research agenda, guides the flow of information between Dene and anthropologist. Moreover, this information very often takes the form of stories, whose significance at first simply escapes the ethnographer. R. Ridington (1988, 31) writes that in the early stages of his fieldwork among the Dunne-za he "did know enough to watch and listen carefully to what people said and did" and to recognize that "their teachings were in their words and actions, not in responses to direct questions." Guédon (1988, 6–7) notes that her Nabesna informants most often offered explanations of events in the form of a story or a myth, which at first she did not understand. Similarly, Bearlakers did not provide concise definitions of the concepts Rushforth was interested in. Typically, Bearlakers would "recite a myth, historical narrative, or personal account" (Rushforth and Chisholm 1991, 25) within which a concept was exemplified. Bearlakers left it to the anthropologists to understand the story and determine what positive and negative consequences flowed from behaving, or not behaving, according to Dene ways. Likewise, among the Dene Tha, when I persisted in asking questions that I thought had not been answered, a Dene Tha woman observed, "We tell you these stories for you to think with, as they were given to me for me to think with." Answers were to be found in the careful consideration of "stories." In all these instances the Dene expect the anthropologist to learn as they themselves learn: first from personal experience, second by observation of people who know how to do things, and third "informally by hearing mystical, historical, or personal narratives" (Rushforth 1992, 488).

FIELDWORK: COLLABORATION AND CONFRONTATION

In July 1979 I traveled to Chateh to communicate to the Dene Tha my interest in pursuing long-term research among them. At a meeting I asked them if they would be willing to teach me their language and their way of life. I would be coming back to live among them in January 1980 for six consecutive months, and would continue to do so for an indefinite number of years, as part of a research project sponsored by the Canadian Research Centre for Anthropology. I would thus alternate between being their student in Chateh and being a university professor in Ottawa. At the end of the meeting a Dene Tha Elder came up to me and shook my hand. He said, through an interpreter, that they would indeed be willing to teach me as I was asking them to do. In the years to come I would grasp the nature and extent of that commitment, which encompassed a complex process of incorporation into the local Dene Tha structure of knowledge and power.

The first two periods of fieldwork were spent mainly in the study of the local dialect, which eventually made possible regular interaction with monolingual Dene Tha. I came to deal directly with Dene Tha Elders and was instructed by them without interpreters. To help me along in my learning, they regularly called on me as their interpreter in their dealings with nurses, store managers, police officers, teachers, and visitors. In the beginning they would always have a bilingual grandchild with them who would assess the reliability of my interpretation and assist when need be. Although I progressed considerably in the language, I could easily lose the sense of conversations if people chose to speak in a manner and with a vocabulary they knew was beyond my reach. Dene Tha were continually evaluating my skills and communicating with me using the vocabulary they knew I had mastered.

Richard Slobodin (1969, 85) reports a similar experience among the Kutchin when he joined a trapping party in early 1947. He acquired enough of the local language "to follow and participate in conversations in everyday matters," but his limited knowledge seemed to vanish when he went on a hunting expedition in the mountains. When the Kutchin moved into the bush, their vocabulary, and to some extent their syntax, changed. As all anthropologists learn, one's linguistic abilities are always bound to certain social environments outside of which one's relative competence rapidly wanes.

→ Conversations in Dene Dháh with Dene Tha Elders were sometimes taped, transcribed, and translated to the best of my ability and then revised with bilingual informants. Much information was also drawn from conversations in English and in Dene Dháh with Dene Tha men and women between thirty and fifty years of age. They allowed me to write down verbatim much of what they told me, but they resented my repeating a question or probing their accounts with more and more queries. For instance, a question to a Dene Tha father of four was followed by a long period of silence. Five minutes went by, and then five more. Thinking that he had not quite heard me or understood the question, I repeated it. He turned his head toward me, saying: "Do you think I am deaf? Can't you see that I am sitting here thinking what is the best answer to your question?" I was at an early stage of fieldwork and could not yet appreciate the rhythm and conventions of conversations. In another instance, when I expressed difficulty at believing what a Dene Tha man and his wife were telling me, he quickly reminded me of my position: "We teach you, we say everything to you; if there is a guy who doesn't know anything, if you don't say the right words, and we don't like it, you are in trouble. Like you write what we tell you, we could walk away, we go away, what do you do? Nothing, you can't write anymore." I had to learn when to ask, when to remain silent, and what to consider a response to a question.

These episodes, like many similar ones over the years, demonstrate how "the 'move toward ethnographic knowledge'" often goes hand in hand with "resistance in the form of incomprehension, denial, rejection, or, why not, simply Otherness" (Fabian 1991, 394). Often enough, as anthropologists, since we cannot begin our investigation "simply by turning our gaze on objects that are given," we must initiate it "by *confrontation that becomes productive through communication*" (Fabian 1991, 394; emphasis in original). In this sense, "one's experience of the process of gradual understanding—and indeed of misunderstanding—in the field is still both the means to comprehension and the source of [ethnographic] authority" (Hastrup and Hervik 1994, 5).

Dene Tha tended to offer me information or explanation in the form of stories, according to canons of Dene instruction experienced by other fieldworkers among Northern Athapaskans. Dene Tha individuals also insisted on the confidentiality of many of the stories they told me. Stories of songs and a power received at the time of a vision quest or in a dream are considered personal stories and songs. They may be heard by others under certain circumstances, but they are not to be repeated except by the one who holds them on the basis of direct, personal experience. In the course of many conversations Dene Tha Elders, as well as other Dene Tha adults, would sometimes tell me to stop taking notes and simply listen. Dreamers and Dene Tha speakers would say *edu kedadondi íle*, "you shall not tell this to others." Others would simply tell me, "This is for your ears only." Dene Tha Elders would often conclude a session of narrative two to three hours long with the words *wontsedle ndedehsi edawondíhi ka*, "I tell you a little bit so that you may know." The request not to write down certain statements is motivated by Dene Tha notions of "power" and of views of "authority" over stories or accounts of life experiences. The information I was asked to keep to myself most often dealt with experiences of dreams, visions, or encounters with animals that played a formative role in an individual's development as a person with a strong mind or with a power. In the view of the Dene Tha parts of the conversations we engaged in, and the information discussed in them, do not belong to the public record.

The implications of these views for an ethnography of Dene ways of living are important. If we accept the Dene conviction that experience must have precedence over instruction, and if we respect the request that the information given for one's own sake not be communicated to a wider public, we must leave the ethnographic record somewhat incomplete. This incompleteness also follows from the basic principles guiding the professional responsibility of anthropologists when faced with "choices among apparently incompatible values" (American Anthropological Association 1989). When conflicts of interest arise, "the interests of these people take precedence over other considerations," because the "anthropologists' first responsibility is to those whose lives and cultures they study" (American Anthropological Association 1989). To ignore the Dene Tha directives not only would be unethical; it would also undermine all possibility of continuing meaningful long-term fieldwork and interaction.

Throughout my research and my writing I have tried my best to show respect for the Dene Tha, for their way of learning, and for the profession of anthropology. I gave pseudonyms to Dene Tha individuals to protect their anonymity. I wrote down, in the presence of Dene Tha, only what they felt I should write. While in Chateh I went over statements made by Dene Tha with them to ensure the accuracy of my notes, and I consulted with Dene Tha concerning my understanding and/or misunderstanding of events. I asked Pat Moore and a Dene Tha to go over all quotations in Dene Dháh for accuracy in orthography and translation. On ethical grounds I withheld from friends, colleagues, and the public what Dene Tha speakers asked that I keep to myself. As suggested by Dene epistemology and by colleagues who engage in experiential anthropology, I made accounts of personal experiences an integral part of an ethnography. In all this I hope I have found the means to treat people with respect and to honor long-standing ethical professional standards.

The Dene models of learning and their guiding principles in the transmission of knowledge need not be seen only as obstacles, however, or as insurmountable barriers to making contributions to anthropological knowledge. Rather, as Wikan (1991, 286) argues, we can also consider that "we stand to gain by taking up challenges posed by ways of knowing alien from ours." In the same vein, Paul Stoller (1995, 356) maintains that it is productive to "pay serious attention to non-Western theories of eth-

nographic authority." Given his "long-term implication and embodiment in things Songhay" (1995, 354), Stoller recognized that
Songhay Elders saw ethnographers in the light of Songhay
griots, who train for as long as thirty years before imparting their
people's history to the next generation. According to Songhay
Elders, griot and ethnographer must produce "words and images" that "enable the young to uncover their past and discover
their future" (1995, 354). This expectation impelled Stoller to
write *In Sorcery's Shadow* with his wife, Cheryl Olkes (1987).[10]

The Dene view of true knowledge as personal knowledge challenges us to produce stories much as they do, ones that express
life experiences in the world as they conceive of it and seek to live
it. The task is to generate stories that are good to think with. The
ethnographers' stories should induce the listener or reader to
grasp important dimensions of the Dene way of knowing and living. The fact that R. Ridington (1988), Sharp (1988a), D. Smith
(1993), and Guedon (1994a) all assume the role of storyteller in
order to offer their interpretation of Dene lifeworlds is not acci-
dental. As argued by Sharp (1988a, xx), "the narrative essay,"
more adequately than other literary forms, "represents the way
events are lived by specific individuals." The Dene emphasis on
processes of living and learning, writes Guédon (1994a, 61), is expressed in the use of "'my story,' the very process of my own socialization into the Nabesna communities, as a major source of
data in the light of which one may uncover aspects of Dene life."
In this respect, she adds, "the manner in which I tell and use a
story will say as much about my participation in the Dene Ways
(my Dene identity) as the story itself" (1994a, 61). In other words,
since the acquisition and transmission of knowledge is "mediated
by experience," we must accept that "ethnography is connected
to (auto)biography" (Fabian 1991, 382–83).

NARRATIVE ETHNOGRAPHY AND ETHNOMETHODOLOGY

To make one's experiences an integral part of an ethnography is
to challenge the canon of modern ethnography whereby "the engagement called for in fieldwork" ought to give way to "the self-
effacement called for in formal ethnographic description" (Pratt
1986, 33). Modern ethnographers might briefly portray themselves in their first encounters with "Others," but they invariably

xxxvii

vanish from the text once beyond the opening passages of their publications. The self-effacement of the ethnographer is true of both the interpretive anthropologist in search of meaning and the scientifically minded anthropologist in pursuit of causal explanations. Both anthropological traditions relegate "the personal to the periphery and to the 'merely anecdotal': pejoratively contrasted in positivist social science with generalisable truth" (Okely 1992, 9).

Being unwilling to challenge that canon, Cornelius Osgood clearly separates his ethnographic work, contained in numerous monographs, from his first-person narrative (1953) of his first year among Northern Athapaskans, in 1928. Likewise, Robert Lowie reserves for his posthumous memoirs (1959, chap. 3) the account of his personal experiences during his first trip to Lake Athapaska in 1908, at twenty-five years of age. Moreover, Lowie kept accounts of his dreams and visions while in the field for an essay published posthumously by his wife in *Current Anthropology*. Here he describes himself as a "chronic and persistent dreamer" (1966, 379) who often heard voices or had visions when resting, eyes half-closed. He remarks that these experiences greatly helped him in his work with Native Americans. He never risked such an admission during his remarkably productive career as a professional anthropologist, however. As Edith Turner et al. (1992, 4) note, to this day, anthropologists are generally embarrassed to report and use their own dreams and visions in their work.[11]

In 1979, when I began fieldwork among the Dene Tha, I was still uncritical of classic ethnographies. I believed engagement in the field ought to give way to self-effacement when it came to writing about Others. This belief was deeply challenged by the concept of knowledge held by the Dene Tha and my sustained involvement with them over the course of many years. I came to realize that the standard separation of the personal from the professional creates "a false dichotomy, which only makes sense if one believes that the data are independent of how those data were acquired" (Bruner 1993, 4). Why strive "to maintain the illusion of disinterest and disconnectedness" (Brady and Turner 1994, 9) characteristic of past ethnographies? Why not acknowledge both my involvement in another society and my active role in the constitution of ethnographic knowledge?[12] It is with these questions in mind that I broke with anthropological conventions and wrote "Ways of Knowing: Towards a Narrative Ethnography of Experience among the Dene Tha" (1994a), the prelude to this book.

Experiments in participation in the lifeworlds of others lead to narrative ethnography. Narrative ethnography recognizes that the choice is not between writing an autobiography focusing on the Self or producing a standard realist ethnography about the Other. That is why the emphasis of narrative ethnographies is "on the character and process of the ethnographic dialogue or encounter" as the context in which experiences arise and data are generated (B. Tedlock 1991a, 78). In other words, "to experiential ethnographers the self and especially experiences in the field are 'epistemologically productive' (Kulick 1995, 20)" (Poewe 1996, 179). Barbara Tedlock's *The Beautiful and the Dangerous* (1992), John Farella's *The Wind in a Jar* (1993), and Claire Farrer's *Thunder Rides a Black Horse* (1994) are recent examples of narrative ethnographies written by anthropologists who have worked intimately with Native North Americans from the Southwest. These books, writes Antonia Mills (1995, 11), are reflexive in the sense that they "evoke the sights and scenes and experiences not only of the Southwest First Nations, but of the anthropological encounter," including accounts of "painful experience and soul searching." Kirin Narayan's *Storytellers, Saints, and Scoundrels* (1989), Dorinne Kondo's *Crafting Selves* (1990), and Smadan Lavie's *The Poetics of Military Occupation* (1990) are similarly reflexive. In each case, writes Edward Bruner (1993, 7), "the ethnographer becomes part of the text that she is producing as she interacts with the people studied."[13] The same form of narrative is found in the work of Young, Ingram, and Swartz (1989) with a Cree healer; in the presentation of contemporary Australian aboriginal life by Jackson (1995); and in the ethnography of healing among the Inupiat of Alaska by E. Turner (1996).

Experiential journeys into the world of "Others," in coactivity with them, goes hand in hand with reflexivity understood as "a reflex action or process linking self and other, subject and object" (Babcock 1980, 2). To be conscious of oneself as an other is to be reflective; to be "conscious of being self-conscious" of myself as an other, and hence to be able to detach myself from "this initial experience of alienation"—being another—is to be reflexive (Babcock 1980, 2). In fieldwork a reflexive observer apprehends himself or herself as his or her "own instrument of observation" (Lévi-Strauss 1976, 36). In other words, the observer "must learn to know himself, to obtain from a *self* who reveals himself as *another* to *I* who uses him, an evaluation which will become an integral part of the observation of other selves" (Lévi-Strauss 1976, 36; emphasis in original). This conscious use of oneself as an instrument of observation explains the shift in ethnographic work "from participant observation to observation of participation" (B. Tedlock 1991a).[14]

Narrative ethnographies provide rich portraits of the anthropologist's involvement with particular individuals in a given place over a given period of time, but they generally fail to examine how the phenomena they describe are actually constituted by those for whom they are real, in the sense that they confront them and cannot be wished away. In this respect, authors of narrative ethnographies, like interpretive anthropologists, are remiss in being inattentive to ethnomethodology, "the deeply germane work produced by those social scientists whose very project it is to describe how people collectively constitute a sense of an external and objective reality" (G. Watson 1991, 75).[15]

In 1995, when I began to write this book, I decided to range beyond narrative ethnography and to couple first-person accounts of experiences with ethnomethodologically inspired analyses.[16] What I have found particularly useful in writing this book are ethnomethodology's concepts of indexicality, reflexivity, and competency. Indexicality refers to the fact that meaning is context-dependent. The sense of a word or a statement (and of silence) depends on the context and timing of its production, on the identity of the speaker, on the place where it is spoken, and so on. Throughout this book the interpretation of verbal and nonverbal interaction highlights the importance of context in the determination of the meaning of words and deeds between Dene Tha, or between Dene Tha and anthropologist. The discussion of accounts of experiences in the Dene Tha world also draws on the ethnomethodological concept of reflexivity. This concept differs radically from the notion of reflexivity discussed earlier as found in narrative ethnographies. In the vocabulary of ethnomethodologists, reflexivity refers to an essential property of accounts and the settings they describe: descriptions "are simultaneously in and about the settings they describe" (Leiter 1980, 139). Accounts and settings elaborate each other in the sense that an "account makes observable features of the setting—which, in turn, depend on the setting for their specific sense" (Leiter 1980, 139). This feature of accounts, ethnographic ones included, leads us to the notion of competency. In a setting new to him or her, an ethnographer is unable to "characterize things for what they 'really are' in the setting under study" (Sharrock and Anderson 1986, 52). To be able to characterize things for what they are, the ethnographer "has to learn to correctly, *competently*, describe the setting" (as it is available to the people who constitute it); and thus the ethnographer "has to learn this from the people who live its life" (Sharrock and Anderson 1986, 52).

These ethnomethodological concepts and their application to analyses of accounts of experiences, mine and those of the Dene Tha, show how all linguistic descriptions of events and actions are meaningfully related. A consistent attention to the essential reflexivity of language in accounts of events establishes without doubt that contemporary Dene Tha operate on the basis of epistemological principles and ethical values that are not shared by Euro–North Americans. Like ethnomethodologists, I am interested in how people constitute settings in which phenomena are seen "as objective or not, that is as existing (or not) prior to and independently of their discourse about them" (Watson and Goulet 1998, 97). For instance, "if people report seeing a ghost or sighting a previously unknown stellar constellation, ethnomethodologists do not attempt to explain away the sightings as delusions; neither do they speculate about the ontological status of ghosts or constellations" (Watson and Goulet 1998, 97). Rather, the concern of the ethnomethodologist is with "the methods by means of which the sightings [of a ghost or stellar constellation] are made available as sightings of objective phenomena" (Watson and Goulet 1998, 97). To engage in an ethnomethodologically inspired analysis of accounts given by Dene of their experiences is to refuse to consider any socially recognized phenomenon "as existing prior to and independently of any actual episode in which it is exhibited and recognized" by the individuals orienting to this phenomenon (Watson and Goulet 1998, 110). The decision not to categorize Dene Tha propositions and behavior that outsiders would see as religious or mystical is but one manifestation of my intention to follow as far as possible the Dene Tha in *their* constitution of social phenomena.

I have also found in the work of ethnomethodologists an opportunity to move beyond the framework of interpretive anthropology which informed my early writing on the Dene Tha (Goulet 1982, 1989). Interpretive anthropology sees culture as consisting "in the sorts of interpretations the members of a society apply to their experience, the constructions they put upon the events through which they live" (Geertz 1971, 90). In this formulation, interpretation and experience, construction and event, are distinct, at least analytically. Cultural constructs are seen as part of the public system of symbols of significance, or the stock of knowledge at hand that one applies to diverse occurrences in various life circumstances. Ethnomethodologists take a different view of things: culture, ethnicity, gender, values, and the like "are not *things*, but processes—processes manipulated or, more radically, composed during the course of interaction" (Moerman 1988, 2). Clifford Geertz and like-minded interpretive anthropologists see cultural forms as extragenetic sources of information or public systems of meaning that determine, influence, or shape human behavior. Harold Garfinkel and his disciples see cultural forms as the "ongoing accomplishment of the concerted activities of daily life" (Garfinkel 1967a, vii), "endogenously and collectively generated" within interaction itself (G. Watson 1992, 1). Ethnomethodologists, therefore, describe social interaction and talk as "work," in that these are the means through which human beings accomplish their identities and constitute the events they live through.[17]

In the following chapters ethnomethodologically inspired analyses of accounts of experiences in our land and in the other land, those of the Dene as well as those of the ethnographer, show to oneself and to others how a reality is "constructed," or, less pejoratively, "produced" or "made available." Since ethnomethodology "is concerned to see *how people determine, to their satisfaction, how things really are*, it can suspend interest in the question of whether they are in any ultimate sense right to be satisfied in that way" (Sharrock and Anderson 1986, 56; my emphasis). This is a relativist position. There is much diversity between people's view of how things are. Ethnomethodologists, like anthropologists, are concerned with a particular people's view of how things are for them. Ethnomethodologists and anthropologists are not interested in metaphysics; they are not in the business of determining how things really are in truth. As Graham Watson (1991, 87) writes, "To Ian Jarvie's taunt (1987: 273), 'The *real* question in all this is what has happened to truth,' we may offer, as rejoinder, Bruno Latour's vigorous assertion (1988a: 156), 'Relativist sociologists are not sawing the branch upon which they sit because they are not seated on it, and no one is or has ever been; the strength of any science, and indeed of any argumentation, has never come from non-local, non-human and non-historical allies.'"

In the process of ethnomethodological analysis, one simultaneously shows that reality is constructed, thus undermining the implicit claim that reality exists prior to and independently of the discourse that constitutes it (G. Watson and Goulet 1992). The methods used in the construction of social knowledge—including scientific knowledge—can be identified and described. To describe Dene Tha methods of constituting their world is not to privilege our discourse, or that of the culture to which we belong, at the expense of the Dene Tha: we are all in the same boat. So, in the following chapters, to make explicit the fact that the Dene Tha, as much as the anthropologist, constitute meaning is to show "that culture, far from being a given framework that lies behind and is expressed in activities, is, rather, . . . a flexible repertoire of interpretive resources drawn upon by participants in accounting for action" (G. Watson 1991, 89). Culture is that which individuals invoke, activate, get to work, and realize in their lives. Culture, in this sense, "cannot be set over or against the person" (Jackson 1996, 11). Such a view of culture allows us to see individuals "not as automatons programmed according to 'cultural' rules or acting out social roles" but as people living their lives and, in the process, "wondering what they should do, making mistakes, being opinionated, vacillating, trying to make themselves look good, enduring tragic personal losses, enjoying others, and finding moments of laughter" (Abu-Lughod 1993, 27, cited in Jackson 1996, 23).[18]

*

In brief, this book is a case study in radical participation, a means of investigating social realities advocated by proponents of experience-near anthropology. The experiential knowledge gained in the course of engaging in the daily lives and ritual activities of the Dene Tha is therefore integrated into the ethnographic description, as is characteristic of narrative ethnography. While advocating the merits of an experiential approach in the quest for anthropological knowledge, the book shows the value of ethnomethodologically inspired analyses of accounts of experiences, those of the Dene Tha and of the anthropologist among them, for illuminating the manner in which Dene Tha realities are socially constituted.

1. Stories from the Field

＊

Twice you have made us happy, can't you make
us happy a third time? —Dene Tha Elder

"The authenticity of ethnographic knowledge," writes Michael
Jackson (1995, 163), "depends on the ethnographer recounting
in detail the events and encounters that were the grounds on
which the very possibility of this knowledge rests." One can never
tell all that has occurred in the field, however, but must necessarily select what events and encounters to narrate. Moreover,
the telling of the account is always from the perspective of the
ethnographer, who highlights certain features of incidents and
draws out their implications for the research. The seven stories
from the field included in this chapter are such a selection. They
show how the Dene epistemological position that learning ought
to occur primarily through personal experience led me to an experiential investigation of Dene Tha social realities, including
what Euro–North Americans would consider their religion.

These stories demonstrate that "radical participation in other
people's lives generates not only 'observations' but also conceptualizations and insights that are clearly a joint creation of the anthropologist and his/her local partners in interaction" (Barth
1992, 65). These stories also provide insights into the process of
fieldwork and teach "about not only the experiences of an author
living in a foreign setting but the mutual interaction between author and the host community, illuminating the Other as much as
the self" (Gottlieb 1995, 571). This being the case, the us/them dichotomy that separates the observer from the observed in classical ethnographies gives way to more reflexive perspectives characteristic of narrative anthropology. Such perspectives are
consistent with Dene views on epistemology—the nature of
knowledge, its acquisition, and its transmission.

Stories from the field emphasize the importance of nonverbal
communication over discourse as the starting point for the journey to anthropological knowledge (Hastrup and Hervik 1994, 6).
"Language events" (Clifford 1988, 41) or "dialogue" (B. Tedlock

1991a) are but a fraction of what anthropologists must take into consideration if they are to become at all competent in their new environment. Newcomers to a social field "absorb new sights, sounds, rhythms, silences, feelings and tastes" when "the language of the society they are trying to enter is incomprehensible" (Kohn 1994, 13). Possibly, these early experiences "are in large degree responsible for the material that ends up being seen as important or 'ethnographically rich'" (Kohn 1994, 14). In the first stage of fieldwork, differences in the background of the anthropologist and the local people are certainly at their greatest. The contrast between self and others is likely to steer the attention of the researcher toward the unfamiliar and the unexpected. In turn, these initial experiences of otherness set the track for what the ethnography comes to be about.

In the process of learning about each other, anthropologist and Dene Tha, like social actors everywhere, constantly direct, check, bend, and transform "their lines of action in the light of what they encounter in the actions of others" (Blumer 1969, 53). This chapter therefore highlights a key property of contemporary Dene Tha social life: the ability of Dene Tha to act according to Euro-Canadian patterns of behavior in some contexts (when interacting with transient or resident Euro-Canadians) and to behave according to Dene patterns of conduct in other contexts (when interacting with fellow Dene among themselves). The Dene Tha can do so because, as mentioned in the introduction, they have acquired considerable insight into Euro-Canadian values and mores over more than a century of participation in numerous Euro-Canadian institutions—economic, religious, educational, medical, political, and judicial. The Dene Tha also do so because they accept cultural differences and willingly communicate with non-Dene according to non-Dene ways. Given my anthropological agenda, this characteristic of Dene Tha social life posed a particular challenge. As I observed familiar patterns of social life and heard Euro-Canadian mainstream views on a wide variety of issues, I realized that I could easily find myself interacting with the Dene according to Euro-Canadian ways. I also found that, if I attempted to interact with the Dene as they do among themselves, I noticed different patterns of life and heard distinctively non-Euro–North American views about all aspects of life. As I became increasingly incorporated into the social world of the Dene, I grasped more of their point of view, their relation to life, in effect realizing more and more how they view the world. The following seven stories from the field illustrate how this process of incorporation was negotiated in the course of unforeseen crises and opportunities.

In January 1980, as soon as I arrived in Chateh, I reestablished contact with the Dene Tha dreamer and his extended family who had promised to teach me their language and their ways. The first task I had in mind was to learn the language. Tape recorder, pad, and pencil were soon put to use in daily hour-long sessions with Dene Tha speakers in their homes. In the course of a session I would write down a brief account in English and in Dene Dháh. The instructor would then record his or her account in Dene Dháh. Later in the day I would transcribe and analyze the recording for its phonemic, syntactic, and semantic features. On the following morning I would listen to the tape and memorize the story, thus progressively building a range of vocabulary and a series of phrases to use as best as I could in my daily visits to families. Within two weeks of my arrival in Chateh we had established a clear pattern of collaboration. Every afternoon I would arrive in the midst of a family and ask if anyone could teach me. If not, I was given the name of another individual from another family who was invariably available. I never had to stop at more than two homes to find an instructor, who was always a competent bilingual young adult between twenty and thirty-five years of age. Sessions with these instructors were often followed by conversations with their monolingual parents or grandparents, who would often talk to me at length, knowing I understood little but confident that in the long run I would know more and more. The referral system was totally reliable, an indication that the Dene Tha were making themselves available to me in a coordinated manner. They were, indeed, living up to the Elder's assurances that they would teach me.

In the second week of March 1980 the pattern of cooperation that I had come to take for granted suddenly changed. On that day the first person whom I asked for assistance replied that although she could not teach me, Paul would certainly be happy to do so. The mention of his name came as a shock. I had always avoided his family, having heard early on of heavy drinking and fighting, including a knifing incident at his home. In the course of the two and a half months that I had been learning the language no one had ever referred to Paul as a potential instructor and I had been quite happy at not having to visit his home. The sudden mention of his name took me absolutely by surprise. I expressed my regrets to the speaker and proceeded to the home of another favorite instructor. To my surprise, he also told me he was unavailable and mentioned Paul as someone willing to teach me. Determined not to come face to face with Paul, I tried another instructor, who responded to my request exactly as the other two had done. Despondent, I returned home, angry at the Dene Tha instructors for their apparent sudden withdrawal of cooperation.

During the subsequent days this sequence of events repeated itself. One after another, past instructors announced that they were unable to assist me but that Paul would be happy to teach me. Again, rather than meet with Paul, I returned home, annoyed at my instructors' refusal. After four days of failed attempts to engage my instructors' assistance I realized that I had to come to terms with the fact that my instructors were unanimous and consistent in their message that Paul be included among the ones instructing me. I wondered at my deeply felt fear to come face to face with Paul. I was afraid to take that step, for reasons unknown to me. Later I discovered that the fear had been triggered by repressed childhood memories of two drunk men fighting, one bashing the other's head on the cement sidewalk and finally leaving him unconscious in a pool of blood. But I did not understand my behavior during that month of March while among the Dene Tha. Firm in their resolve, my instructors remained polite and patient with me, never asking why I was not acting immediately on their suggestion as I had always done in the past. Finally, I concluded that unless I overcame my fear, instruction in Dene Dháh would simply cease. There was no other way but the one they indicated.

The next morning, I went to Paul's house and met my new instructor on the doorstep. Scars on his face and an arm in a sling caught my attention first. Then I noticed his bright eyes and appreciated the deep tone of his voice as we introduced ourselves in English.

"I do not know you," I said. "But others have told me you would be willing to teach me Dene Dháh."

"Yes, I don't know you too."

Paul extended his hand and with a firm handshake invited me into his home. Inside, he proceeded to clear the table of the fur and blood of animals he had skinned in the morning. His was definitely the home of a hunter and trapper: moose meat was suspended from rafters running across the ceiling to dry; stretched pelts from beaver, muskrat, and mink were lined against the walls; and fish was lying next to the stove, as were half a dozen frozen hare.

Paul had me sit down at one end of the table, where he said I could put my tape recorder and writing pad. "I have things to tell you," he said. "I will first tell you in Christian [English] and then in Indian." He obviously knew how we would proceed through our session, which we did at a leisurely pace, over the background noise of a radio station. Twenty minutes into our session he suddenly interrupted our work at the mention on the radio of jobs in Rainbow Lake, a white settlement approximately thirty kilometers west of Chateh. Animated, Paul immediately launched into a passionate speech in English about the importance of education in gaining access to jobs such as the ones advertised on the radio. As I listened, I could see his children playing outside the house. He punctuated his speech with numerous references to his children, claiming that they were too stupid and lazy to take advantage of the schooling system on the reserve. He emphasized the government's effort to make education accessible to his children, sending a school bus right to their home, a bus that his children were most often just too lazy to board. On and on he went for fifteen minutes. A minister of education could not have spoken so eloquently about the necessity of education in the modern world, but why would a father so berate his children to a newcomer to the community? What was I to answer?

"Paul, I have been to many places around here but never have I seen so many beautiful things gathered together in one place," was the comment I spontaneously voiced. "Look at all the fur and meat you have here."

Paul's eyes immediately gleamed with light as he broke into a smile, saying: "You know, these things do not come here by themselves. We have to trap them and remove them from the traps before other animals get at them. And I do that with my children before five o'clock in the morning."

Paul explained how he was teaching his children skills they would never learn in school. He praised them for their ability to move in the bush along his trapline and for their growing skills in skinning animals. He understood that the jobs advertised in Rainbow Lake usually came and went according to the boom and bust of the economic cycle: "People who do not love the land come to these jobs for the money," he said, "and when the jobs are gone, they leave too. But we are Dene Tha; we love this land; we must know how to live from the land." Paul then led me into an exploration of local knowledge and practice that was quite unanticipated given his earlier speech on the necessity of schooling and his derogatory remarks about his children's truancy.

In this first meeting Paul and I were implicitly setting the stage for many conversations to come. In his response to the radio broadcast Paul showed that he was quite familiar with the social world constituted by the dominant society, proclaiming the need of education to get good jobs. He knew I belonged to that dominant society and earned my living in the field of education. It is conceivable that I could have endorsed his earlier statements on the virtue of schooling and sought to find ways to get his children to attend school on a more regular basis. I could have made this theme the topic of further investigation and pursued interviews on the same topic with Dene Tha in other families. Presumably, I could have gathered a substantial number of statements on the part of Dene Tha parents, all reflecting the dominant society's discourse on education. A number of papers and publications might have followed. None of this happened, because I followed up on his speech with a comment on the wealth of meat and fur collected in his house. I did so out of intuition, based partly on the presumption that a father would not truly berate his children before a stranger in the way he was doing, and partly on the anthropological practice of paying more attention to what people do than to what they say. I was obviously listening to a man who was deeply involved in hunting and trapping, hence my comment on the fruits of his labor. Not in the least offended by the fact that I was not pursuing the theme he had so passionately embarked on, Paul took my comment as an opportunity to inform me of things he and his family clearly had at heart.

This whole episode can be seen as a social drama. In V. Turner's sense of the term (1985), it is a complex social process initiated by a breach of norms, followed by attempts at redress, and concluded by either a schism or a reincorporating of social actors in a reinstated structure of knowledge and power. In the eyes of the Dene Tha my behavior constituted a breach of norms. In July 1979, when the Elder said "We will teach you," he meant that I would learn from all of them. It was not up to me to pick and choose from among them whom I would or would not work with. They had committed themselves as a whole to teach me their language and their ways, but I persisted in excluding a member of their extended family as an instructor. The breach was followed by an effort on the part of the Dene Tha to redress the situation. Unanimously, clearly and firmly, their actions communicated the following: "We will not teach you until you meet with Paul. You cannot keep on as you are doing." They did not tell me so in so many words, for that would have violated the Dene Tha expectation that one ought to learn by observing people's behavior. This was my responsibility. When I finally went to Paul's home, the other instructors again became available to teach me. My visit to Paul led to my reintegration into an extended, reliable network of instructors who were obviously teaching me much more than their language. They were teaching me the subtle forms of concerted actions that Dene engage in to get people to behave in certain ways.

The response Paul made might also have been taken as an invitation to join him and his family in their bush activities. D. Smith (personal communication 1997) has suggested that everyone insisted that I meet Paul precisely because he was highly qualified to become my mentor in experiencing firsthand how one becomes at home in the bush, hunting, fishing, and trapping. Being at home in the bush also implies experiencing animals as intelligent beings able to communicate with human beings. It is also in the bush that one meets one's animal helper, a meeting critical in the shaping of one's identity. Being at home in the bush was not on my mind when I met Paul, and so I was blind to an opportunity to seek him as my mentor in that environment. In fact, in my years with the Dene Tha I have spent very little time away from the settlement, save for a few day-long journeys with Elders to collect birch bark for basket making, or with younger Dene Tha men to hunt ducks. This lack of life experience in the bush is of course reflected in the kind of stories from the field that I can tell. Had I a rich experience of life in the bush there are undoubtedly many aspects of Dene life that I would write differently about.

PLEASE SMILE AND SAY THANK YOU

The encounter with Paul revealed a feature of interaction that characterized my fieldwork among the Dene Tha from the beginning. Dene Tha could always switch from one pattern of interaction to another, one moment interacting with me in English according to well-mastered Euro-Canadian ways, the next moment reverting to Dene Dháh and behaving according to their ways. Conversely, although I wanted to learn Dene Dháh and sought earnestly to learn the Dene Tha's ways, the seesaw between the motivation to immerse myself in a new culture and the desire to live according to my home culture never ceased. The oscillation between their world and mine manifested itself in surprising ways, as in the following experience.

I had returned home after a long day of visiting Dene Tha families. Tired, I rested comfortably in a reclining chair. Within a few minutes I felt myself drifting away in a dreamlike state. Eyes closed, half awake, half asleep, I began watching, as in a lucid dream, a revolving procession of familiar Dene Tha faces. Well lit and readily identifiable, the faces followed one another in a regular circular movement, as if they were part of a carousel, each appearing on the screen in turn. As I looked at these faces, I felt my own facial features alternate between smiles and frowns. Surprised, I kept my eyes closed, paying close attention to the process that was unfolding. I examined the faces, wondering why these particular faces appeared at this particular time. It suddenly dawned on me that all these faces were those of individuals I had picked up along the road and had given a ride to in the preceding weeks. I realized that the faces I was smiling at were those of individuals who, when taking leave, had looked at me and said either thank you or *mahsi chon*, from the French word "merci" and the Dene Dháh word *chon*, meaning big. The faces I was frowning at were those of individuals who had simply stepped down from the vehicle and walked away without a glance, a nod, or a thank-you.[1]

In a waking dream "the imaginative world is experienced as autonomous," that is to say, "the imager does not have the sense that he is making up these productions, but feels that he is getting involved in an already created process" (Price-Williams 1992, 249).[2] My own waking dream revealed a subconscious process of approval and disapproval. The good Dene Tha were being separated from the bad. I smiled at the ones who rewarded me with the smiles and words of appreciation I had grown accustomed to in my culture. I frowned at the ones who treated me as they treated each other at the end of a ride. I realized that I was unconsciously discriminating between the Dene Tha on the basis of whether they conformed to patterns of behavior I was familiar and comfortable with. To understand my waking dream one needs only remember how Euro–North American children who are always told to say please and thank you are praised when they say these words on their own. I realized that unless I cultivated relationships with those individuals who did not meet my expectations, I would never get to learn an important set of Dene Tha patterns of thought and behavior.

To associate myself on a more regular basis with these Dene Tha individuals often brought about intense feelings of frustration and anger. Such was the case, for instance, when some of these Dene Tha, who had worked part of the year off the reservation, asked me if I could help them prepare their income tax reports. Not thinking much of it, I said yes and spent a little over an hour doing so. Word of what I had done soon got around, and I suddenly had a stream of Dene Tha coming to my house asking for the same service. One evening as I was preparing dinner, a Dene Tha couple came to my house with their papers. Would I do their report? Although tired, I said that I would. We sat at the table, and two hours later we were done. Tired, I gave them their papers back. Then, without even a glance in my direction, as they got up, the husband said in Dene Dháh, *dótáh*, "let's (us two) go," which is customary to say on leaving someone. As I heard them heading away on their skidoos, I felt angry at them and also somewhat exploited and unappreciated. Unexpectedly, within a few weeks their daughter came by with two large moose steaks, saying, "My mom and dad thought you might like this." They were expressing their appreciation in their way.

I reflected on the Dene Tha whom I tended to like because they thanked me in the customary Euro-Canadian fashion. I remembered reading in the missionary records a speech of French Bishop Breynat observing that lack of gratitude was one of the many negative traits found among the Dene. Bishop Breynat offered as evidence the fact that in their native tongue the Dene did not have any word equivalent to "merci," hence his pastoral admonition to missionaries to instill in their flock the sentiment of gratitude and to enrich their vocabulary with "merci." Since the phoneme r is absent in Dene languages, "merci" became *mahsi*, and "merci beaucoup," thank you very much, became *mahsicho*, literally "a big thank-you." Such expressions are widely used but only in interaction with non–Dene Tha, for only they expect it. My predecessors in Dene communities, missionaries, teachers, social workers, nurses, and other professionals, have all taught the Dene, young and old, Euro-Canadian rules of polite and correct behavior. Many Dene Tha abide and behave according to these expectations when in the presence of non-Dene. The Dene have not, however, forgone their own ways, for among themselves, and occasionally with some non-Dene, they behave according to their own notion of appropriate behavior, as illustrated here and in the following stories.

ARE YOU UP FOR A FIGHT?

Giving rides to Dene Tha led to other surprising developments in my relationship with different factions on the reserve, leading me to confront unexpected foes and meet unforeseen allies. Early in the spring of 1980 I went to the town of High Level to run some errands. Driving along with me were Albert; his wife, Mary; and their sixteen-year-old daughter, Rose. Water from melting snow had filled deep ruts in the more than ninety kilometers of dirt road we had to travel. One could easily slide off the road, become stuck in axle-deep gumbo, or be obliged to stop behind other immobilized or impaired vehicles. When we reached our destination it was, therefore, with a sigh of relief. We took a few hours to complete our errands and were preparing to return to Chateh when we met Roger and Lucy and their six-year-old son. The parents were obviously drunk, hardly able to keep their balance as they asked for a ride back home. It was late and very cold. I hesitated to take them on board because of their drunken state but nevertheless decided to do so for the child's sake. The grateful parents promised that they would behave themselves and cause no problems. And so off we went, with me in the driver's seat. Albert sat next to me in the front passenger seat while Mary, Rose, and the boy sat in the back seat. The boy's parents sat on the floor in the rear section of the vehicle.

It was midnight, and we were driving down the long steep hill leading into Chateh when Rose suddenly yelled that she did not want to return home. She instructed me to drive her back to High Level to buy liquor. Her parents and I realized that over the last two hours Roger and Lucy had given her alcohol to drink. Albert told his daughter to calm down, saying that going back to High Level was out of the question. Rose then lashed out verbally at him and smashed an empty bottle of liquor against the side window behind my seat. Shattered glass flew across the vehicle. Waving the broken bottle in her right hand, she told me that if I did not stop to let her out, she would make her own way out of the vehicle. The six-year-old boy broke into tears and was crying out loudly as Albert tackled his daughter on the back seat, restraining her lest she hurt herself or others. Albert's stern warnings, the young boy's cries, and Rose's swearing and angry words were soon joined by the voices of Roger and Lucy disclaiming responsibility for Rose's drunkenness. I was tense and tired and thinking that a few kilometers away from here I would be able to drop Roger, Lucy, and their son at their place and that it was a matter of only a few additional minutes before I could do the same with Albert, Mary, and Rose.

Once we had pulled over on the roadside close to the path leading to their house, Roger, Lucy, and their son slowly stepped out of the vehicle. Before I could pull away, however, we were approached by young Dene Tha men who were drunk and out looking for adventure. They peered into our vehicle and at the sight of Rose immediately asked for her. One of them pressed on the handle to open the driver's door to take her away. Happily, the door was locked. Albert immediately asked me to take them to his house. As we pulled away, I was startled by the sight and sound of a large fist smashing into my side window. Luckily, no damage was caused. Leaving the angry young men behind, we proceeded to Albert's house, which was less than two kilometers away. Once there it took more than ten minutes for Albert and his wife to tear their screaming and fighting daughter out of the vehicle. For me, a very emotional evening was finally drawing to an end.

As I prepared to pull away, I saw, in my rear-view mirror, lights rapidly coming toward me. I soon recognized the familiar sound of skidoo engines racing over the snow and through mud patches from different directions. Immediately, I thought of the frustrated young men I had left behind nearly half an hour earlier. I presumed that they and some of their friends were trying to catch up with me to get what they had wanted in the first place. Since I could not avoid them, I decided to step out of the vehicle and meet them face to face. Blinded by the circle of skidoo headlights now stationed a mere twenty feet away, I waited anxiously for their move. Motors were stopped, and headlights were turned off. Silence. Then the silence was broken: "We heard that you were having some problems and we came to see if we could help you," said the friendly voice of one of my instructors in the language. I took a deep breath and let go a sigh of relief. Anticipated foes had turned into unexpected friends.

Unknown to me, neighbors of Roger and Lucy had witnessed the frustrated youths assault my vehicle. These neighbors dialed up the family of an instructor to inform them that I might be in trouble. The instructor immediately called on his brothers and cousins to race to my rescue. Deeply relieved, I laughed and told them I was OK. As I drove back home, I felt the support of the tough young men at "my" end of the reserve. Their response in the middle of the night indicated a degree of incorporation in the community that I had not suspected. Not only was I being taught; I was also being protected. Youths from other parts of the reserve now knew that if they took me on, they would also have to take on my instructors and their friends. The checks and balances between rival groups of youth in the community guar-

anteed my ability to move relatively freely around the reservation any time of the day or night.

TELL ME: WHAT HAPPENS TO PEOPLE WHO DIE DRUNK?
Even though I had been spared the anger of a group of drunken
young men, victims of violent aggression associated with the con-
sumption of alcoholic beverages, mostly beer or whiskey, were a
regular feature of life in Chateh. To this day, this state of affairs is
deeply troubling to most Dene Tha. The very first question I was
asked in a Dene Tha family when I arrived in Chateh in January
1980 was whether I knew how to stop people from drinking and
destroying their lives. I answered in the negative, telling them of
my long-term experience with an alcoholic friend who had ru-
ined his life and career despite intense and sustained efforts by
all his friends to have him change his behavior. I concluded by
saying that I thought alcohol abuse was not a simple issue that
could be easily resolved. They concurred.

During the winter months of my first period of fieldwork, not
a week went by without my coming across men and women with
swollen and bloody faces who would tell me how they had been
beaten up by friends, kin, or spouse. Not a winter month went by
without my hearing of someone who had lost part of a limb or
who had frozen to death as a result of having wandered outdoors
inebriated in the middle of the night. Among the families of my
instructors, one family seemed to be free of alcohol-related incidents until one day when I found their door locked and their
house empty. I was told that in the night a brother-in-law had
come into their house with other friends to drink. In the early
hours of the morning a fight had ensued, and one of the men had
stabbed a knife into the abdomen of his brother-in-law. The police had been called and the victim flown to a hospital where
blood transfusion and emergency surgery saved his life.

In Chateh people commented that a non-Dene would certainly have died from such a wound. They explained that the victim had survived because he was a Dene and that Dene have
strong blood. Some people also expressed the view that I might
be in some way associated with the eruption of violence in their
homes. Two days later, as I was concluding a language session in
the house next door to where the stabbing had occurred, the

13

mother of my instructor glanced in my direction and then told him something in Dene Dháh. I asked him what she had said, and he answered, "She tells me, 'Don't spend too much time with him; you know what happens when he spends lots of time somewhere.'" I had, indeed, spent more time receiving instruction at the home of their next-door neighbors than at any other home. He had been my favorite instructor and the one that I would most often call on first. I tended to go to others only after he had told me he was unable to teach me on a particular day. His pronunciation was clearer than that of most of the others, and his ability to explain sentence and verb structures was superior to anyone else's. Sessions with him always seemed relaxed and productive. He was friendly and had a lively family of four children whom I also enjoyed very much. Had I spent too much time with them? Was I unknowingly pushing the limits of Dene Tha hospitality? I took the mother's comment as an admonition to spend my time more equally among the families of my instructors.

It was in this context that people began asking me what happened to people who died while drunk. When an instructor first asked the question, I said I did not know and asked him the question in return. I did so thinking that, surely, the Dene Tha had an answer or a set of possible answers to such a vital question. I was interested in learning their view of the afterlife. Rather than answer my question, the instructor also claimed that he did not know the answer. The question surfaced again and again in the course of the weeks to come but consistently led to the same result. My instructors and I all remained firm in stating that we did not know the answer. Intrigued by this turn of events, I visited the instructor who had first asked the question and asked him what one could do to know the answer. He told me that I should talk to the dreamer, the one who had shaken my hand and expressed their commitment to teach me when I had first come to them.

I therefore went to the dreamer's house and sat at the kitchen table, where he was eating moose meat, a portion of which he gave to me. We shared various bits of information, and then I asked him the question, What happens to someone who dies drunk?

The dreamer went to his room and came back with a piece of paper and a pen. He first drew a path leading diagonally from one end of the paper to the other. He then added a second path turning left from the main road less than a third of the way along that road. Near the fork he drew a cluster of small lines representing a fire with three small figures around them. These were *yake wodené*, "people from heaven," he told me. He then drew two additional human figures on the main path, which, he said, was the road leading from this earth to heaven. People who died drunk, such as the two figures he pointed at, could make it to heaven, but if they made it there, *Ndawotá*, "God," turned them away. Imitating the godly figure, the Elder covered his eyes with his left hand and pointed away from him with his right hand. He then said in a strong voice, "Go away, I don't want to see you, I don't know you!" When this happens, the Elder said, drunken people have to turn back. When they reach the fork in the road, they will be taken by the three *yake wodené* standing there and thrown into the fire to burn. This, he told me, is what happens to people who die drunk.

I thanked the Elder for his answer and in my anthropological fervor asked if I could have his drawing. He said I couldn't and tucked it into his shirt pocket. He then began speaking of the hunting and trapping expeditions of his youth. Half an hour later I thanked him again and said I would return home. I had come for a Dene Tha answer to an important question. I was leaving not knowing the exact nature of the answer I had been given. The dreamer's answer called to my mind the lessons of catechism I had received as a child. It appeared that the Dene Tha Elder had given me the answer he had been taught by priests and missionaries as a Roman Catholic. But had the dreamer thoroughly accepted the Roman Catholic Church's teachings? He had kept his drawing, the only evidence of our conversation. What had I learned?

A few weeks later, on the occasion of another visit to the same dreamer, I commented on the recent Prophet Dance in which I had been invited to participate. I told him that I appreciated very much the opportunity to take part in the offerings and the dancing. He then took his previous drawing, which he had close at hand, to tell me what the Dene Tha thought happened to people who died drunk. He drew another line representing the path to heaven. This straight line, however, did not have a fork leading to a fire. Rather, the line that he now drew was broken at midpoint, where, he said, most people find it difficult to go farther, particularly if they have died drunk. Because of the difficulty, most people who die in a drunken state give up walking on the road to heaven when they reach this point, and they turn around to come back to this land, where "they are made again." They are born, grow, and live a new life among their kin. This view of things, as I was to learn (and which I describe fully in chapters 6 and 7), informed the manner in which Dene Tha interpreted sightings of ghosts in dreams or visions; the manner in which they identified newborn babies as someone who, having died, had decided to come back to be made again; and the manner in which they constructed one another's life histories. The dreamer was giving me quite a different view of the afterlife than the one he had previously offered. This second view was not the one, typically offered by missionaries, that he had so effectively dramatized earlier. Answers from two distinct religious traditions were available to him, and he had put both up for my consideration.

Once again we can see that "information is not there, ready in the native's head to be called up and expressed in discursive statements which can then be collected by the ethnographer and taken home as 'data'" (Pool 1991, 70). In this instance of interaction with a Dene Tha dreamer, as in my discussion with Paul on the value of Western education in the modern world, we see Dene Tha astutely answer the anthropologist's queries with opinions and views from mainstream Euro-Canadian society. The Dene Tha then wait to see the anthropologist's response. His own move has to be created in situ. When the anthropologist shifts the focus of the conversation away from taken-for-granted, dominant Euro-Canadian views, the Dene Tha follow suit. The Dene Tha then offer a non-Euro-Canadian perspective on education or the afterlife, the perspective that the anthropologist is actively seeking since it is the one he is interested in all along. In both instances "knowledge was being produced rather than simply being called up from some cognitive reservoir" to be tapped by the anthropologist (Pool 1991, 71). It is through such social processes that ethnographic data are generated.

YOU ARE TAKING MY POWER AWAY FROM ME

As stated in the introduction to this chapter, my view of social reality is one of ever-shifting outlooks and positions within and between social actors. Situations are always evolving and being re-interpreted, giving rise to new opportunities for agreement or conflict between actors, and fresh alternatives as to possible courses of action. So when my first period of fieldwork was nearing its end and a friend told me that a Dene Tha healer and his extended family thought I was partly responsible for the loss of their power to heal, I was shocked. How could they lay the blame for their diminished power onto me and onto the Elder among whose extended family I had found the instructors to learn Dene Dháh? In their view I had contributed to making the distressed healer and his family more vulnerable to other Dene Tha and less able to assist those who might come to them for healing or protection.

Word of this accusation came on the heels of numerous conversations with Dene Tha about their suspicions with respect to the causes of misfortune in their lives or those of close relatives. Car accidents, death by drowning, work- and hunting-related injuries, and serious physical abuse at the hand of one's spouse were all seen as part of a complex web of jealousy, evil intentions, and the desire for revenge, which always involved the use of a power received from one's animal helper to defeat another's aspirations and goals (more on this topic in chapter 5). The suspicions, accusations, and counteraccusations that informed Dene Tha perceptions of one another had come to cloud my own view of the individuals who were welcoming me into their homes and assisting me in various ways. For every Dene Tha that I had come to see as caring and trustworthy, there was another Dene Tha telling me how dangerous and evil that individual was, laying on him or her the responsibility for the suffering and even the death of others. I had reached a state of great confusion concerning all this, and I had to come to grips with the fact that I too was caught up in the web of suspicion and accusations. What to do?

Questions rushed to my mind. Had I unknowingly become an accomplice to an Elder using his power to wrong others? If there was no basis for this accusation, what was the basis for all the other accusations I had heard over the past few months? Were all the accused innocent of actually wishing and attempting to bring misfortune on others? If so, what did all the accusations stand for? Were they the result of the pain of misfortunes unexplained? Or, perhaps, a means to get attention? Attempts to disrupt associations between individuals? All these questions and more left me perplexed and disoriented. How was I to respond to this latest development in my relationship with the Dene Tha?

I left Chateh with all these questions in mind to follow up on an invitation from neighboring Cree to join them in Pipe and Sweat Lodge Ceremonies in their local community. These were Cree who knew the Dene Tha well, who had relatives among them, and who even consulted Dene Tha healers when in need. Around the campfire one night I described the point that I had reached in my relationships with the Dene Tha. As soon as I had finished my account, a Cree said that it was all very simple. His explanation went as follows: the Dene who were accusing the Elder and myself of taking their power away from them thought this was happening because they were not feeling their power as often as they had in the past. He suggested that this was so because fewer Dene Tha were calling on them for assistance, preferring to call on the Elder with whom I was closely associated. Clearly, more Dene Tha were turning to this Elder because he had gained prestige through my intense involvement with him and his extended family. To redress the situation, I had to involve myself equally with all the segments of the community; otherwise accusations of my taking part in local medicine fights would rise and could possibly lead to my eviction from the reserve.

The explanation offered by the Cree went directly to the sociological root of the accusation. The healer and his extended family who had voiced the accusation were, indeed, the group I had visited the least during the past six months. When I initiated my fieldwork, learning the language had been my first preoccupation. More than 80 percent of my time was spent with the Elder and the extended family that had offered to teach me their ways and their language. In the process, I had neglected to establish and nurture relationships with many other groups in the community. In the idiom of accusation the Dene Tha were telling me that I had upset the balance of power between different healers residing in various segments of the community. I had unknowingly disturbed the complex and delicate network of local healers. Redress was called for. I had to extend my involvement to include dreamers and healers whom I had so far neglected to visit. This was the first thing I did when I returned to Chateh in January 1981 after my first absence of six months. As a result, the accusations of the previous year disappeared.

MAKE US HAPPY ONE MORE TIME

As I widened the circle of Dene Tha families that I involved myself with, I came to share in many of their activities and to learn much about their concerns. In 1983, the healer who two years earlier had accused me of causing the loss of his power was worried about his granddaughter, Diane. A few years earlier, torn with grief when her husband had been found frozen to death near their house, Diane had begun to drink more heavily than ever before. She drifted away from Chateh, first to High Level, then to Edmonton, and finally to Montreal, where she was living as a prostitute at the hands of French Canadian pimps. Her children were in the care of her grandparents, who maintained regular contact with her by telephone. One evening in May, following a long conversation with Diane, her grandfather said to me: "Twice you have made us very happy. Can't you make us happy a third time?" He was referring to two previous occasions on which I had been in a position to help his family. He was suggesting to me that since I was leaving in early July to return to Ottawa, I could contact Diane in Montreal and arrange for her to come back with me in January of the following year. An unexpected and daunting task, to say the least.

I felt that they failed to appreciate the nature of their assignment. My objection was that if Diane was deeply involved in a drug and prostitution ring in eastern Canada, as they knew her to be, it was doubtful that her pimps would let her go. They responded that surely I could find a way to bring her back. I pointed out to them that Montreal was a very big city, that I did not know where she was, and that it might be impossible to locate her. They retorted that Montreal was in my land and that surely with Diane's phone number I could trace her. They handed over a piece of paper with Diane's phone number on it and asked me to talk to her over the phone to find out where she lived. That, I thought, was the least I could do. And so, when I left that year for

Ottawa, I wondered if it would be at all possible to make my Dene
Tha friends happy for a third time. Unexpectedly, I had to come
to terms with the fact that the Dene Tha social world I had been
exploring extended as far away as eastern Canada.

A month after my arrival in Ottawa I dialed Diane's phone
number. A male voice answered in French. I explained who I
was, how I alternated between living in Ottawa and in Chateh,
and how I had come to know Diane and her family. I asked if I
could speak to Diane since I had just arrived from Chateh. The
man proceeded to explain at length how dearly he loved Diane,
how much he valued her, and how well he looked after her. He
stressed, over and over again, that he was very happy to have her
around. This discussion confirmed my suspicion that he was not
prepared to let Diane go. I reassured him that all I wanted to do
was talk to Diane for a while to transmit news from her family
and her friends in Chateh. A few seconds later Diane was on the
phone speaking in Dene Dháh. She told me that she was just out
of the hospital, where she had been treated for a fractured skull,
the result of an ugly fight with a pimp and a friend of his. I gave
her news about her family and asked if she knew that I would be
returning to Chateh in January. She said that she knew this and
told me she would appreciate it if I called her once in a while. I
assured her I would do so, and she hung up the telephone.

During the following five months I phoned her at least once a
month. I never asked her if she wanted to come back to Chateh
with me, nor did I tell her that her grandparents would very
much like her to do so. I thought that if she was to come back with
me at all it was best to proceed in typical Dene fashion. I was in no
position to organize a rescue mission, nor was I inclined to ask
the police to raid her place and rescue her. I felt that the onus was
on her to persuade her pimp to let her go, if she was truly determined to do so. According to Dene Tha convention, the simple
fact of informing her that I was to leave for Chateh constituted
an invitation to join me if she wanted. Perhaps the grandparents'
dream would become reality after all.

In November Diane invited me to visit her in Montreal, and I
accepted. She gave me the address to her apartment on the seventh floor of a high-rise building in the center of Montreal. I
rang the doorbell with a certain amount of anxiety. The man who

opened the door was the one to whom I had spoken on the phone earlier, and he offered me a beer, which I accepted. I was soon engaged in two conversations, one in Dene Dháh with Diane and the other in French with the man who "looked after her." Diane talked about the main street on which she worked, the well-known rue Saint Laurent, which she called *eteneh dzahdonhti*, "the bad road," in Dene Dháh. She described different fights and knifing incidents she had witnessed in local bars and explained in detail how she had nearly been beaten to death one night. She pointed to her fractured skull and indicated she had been skillfully looked after in a local hospital. The man asked questions about my work and about my activities in Chateh. Diane switched to English, which the man understood, to tell me that he wished to join her in Chateh if she went back to her family in January. The man repeated in French that he loved Diane so much that he would be ready to marry her in Chateh if she ever went back there. I said that I looked forward to the day when they would visit me in Chateh, and I talked a little bit about the place and the people. When I was preparing to leave, I thanked them both for their hospitality. Diane reiterated, in English, that she would like to go back to her children and family. I told her that if this was the case, I could come and pick her up at her Montreal apartment in early January. And so we parted.

In the telephone conversations that followed, Diane repeated her intention to return to Chateh and we set the date for me to pick her up in Montreal. On the day I showed up at her apartment she was dressed in her winter coat, standing next to her suitcase and ready to go. On each side of her and right behind her stood three men, each over six feet tall and dressed in long winter coats. I greeted the man I already knew, who introduced me to his two friends. I asked, "So, are you ready to go?" Diane picked up her suitcase and said yes, and we all walked toward the elevator and waited in silence. Once in the elevator, tears started to run down the cheeks of the three men. With a choked voice one of them told Diane, "You know, if you do not want to go, we can stop him from taking you anytime you want us to." She answered, "No, it's all right. I want to go."

A few days later, at two in the morning, in the middle of a snowstorm, we were entering the driveway to her grandparents' house in Chateh. The trip from Montreal to Ottawa and from there, via Edmonton, to Chateh had been a pleasant one. The only tense moment came when we neared the turnoff to Chateh. At that point Diane asked me to continue to High Level, where she wanted to greet her Dene Tha friends at the local bar. I told her I thought it was a better idea to return immediately to her grandparents' house. She insisted that it would be only a short stop in High Level, that she felt tense, and that a beer or two would do her good. I said that it was late, that I was getting tired and would rather not extend our trip. As I said so, I turned left onto the dirt road that would take us to Chateh. Diane told me in a stern voice, "You know, I could throw a fit here and make life very difficult for you." I answered, "I know that, but you told me all along that you wanted to go back to your family and that is what we are doing now." She kept silent. I talked to her about her grandparents and how they had helped me. Surprised at this comment, she asked how. We continued to talk in this manner for an hour and a half and then pulled into the driveway of her grandparent's house, where everyone was up waiting for her arrival.

REMEMBER, THE GIFTS ARE TO GET YOU TO OTTAWA

The next story, of how Diane's grandfather helped me with his power in the Dene way, begins with my attempts, early in the course of my second period of fieldwork, to establish a relationship with Alexis Seniantha, the leading Dene Tha dreamer. At that time I paid a visit to his son and daughter-in-law. During the visit I mentioned once to Alexis's son that I wondered if his father knew that I was interested in learning the Dene Tha way of praying. The remainder of the visit was spent talking about local events, trapping, education, and so on. A few days later Alexis himself stopped for tea at my place while on his way to the band office for business. We conversed for more than two hours. He did most of the talking, given my limited ability to express myself in Dene Dháh at that time. Twice Alexis mentioned that he prayed in the way of the Dene Tha at his house at ten o'clock in the morning on Sundays. Consistent with the Dene patterns of interaction described previously, I listened but said nothing to the effect that I would be pleased to join him.

That was the first time I had interacted with a Dene Tha dreamer in this manner. I therefore went to some Dene Tha friends and told them what I had done, describing my visit to Alexis's son and daughter-in-law and summarizing Alexis's visit. I asked them what would happen if I did not show up on Sunday at his place. Immediately, they answered that he would conclude I "had no ears." To them, I had been told in unambiguous terms to come to his house around ten o'clock on Sunday morning. In the eyes of Euro–North Americans, the manner in which Dene offer information and extend invitations appears restrained and indirect. In the eyes of the Dene Tha, however, their style of communication is clear and straightforward. It is respectful of each person's right to decide on his or her own activities without feeling the imposition of another person's will. Thereafter, I joined Alexis in his house every Sunday morning for many months to come. And so began a long series of meetings that included accounts of the dreams and visions he had experienced in his life, accompanied by numerous performances of drumming and singing. When I received a drum from a Dene Tha drummer, I brought it to Alexis, who added two prayer ribbons to the side of it. The ribbons, one purple, the other green, were approximately two centimeters wide and thirty centimeters long. The sessions with Alexis soon led to similar ones with other Dene Tha dreamers and healers, including Diane's grandfather. As I spent more and more time learning about Dene Tha ways in this manner, I came to the point of offering gifts to Diane's grandfather and to Alexis Seniantha when asking for their help. On the occasion of an important meeting I was about to have in Ottawa, I proceeded in the culturally appropriate manner to buy them gifts. Such gifts are usually tobacco and various objects—shirts, moccasins, a piece of tanned moose hide, gloves, knives, ribbons, and so on. The gifts, which vary from person to person, are said to be for the animal helpers on which the dreamers and healers call to assist the one who brings the gifts.

I presented my gifts to each of the two Elders in his home. Each eagerly took the gifts and told me he was quite happy that I was taking this step. Each went into his bedroom to get his drum and began a session of instruction and intercession for me. A few days later I traveled the more than eight hundred kilometers to

Edmonton, where I stayed at my brother's house before taking the plane the next morning. When we went to bed in the early hours of the morning, my sister-in-law said not to worry, for she would wake us in time to get to the airport. In the morning, to my surprise, I awoke to the sound of drums. My eyes still closed, I paid attention to what was happening, and I saw the faces of the two healers to whom I had brought gifts. They were drumming and smiling at me, and one of them was saying, "Remember, the gifts were to get you to Ottawa." I opened my eyes, looked at my watch, and realized it was 6:45 AM. Somehow my brother's alarm clock had not functioned properly, and everyone in the house was sound asleep. I woke my brother, and forty-five minutes later we were at the airport just in time for me to board the 8:00 AM flight to Ottawa.

I don't believe this dream would have occurred had I not been deeply involved with Dene Tha dreamers and healers. To them my experience was a simple case of "knowing with the mind," a normal and recurring feature of nonverbal communication in their lives. My waking dream had occurred at the most propitious moment. Euro–North Americans would claim that it was the product of my mind's unconsciously keeping track of the passage of time and in effect creating a dream that would pull me out of sleep. Dene Tha, on the other hand, would say that it was the product of the power of the healers drumming up sounds and showing me images that would stir me. Both accounts are reasonable within their distinctive interpretive communities; the differences in interpretations need not concern us here. It is sufficient to note that the deeper my involvement became with an ever-expanding circle of dreamers and healers, the more I experienced dreams and visions that the Dene Tha saw as instances of teaching and communication through the medium of images rather than the medium of words. Having entered into meaningful conversation and interaction with others on the basis of such accounts of dreams and visions, I could ignore them in the presentation of my work or attempt to incorporate them in my ethnography. To do so is to range beyond Geertz's directive that as ethnographers "we can but listen to what, in works, in images, in actions, [others] say about their lives" (1986, 373).

Episodes such as those narrated above also show that vulnerability is an important feature of fieldwork. In this respect V. Turner (1985, 205) correctly claimed that to understand others and grasp their sociocultural environment, one ought to make oneself "vulnerable to the total impact not just of the other culture but of the intricate human existences of others." In the words of Favret-Saada (1990, 195), to accept vulnerability as a condition of one's ethnography is to recognize "that ordinary ethnographic communication—a verbal, voluntary and intentional communication, aimed at learning a native system of representations—constitutes one of the poorest varieties of human communication. It is especially unadapted to give the kind of information on the nonverbal and involuntary aspects of human experience." To become vulnerable to the intricate lives of others is to embrace "'passion'—understood as drive but also as suffering—as a condition of knowledge, hence of objectivity" (Fabian 1991, 400). Moments of vulnerability, however, are not deliberately chosen. They are lived in the midst of the unanticipated crises that are part of any life and relationship. It is the sustained day-to-day involvement with others that allows for a greater appreciation and a deeper understanding of the manner in which Dene Tha see the world and seek to live their lives within it.

*

To "use 'participation' much more radically as a method than most interpretivists have imagined" (Barth 1992, 66) involves making oneself vulnerable to the complex human existence of others, exploring new forms of knowledge, recognizing unanticipated local structures of power, and engaging in practices consistent with a local body of tacit understanding that informs the interaction of individuals, constituting their reality in coactivity. As I became part of the Dene Tha social world, I began to recognize the fundamental premises and rules of communication that underlie it. Each story from the field illustrates the process whereby Dene Tha and anthropologist reproduce a local structure, that is, the routinized practices that are based on tacit understandings and are carried out or recognized by the majority of members of a collectivity.

Stories from the field show that fieldwork is an experience in socialization. One withdraws from one's usual social environment and approaches others to learn how they think, feel, and behave. One leaves a society whose conventions one has mastered and enters the society of others who become one's teachers. To become socially competent among the Dene involves verbal and nonverbal skills, including the ability to experience waking dreams or visions that appear to flow into one's own stream of consciousness from one's immersion in their social world. But in the end, however sensitive one is to local realities, however fluent one becomes in a new language, and however at ease one is with new patterns of behavior, the ethnographer can only, at best, "be one with them, but not one of them" (Obeyesekere 1990, 11).[3]

2. True Knowledge and True Responsibility

It's up to this certain person to make up
their mind. No one else is going to make
up their mind.—Dene Tha speaker

Dene expect learning to occur through observation rather than instruction, an expectation consistent with the Dene view that true knowledge is personal knowledge. The Dene prefer this kind of knowledge since it is the form that has the most secure claim to being accepted as true and valid. Students of the Dene have often commented on the fact that this theme goes hand in hand with the premium Dene place on "noninterference" or "nonintervention" in the lives of others (Helm 1961, 174–76; Scollon and Scollon 1979, 185–209; R. Ridington 1987, 15; 1988, 46; Rushforth 1992, 485–88; Goulet 1994a, 114–19).[1] June Helm (1961, 173) refers to the constellation of Dene traits of behavior and sentiments with which we are concerned here as "the cultural theme of autonomy," in lieu of the cultural theme of "individualism" favored by J. Alden Mason (1946) and John Honigmann (1946, 1949, 1954). Unfortunately, both these expressions suggest a form of self-assertion that ignores the presence and well-being of others. To think so is to ignore an essential aspect of Dene life. True, Dene foster autonomy in one another's lives to the greatest extent possible, but they also "go far out of their way, even if it require[s] substantial camouflage, to prevent others from undertaking activities that might bring them harm" (Sharp 1994, 40) or to protect them from potential harm, as my instructors did in the middle of the night when they thought I might be in trouble. I therefore refer to the ethical principle of personal responsibility for one's life and that of others where in the past the expression of "noninterference" was used.

The Dene responsibility for one's own life is accompanied by a well-developed sense of one's position relative to others. Everywhere the older and more capable individual has a responsibility to exhibit competent and respectful behavior for younger individuals to observe and learn well. First, everyone's position in a family is defined in relation to the firstborn child. This child receives a name, and its parents, and its siblings, if any, are referred to as the father, mother, brother, or sister of that child. Second, kinsmen and friends keep an eye on one another to offer protection, important information, or food, when needed, without being asked. Parents are also careful to store firearms and ammunition away from the reach of children. Third, stories are repeated again and again to illustrate the kind of behavior that leads to well-being and the kind that leads to undesired consequences or disaster. And so one learns that generosity brings general esteem, that consideration for the well-being of others and for the community may entail subtle forms of nonverbal communication to elicit a change of behavior, and that true knowledge is personal knowledge.

The Dene promote access to this kind of knowledge as they insist on one another's autonomy and on one's ability to learn independently, by oneself. According to Rushforth (1992, 484), "the significance of the Dene preference for experiential knowledge is, despite some recent attention, underemphasized by ethnographers. It has yet to be fully comprehended." I attempt to redress this underemphasis in this chapter, and in the book as a whole. To consider true knowledge to be personal, firsthand knowledge, and to foster autonomy as much as possible in all domains of life, has profound implications for what Dene consider the proper way to teach or inform not only their children and one another but also the inquisitive ethnographer who approaches them to learn about their ways of knowing and living. In this chapter I examine aspects of Dene epistemology and ethical stance to demonstrate that they call for an investigation of Dene Tha social life in the experiential mode that Barth, Jackson, Tedlock, V. Turner, and others have referred to as "radical participation."

THE PREFERENCE FOR EXPERIENTIAL KNOWLEDGE

Among the Dene, learning proceeds with what, from the Euro–North American point of view, appears to be a minimum of intervention and instruction. To them "knowledge that has been mediated is regarded with doubt. True knowledge is considered to be that which one derives from experience" (Scollon and Scollon

1979, 185). An outsider might view this conception of true knowledge as strong social pressure against freely dispensing knowledge, but such a perception betrays the outsider's expectation that information or knowledge be imparted through instruction. This expectation contradicts the Dene view that the first responsibility everyone has in life, including the incoming ethnographer, is to learn individually and personally through observation and imitation. Concerning such an attitude to learning, D. Smith (n.d.) comments, "As Thomas Buckley writes concerning the Yurok (1979: 3) so also for the Chipewyan: 'To explain too much is to steal a person's opportunity to learn.'" To state that true knowledge of the Dene way is firsthand knowledge should not detract our attention, however, from the fact that personal experience is informed by a rich tradition of stories about powerful individuals and animals (Asch 1988, 1–3; Blondin 1990; Moore and Wheelock 1990; R. Ridington 1990; Smith 1985; Sharp 1988a), stories that legitimate the individual pursuit of true knowledge.

Consider the following observations made by a number of anthropologists, beginning with Honigmann, who remarked that, among the Kaska, an adult's instruction and direction are rarely explicit when trusting a child or the ethnographer with a task: "'Do this,' is the formula, and the child is left with the task of working out the details of an activity for himself. . . . The same kind of teaching was used for the ethnographer. Activities were illustrated but never explained in detail, the exposition of principles being ignored." Thus, to Honigmann's surprise, on the second day of a journey with dog team and toboggan, Dene entrusted him with the handling of the vehicle "without a word of instruction regarding the technique of managing the dogs" (Honigmann 1949, 185). They were confident that he would have learned the techniques entirely from observation, as indeed they had done in their youth. Compare Honigmann's report to the following by James Van Stone. While on a trip in the bush with a Kutchin family, Van Stone noted that boys were allowed to do very little except observe. Finding it "difficult to detect the ways in which children learn the techniques of sub-arctic living" under such circumstances, Van Stone concluded that "*if a boy learns anything* on trips of this kind, *he does so entirely from observa-*

tion" (1963, 44; my emphasis). Van Stone seems to have doubted that much learning could occur under such conditions. The Dene, however, are absolutely confident that these are the proper circumstances for serious learning.

Illustrative of this Dene learning strategy is the report of a Chipewyan who learned how to operate a road grader by sitting for several days at the roadside carefully watching a grader in operation. Although the man could then drive the road grader without any difficulty, he observed "that he could not say how he did it" (Scollon and Scollon 1979, 186). In a similar manner, Marcel, a Lynx Point Slavey, had come to excel at repairing clocks, radios, motors, and any other mechanical device. Impressed by his skills, Helm (1961, 184) commented that "it was a pity he had never had the opportunity for any technical training." In typical Dene fashion, Marcel responded, "Well, things often look hard, but if you try them, sometimes you find out it's not so hard after all" (Helm 1961, 184).

As noted by Rossalie Wax and Robert Thomas (1972), the preference for learning by observation rather than by instruction is found in all Native North American societies. For instance, Wax and Thomas cite Manning Nash (1958), who noted how in a factory a Maya girl silently observed the operators of weaving and spinning machines until she felt competent enough to take over and run the machines herself. According to Nash (1958, 46, in Wax and Thomas 1972, 33), the girl learns on her own, without asking any questions, "because that would annoy the person teaching her, and they might also think she is stupid." The Maya girl acts only when she feels competent, "for to fumble and make mistakes is a cause for *verguenza*—public shame," writes Nash (1958, 46, in Wax and Thomas 1972, 33). Like the Maya girl or the Chipewyan man, Native North Americans generally learn to act competently on their own through silent observation. Consequently, Native North Americans rarely "exhibit clumsiness or ineptitude before others" (Wax and Thomas 1972, 33).

Among Native North Americans generally, and among the Dene specifically, knowledge is not a commodity to be objectified in instruction; it is an expertise personally absorbed through observation and imitation. In all Dene communities, as among the Hare, "children receive little guided instruction as they learn to develop various kinds of competencies, whether the latter be expressive or instrumental in nature" (Savishinsky 1982, 127). This absence of "directed learning," writes Joel Savishinsky (1982, 127), means that "children acquire skills and self-control in more informal ways, including trial and error, imitation, modeling, participation and observation." Savishinsky (1982, 127) characterizes this kind of learning as "observational and vicarious." Among the Dene it is greatly facilitated "by the openness of the village and camps, by the freedom of movements and access accorded to children, and by the lack of visual and auditory privacy within dwellings" (Savishinsky 1982, 127).

Guédon (1994a, 49) writes that when she wanted to learn how to weave beaded headbands and sew moccasins, her Nasbena friend "made it clear that I was not going to go very far by asking questions. I was to keep quiet and watch her hands." One learns not by asking questions but by watching, silently observing how a trap is set, how a hide is tanned, how a rifle is shot, and so on. "When I was learning to embroider moccasins," writes Guédon (1994a, 50), "I was learning to become a moccasin embroiderer. I was not simply taught hunting techniques; I was imitating a hunter. I was not transmitted a skill, I was presented with a whole person shaped by that skill." Jillian Ridington experienced the same learning process among the Dunne-za. Over more than a decade, beginning in 1978, she was taught many Dunne-za skills, including how to make bannock, tan hides, and snare rabbits. Summarizing all she learned from her Dunne-za friend Daeda Davis, J. Ridington (1994, n.p.) writes: "More importantly, she taught me how to learn the Dunne-za way; not by asking questions and reading books, but by listening and watching, then fitting the answers together until I had all the information I wanted." Likewise, when I expressed my interest in dancing the Dene way in the Prophet Dance, a Dene Tha friend invited me to follow him in his footsteps around the fire. It took three years of dancing with Dene Tha before I was told, "Now you are dancing; your body moves just like ours." In such cases the knowledge gained through one's imagination, senses, and practices involves a personal transformation. To know is effectively to become a dancer, a hunter, or an embroiderer.

This pattern of learning by observation, without asking questions, is also reported by Crow Spreading Wings (1987) in her study of Agnes Vanderburg's camp in Montana. Agnes is an elderly full-blood member of the Montana Salish (Flathead) who opens her camp to Indians and whites who want to spend part of the summer living the Indian way while learning how to do beadwork, tan a hide, make a drum, and so on. When they arrive at the camp, whites are inevitably disconcerted at the lack of instruction and direction. When white visitors express an interest in beadwork or in making a drum, Agnes tells them: "Just do it. . . . If you don't do it you're never gon' learn" (in Crow Spreading Wings 1987, 42). Steadfast to their Native ways, Agnes and her Native campers carry on with their activities and offer a minimum of verbal instruction. They expect the newly arrived visitor to learn by observation of those who already master these skills.

When a Dene Tha Elder tells me that "long ago girls were with their mom, and boys with their dad," that "when the mother would do something she would teach the girl," and that one always followed "the one who worked," he is describing a process of learning by observation that is still prevalent today. The activities that a boy and a girl observe differ because of the division of labor: men hunt big game in the bush, while women may fish, snare small game, and pick berries closer to home; indoors women look after clothes, while men repair hunting gear and machines; men operate large equipment on the reserve, while women become local store clerks or secretaries. Since the productive activities of men and women differ, "men and women have access to different experiences and different primary knowledge" (Rushforth 1992, 496 n. 26). It also follows that since I am a male anthropologist, there are many aspects of Dene social life that I simply have not had the opportunity to observe or experience and that have, thus, remained beyond my reach.

When I began fieldwork among the Dene Tha, I took up a twenty-year-old Dene Tha woman's offer to teach me how to cook bannock—an activity that Dene Tha men are likely to engage in when on their trapline but not when at home. She came to my house and once in the kitchen proceeded to mix flour, water, and lard and to bake the resulting dough without offering a single word by way of instruction. One hour later, while we shared the freshly baked bannock, I asked if she was going to give me the recipe or the instructions necessary to replicate her baking. She immediately told me, "I just taught you—you've seen me do it!" Obviously, I had not watched as a Dene Tha would have watched. A forty-year-old Dene Tha father asked me once how many sports I could engage in. I mentioned swimming, white-water canoeing, scuba diving, skiing, and skating. With tears in his eyes he said that we non-Dene Tha could learn so much because we had instructors to teach us all manners of activities, whereas the Dene Tha must take the much longer and more arduous route of personal observation and imitation.

These cases, along with many others, show that from a Dene perspective "learning comes by direct experience and perception, not through the mediation of thought or conscious planning" (Scollon and Scollon 1979, 186). The same principle applies to the learning of social and ritual behavior. This is how, for instance, Tlingit women learn the process and meaning of traditional ceremonies. There, as among the Dene Tha, "the onus was on a child actively to learn what each of the greetings, exchanges, songs, and dances meant rather than on adults to provide elaborate explanations of each component" (Cruikshank 1991, 33). By the same token, when Dene Tha Elders eventually entrusted me with setting up a performance of the Prophet Dance, they brushed aside my hesitation with the remark that I had been with them in Prophet Dances often enough to know how to do it properly (see chapter 8 for an account of this experience). Although their initiative surprised me, they were acting in a manner fully consistent with Dene assumptions about learning, ones that I had not fully appreciated at the time.

The view that direct experience is the essence of all true knowledge also finds its expression in the manner in which Dene Tha convey information, be it of our land or of the other land. In conversations with monolingual Dene Tha individuals I noticed how they tended to construct their statements carefully so as to declare whether the information they conveyed was first or secondhand. The following excerpt from a conversation with a Dene Tha Elder illustrates this pattern and is related to the Dene Tha conception of knowledge, its acquisition and transmission.

True Knowledge

$\overset{1}{tu} \overset{2}{kaot'} \overset{3}{ah} \overset{}{ghedi} \overset{4}{ghats'} edi \overset{5}{iin}," \overset{6}{\acute{e}hdi} \overset{7}{wonh'} a \, adehsi$

水 for we go they say it is said he says because I say

Converted to English phraseology, the informant's statement reads as follows: "I say they say 'we are going for water' because he [my son] says this is what is said."

When asked whether the original speakers actually said, "We are going for water," the Elder said he did not know, for he had not actually heard them say this. What the Elder knew is what he heard with his own ears from his son. Asked whether his son knew if the original speakers said, "We are going for water," the Elder answered in the negative, for his son, also, was relating secondhand information. To know is to perceive directly with one's senses or with one's mind. What one has not experienced or perceived directly, one does not know. Much of what is said and repeated in conversations is, therefore, not knowledge, in the strict Dene Tha sense of the term. It follows that the credibility of individuals identified as links in the chain of transmission of information is crucial in evaluating the truth of whatever is said. That is why, among the Dene Tha, one is careful to identify the source of whatever information is conveyed.

Others have also remarked on the significance of firsthand knowledge for the Dene and their Algonkian neighbors in the eastern subarctic. Richard Preston (1975, 144) notes that the eastern Cree "define certain truth value on the basis of what a man can see with his own eyes, complemented by what he may perceive with his 'mind's eye.'" In her study of Chipewyan mapmaking Helm (1989, 28) quotes David Pentland's observation of a "crucial difference" between maps drawn by European mapmakers and the ones drawn by North American Indians: "On the European maps the simplified features are usually imaginary. Indian maps are founded on actual experience—areas not known to the mapmaker are entirely omitted" (Pentland 1975, 153; quoted by Helm 1989, 28). Helm (1989, 32) notes that features known to Matonabbee, a Chipewyan mapmaker, such as the outline of Great Slave Lake, is "so proportionately realized as to be immediately recognizable." "One marvels," writes Helm, "how their minds' eyes grasped the shape of this great body of water, some 300 mi long and encompassing over 10,000 mi^2" (1989, 32). Whereas European mapmakers "completed" a map with features of the landscape they "imagined" to be there, Indian mapmakers of the subarctic refused to do so, because they did not "know." They did not claim more than they could vouch for, for that would have risked their reputations as authoritative sources of information. As a Dene Tha once told me: "I could tell you another story, but don't write that one down, I have to find out if it's really true. Then I will tell you." Nabesna also give with as much precision as possible the source or sources of the information they are transmitting (Guédon 1994a, 50): "'I learned this from my dad. . .' or 'My auntie used to tell me about her grand'ma going there when she was a kid. . .' or 'Me, I tried it this way' or 'I heard it last year from someone, somewhere down Mentasta.' One always knows the relationship between the information and the person transmitting it." To this day, one's reputation as an accurate source of information is one of the most important social assets a Dene may enjoy. Indeed, the two worst things that can be said of a Dene Tha is that he or she is stingy and that he or she lies. To be considered truthful and trustworthy is a very important consideration in Dene Tha lives and social interaction.

Pat Moore and Angela Wheelock (1990, xvi) similarly note that "Dene storytellers usually start by naming the people who told them the stories." Dene storytellers clearly present themselves as "intermediaries" between an original speaker long ago passed away and a contemporary audience. One storyteller told Moore and Wheelock (1990, 12): "I'm not always comfortable telling these stories. Why is that? How can I be certain that I am telling the truth about events that happened before my time? That's why it sometimes seems to me like I'm burdening myself with a lie. That's the way it may appear, and I don't want to tell something which I can't be sure is true." Lisa Valentine (1995, 194) reports the same for the Severn of northern Ontario, where "dubitative verbs . . . , common in legends, carry the story into the realm of hearsay. . . . The narrator using this form makes no statement about the absolute truth value of that story; he is free to report what he has heard without being held to its veracity." This is in contrast to storytelling in which the speaker reports what he has seen with his own eyes. The speaker then makes "it quite evident that the story is from his own personal experience which functions to invest him with the authority to tell this story" (1995, 179).

Among Northern Athapaskans and among Northern Algonkians, in the absence of authority based on direct observation and experience, confidence in one's words wanes, lines on a map are not drawn, or a ceremony is not performed. It follows that to speak and act with confidence, one has continuously to update one's knowledge through active involvement in productive activities, including, from the Dene point of view, dreaming and participation in ritual activities. Otherwise, one's competence and authority wane and with it one's status in the community. To submit that "such participation is an unintended consequence of the pursuit of primary knowledge" (Rushforth 1992, 496 n. 30) is to suggest causality where there is none. The pursuit of primary knowledge and the participation in productive activities are two sides of the same coin, or, to use another image, they belong to a single gestalt in which each element constitutes the other in a back-and-forth process.

TO BE A COMPETENT INDIVIDUAL

Anthropologists use the term "nonintervention" to characterize Dene social life because they do not see Dene adults intervene where Euro–North Americans would do so: for example, instructing someone how to accomplish a particular task; stopping a year-old child from approaching a broken windowpane; taking a chainsaw and a new pair of gloves from a boy before he destroys them; or snatching liquor away from young children who are drinking it. To affirm that "the behavioral mode by which the autonomy rights of others is observed can best be summed up as non-interference" (Helm 1961, 176) is to view them as *not* acting as we would act. To engage in this kind of description is to miss the point that in behaving as they do, the Dene promote *their* values and view of life: they consistently maximize the number of occasions in which one can learn by oneself and for oneself what it is to live an autonomous life competently. Since it is the Dene world that we strive to grasp, the onus is on us to write, as much as possible, in a manner that conveys their world view and their

ethos. We should, therefore, write about the Dene ethical princi-·
ple of personal responsibility for one's own life, where in the past
the expression "noninterference" was used.

The right to one's autonomy and the obligation to respect the
autonomy of others—specifically, the obligation not to diminish
other people's ability to realize their goals on their own, including the acquisition of personal knowledge—are two sides of the
same coin. This ability is nurtured and respected throughout
one's entire life. The respect for one's autonomy is experienced
by the year-old child who moves toward a broken window, pulls
himself up onto a chair, moves his hand through the gaping hole,
feels the cold outdoor air, and safely withdraws his hand without
touching the windowpane's jagged edges. All along, the child's
parents and grandparents quietly observe as they carry on with
their own activities, while I, not believing my eyes, silently cringe
at the thought of an impending injury. At the other end of life,
the consideration for one's right to accomplish one's goals on
one's own is experienced by elderly people who in their seventies
climb aboard pickup trucks unaided. It may take them several
minutes to pull themselves partially up, slip down, and pull
themselves up again, sweating and breathing heavily in the process. As they do so, able-bodied adults casually carry on with their
conversation in the vehicle, while I wonder if it would not be
more respectful, and easier for everyone, to give the old person a
helping hand.

The differences between my spontaneous view and that of the
Dene Tha reflect our very different upbringing. As Wes Sharrock and Bob Anderson (1986, 51–52) insist, we do not enter into
a new setting "with the capacity to adequately identify and describe the activities which make up its daily life and round," and
although we "can of course make *some* description of what is happening," this characterization will initially fall short of defining
things and events as "they 'really are' in the setting under study";
a correct and competent description of the setting has to be
learned "from the people who live its life." According to the
Dene Tha, to interfere with the child's exploration of his environment would violate his right and ability to pursue and achieve
his goals. According to my point of view, to stop the child from
approaching the broken window is to protect him from possible

injury. I must, however, acknowledge that over the years the accidents and the injuries that I expected in the course of the Dene Tha children's free-ranging explorations did not occur. This fact, I believe, accounts for the relaxed attitude of Dene Tha adults who supervise their children with a minimum of interference in their activities. They know that at a relatively early age children can handle knives, axes, and chainsaws without getting hurt. The children proceed with confidence in their exploration, secure in the knowledge that no one will interfere with their activity. Similarly, to help an elderly individual get into a vehicle would be insulting, for it would suggest that he or she cannot climb on board the vehicle on his or her own. What outsiders see as noninterference in other people's lives, Dene see as preserving the other's ability truly to live one's life to the fullest extent possible.

Everywhere, the ethical principle of personal responsibility for one's knowledge and behavior informs the way parents raise their children. I often heard Dene Tha parents tell a child "Don't do this!" or "Leave that!" but I never saw a parent impose his or her will on a child or take something away from a child. Helm, who reports the same for the people of Lynx Point, illustrates this pattern of behavior with the following account (1961, 87). Carterette, Helm's coinvestigator, complained to a Slavey friend, Cora, about a four-year-old boy, Benny, who bombarded their cabin with rocks and sticks all day long despite their frowns. Cora's reply was to say that Benny had been the same at their house. Benny "had spent that morning pounding at the wall with an ax and culminated his labors by striking Cora's four-year-old daughter on the head with the blunt end." Shocked, Carterette asked, "'Good heavens, what did you do?'" Cora replied, "'Well, I told him to go home, but he wouldn't.'" Although this was not stated, I assume Cora's four-year-old daughter was simply told to withdraw from Benny, if she had not already done so on her own.

Among the Chipewyan, David Smith observed children play on the partially collapsed roof of a dilapidated two-story building. These children, "some of them very young, loved to slide down the remaining roof on pieces of cardboard, braking with their feet just before they shot off into space" (Smith, personal communication, 1997). Smith, who thought this a very dangerous activity, never saw any Chipewyan parent or adult intervene to stop it. "I struggled with myself daily," writes Smith (personal communication 1997), "wanting to rush out saying: 'You kids get the hell off that roof before somebody gets killed.' Fortunately, I didn't; no child was ever injured." Smith's spontaneous feelings and inclination to intervene were typically non-Dene, as were mine and those of every Euro–North American who visits a Dene community.

In Chateh I observed a seven-year-old child decide to work with his father's chainsaw. The boy took the chainsaw and walked out of the house with it, although his father told him not to do so. The boy tried to start the chainsaw, but when he realized there was no gasoline in it, he brought it back into the house to fill it. He found the container of gasoline but could not open it. He asked me, then his father, then his grandmother, and finally an uncle to help him open the can. Everyone declined. The boy's father and grandmother each told him, in a soft voice, to leave the container alone. The boy quietly persisted in his task and eventually managed to open the container on his own. He filled the reservoir of the chainsaw and carefully put the caps back on the container and the chainsaw. Then, looking for a pair of gloves, he found his father's and put them on. As he went out, chainsaw in hand, his father told him in a low voice, "Don't do that! You will probably tear my gloves." All along, the father and the other adults carried on with their own activities, preparing food, filing an ax, working on a beaver pelt. Outdoors the boy spent fifteen minutes trying, without success, to start the chainsaw, which he eventually abandoned on the snow in order to go play with his cousins. In the eyes of the parents, uncle, and grandparent, it was better to let the child carry on with his project than to interfere and frustrate him. How else was he to learn, as indeed they themselves and every other Dene Tha had learned, if not by minimal instruction, careful observation, and imitation? "Social actors acquire not only a sense of what is natural, they also acquire strongly motivating senses of what is desirable. They do not only know, they also care" (Strauss and Quinn 1993, 3). Since "access to knowledge is a function of access to experience" (Rushforth 1992, 490), Dene parents impose few restrictions, if any, on their children's access to experience.

True Knowledge

The same regard for one's ability to live one's own life competently is extended to individuals who, in Euro–North American society, would be classified as mentally handicapped. In one instance, the parents of five Dene Tha children introduced them to a friend, explaining that in the case of the second son there had been complications at birth. "Luckily, it was only brain damage," the mother said. I was astonished at hearing this. I had always thought of brain damage at birth as a serious impediment in life. Not so, according to the Dene Tha, for whom life comes in many forms, none necessarily superior to others. The parents explained that although the boy attended school along with his siblings, he could barely understand or remember anything that had been taught during the day. He could, however, speak and make himself understood. He assisted in many household chores, hauled in the wood and the water, and helped skin animals. He was, above all, a joy to have around as a companion. He too had learned many skills through observation and was treated as an independent and competent member of his household.

In the eyes of the Dene Tha, to be a responsible parent is to act in the knowledge that one's children are responsible for their actions and, thus, to interfere minimally with their decisions, as illustrated in the following conversation between a Dene Tha mother and a visiting Euro-Canadian teacher. The mother tried to bring her two-and-a-half-year-old daughter into the bedroom for a change of diaper, but the child resisted and began to cry.

"She never listens to me," the mother said, letting the daughter go.

"You know, if you don't teach her to obey now, when she is ten or twelve, you will never be able to do anything with her," said the teacher. "She is still small. It is time to make her do what you want to do."

In typical Dene Tha fashion the mother sat motionless as she listened to the comment. She said nothing. Ten minutes later, without saying a word, she picked up her daughter and, in spite of the child's screams and kicks, took her to the bedroom and changed her diaper. Afterward the child came back into the kitchen, kicked the carpet, hit the table, and threw a tricycle over on its side. In the mother's eyes, the obvious lesson was that the teacher's advice was counterproductive. "You see, and if you don't watch her, she will hit the baby," the mother said.

The Dene attitude is further expressed in the words of one forty-year-old Dene Tha mother: "At home I pretty much let them do what they want to do." What Dene strive for, and to a large extent obtain, is a form of power understood as "the ability to accomplish one's own choices, but without any implication that to do so necessitates control over the actions of others" (Sharp 1988a, xv). This is true, for instance, in the case of letting a child eat whatever he or she wants to eat when hungry. In one family, for instance, I observed a five-year-old boy announce to his parents and five other children that he would eat eggs. Frying pan in hand, he approached the wood stove. His dad said simply, in a very low voice: "Careful, it's hot." The boy fried four eggs on his own, added salt and pepper, and ate them. Still hungry, he fried four more eggs. All along, his parents were quietly busy with their tasks. The mother was mending clothes, and the father was repairing a snowshoe. At no point did anyone say, "I would like some too." At no time did the parents suggest, "Two are enough; leave some for others to have later." No one else was hungry then, so no one else ate then. Having eaten to his satisfaction, the boy joined his companions to continue playing.

In March 1980, while I was visiting the family of one of my Dene Dháh instructors, he and his wife told me how exhausted they were, because their children and the children of their neighboring kinsmen played and ran about in the house all evening and into the early hours of the morning. Night after night, the family of six had gone to bed at four or five o'clock in the morning. Unfortunately, the parents had had to get up early to do some work and look after the house. As I felt their exasperation and understood their exhaustion, I could see their four children, aged two to six, sleeping on a king-size bed in a room across from the kitchen. It was eleven o'clock in the morning. My first response was to ask, "But why don't you wake them up and put them to bed earlier tonight?" As soon as I asked, I realized that my question reflected my values and not those of these parents or of fellow Dene. I remembered the general pattern of family life that I had noticed within a few weeks of my arrival in Chateh: there was no mealtime, for people ate whenever they felt hungry; there was no bedtime, for people slept when they were tired—a pattern of socialization also reported by Minnie Freeman (1978) for the Inuit.

Bossiness, that is, "giving orders, demanding, telling another person what to do," is not often seen, writes Helm (1961, 176), for everyone is considered his or her own boss. In fact, the only instances of "bossy behaviour" she observed were on the part of drunk men. Although the individual is expected to be self-reliant and self-sufficient as much as possible, every household member knows what he or she is expected to do. No one is told what to do because, by and large, everyone does what he or she ought to do. During his stay with a Dene family in their bush camp at the beginning of the trapping season, René Fumoleau (1995, 153) writes that he "never heard anybody giving an order to anybody else, or telling the children: 'Do this,' or 'Don't do that'." While cooking, the mother would say: "'There's not much water left in the barrel' which meant that someone had to grab a pail and go down the river bank for water." Or the father, without looking at the two boys: 'We're running short of firewood.'" In due time the boys would fetch the wood, and thus family life would unfold smoothly as everyone carried on with his or her responsibilities.

Dene Tha parents let their children make decisions that non-Dene parents or professionals would never consider letting them make. For example, when a six-year-old girl was bitten by a dog, I expressed my concern about rabies to the parents and suggested the need for a medical examination and, possibly, a vaccination. I offered, if they wished, to take them to the nursing station in my vehicle. The parents listened and sat in silence for a few minutes. They then told me that their daughter did not want to go and that they could not and would not take her for medical attention against her will. The girl looked at me with a smile. She knew that it was up to her to make up her mind and that, once she had done so, everyone would respect her decision. A week later the wound had properly healed, and the girl could be seen merrily playing with her siblings and cousins.

I observed a similar situation one afternoon when a doctor and a nurse came into a Dene Tha home asking where they might find the eight-year-old girl who was at risk of contracting tuberculosis. The doctor explained that they had flown to Chateh specifically to vaccinate this girl and a few other children also known to be at risk. It happened that the girl they were looking for was in the house at the time. The five Dene Tha adults who were present remained silent as six Dene Tha children quietly moved around. The nurse asked if the girl they were looking for was in the house, but no one answered. Growing impatient, the doctor explained that he was on a tight schedule and would soon have to leave. He reiterated that without the proper vaccination the girl could become very sick. He obviously expected the adults to cooperate and to answer his questions. From the Dene Tha point of view, however, it was the girl's responsibility to identify herself to the doctor. The girl knew that no one would point her out to the doctor. In the end the doctor and nurse had to leave without having identified the girl they were looking for. The parents of the girl looked at me with a smile, happy that I had not stepped in to undermine the child's ability to make up her own mind on this important matter.

TO BE RESPONSIBLE FOR ONESELF AND OTHERS

The same ethical principle informs the Dene Tha response to self-inflicted misfortune. For example, at nine o'clock in the evening, Jack, who was eighteen years of age, ran into his parents' house, hand over his mouth, blood dripping through his fingers. His mother followed him into the house and told everyone, "He drove his snowmobile through the metal wire of the fence." Everyone in the house immediately broke into laughter. I was stunned at the sight of Jack and at the response of his parents and siblings. No one got up quickly to attend to his injury. On the contrary, he was left to look after himself. Visibly in pain, he walked around the living room twice and then went to wash his face and stop the bleeding by holding a cloth soaked in ice water onto his wound. Meanwhile, everyone continued to laugh heartily.

In the following days I realized that Jack's misadventure had become part of the local folklore. I observed that the Dene Tha account of the event differed markedly from the one I had written down in my fieldnotes. When a Dene Tha told the story, the blood running from the wound was barely referred to, the laughter of parents and siblings was never brought up, nor was the fact that no one assisted Jack. The Dene Tha account reported the event as follows: Jack knew the fence wire was there as he had stopped to pass underneath it earlier on his way to his girlfriend's house. On his way back home, in his hurry, he had completely forgotten about the wire. Thus he drove right into it and badly hurt himself. At this point in the story the Dene Tha narrator and audience invariably break into laughter. How can one drive into an obstacle one is already aware of? Everyone understood that it was the responsibility of Jack to avoid the accident he had gotten himself into and that it was equally his responsibility to have looked after himself. Listeners, old and young, were reminded that they were all expected to behave responsibly and look competently after themselves lest they too make themselves the laughingstock of the community.

On another occasion, late at night, as I was driving a Dene Tha man and his grandson home from a Prophet Dance, we slowly drove by two drunken men involved in a fistfight. Because of his poor eyesight the grandfather moved closer to the windshield, but he could not make out who was involved. Asked who was fighting, the grandson answered with the name of the man with the bleeding face. As soon as he heard the name, the grandfather broke into laughter, saying: "He is just making life more difficult for himself. He might learn." When his laughter subsided, the grandfather instructed me to continue on our way to his home. When we drove by the R.C.M.P. station, there was no thought of informing them of the ongoing fight, for it was clearly the responsibility of the men involved in the fight to learn that their behavior would simply make their lives more difficult. The grandfather, like Jack's parents and siblings in the preceding story, responded to the sight of self-inflicted misfortune in a typically Dene Tha fashion.

It is a basic premise of Dene Tha thought that one learns from the hard lessons of life. As one Dene Tha mother said of her daughter: "She has to learn the hard way." Fumoleau tells the story of Jennie, who was leaving her family to follow a young white man who had arrived at their village for the first time four days earlier. This young man had fallen madly in love with Jennie and wanted to marry her. Jennie was willing to leave with him. Although many fellow Dene thought her move was foolish, they left her to herself to make up her mind. "In the midst of their sadness," writes Fumoleau (1995, 143), the parents said:

"We have trained our daughter to be responsible for herself and to make her own decisions. This is her life. And if it doesn't work out, she'll know we still respect her, and she'll come back."

Sharp (1986, 261) reports a similar case, in which the mother decided to intervene in her daughter's decision to leave with a man named Magic Boy. As soon as the daughter had moved in with Magic Boy, the mother voiced her opposition. When the mother publicly expressed her disgust for Magic Boy, "most people felt that Magic Boy was showing a great deal of restraint by not taking action and said that, if she would only cease complaining in public, she would suffer no harm" (Sharp 1986, 261). The mother persisted in her opposition to Magic Boy's relationship with her daughter. When Magic Boy and the daughter boarded the plane that would take them to their new place of residence, the mother also embarked on the plane and forcefully retrieved her daughter. Magic Boy did nothing. He said nothing to the mother, who swore at him and slapped him in the face. "He only looked at her. In the eyes of the [Chipewyan] audience it was a death sentence. Within the year she was dead and her daughter, pushed drunk and naked from a car at the city dump, was an abandoned rape victim who froze to death" (Sharp 1986, 261).

The consequences of actions, not prohibitions from parents and relatives, teach one to modify one's behavior on one's own. From this perspective the Dene Tha would have no difficulty approving of the conduct of a young man I call John, who had let his young cousins get drunk while he himself was deciding to give up drinking. Entering his house one morning, I found it empty except for John. He was sitting on his bed half drunk. Two empty whiskey bottles and several bottles of beer were scattered around the floor. When I asked how he was, he replied that he was happy because he had decided to stop drinking in the course of the night. John had been drinking with friends and had returned home in his car, with bottles of beer and whiskey left to drink. Thinking that drinking was bad and that he should quit, he nevertheless kept on drinking in his room, where he silently observed his younger cousins, children eight and ten years old, get drunk as they helped themselves to some of his liquor. He eventually decided to rid himself of the remaining liquor and poured it on the ground outside the house. He then fell asleep.

True Knowledge

As I listened to him, I thought of the contradiction between his words and his behavior—between his opinion that drinking was bad and his letting his young cousins get drunk with his liquor. Intrigued by his attitude, I decided to find out from other Dene Tha what they thought. Without revealing John's identity, I informed Dene Tha friends of what I had seen and heard and asked them what John had been doing. They immediately answered: "He was setting an example. This is how you stop. He wants them [his young cousins] to see how it was with him when he was drinking. He wants them to take some of the medicine he had. It's up to this certain person to make up their mind. No one else is going to make up their mind."

To drink or not to drink is one's own responsibility, so to take the liquor away from the children would have been to make that decision for them. This would be a most irresponsible thing to do. I commented that in my experience, there was a striking difference between a Euro-Canadian family and a Dene family, because white parents would take the liquor away from the children. The Dene wife and husband immediately replied, "Yeah, just like the missionaries did with us." They looked at each other, surprised at having said the same thing at the same time.

To clarify what she meant by letting each person, child or adult, make up his or her own mind, the wife offered the following example. Because she was a Dene Tha teaching assistant, the local priest had asked her to prepare a group of six schoolchildren for their First Communion. Other, non-Dene teachers were asked to do the same with similar groups of children. While the non-Dene teachers immediately scheduled formal religious instruction after regular school hours, the Dene Tha teaching assistant asked her own three school-aged children to invite the children she had been assigned to her home. In preparation for their arrival she laid out religious books and pictures on the living room table together with food and beverages. While the children sat down to eat, she retreated to the kitchen to listen to their conversation and to observe their behavior. She was prepared to answer questions they might raise about the books and pictures but not to question them herself or to attempt to direct their attention to anything in particular. It was up to them to seek information from her if they saw fit. Although she knew that these children would be prepared for First Communion quite differently from their peers in the hands of non-Dene teachers, she proceeded in her own way, according to Dene Tha principles of learning, without informing the local priest or the other non-Dene teachers that she was doing so.

In brief, the following statements reflect the Dene attitude toward their children and fellow Dene: "At home I pretty much let them do what they want to do." "It's up to this certain person to make up their mind; no one is going to make their mind." "The kids should learn for themselves." These sayings, and countless similar ones, serve as a constant reminder that the right to one's autonomy and the obligation fully to respect that of others, irrespective of age, are the cornerstones of Dene Tha social life. The following generalization about Native North Americans by Wax and Thomas (1972, 35) applies perfectly to the Dene: "From earliest childhood he is trained to regard absolute non-interference in interpersonal relations as decent or normal and to react to even the mildest coercion in these areas with bewilderment, disgust, and fear."

TO BE WITH NON-DENE THE DENE WAY

The Dene view of responsibility and socialization of children is obviously not one shared by non-Dene. What happens, then, when Dene Tha interact with non-Dene who, because of their upbringing, view responsibility and accountability quite differently? By and large they behave as they do with one another, respecting the autonomy of those who come to them with distinct professional and personal agendas. A Dene Tha mother observed non-Dene parents take an ashtray or periodicals away from their children in the lobby of the hospital. She said she felt "like going over there and give it to the kids" but did nothing of the sort. She wondered why the parents were so mean. Why did they not let the children learn themselves? She kept her thoughts to herself. She would never admonish the parents to amend their ways. That would constitute interference in their lives.

Consider the interaction between the Dene Tha and the local non-Dene teachers who ran the yearly spring carnival. The event included dogsled races, snowshoe races, and various competitions to determine who could most quickly saw a log, eat a pie without holding it with one's hands, or light a fire and bring a cup of water to a boil. The event drew two to three hundred Dene Tha of all ages who were happy to witness all the activities and consume the hot food and beverages that were available at different stands. From 1980 to 1983, the first four times I participated in the carnival, the local teachers were clearly in charge of the program and of the activities. Using loudspeakers, they would call in English on Dene Tha children and adults to engage in contests or races. Later they would announce winners and give out prizes, again all in English. The teachers often complained that the responsibility for the carnival rested on their shoulders, and they were adamant that without them nothing would get done. Hence in 1984 they decided to stop running the show and to leave the reservation on the weekend of the scheduled carnival.

Once the decision of the teachers was known, the names of approximately a dozen Dene Tha in their early thirties, mostly men, began to circulate in the community as the ones who were to organize the carnival. The carnival was to have taken place as scheduled, but on the eve of the event the Dene Tha men got drunk, and most of them ended up in the R.C.M.P. holding tank on the reservation. On the morning of the day set for the event only a few individuals wandered around on the carnival grounds, whereas in the previous years at that time school-teachers had been busy putting Dene Tha helpers to work setting up the stage for various competitions and setting up stands for hot food and beverages. Shortly after noon approximately forty Dene Tha adults and children arrived on the site and began setting up food and beverage stands. Pickup trucks went back and forth from the site to the community. The crowd grew larger. The voices of men in their late forties and early fifties were soon heard over loudspeakers as they began to call the various events. From beginning to end no English was heard; all was in Dene Dháh. People seemed more relaxed than in previous years. There was much laughter and teasing. There was no predetermined schedule to follow. Later in the afternoon the would-be-organizers appeared to mingle among the others and take part in events of their choosing. In stark contrast with the previous years this was clearly a Dene Tha Carnival run by the Dene Tha for the Dene Tha. In the preceding years no one had told the teachers to stand back and let the Dene Tha organize the event. That would have been confrontational. The Dene Tha had simply let the teachers run the day as long as they wished to. Once the teachers had withdrawn from the community, however, the Dene Tha happily took over the carnival.

The Dene view that one should not control the actions of others also shapes their view of hospitality—an outlook so foreign that Euro–North American visitors to Chateh told me they considered Dene Tha hospitality to be nonexistent. Their opinion coincided with Helm's report (1961, 86) that among the Slaveys of Lynx Point, "manners are manifested only in a negative sense, that is the *lack* of special recognition accorded an individual or a situation." In Lynx Point "a visitor to a house is ordinarily accorded no acknowledgment upon arrival; in turn, he does not proffer any, nor does he knock or in any way indicate his presence before entering a dwelling" (Helm 1961, 86). Once one is inside a Dene dwelling, "no offer of food or non-alcoholic beverage is made" (Helm 1961, 86). Again, Dene are described as *not* behaving as we would. To describe the process of welcoming in Dene homes as consisting of a lack of recognition accorded to an individual is to emphasize what is not there from an Euro–North American perspective. Dene hospitality goes unrecognized for what it is in the eyes of those who practice it. From a Dene perspective nothing is missing: everyone is there, carrying on with his or her activities, to be seen and observed, leaving the guest responsible for his or her actions.

On the other hand, Cree students who in 1983 visited Dene Tha families with me readily identified "Indian" hospitality by the manner in which we were greeted in Dene Tha homes.[2] They characterized the form of hospitality that they perceived among the Dene Tha, and that they had also been raised with in their Cree homes, as follows:

> In visiting they don't say "Hi, how are you?" They let you come to them. They keep on doing what they do when they visit.
>
> Head down is a sign of respect, like the lady making moccasins, she took a short look at us and looked down, that is respect. Or when that old woman came in that other house,

49

her son-in-law did not look at her; he even turned his head a little. That too is respect.

When we visit, when we leave, the talking starts among them. In the first visit you don't push yourself in, a no-no in Indian culture; you do not push, for example don't walk in someone's room in first visit, don't ask too many questions.

When we meet someone, we don't ask names directly, because it is too personal. In meeting someone, children have a role to play. A woman introduced herself with "This is Andy," showing her baby. The child is shown; it is important to connect through a third party.

The way we interpret listening is different from the way white people interpret listening. To listen one does not have to stop and look at you in the eye.

In houses we went to, people did not offer us anything, tea, chair, or food. The idea is to help yourself. It is up to you.

After a while you get to know somebody. Then you don't ask for tea or food; you take it yourself. They make you feel at home. They are telling you, "Don't be like a stranger; all I have is yours." It is up to you.

In the view of these Cree students, as in my own experience, Dene Tha hospitality contrasts with Euro–North American norms concerning social interaction between visitors. As a result, the visitor to a Dene Tha home often has the impression that he or she has been left standing there and, not surprisingly, may leave thinking that the Dene have shown no sense of hospitality.

Unless one is told about the nature of Dene Tha hospitality and the reasons for their behavior toward a visitor, one will never understand why the Dene Tha carry on with their own activities, avoid eye contact, and first engage in silent observation rather than conversation. Dene Tha drink and eat when they are thirsty and hungry. They believe that it is up to the visitor to feel at home and help himself or herself if thirsty or hungry. The teapot sitting on the stove and the cups sitting nearby are, indeed, there for all to see and use whenever one feels like it. In spite of what Euro–North Americans might think, Dene Tha hosts are expressing respect and are in fact saying: "It is up to you. You may help yourself if you please."

Visitors are greeted just as members of the household returning home are greeted, without a word of welcome, without anyone interrupting his or her activity to greet the one arriving.
Fumoleau (1995, 28–29) offers a fine illustration of the Dene pattern of greeting a family member who has come home after an
absence of a few days. The case concerns Eddy, a fifteen-year-old
from Fort Good Hope. Along with four younger siblings, Eddy
had spent nearly two months trapping in the bush. The father
and Eddy's two younger brothers had come back to Fort Good
Hope by skidoo, while the mother and the two smallest flew back
by small airplane. Eddy was coming back on his own with the
family's dog team. The trip was to take him three days, "setting
up his tent every evening at _40, having to feed himself and the
dogs, aware that nobody was closer than fifty miles, and that any
mistake would be his last one" (Fumoleau 1995, 29). Fumoleau
was visiting Eddy's parents the day they were expecting him
back. A child, looking through the window, was the first to see
Eddy in the distance and to announce his return. Eddy tied the
dogs to their posts and walked into the house. He removed his
parka, dropped it onto the floor with its hood covered with frost,
and rubbed his footwear one over the other to remove the snow.
He then walked to the stove to warm his body, stretching and
flexing his limbs, taking in the radiant heat. All the while, writes
Fumoleau (1995, 28), "life was going on in the house: baby slept
on the couch, two children played on the floor, a boy prepared a
pelt stretcher, and mother watched a pot on the stove while conversing with me. After a while she turned to Eddy: 'You came
back?' 'Yes, I came back.'"

Dene conduct their lives without controlling the actions of
others and without being controlled by others, and they welcome
non-Dene who learn to conduct themselves accordingly. To com-
port oneself in this fashion has far-reaching implications for the
manner in which one truly informs others of one's intentions.
This point is illustrated in the following two examples. The first
is a story told by René Fumoleau, who arrived as a missionary in
Fort Good Hope in 1953 and who has since assimilated Dene
values to a rare degree for a non-Dene. The story begins at a conference in Yellowknife that Fumoleau attended with numerous
Dene leaders and community members from across the North-

west Territories. During the course of the conference Fumoleau expressed to a Dene friend his wish for an opportunity to spend time in the bush. Fumoleau knew his friend would leave in the fall to spend an extended period in the bush. Proceeding with typical Dene sensitivity to not imposing oneself on others, Fumoleau expressed his interest to his friend without expecting an immediate response. At the end of the conference he did not know what the result would be. They were soon hundreds of kilometers apart, he in Yellowknife, north of the Great Slave Lake, and his friend in Fort Good Hope, down the majestic Mackenzie River.

A few weeks after the conference a Fort Good Hope resident stopped by Fumoleau's house to visit and have tea. In the course of their conversation the visitor mentioned that Fumoleau's friend was soon to spend a few weeks in the bush. No more was said on the topic, but Fumoleau understood he was being told that the opportunity was there for him soon to join his friend if he so wished. A few more weeks went by, and another visitor from Fort Good Hope stopped by Fumoleau's house. This visitor mentioned, in passing, the exact date on which Fumoleau's friend had chartered a small plane to be flown with his family to their trapline. Here was the invitation to go along. Fumoleau packed his suitcase and boarded a plane that flew him to Fort Good Hope. Then his friend, who was expecting him, took him aboard his chartered plane, and they left for the bush.

Scott Rushforth and James Chisholm (1991, 50–51) note that Bearlakers tend to visit the person of whom they have a request to make, and the more important the request, the more likely the one making it will leave before receiving a verbal response from the addressee. For example, a request might consist of a simple observation, in the course of a conversation, that if one had a motorboat, one could go visit one's fishing net. The addressee will never answer verbally, nor will he or she signal that the request has been heard. The response is given later "through subsequent compliance or noncompliance with the request" (Rushforth and Chisholm 1991, 51). The one needing the boat, for instance, "might find that his request was successful only after the addressee's son moves the boat to a spot in front of the requester's warehouse a few minutes or even hours later" (Rushforth and

Chisholm 1991, 51). And so when Fumoleau showed up at the appropriate time to leave with his friends, they knew that he really wanted to go with them.

On the strength of Fumoleau's story and on the basis of many similar stories heard over the years, I communicated in this fashion with the Dene Tha in Chateh, as can be seen in the following case involving myself, a man named Steve and his wife, Rose. They opened the door to my house without knocking, much as I do when I visit them in their house, because knocking suggests that the other person may have something to hide. They came in, sat at the table where I was writing, and placed on the chair next to them the bag they carried with them when they have artifacts to sell. Both Steve and Rose were intelligent and skilled artisans. They did not show me the contents of their bag, nor did they speak of selling. They had already been as explicit about their intentions as was necessary and proper from a Dene Tha perspective. We sat together, drank tea, and talked about other things, all along knowing that an offer to buy was being made and considered.

With us was another Dene Tha man who had also come in to visit. He described at length a small-scale canoe he had just carved. It too was for sale, but he never asked me directly, or anyone else, if we wanted to buy it. When the man mentioned that he had had a hard time carving this canoe because he didn't have the proper knife, Steve said that he and his father's brother had very good carving knives. Steve told the man that he should ask his uncle what kind of knives he had. What the man did not know was that Steve had recently made knives, which were on sale at the local store. At first, the knives at the store were not selling, and Steve had wondered why. Steve then offered a knife to his uncle, who was carving the wooden frames of snowshoes. Delighted with the knife, the uncle said so to everyone who would hear him, at home, at the local store, and at the band office. In no time, all the knives in the store were sold and an order for additional knives received. Steve then told me, "I guess this is the way to sell things around here." One sells things by word of mouth, through third parties who have had a direct experience of the quality of the goods offered for sale. They truly know.

Thus the only thing Steve said to the man complaining about his carving knife was that he should talk to someone else who had a good carving knife. In a similar way, the man with the canoe to sell wondered aloud, in a soft voice, if the teacher who lived across the road might be interested in buying it. He was suggesting that unless I made an offer, I would lose the opportunity to buy. He would soon be looking for other buyers. Without establishing eye contact, I said that I was unable to buy at this time. Steve and his wife immediately got up, thanked me for the tea, and told me they had other visits to make. They understood that my answer to the other man was also meant for them. All the necessary information had been conveyed in the proper, nondirect manner, through verbal and nonverbal cues. No one was told what to do or pressured to do anything. All were informed and made up their own minds on the basis of that information.

Over the years I became more and more sensitive to what outsiders characterized as an indirect way to approach others. In their detailed and informative analysis of directive speech acts among Bearlakers, Rushforth and Chisholm (1991, 38–63) proceed on the basis of technical distinctions. They classify speech acts as indirect or direct, and intended meaning of speech acts as implicit or explicit. Bearlakers, however, distinguish between their speech acts according to other dimensions of contrast, for instance, those of relative strength and/or control. Bearlakers consistently characterized "the most direct and explicit kind of utterance" as "the strongest and least controlled type of directive" (Rushforth and Chisholm 1991, 43). To lack control in one's speech is to issue a command to someone else. To show control is to speak and act in a manner that avoids the impression that one is interfering, or wishes to interfere, in the lives of others. The Dene Tha believe that their way of approaching others is very direct. They claim that outsiders are too often without ears to hear or eyes to see. From their point of view a successful exchange depends greatly on the observation skills of the parties involved, for much communication is nonverbal rather than verbal. While clearly communicating their intentions in this way, they are patient, for they know that each party to an exchange needs time to consider his or her response.

IMPLICATIONS FOR RESEARCH STRATEGIES

Given the Dene approach to communication, it is clear that interviews are a poor means of investigation among the Dene. Con-

True Knowledge

sider, for instance, the following transcript of a conversation between a local teacher and a Dene Tha man in his mid-thirties:

> Someone told me that when a man prays in the bush while hunting, he faces the sun. Do people do that?
> I don't know much about the Indian way. . . . I never asked.
> Would you like to know so that you could pass it on to your children?
> Sure, I would like to know, but some of those things you don't ask. Like it's impolite to ask or improper to ask.
> Is it improper for me to ask these questions about prayer?
> Like I said, some things are improper to ask.

The Dene Tha reply to the outsider's request for information about the Prophet Dance can be summarized in a few words: "I never asked" and "You should never ask." Why? Because one learns these things by observation, by involvement in the ceremony itself, and by careful consideration of the stories that dreamers and older people will eventually tell.

The Dene Tha man's response to a direct inquiry is characteristic of the Dene in general. Early students of northern Native culture reported frustration at their failure to engage Northern Athapaskan informants in controlled systematic research (Scollon and Scollon 1979, 204–5). In 1908 Lowie found the people of Fort Chipewyan "highly suspicious" and, in some cases, "uncompromisingly refractory" (Lowie 1959, 31). In 1913 Mason (1946, 3–7) experienced great difficulty securing the services of interpreters in four Northern Athapaskan communities. Many of those who promised to interpret never materialized. In 1928 Osgood faced similar difficulties, as did Honigmann at Fort Nelson in 1943 and at Lower Post in 1944–45, despite having been warned earlier by Osgood that Northern Athapaskans may be difficult to approach.[3] Helm (1961, 3) writes that to overcome "the unapproachability of the Interior Athapaskan [which] is well known in anthropological lore," she and her coinvestigator, Carterette, offered their "services as school teachers in return for the aid, ethnological and practical, that we might ask of the community."

R. Ridington (1988, 46) writes that in the first stages of fieldwork among the Beaver, his training in the methods of social sciences blinded him "to the fundamental cultural reality that asking direct probing questions is both meaningless and insulting to the Dunne-za intelligence." I have found the same among the Dene Tha. To seek interviews in a local dialect, rather than through an interpreter, is seen as equally insulting because it totally misses the point that learning ought to occur primarily through observation and direct experience as opposed to the mediation of explicit instruction and guidance. To enlist the assistance of a young translator is also counterproductive, for Dene Elders expect a young person to "wait until he or she is told something, as it is up to the elders to decide when a young person is ready to hear things" (Beaudry 1997, 75). The same applies to the visiting anthropologist, regardless of his or her research agenda and grant deadlines.

Shepard Krech's opinion (1980, 94) that progress in the investigation of Northern Athapaskan religion "will come only from those who work with ease in Northern Athapaskan language" must be qualified. Fluency in the native tongue is not in and of itself sufficient to ensure the sought-after progress in the ethnography of the Dene way of knowing and living.[4] As Ganath Obeyesekere (1990, 230) observed, "There are people who are thoroughly fluent in an alien language but are quite incapable of understanding the alien culture." Command of the native tongue is certainly important in working directly with Dene Tha dreamers and in gaining access to the Dene Tha categorization of their universe, but it will not by itself give the fieldworker an entry into the rich social life of the Dene.

Ronald Scollon and Susan Scollon (1979, 203; 1983, 15) attribute the general taciturnity of the Dene, independently reported by numerous investigators, to a number of factors, including the Dene avoidance of social contexts in which personal reality and opinion are open to challenge and negotiation. Since Dene "avoid conversation except when the point of view of all participants is well known," it follows that they are more talkative in contexts "where there is no threat to the speaker's view of himself or the world" (Scollon and Scollon 1983, 15–16). To the Dene, it follows that the outsider attempting to establish rapport through talk appears aggressive: "The more the researcher relies on talk to negotiate this 'rapport,' the more aggressive he or she is felt to have become and the greater the resistance and general taciturnity become" (Scollon and Scollon 1979, 207). This explains how the largely silent encounters with the Dene Tha that characterize the early stages of fieldwork progressively give way to lively conversations about a wide range of issues, some mundane, others more central to the lives of those concerned. As illustrated in chapter 2, this shift occurred as I engaged in events with Dene Tha in a manner that did not challenge their values and perspective on life.

Northern Athapaskans communicate with visiting anthropologists on the basis of their estimation of the ethnographer's experience and knowledge. As stated earlier, this estimation is a key factor in determining the flow of information between the two. An old Hare informant told Sue Hara that "Indian people know things by dreams. But *this, the white people do not understand*" (1980, 220; my emphasis). A Career Indian expressed a quite different point of view to Guédon: "You understand, *we can only explain [dreams/visions] to people who can understand*" (1988, 6; my translation and emphasis). This view was vouchsafed to Guédon only after she had become a mother and had shared personal dreams with her informants. Fifteen years of ethnographic work among Dene convinced Guédon that "her informants adapt their information to her age and to her experience" (1988, 5; my translation). Guédon's informants transmitted to her what they considered important in light of their assessment of her level of experience and understanding. Not surprisingly, the ethnographic record shows that through a process called *recipient design* (Sacks and Schegloff 1979), Dene Tha speakers, like speakers everywhere, "design their utterances for certain aspects of the context, especially for who the other participants are and what they have just said" (Nofsinger 1991, 9). And, one must add, for what other participants have done or not done.

Throughout the course of my stay among the Dene Tha, I always had the impression that Dene Tha dreamers in particular were relating to me with what they knew were my abilities and my knowledge of the language. Although they could evaluate my expertise in the Dene Tha world, I could never truly do the same with theirs, for it far exceeded the reach of my experience. For example, in my third consecutive field trip to Chateh, a Dene Tha dreamer told me that although I had reached a high level of knowledge according to the white man (*Egeeyah*), I was still comparatively far behind in the Dene way. Lifting his left hand from his knee up to the height of his shoulder to suggest the level of knowledge attained in the white man's way, *Egeeyah k'ihhin*, he lifted his right hand in parallel to the left, but only a third of the way. This was how far I had come, and how far there was to go, in "the Dene Tha way," *Dene Tha k'ihhin*. Assuming that I have progressed a little more on this road since, I am deeply aware that I am attempting to understand the Dene and that I am writing this ethnography from a position of relative knowledge and ignorance, unaware of all that I have been unable to grasp.

*

The epistemological stance that privileges direct, personal knowledge over any other kind of knowledge, and the ethical position that promotes "the inherent right of individuals to govern themselves freely and independently," are intimately associated (Rushforth 1992, 483). The Dene way of knowing and living is an expression of great confidence in the human ability to learn to live responsibly and competently without diminishing other people's opportunity to live in the same way. Everyone is expected to learn by mindful observation and careful consideration of the consequences of one's actions. The ethical principle referred to in the literature by outsiders as noninterference in other people's lives is, from the perspective of the Dene epistemology, one of personal responsibility for one's own life.

Because the Dene consider true knowledge to be personal, firsthand knowledge, they learn in a manner that emphasizes the nonverbal over the verbal, the experiential over the exposition of principles. In this way they foster one another's ability to learn and live competently. They promote the sense of one's autonomy and competence over the sense of one's dependence and incompetence. Among the Dene the ability to learn through observation and imitation and the power to accomplish one's own choices by oneself are nurtured and respected throughout one's entire life. We have seen Dene interact with their children, elderly individuals, and non-Dene in this fashion. They expect everyone who has ears to hear and eyes to see to learn and live in this way, and that includes the inquisitive ethnographer. Dene epistemological views and ethical values thus lead to an investigation of Dene social life through what Jackson, Tedlock, V. Turner, Barth, and others have referred to as "radical participation." The nature and extent of this participation become clear over the course of the following chapters.

3. Powerful Beings and Being Powerful

*

It all goes back to the time when animals
were like human beings, they could talk
and everything.—Dene Tha speaker

The Dene Tha, like any other human population, live "not directly or nakedly" in their environment but within a body of assumptions and taken-for-granted propositions developed within their historical and social situation (Frye 1982, xvii). We all perceive our environment and its inhabitants according to our notions, however implicit, of personhood, nature, or animal. The following statement by Stanley Fish (1980, 370) applies equally to the Dene Tha, to the writer of this book, and to its reader: "Whatever seems to you to be obvious and inevitable is only so within some institutional or conventional structure, and that means that you can never operate outside some such structure."

The purpose of this chapter is to uncover part of the Dene conventional structure concerning powerful beings and the process of becoming a powerful person. Among the Dene Tha, as elsewhere, including among social scientists, notions of power and powerfulness encode "ideas about the nature of the world, social relations, and the effects of actions in and on the world and the entities that inhabit it" (Arens and Knapp 1989, xii).[1] Dene Tha, like many other Dene, "frequently refer to knowledge, power, and their use by individuals when explaining how and why events take place" (Rushforth 1992, 486). The concept of powerfulness that Dene have in mind, however, is not the one we usually associate with the legal and political realm, consisting in the ability to impose one's will on another; nor is it the one we examined in the first chapter, where, following Sharp, we defined power as the ability to accomplish one's goal by oneself without compelling anyone else to act in a certain way. When Dene speak of a power, they think of a powerfulness inherent in plants, animals, or other substances, which can affect human beings knowingly or unknowingly. This powerfulness can be tapped by human beings to change the course of events in their lives or the lives of others.

To the Dene this notion of powerfulness is through and through an "experience-near" concept.[2] The validity of propositions concerning powerful beings comes to the Dene Tha not through instruction or argumentation but through lived experiences. By the time a Dene Tha child has reached the age of five, he or she has experienced with his or her immediate family and relatives countless numbers of events that are repeatedly seen as evidence that other-than-human powers are at work in human lives. These powers bring about success or failure in the hunt, cause an illness or an accident, shield or fail to shield one from the evil intentions of others, and so on.

POWERFUL BEINGS

We already know that, to the Dene Tha, the following propositions are obvious and certain: human beings, animals, and plant forms live in "our land," *ndahdigeh*, and in "the other land," *ech'uhdigeh*. Animals and plants found in the bush are powerful, sentient beings. They are the material manifestations of the same life forms found in the other land. For all Dene Tha, dreams and/ or visions are the ordinary means of communication with inhabitants of the other land, whether humans or nonhumans. Respectful behavior toward all life forms maintains the continuous flow of the gift of life to human beings.

Respectful behavior is extended to *yú*, those parts of animals and plants that bestow their healing powers on humans. For instance, beaver testes are often seen hanging up to dry in Dene Tha homes. The gumlike material inside is used for toothaches, or the whole can be boiled and the potion drunk for a chest cold. It is also used as a very efficient bait for lynx. Rat root is used for stomachache and head colds, poplar bark is used for headaches, and so on with a wide variety of parts of animals and plants. Dene *yú* is therefore in the public domain. It is part of the knowledge of every domestic unit and is easily accessible to any adult who cares to go into the bush with the proper attitude. To benefit from the medicinal power of these entities, one does not simply take them. One places tobacco where an uprooted plant stood or by a tree from which a part is taken. In the words of a Dene Tha woman (Dene Tha Band of Assumption 1990, 25): "If you pluck a 'rat eye' or stinkweed (special roots used for medicine), you don't just take it. You have to put a gift there to replace what you took." Without this acknowledgment of the gift to come, the plant's medicinal power would be withheld.

Dene Tha also apply the term *yú* to Western medication—the pills, syrups, and ointments bought in drugstores or administered by doctors and nurses, who are referred to as *yú dené*, "medicine person." *Yú kóan*, "medicine house," refers to the local health clinic and to the hospitals in urban centers, where Dene Tha are often taken for medical tests and surgery. Dene Tha never refer to a fellow Dene as *yú dene* or to a particular dwelling of theirs as *yú kóan*. Some Dene Tha men and women are nevertheless reputed to gather herbs and parts of animals and to keep them properly. These are dispensed to others for medicinal purposes in exchange for an appropriate payment in tobacco, other goods, and sometimes cash.

The administration of Dene Tha medication is based on an exchange between parts of plants or animals on the one hand and human beings on the other. Without a gift one cannot be healed. For instance, during my first winter among the Dene Tha, I had a bad cold, and a grandmother offered muskrat root to cure it. I thanked her and chewed part of it as prescribed for the next few days. When I visited her again, I still had a runny nose. The grandmother immediately said to her grandson: "Where is his tobacco? He did not give me any tobacco; how can he expect to get well?" I gave her some tobacco, which she happily accepted, and soon thereafter my cold was gone.

Respect is, therefore, extended to animals, seen not only as game but as powerful, sentient beings who freely go out of their way to contact humans to give them a power or information that they would otherwise not possess. To the Dene Tha an animal is, to use Irving Hallowell's (1976, 405) phrase, an "other-than-human-person." Dene refer to a time when the boundaries between animals and humans were not as definite as they now are. In this "Distant Time" (Nelson 1983) animals and human beings spoke the same language, married, and cohabited. Although this is no longer the case, animals and human beings continue to entertain very intimate relationships.

Powerful Beings

Dene Tha share a deep sense of dependence on animals, to which conventional signs of respect are faithfully given lest animals stop offering themselves to hunters who seek them as game. A Dene Tha child learns this respect from his parents as they dispose properly of the bones of animals or the feathers of fowl and as they avoid talking negatively about animals (animals know how one talks about them and will not present themselves in the bush to the hunter or trapper who speaks negatively about them). Children learn that there are little feathers at the end of a duck's wings that are not to be burned: "If you burn that little feather, real pointed ones, if you burn them, you don't shoot ducks as you would like to; you miss them. You don't burn them, you keep them good. You don't throw them to the dogs. You throw them in the bush or in the water. If you throw them to the fire, you do not shoot right." And so the child is sent to drop the feathers in the creek behind the house. The guts are removed from a dead moose and its eyes pierced before its head and brain are put high in a tree. "This is so he will not see where we go. If he knew, he would be mad at us and we would not shoot moose next time around," says the hunter. The hunter's wife adds: "It's always been like that. If you kill something, you take its guts out and pierce its eyes." In the case of a whooping crane, it is gutted in a hurry and its gizzard buried as fast as possible; otherwise "it will rain real hard, rain a lot." Eagles are never killed, for they tell hunters where the moose are and in some cases fly very low to look at people and communicate with them. A woman commented: "We are afraid of the eagle; we do not kill it. If we kill it in the fall, then it comes and kills one of the family the same year. It all goes back to the time when animals were like human beings, and they could talk and everything. My dad knows lots of these stories."

The relationship between human beings and animals, or other-than-human persons, is a social one. Dene Tha and animals are bound in a cycle of reciprocal exchange in which the animals have the upper hand. One can never demand or take what is up to the animal to give freely. Humans cannot coerce other-than-human people to act in a certain way. At best, Dene Tha must treat the animals with respect, and then the animals will make themselves available again as game or will choose to whom they will give leftover powers. Animals are likely to do so when they see the pitifulness of the one they choose to help.

BECOMING POWERFUL: THE VISION QUEST

Until very recently, almost everyone in Chateh went on a vision quest and experienced, before the onset of adolescence, encounters with animals that gave them a power and therefore became their helpers in life. Even Dene Tha men and women in their mid-twenties, early thirties, and forties were known to have an animal helper, despite their having been sent to residential school at the age of five or six for as long as ten months of the year and having returned to their community in their early teens. As one former residential school student commented, "You need an animal helper to survive in this community." Dene Tha Elders also teach "that other people—not just Dene—can have dreams and have a vision" (Dene Tha Elder, in Moore and Wheelock 1990, 75). Not all Dene, however, deliberately seek a power. Among the Mission Chipewyan, for instance, power cannot be sought, and it is the animal who seeks a recipient on whom to bestow a power. Mission Chipewyan also vehemently deny that women have or may have a power, but Chipewyan women with a power are reported in other Chipewyan communities by D. M. Smith and J. G. E. Smith (Sharp 1986, 258). What I am reporting for the community of Chateh may not obtain among other populations known as Slaveys.

Among the Dogrib, writes Helm (1994, 69; emphasis in original), "*ink'on* adepts come to know something that *empowers* them to *compel* change in human beings or in circumstances that affect human beings." Helm (1994, 77) argues that when thinking in English of *ink'on* among the Dogrib, it is better to conceive of it "as 'a power' or 'a powerfulness' rather than as 'power' unqualified by an article." I agree with Helm, and I follow suit when translating the Dene Tha word *ech'int'e* as "a power." *Ink'on* among the Chipewyan (Smith 1973) and among the Dogrib (Helm 1994), like *ech'int'e* among the Dene Tha, is an adjunct to an individual's personality. It is a quality that a person receives as a gift from animals conceived of as humanlike. To have a power is to enjoy special resources on which to draw to bring good fortune and ward off misfortune.

Powerful Beings

Although there is a rich tradition of vision quest among many Native North American populations, Ruth Benedict noted significant exceptions.[3] Among the Pueblo communities, for instance, characterized by intensive communal living and collective agriculture, all forms of individualism were deemphasized. Direct contact with other worldly powers was not sought and was not welcomed. The vision quest complex was, therefore, absent among them. Indeed, as Benedict writes (1959, 87): "If a Zuni Indian has by chance a visual or auditory hallucination it is regarded as a sign of death. It is an experience to avoid, not one to seek by fasting." Not surprisingly, among the Zuni, dealings with other-worldly powers were the prerogative of priests and religious societies. Not so, however, among the Dene.

To this day, Dene Tha view animals as having powers superior to those of humans. Encounters with these animals and communication with them in dreams or visions are not only desirable but essential to the well-being of the individual and the community. Animals reveal themselves to human beings. Animals give human beings information about events unfolding in this land, and songs and power to influence one's fortune in the world. To be the recipient of such gifts is to become someone who knows an animal. This knowledge, however, is always limited. In the words of Jean-Marie Talley, a Dene Tha dreamer: "People may think that they know about animals, but it isn't true; a human's powers are insignificant. We are people; we know only a little about animals and their ways. Animals have special abilities which they depend upon to live, giving us only the powers which they no longer need. . . . An animal chooses someone to receive these leftover powers, a person who has treated the animals with respect" (quoted in Moore and Wheelock 1990, 7). A Chipewyan elder expressed the same view to D. Smith (n.d. 16): "By *inkonze* the people helped each other to live before. It's the animals that give *inkonze* to the people. Animals are always the best medicine people."

When discussing animal helpers and associated phenomena in English, Dene Tha often use the word "superstition." Nevertheless, though English-speaking Dene and anthropologists may have a common vocabulary, the meanings of the words may differ radically. Dene Tha speakers do not use the term "superstition" as defined in Webster's as "a belief or practice resulting from ignorance, fear of the unknown, trust in magic or chance, or a false concept of causation." When translating "superstition" to Dene Dháh, Dene Tha always give the phrase *dene wonlin edadíhi*, "a person who knows an animal." In this case, as in many others, the simple process of translation back to Dene Dháh uncovered the Dene meanings attached to English vocabulary.[4] These Dene meanings belong to a world view that is, to a large extent, shared by old and young Dene alike and taken for granted by Catholic Dene in their daily lives.

In Dene thought, powerful beings are more likely to come to individuals who are pitiful, or without the resources to sustain themselves on their own. Spending time in the bush with few provisions attracts the attention of animals. It is a common theme among Native North Americans that other-than-human-beings with greater powers than human beings are "willing to share a surplus of their power with the less fortunate, just as the wealthy and powerful within the human community are supposed to share their wealth with their 'poor' relatives" (Irwin 1994, 110). Central Algonkians who received power from these beings would say that they were "pitied by the spirits" (Benedict 1964, 27). Concerning the Ojibwa, Mary Black-Rogers (1986, 367) similarly concludes, "To be pitiable . . . is the correct state for a person who wishes to receive a gift of power—a promise of help in getting through life." Indeed, for the Ojibwa, to "be pitied" and to "receive a gift" from a powerful being were one and the same (Black-Rogers 1986, 367). An Omaha youth seeking an encounter with these beings "was expected to learn the one prayer to be chanted by all during the fasting period: *"Wakonda!* Here in poverty he stands, and I am he!"" (Irwin 1994, 106).[5] Dene Elders always emphasized how pitiful they were when they encountered their animal helpers. The poverty and pitifulness in question is not so much a material one as an existential one. The recognition of one's existential poverty compared to other beings is the necessary condition to become the recipient of gifts and powers from these other beings.

As a vision comes hand in hand with a song, "a young person who is sent to seek a vision is often told *shin kaneya* (go for a song)" (Moore and Wheelock 1990, 59). When he sought his vision,

Alexis Seniantha was told that it would be good for him to sleep beside a tree that had been split by lightning and struck by the Thunderbird. Lightning and thunder originate from giant birds that fly around in the sky. Julian Hardisty, a Slavey from Fort Simpson, was told of a place high in the mountains where Thunderbirds nest. Julian explains: "There are trees up there all burned up on the top of the mountain—that is where they have nested. *It's hard to believe until you see it*" (in Waugh and Prithipaul 1977, 64; my emphasis).[6]

Dene Tha "describe a vision as something 'appearing in front of someone,' *mendayeh wodekeh*" (Moore and Wheelock 1990, 59). A young Dene Tha healer translated this expression as "in front of your eyes your power has done its work for you." "Your power comes to you. It is just like a movie you look at, and when the show is finished, it is your power," he explained. The young man claimed a steel unicorn horse among his animal helpers. It had come to him in this way: "I used to see a horse, a unicorn horse, steel horse, that used to come to me, and it made some kind of a show, some action for me. It became my power." He was therefore someone who knew steel and who could help individuals affected by steel objects. "Because I know steel," he said, "a person could shoot me, and it [the bullet] would all go flat on my hand and I could show it. That's what could happen, if the power is strong. I can't do that yet. I am still a kid [in his mid-twenties], but I can help the sick with it."

The apparition of a steel unicorn to a Dene Tha on a traditional vision quest suggests that the spectrum of powerful beings who show themselves to a Dene has broadened over time, much like the Dreamtime Beings of the Australian Aborigine, which now include figures such as John Wayne (Poirier 1996, 135–36). The metaphor of a movie to convey the experience of an encounter with a power may suggest more passivity on the part of the viewer than is the case. For instance, independently of each other, two men told me that during their vision quest their power taught them to fly. One young Dene Tha healer in his later thirties told me, "When I am young I fly. They [my power] help me fly. Do you believe that? Even now, if I am alone in the bush, I could fly. That's the way it is. Me and my brother we know swan. We can fly." Without identifying his animal helper, the other younger healer said, "I could fly. My power had me fly. It can teach me that."[7]

Consider also the following account of a transformation reported by Sharp (1986, 260). The case concerns a Chipewyan named Magic Boy:

> Before dawn, after a snowfall had ceased he [Magic Boy] left his house. No one in the village saw what happened but several people became curious at his departure and later return. Shortly after dawn they followed his tracks out of the village toward the ill-kept airstrip at the edge of the surrounding bush. Between town and the airstrip the footprints of a man were replaced by those of a wolf. The wolf tracks led to the airstrip where they were joined by two other sets of wolf tracks coming from different directions. The airstrip was covered with tracks from the three wolves romping. Two sets of wolf tracks ultimately led back into the bush while the third started back towards the village. En route these wolf tracks were replaced by human footprints that led directly to the house where the Magic Boy was staying.

Identification of an individual with his or her power, either in the course of the vision quest or afterward, is very deep and strong.

Among the Dene Tha, as among the Beaver, "power can only be acquired between weaning and puberty, a time in which organic ties with the mother have been severed and sexual ties with a wife have not yet begun" (Ridington and Ridington 1975, 199). Today many parents still encourage their young children to spend time wandering in the bush in the hope that they will come back with an animal helper. A mother of five children, aged six to fourteen, said: "Like our children, if they are out in the bush, away from people, we do not call them back, because if we call them and their vision disappears they do not regain it." Parents are happy rather than worried if their child stays in the bush overnight. There are just so many years during which to receive a power. A mother said that while on a vision quest "the animal, a dead skull, or a live animal, they act like humans." The animal moves, speaks, and instructs. A father explained that how long one spends in the bush "all depends on the spiritual helper, how much power it wants to give to you."

Powerful Beings

Although some Dene Tha children still go for a song, many Dene Tha parents despair that their children will ever get a vision. As one young woman expressed it, pointing to her young son and nephew, who were listening to our conversation: "They are always on the road. You get that kind of thing [the vision] in the bush, not on the road." Voicing her opinion in this manner, the woman was not only criticizing the children; she was reminding them that they should get on with it and go for a song. This Dene Tha view mirrors that of the Chipewyan, for whom "it was life in the bush which most needed to be experienced, not just talked about, since it is the home par excellence of the animals, sources of knowledge cum power" (D. Smith, personal communication 1997).

In another Dene Tha family, teenagers admitted that although their grandfather had often told them "to go and look for medicine, to learn what they had to do and receive a song to sing on people," they had been too scared to go. These adolescents were growing up without a power but in the company of parents and other siblings who had an animal helper. Every Dene Tha knows someone who has had a vision and has received a power; everyone knows a relative or a friend whose health has recovered through the assistance of someone with a power to heal. I would dare say that when in need, every Dene Tha calls on a fellow Dene Tha with a power to help.

The Dene Tha view of true knowledge as that which is perceived directly with one's senses or one's mind applies to the knowledge obtained in the vision quest. It is only through one's personal and private encounter with an animal that one knows the animal and receives a song and a power. In all contexts, what one has not experienced or perceived directly one does not truly know. Much true knowledge is acquired in solitude when an adult dreams or has visions or when a child, wandering alone in the bush, finds his or her tutelary spirit. "When they come back they are not supposed to tell you; if they do, their power just goes away," confided one informant. And the curious may not investigate: "If you are in the bush and the animal is talking to you or coming to you and someone comes your way, then the animal disappears." The scope for empirical investigation in these circumstances is nil.

69

Dene are reticent to talk about animal helpers at length, if at all. For instance, when asked what it means to know an animal, a woman answered as follows: "I don't really know. Like my older brother, he never talks to us about it, but my mom told us once that one day Frederick went in the bush with little provisions, and was supposed to come back the same day, but stayed two days and two nights. On his way he met wolves who had come to meet him; and he had been with them all that time. I guess they became his helpers. But that is all I know. We do not talk about these things." Back home, Frederick eventually became known to his fellow Dene as someone with *ech'int'e*, "a power," or as *dene wonlin edadihi*, "someone who knows an animal."

One is prohibited from killing or eating animals representative of one's animal helper under threat of severe illness or even death (R. Ridington 1978, 114–15; Goulet 1982, 8–9). People say that "when you have a power, you do not eat that kind because it can kill a person," or that "the power will be too strong for him. He will go crazy if he eats it." "People with power are always allergic to something that makes them have the power," explained a Dene Tha woman. The avoidance of certain foods is, therefore, a clear indication of the identity of one's power. For instance, when I dish out pieces of cake to a group of trappers who have stopped by to visit, and one of them asks, "Are there any eggs in it?" everyone understands that he is not to eat eggs because his animal helper is a fowl. It is through such avoidances that one reveals the identity of one's animal helper and, in this way, bridges the gap between the private world of a vision and the public world of social interaction. To know a Dene Tha individual is to know a range of foods, beverages, sounds, or other phenomena he or she must avoid to maintain a healthy relationship with his or her power. To respect such an individual, one does not offer him prohibited foods or expose him to sights, sounds, or objects that would similarly disturb his relationship to his animal helper and so endanger his life.

Dene who have a power keep a pouch next to their bed containing a piece of fur, a bone, or some other part of the animal who is their helper.[8] The only Dene Tha to have shown me the contents of this pouch was Alexis Seniantha. He did so twice. His pouch contained bones from fish, birds, and other animals. Alexis would take each item out of his pouch, one at a time, to hold it preciously in the palm of his hand. Each item was a memento of a special moment in his life, of "an experience" that "like a rock in a Zen sand garden, stands out from the evenness of passing hours and years" (Turner 1986, 35). Alexis would tell me how, in a dream or a vision, he had been instructed to go to a specific place in the bush to find a particular animal. The animals that were given to him in this fashion revealed a peculiar bone formation, and it was this atypical bone that had found its way into his pouch. Each animal part was associated with a specific area either on land or on the shore of a lake or stream. Alexis could describe each place where he had encountered the animal in rich detail. Each consideration of an animal part also evoked vivid memories of a particular period of his life. Alexis would say whom he was then living with and/or trapping and hunting with. Each feather or bone was a testimonial to his increasing ability to orient himself in this world on the basis of gifts received from animal helpers.

To describe such an apprehension of one's life in the world, D. Smith follows Walter Ong (1969), who "suggests that in oral cultures it is more accurate to speak not of world-as-view, but rather of world-as-event" (Smith n.d., 11). I agree. Dene "experience themselves as participants in a meaningful, eventing actuality," and their languages "stress action so heavily that even most nouns are really nominalized action verbs" (Smith n.d., 11). That is why the Dene consider that "first-hand experience-as-action is an epistemological *sine qua non*" for a true apprehension of oneself and of other beings (Smith n.d., 11). That is also why the Dene consider it inappropriate to speak extensively about their experiences with animal helpers, in dreams or in visions.

Commenting on the Huichol Indian prohibition against discussing their peyote-induced religious visions "because they are personal to each individual," Barbara Myerhoff (1990, 245–46) notes that "recently, physiological studies of ritual have suggested that the ineffability of intense emotional, transformative states may be due to the dominance of right brain activity. These states, like dreams, are fundamentally non-linear, non-discursive, non-linguistic, and are distorted beyond recognition when rendered in collective, verbal, conscious categories." Malcolm

Crick (1982, 292) and V. Turner (1985, 259–60) suggest that there is also a neurophysiological basis for people's reticence to discuss openly their visions or extraordinary experiences. This may be true of the Dene Tha. Personal experiences lived within transformative states are nevertheless partially amenable to verbalization. The Dene Tha prefer to suppress any such verbalization lest it undermine their view that individuals ought to learn primarily on the basis of personal experience and observation of one another's behavior.

REVEALING THE IDENTITY OF ONE'S ANIMAL HELPER

In light of these facts of life, relationships between spouses and in-laws are initially fraught with danger, because individuals who now share in commensality may not know precisely about one another's powers and the associated prescribed avoidances. For example, a woman learned the identity of one of her husband's powers on the day they were going to her mother's house. As they approached the house, the man became nervous and told his wife that he could go no farther. She insisted they go on, but by the time they got to the house, her husband was shaking and throwing up. The woman took him back home, where he told her that as they approached the house, he had smelled ptarmigan, his animal helper. The woman then went to her mother's house, where ptarmigan was, indeed, being cooked. "I told Mom," the woman said, "and they got rid of all the ptarmigan." Henceforth, an important aspect of the identity of the man who knew ptarmigan was known to his spouse and his in-laws. They modified their hunting and eating behavior accordingly in order to incorporate him into their circle. The man behaved in a manner that allowed his fellow Dene Tha to infer what they must avoid doing if they were not to jeopardize his health and life. In return, these relatives could now call on this man's power to heal their young children, for they know that the ptarmigan empowers those who know it to help children less than a year old.

Among the Dene, attribution of a power is not given lightly. As noted by Sharp (1986, 264), and as is amply demonstrated in the following two chapters, any attribution of a power localizes in a fellow Dene "the ability to change the course of the most intimate parts of one's life and perhaps to terminate life itself." This attribution of a power to a particular individual "is made up of such individual and family decisions as from whom to seek help for a critically ill child, where to seek succor from the maddening itch of refractory skin conditions, or from whom to seek protection when all that is of value in life is collapsing and death stalks around you" (Sharp 1986, 264).

When one begins to use a power to help people, one does so with some degree of anxiety, not knowing if one has received all the power one actually needs to help others without causing harm to oneself: "Like an animal, if he tells you all how he is from beginning to end, you help someone, you cure him. Like when you are young, you go alone in the bush and you stay there and an animal comes to you. He talks to you just like we do now [we are sitting next to each other], and he tells you about him and with his power. He gives you his power to heal other people. With it you heal people. If it tells you all how he is from beginning to end, you help someone, you cure him. If he does not tell everything, and you do not know all about him, then, when you help someone, you cure him, but you get the sickness." In this account, as in other Dene Tha accounts of vision quests, we find the view, typical in societies of hunters and gatherers, of animals as fellow persons with whom one entertains relations of reciprocal exchange and cooperation (Ingold 1988, 15; Tapper 1988).[9] As the Dene Tha speaker describes, the animal and the person on a vision quest talk to each other just as we talk, elbow to elbow at the kitchen table, where I write down what I am being told. In the vision quest a relationship to endure throughout one's life—and, indeed, beyond one's life in our land—is sealed in the intimacy of a secret encounter in the bush.

The dramatic revelation of one's relationship with an animal is also manifested in the following cases, two from the Dunne-za of northeastern British Columbia, the other from the neighboring Dene Tha. R. Ridington tells of a white woman who attempted to take a picture of a Dunne-za Elder with a flash camera. As she rose to take the picture, the young people told her that the Elder did not like that kind of camera with a flash. The white woman did not heed the young people's hint. As she prepared to take his picture, the Elder dove out of sight beneath a sleeping robe. His action reinforced the white woman's "belief that Indians are child-like and superstitious" (R. Ridington 1976, 115).[10] To every Dunne-za present, however, the old man had "demonstrated his power, not weakness." He had been brave rather than fearful. According to R. Ridington, the key to the old man's reaction to a flash camera lies in the Dunne-za myth of the Giant Eagle, "whose flashing eyes still penetrate from heaven to earth in time of storm" (1976, 115). The flash of a camera, like lightning, is comparable to the "flashing eye" of the Giant Eagle. The old man had to avoid the flashing eye of his animal helper. To do otherwise was to risk becoming Wechuge, the person-eating monster that the animal helper was in ancient times.

If one becomes Wechuge, one does not turn into "an unspecified Person-eater"; one turns into "the particular Person-eating monster that is a person's friend" (R. Ridington 1976, 114). A Dene who knows an animal is acting responsibly when he or she avoids dangerous situations. For instance, among the Dunne-za, if Spider is one's helper, then the sound of a vibrating taut line (rawhide, string, rope, or guitar) "can potentially send the individual into a state where he identifies with the Giant Spider, eats his own lips and begins killing and eating the people around him" (Mills 1982, 43). Thus, when Charlie Yahey, the last of the Dunne-za prophets, was riding with Antonia Mills and Robin Ridington in their car, he abruptly turned off their radio "when country and western music began playing," Spider being "one of his medicines" (Mills 1982, 43). The avoidance of certain foods, actions, sounds, smells, touch, and so on underlies every situation in which a Dene who knows an animal finds himself or herself. It is precisely situations involving Dene individuals with a power that we are concerned with here, as in the following event, witnessed in Chateh in March 1980.

A dozen Dene Tha were attending mass along with a white visitor and myself. The visitor proceeded to take pictures of the congregation with a flash camera without making his intention known in advance. As he took the first picture, the entire congregation turned toward him in apparent shock. As a second picture was taken with a flashbulb, a Dene man in his early sixties dashed out of the church, rosary in hand. Later I was told that he could not stand a flash camera because that was his "superstition." People said the man might have died if more flashes from the camera had hit him. The man had reacted appropriately in taking flight and seeking the aid of another Dene with a power to help him recover from a serious breach in his relationship with his animal helper. One Dene commented: "It's always difficult when there's somebody who is not from us. People tell us their fears and we protect them." Others explained that this man was not alone in being afraid of a flash. They referred to a picture taken with a flash of a powerful old woman. In this picture, which I had seen hanging on the walls of some Dene homes, as well as in the church, the woman is seen holding her rosary high in front of her chest. "She is holding her rosary because she is afraid of the flash," Dene Tha explained. As described in chapter 8, the Dene Tha know that the rosary is an effective means of deflecting a power that threatens them.

AN ANIMAL HELPER FOR LIFE

The relationship with one's animal helper may (but does not necessarily) endure throughout one's life—and beyond one's life on our land. The psychological reality of this view and its impact on the Dene Tha perception of the environment came most forcibly to me in a visit to a cemetery, where a person's animal helper appeared. The event occurred in the first months of my initial period of fieldwork. Andrew and his mother invited me to join them on a visit to the small, fenced-in cemetery near his home. Andrew and his mother belonged to an extended family that, in the mid-1970s, was the last to bury relatives in its own burial ground, according to Dene Tha custom, without having the deceased brought to church for a funeral mass. In the early 1970s, at the age of twenty-two, Andrew's brother, David, had died in an oil rig accident. He had been buried next to his grandfather. In the cemetery we knelt by David's grave and prayed a rosary in English. We concluded with a sign of the cross and rose to our feet to return home. I had the impression of having accomplished a typical act of Catholic devotion for the deceased. But the unexpected occurred.

As we were proceeding to the gate of the cemetery, a deer appeared at the edge of the bush. It bounded toward us and stopped fifty feet away, looking straight at us. At the sight of the deer Andrew's mother threw herself to the ground, crying loudly as she pounded the earth with clenched fists and then pulling the grass out of the ground in rage and tears. In the meantime, Andrew addressed the deer in Dene Dháh. The deer stood there, moving its ears only, as if better to understand Andrew. Twice Andrew turned to me, saying, "It's our brother's power, he knows we are here, he sends it to us." The conversation with the deer seemed to last a few minutes. Then the deer turned around and quietly reentered the bush. Andrew looked at his mother still prostrate on the ground, crying loudly. He told her to quiet down and not to cry lest she bring death on another member of the family. Immediately, the mother subdued her cries and lifted her head toward us.

One moment we were in a rather peaceful mood, talking together as we headed back home, and a moment later, in a abrupt change of mood and behavior, the mother shed tears and broke into wailing while her son solemnly addressed a deer. Why this sudden transformation of mien and mood? On the evening of our visit to the cemetery I returned to Andrew's home to find answers to my questions. I carried a tape recorder and a notebook with me and, in what I soon recognized as a rather rude way, asked Andrew if he would put on tape an account of what had occurred in the afternoon. Could he explain in particular what he had meant by telling me, "It's our brother's power, he knows we are here, he sends it to us." Avoiding my eyes, Andrew looked over my shoulders and said, "We do not believe in these things anymore; I do not want to talk about it." He was obviously tense and uneasy about my asking this question. I did not insist, and we turned to other topics of conversation.

Nearly a year later, during the course of my second period of fieldwork, I again raised the question with Andrew and his cousin. Now they were ready to answer, and Andrew recapitulated the event in the following words: "Last year we all went to where my brother is buried, and we prayed the priest's way. As we came back, from over there came a deer, my brother's power was coming to visit. My mother sees it and starts to cry very loud. Me too, I feel sad, I feel sad. It was my brother's power. In 1970, before my brother died, his power came up to him and told him, 'Now you are almost dead.'" Early in his childhood David had encountered deer when on his vision quest. When in his early twenties he had reported to his parents and siblings another encounter with his power in the bush. The deer had told him, "I have come to say farewell, for this is the last time I will see you in this world; you are almost dead." Two days after reporting this incident to his family, David died. Ten years later he sent his animal helper to his grave to remind his relatives that he appreciated their continuing attention.

Andrew's cousin added that almost everyone in Chateh experiences encounters with animals that become one's power or guardian. When in danger one can always go back in one's mind to the first encounter with one's animal guardian and receive the necessary strength to avoid a drowning, an attack by an animal, or a death by exhaustion when lost in the bush. In David's case his animal guardian had come to inform him of the inevitable death soon to follow.

To illustrate what it means to send one's power to someone else, David's brother shared the following story that goes back to 1973. His grandfather was reported to be sick on his trapline, away from the reservation. David's brother decided to send his power over there to help his grandfather: "I sent my power to him over there, and two times it flew to him over there. He saw it, but he doesn't know who it was [sending it]. Then it came back." What the grandfather saw was a Canada Goose, David's brother's animal helper. What had been sent was not a Canada Goose but the power, which "became a Canada Goose" on its way to the grandfather, for him to see and find comfort in. Similarly, with the deer at the cemetery, it was David's power sent from the other land and materialized in our land that appeared before the eyes of his mother and brother to reassure them that he was alive and well.

Mistassini Cree are also reported to develop friendship ties with members of animal species. The animal is referred to as "u:wi:ciwa:kan 'friend' or awhaka:m 'pet'" (Tanner 1976, 248–49). Adrian Tanner writes that, shortly after the death of a man at the post of Mistassini, a goose from a high-flying flock descended on the village and flew between the houses. When the same phenomenon recurred a few days later, young men were instructed not to shoot it, because it was the deceased's friend. Similarly, when Andrew saw the deer in the cemetery, he did not see game to report to his relatives and to track down to kill. He saw the deer as his brother's power. Sighting a goose or a deer as an animal helper to respect and not as game to hunt involves "membershipping," that is, the activity "by which persons in social settings categorize objects of knowledge, incidents, events, and other members" (Anderson and Lee 1982, 290).

Andrew and his mother did not first see the deer as a deer and then work out that it was the dead man's power. To them the deer was that power. All realities are socially generated, and the process of generation involves work, described as "membershipping" by Anderson and Lee. The scene, consisting of the co-occurrence of David's mother and brother at his graveside and the appearance of the deer, is constituted by communicative acts, the mother's lamentation and the son's declaration that "it is our brother's power." These words express the standardized Dene Tha way of accounting the flesh and blood animal as someone's power, in this case David's. In turn, the scene as formulated gives specific meaning to otherwise inherently ambiguous gestures and sounds. David and his mother could not see the deer as game to be hunted; other Dene Tha who were not related to David and who would not know the deer as David's animal helper would immediately see it as game to be shot. In either case, membershipping, "the sense in which members of a culture deal with contingent events, and render them into categories such that 'this' may be found to be 'another case of', or 'similar to', or 'the same situation as', 'that'," is involved (Anderson and Lee 1982, 290). It is the making of a contingent event into a socially recognizable one that accounts "'for culturally informed interpretation of experience' (Holland 1992, 75), and thus for the experience of continuity in one's world" (Hastrup and Hervik 1994, 7), whether that be our world or the other world.

Because the relationship between an animal helper and a Dene Tha endures after death, people are careful not to move into the house of a deceased individual until such time, often a year or two, that the person's soul and power have definitely left. To move in earlier is to lack respect toward the deceased individual and his or her animal helper, and so to risk retaliation. A young man who had moved in to live with his wife in her mother's house complained about their living conditions: "It's real hard to find. It is really crowded where we are now. We must be fifteen people in that house. Last night her young brother was drunk and wanted to fight me. I know I could beat him up and I didn't fight him. It is too crowded in there for all of us. It gets on all of us, and we are looking for a place for ourselves." Since there were no new housing units available for them, they asked the Elders if they could move into the house of a recently deceased person but were told not to do so and heeded the Elders' advice. A Dene Tha woman explained what happened when she and her husband ignored such counsel and moved into the house of her recently deceased brother-in-law. Soon after moving in, her husband started to drink heavily, much as her brother-in-law used to do. When in the house she always felt scared, "feeling all the time expecting having a dream." Unable to eat or to sleep, she decided to seek help from a powerful local healer. She was told that they had to move out of the house because the power of her brother-in-law "was still all in the house, like something like a big, big mouth opened like that, and real dark in that." The woman's unease and the husband's uncontrolled drinking abated as soon as the couple moved into another house.

THINGS THAT KNOW GIVE YOU SIGNS

Dene Tha report numerous encounters with moose, fox, coyote, or wolf that unexpectedly show themselves, bark, and run off. These encounters are invariably seen as announcing an impending death: "It's that things like that know what is going to happen, they give you signs," explained a Dene Tha hunter. The animals who warn people of bad things to come are also thought to offer an opportunity to reverse the course of future events. A person may ward off misfortune by immediately shooting at and killing the animal/messenger. Failure to kill the barking animal means that a close relative of the one encountering the animal will die shortly. To the best of my knowledge such experiences have never before been reported in the literature on the Dene.

I heard the first account of such an incident in the course of a session with an instructor teaching me Dene Dháh. His dogs were barking, and I asked him for a sentence with the verb "to bark." He told me *xeda deghoh*, "the moose barked." Surprised at this notion of a barking moose, I asked what he meant. He told me the following: "They [Elders] say if a moose barks at you, it does sound like a dog, they say somebody close to you dies. *Not long after,* two or three months after, somebody dies. It's true. Once my dad and I were hunting, that was when we were living at the other end of the reserve. A moose barked at my dad. He tried to get at it. It got away. Then, *not long after,* my nephew died by lightning. The moose barked in October. He died in June; that's just seven months after. It's true. Animals know. Like bear, it knows too. Like this man, he talked smart about bears, and bear attacked him when he was in the bush. These are Indian legends" (my emphasis). His brief statement is highly structured, beginning and ending with a reference to what the Elders say. When asked what he meant by Indian legends, the speaker said *deetiyi wodihi,* literally "the stories of the elders." This reference frames an account of a personal experience of a moose barking at the speaker and his father on a hunting expedition. This personal account is introduced and concluded with the emphatic "It's true." What is general knowledge among the Dene Tha is given the stamp of authority of a personal experience. His statement illustrates how flexible Dene Tha can be in their interpretation of what counts as "not long after" an animal barks. The speaker begins with "two or three months" and later offers the case of his nephew, who died seven months after the moose barked. The speaker concludes his account with a reference to a Dene Tha man whom we both know to have survived a bear attack that left him severely maimed. In other words, animals expect respect, and they know what Dene Tha say about them, even at home. To mock them is to invite serious retaliation.

Dene Tha have numerous encounters with animals who come to warn them of an impending death and to give them a last opportunity to ward it off. Typically, Dene Tha speakers state the general principle accompanied with a personal illustration of its truth. "It [the animal] knows the close relative of someone is going to have something happen to him. A moose barked at my husband and his dad; the next year my brother [father's sister's son] died," stated a Dene Tha speaker. Referring to a moose who had recently barked at his nephew, a Dene Tha man said: "He shot him but he did not kill him. If you kill him, the bad luck is for the moose, but if you don't kill it, the bad luck is for somebody else close to you. Wait and see, before long something will happen." To substantiate this claim, the speaker added that three years earlier a moose had barked at his uncle, who had failed to kill it. The month following, at carnival time, the man and his nephew had a car accident on their way to High Level. One of the passengers died. The speaker's wife then attested to the truth of his story with her own account: "Last winter my dad was in the bush and he heard a dog bark. He thought it was a dog. It was near. He could hear it, and the next morning when he went to see where he had heard it, it was wolf tracks there. All that time it was a wolf. When spring came, his nephew drowned."

In such accounts we see again and again the theme of animals who know more about human affairs than humans themselves. In the view of the Dene Tha, a barking animal is saying: "My life, or that of a close relative of yours. If you are alert and skillful enough, kill me, for we both know that unless you do so, someone close to you faces imminent death." Only in one case did I hear a story in which the bark of an animal was interpreted as saying, "If you are alert and skillful enough, kill me; otherwise *you* face imminent death." The case concerned Luke, a young man hitchhiking from High Level to Chateh who saw a fox run toward him, bark at him, and then run away. The one who told me the story noted that "when something like a fox, wolf, or coyote barks at you, bad sign." A few months earlier Luke's brother had frozen to death halfway between his house and that of his parents. Dene Tha friends interpreted the barking fox as a warning that Luke might meet his brother's fate. In fact, a few days after meeting the fox Luke was found drunk and unconscious in the snow. Doctors were able to save his life, but they had to amputate part of his limbs. Fellow Dene Tha commented that Luke should have stopped drinking and that in not doing so he had failed to heed the warning the fox had given him.

In other circumstances one is told of an imminent death without having the opportunity to attempt to ward it off. Such was the case when a woman took a shortcut through the bush from her house to the townsite. She was walking on the trail on a perfectly quiet day, without even a breeze, let alone a wind, when all of sudden a tree fell on her path. The fallen tree was seen as an indication that someone close would soon die. The tree knew; it was warning the woman. Soon after, the woman's mother died.

OLD AND YOUNG, YESTERDAY AND TODAY

The situation that I encountered in Chateh in the 1980s can be compared with that reported by Helm for the Lynx Point people (Slaveys), in Canada's Northwest Territories, thirty years earlier. Lynx Point is the fictive name Helm gave the Slavey community "to protect the people's anxiety of being talked about" (1961, 5). In her summary of aboriginal survivals Helm (1961, 117–21) mentions several beliefs, proscriptions surrounding menstruation and hunting practices in particular, that still play as "lively a role in [the] daily life" of the people of Lynx Point as they do in the lives of the Dene Tha today. Concerning animal helpers and a power received from them, however, none of the Lynx Point people under fifty "could be determined to have a guardian spirit" (Helm 1961, 121). Although "knowledge about guardian spirits still persists among the younger adults," writes Helm (1961, 120), her "primary informant," Marcel Renard, then aged forty-five, "denied that he or any of his contemporaries" had obtained a guardian spirit. Although Marcel reported traditional healing rituals that he had seen in his youth, they had been performed by old men who were long since dead. Helm (1961, 121) concluded that "since none of the younger adult generation have guardian spirits, they do not possess the medicine which is derived from it."

Helm's conclusion is questionable. Dene speakers' denial that they have an animal helper should not be taken at face value. Dene are taught not to flaunt their knowledge and power; therefore, they do not speak casually about their animal helpers. When Dene speakers deny they have an animal helper, they do not lie; what they do not like is our asking. Moreover, younger Dene tend to defer to their predecessors and to refer to them as the people with power and the ability to heal. For instance, Sharp (1986, 263) writes that he has never heard any Mission Chipewyan speaking English "state anything but a flat denial that any living person there had the power to kill. That power is always a thing of the last generation or of outsiders."[11] Proof that such statements are not to be taken literally is that generation after generation, there are Dene individuals who heal because they know an animal. Like Helm in Lynx Point, earlier in this century Pliny Goddard accepted the statements of Beaver informants that they were no longer healers with the powers of animals. Yet in the early 1970s Pat Moore was driving Dene Tha Elders to Beaver healers who called on their animal helpers to cure (Moore n.d.c, 21). In the same vein, it might well be worth a visit to Lynx Point to hear what people have to say concerning healing with a power today.

In this matter we must keep in mind that ethnographic knowledge is social knowledge. It is constituted not only by the anthropologist but also by one's informants, who prefer certain representations of themselves over others. Beavers and Lynx Point Slaveys may have spoken to Goddard and Helm as they did to promote a certain image of themselves. Goddard's and Helm's informants may have, for reasons known only to themselves, emphasized their distance from "superstitious" Indians of the past, even if they shared the experiences and beliefs of their ancestors concerning animal helpers.

Indigenous people of old, like contemporary ones, tended to share with anthropologists of their time a narrative structure within which interaction and cooperation proceeded. Shared implicit narrative structures "provide social roles for the anthropologist as well as for the Indian people" and define "what is to count as data" (Bruner 1986b, 140, 142).[12] Before World War II the dominant paradigm was that of Indian cultures vanishing under the irresistible pressure of acculturation. Hence the role of anthropologists became to capture as much as possible of the past through informants, such as Marcel Renard, who had seen the old ways in their youth but who were determined to live according to Western ways in the modern world. "The reasoning in the assimilation narrative is that if Indians are going to disappear anyway, then their land can be leased or sold to whites" (Bruner 1986b, 144). The long-expected assimilation of the Indian has never materialized. In its place, following World War II a renewed Indian politicization sought to denounce the narrative of assimilation with its clear socioeconomic implications. A new interpretive paradigm emerged, one in which the past came to be viewed as exploitation, the present as the time for resistance, and the future as the promise of an enduring and distinct indigenous identity fully reasserted. Not surprisingly, notes Bruner (1986b, 144), "in the ethnic resurgence narrative we are told that if Indians are here to stay, tribal resources must be built up." G. Watson (1979) and D. Smith (1992) offer insightful case studies of how Dene and Euro–North Americans construct ethnicity in the contemporary political context. This shift in paradigms on the part of Dene and anthropologist alike may well account in part for the differences between what Goddard and Helm could detect among the Beaver and the Slaveys and what Moore and I could find among the Beaver and Dene Tha in the early 1980s.

It may surprise some that the Lynx Point people could withhold information about healers and their animal helpers from Helm and Carterette given the fact that Helm spent two months there in 1951, five months in 1952, and an additional week in 1955, and her coinvestigator, Theresa Carterette, remained in Lynx Point for fourteen consecutive months, from July 1951 to August 1952. There was, of course, the language barrier, which limited their meaningful conversations to a few bilingual adults, but they had frequent contact with children eager to gossip with them about what was happening in the community. This does not rule out the possibility that the people had decided to suppress certain information from their guests. As discussed in chapter 8, this is exactly what the Alberta Cree did for ten years with the local missionary who ministered to them, in their native tongue, in the local church as well as in their homes, where he always felt welcome. After he first witnessed the ceremonies that had been hidden from him for so long, Roger Vandersteene noted that it took him many months to admit that such a thing was possible.

Vandersteene's experience is not unique. In the late 1970s I was invited twice by an Algonkian band of northern Quebec to facilitate meetings between band members and Euro-Canadians. The first meeting was held over a period of two days. It involved the band council, Algonkian parents, and Euro-Canadian teachers. On the agenda was the issue of rising tensions between parents and teachers, given their different expectations concerning schooling and children's behavior. Six months later the band chief called me to facilitate a second meeting between the local band council and the local missionary. The one-day meeting was

used by the band council to introduce the local missionary to a set
of various beings who manifested themselves daily to people, either to help or to harm. The missionary had never known such
beings existed among his parishioners. He was suddenly introduced to a subset of vocabulary he had never heard before, despite being fluent in their language and having lived with them
for more than fifteen years. The missionary was dumbfounded.
How could he have missed so much, over so many years, having
spent so much time with local people, in their homes, or they in
his (for he was, indeed, well known for his hospitality)? The chief
simply said that the band members thought that now was the
time for him to know.

Perhaps anthropologists have not sufficiently considered the
possibility that Dene might act according to a Euro-Canadian
pattern of behavior in some contexts (when interacting with
transient or resident Euro-Canadians) and according to Dene
patterns of conduct in other contexts (when interacting with fellow Dene among themselves). By failing to entertain this as a possibility, anthropologists tend to emphasize how the Dene are
being progressively assimilated within the dominant Euro-Canadian society. This tendency is manifest in Annette McFayden's
opening remarks to D. M. Smith's work on *inkonze* among the
Chipewyan. McFayden (1973, vi) commends the author for giving "us a rare opportunity to gain further insight into one aspect
of the richness of *earlier* Athabaskan belief," noting that "at the
present only a pale version of the older beliefs and practices remain in the minds of a few of the oldest inhabitants" (my emphasis). McFayden's statements stand in stark contrast to Smith's
own view of the strength of earlier Athapaskan beliefs among
contemporary Chipewyan and Metis. Smith writes: "Yet, the old
ones still believe. So do many of the young people. Chipewyan
and many Chipewyan Metis are still very Indian in the cognitive
sense. . . . I would not be surprised if beliefs in *inkonze* continue
or even become stronger among the young" (1973, 20). If we
mean by cognitive sense the understanding of events according
to distinct Dene notions of self and of animals, then younger Dene Tha, like their Chipewyan counterparts encountered by
Smith, are still deeply entrenched in the world of their predecessors.

Nevertheless, we must not forget that the beliefs of old do not come quite as naturally to the younger generation as to their parents and grandparents. The younger generation of Dene Tha has the unprecedented task of reconciling the knowledge received from their parents in the course of daily life with the scientific knowledge transmitted through schools and other institutions. In 1991 a young Dene Tha man in his thirties expressed the challenge in the following way: "From school I tell my dad 'the earth goes around the sun [and not the other way around], as the moon goes around the earth.' And my dad says, 'How come then the bear snared the sun one day? Unless the sun went somewhere, it would not have its path.'" The man then asks his son: "If that story was not true, how could you be here now? People who lived by these stories are here now." The young man understands his father to say, "Why create a new school of thought, why reinvent the wheel, when there is already a school of thought that works?" Juxtaposed in his brief narrative are father and son, youth and Elder, traditional knowledge and modern knowledge, or what many Euro–North Americans would recognize as mythology and science. Despite this young man's schooling in the Western sciences, he, like other Dene Tha of his generation, often thinks of his Elders' argument about the truth of their knowledge and stories.

A similar situation is reported by Harvey Feit for the Waswapini young men who take up hunting as their primary activity. They also become aware of the sharp contrast between the views of their Elders and that of their schoolteachers: "The presentation [by the Elders] of animals and natural occurrences as social beings, the emphasis on harvests as gifts to be reciprocated with spirits and kin, and the assertion that power is knowing the future all contradict school learning" (Feit 1994, 436). Although schooling introduces young Cree to the concept of "luck" as "unexplainable chance occurrence," Cree Elders convincingly demonstrate to younger Cree that "good luck" and "bad luck" are "expressions of cycles of power," in the process constructing "for the young hunters a world that the latter's schooling neither taught them to expect, nor is capable of explaining" (Feit 1994, 436).[13]

Powerful Beings

This chapter focused on Dene Tha notions of power and of human and nonhuman agencies that inform their lives. The child who is on a vision quest shares with his parents and relatives a deep sense of dependence on animals, to which signs of respect are constantly offered lest animals stop giving themselves to hunters who seek them as game. In accounts of interactions with animals, the relationship of human to animal is not predominantly one of hunter to prey. Rather, human beings and animals relate to each other as intelligent, purposeful, social actors. Animals constantly monitor the actions and speech of human beings for signs of respect or disrespect toward themselves. Lack of respect toward an animal is followed by retaliation. In the course of a normal ordinary life a Dene Tha is healed by *yú*, following a reciprocal gift of tobacco. He is also visited by animal helpers in the bush who impart knowledge and a power to increase the likelihood of a successful life, and is helped or harmed by the power of individuals who know animals. He or she may be warned of an impending misfortune by animals that know what is going to happen. In all these settings relationships with animals are fraught with uncertainty and danger, even though there is the potential for increased familiarity and reciprocity.

4. Powers to Heal, Powers to Respect

*

*Whiteman have lost their
soul, they cannot be helped.*
—Dene Tha speaker

In the preceding chapter we saw how the successful conclusion of a first healing ritual confirms that the relationship between an animal helper and a particular individual is well established. Because of the success the healer's reputation is bound to grow, along with the number of calls on his assistance to help others. Dene Tha healers do not advertise their power or their ability to cure; it is up to others to find out how a healer can help and what gifts to bring. As one healer said: "It always has been like that. You don't just go help someone; you have to be asked. You bring a gift of their liking, because if they help somebody and that person does not give them something they like, they could get sick themselves." Another, forty-year-old healer explained: "You don't just go around helping, because if you help somebody and that person does not give you something, you could get sick yourself." Or, as another Dene Tha put it, "You give something to the person who helps you; the gift is for the power they have." Gifts vary from healer to healer, depending on what the animal helper has told them it wanted to receive. Gifts may consist of a combination of tobacco, parts of animals, feathers, ribbons, coins, shirts, bullets, and rifles.[1]

Being Sick and Healed the Indian Way

It is part of Dene Tha teachings that "long ago there were no doctors, and people who had visions were like doctors [who] would cure others" (a Dene Tha Elder, in Moore and Wheelock 1990, 75). To cure others, Dene Tha would draw not only on *yú*, animal parts, herbs, roots, bark, and the leaves of shrubs and trees, known to have medicinal properties, but also on *ech'int'e*, which they had received as a gift from their animal helper. Although contemporary Dene Tha consult doctors, they also continue to rely on people who know an animal. This is the case when one is sick the Indian way, beyond the reach of Western medicine. This is also the case when the Indian way provides complementary care to that supplied by Western doctors.

The Man Who Knows Steel

Let us begin with an account in which Lisa credits both the doctor and her father for the recovery of her health. This case, like the ones to follow, is revealing because it portrays Dene Tha as drawing on the best of two proven medical traditions, that of Western doctors and that of the Dene Tha. The case is also interesting because it involves a Dene Tha healer who knows steel, but it is not the man whom we mentioned in the preceding chapter as knowing the steel horse or unicorn.

"My father knows steel, like this," said Lisa, touching the doorknob. She had just returned from the hospital for the final treatment to her jaw, which had been broken two months earlier. The doctors had put steel pins and metal thread in her gums to reconstruct the jawbones, a procedure that had caused her considerable pain. Soon after the operation Lisa decided to enlist the help of her father, since he knew steel. She therefore presented herself to her father as pitiful and deserving of help from his powers. Late in the afternoon, when both her parents were at home, Lisa commented to her father, "I guess you don't love me, that's why you don't come to visit me when I'm suffering." Lisa's father remained silent while her mother took Lisa's head in her hands and cried. Later in the evening, once all the children were in bed, the father went to Lisa's bed. He spoke at length about the power he knew, about his ability to know when steel will hurt, and about his ability to relieve pain inflicted by steel. He then gave her a piece of beaver pelt wrapped in different colors of ribbons and told her to keep it under her pillow. He next blew over a glass of water, which he gave her to drink. "And to tell you the truth," said Lisa, "I did not feel anything after that." When she went back to see the doctor, he told her that he was surprised when she bled very little when he took the steel thread from her gums. Lisa told the doctor, "Maybe you won't believe it, but my dad helped me." Her father could not do what the doctor had done, but neither could the doctor do what her father had done with his power, given his knowledge of steel. In this manner, Lisa, like other

Dene Tha, typically draws on two streams of knowledge to recover her health. In a sense, Lisa claims to be in a better position than non-Indian patients, who have only the Western doctor to care for them.

The notion that someone could know steel and as a result have some power to heal or alleviate injuries caused by metal objects surprised me. On the occasion of a visit to Lisa's house I raised the issue, saying that when I heard of a man who knew steel, I wondered how this could be. "I understand to know an animal, but to know metal, I don't," I said. Lisa's brother then told the following story: "Like there is a story. It happened a long time ago; they say it is true. The first time the white men were around, they were stealing the horses from the Indian and they would have to steal it back, and they got into more and more trouble, and the white people were around them—so one night this old man stood by the fire and with his hands up like this [puts his open hands up near his chest, palms facing outward] he had all their bullets come to him and fall into a plate. Then he had their mind kind of go that other way, and they all left. He knew metal. That's how he could do this." Here, as in many other instances, when seeking information I was told a story. Stories are given for one to think with. They are meant to guide one's thoughts in thinking about a certain matter and to inform one's relationship with fellow Dene and fellow animals. In this case, the speaker's story establishes the fact that his father is not the first one to know steel and that there were such individuals among the Dene ever since they came into contact with the white men.[2] When pressed for additional information, Lisa and her brother would say no more. In this way they showed respect for their father's power: one should not boast about it or tell about its acquisition. I surmised that a steel animal of some sort must have appeared to Lisa's father, much as described by the other Dene Tha healer, who claimed to know steel and who attributed his knowledge and power in this respect to his vision of a steel horse or unicorn.

Other Powers to Heal

In the following account the healing power involved is that of a woman in her fifties, the speaker's mother: "My mother has the power to stop heavy bleeding, and the power to drive a bad toothache away. She did that to my grandmother. She was coughing a lot of blood; a yellow pail was full [of blood]. I called my mother, and she took a glass of water and blew over it. She gave her the water, and the blood stopped right away. She did not spit blood since. My mother likes something red and heavy [as a gift]; the gift is for the power they have." The account concerns the speaker's grandmother, who lived very close to the health clinic. She was visited daily by a nurse and was regularly seen by a doctor. Nevertheless, when she began to cough up blood, the speaker immediately called her mother because of her power to stop heavy bleeding. Although the speaker refers generally to what kind of gift her mother expects, the identity of the mother's power is not disclosed. In Dene Tha healing it is common practice for a healer to blow over a glass of water and give it to his or her patient. In the words of a Dene Tha healer in his early twenties: "If I take the cup of water, I blow on it, you give power to the water, then you give it to the other person, that makes the other person who is sick better. You blow on it, that is power." Another Dene Tha healer explained: "Like if you were sick, I could sing you a song and give you a glass of water. That song is the owl song, and the owl power in the water might make you better."

A Dene Tha woman attributed her sister's survival following a car accident to a Dene Tha healer. Her sister had stopped breathing and was thought to be dead. A Dene Tha used his power, putting his mouth against her throat. She began to breathe again, feebly. He then placed his mouth against the back of her neck, and she started to breathe for good. He had brought her back to life. "In the hospital they use oxygen to breathe; old people, they use their power. It's different," said the woman.

Parents often explained that sores on the skin of their babies and young children were due to events affecting their parents or close kin. When two Dene Tha parents pointed out that their four-year-old daughter was sick with sores in her mouth, they said: "She is sick the Indian way, there is so much killing going around, that is why. She has to be helped. Lots of little kids like her are sick too." These parents knew a healer who was "good for that," and they were busy making a pair of moccasins to bring him as a gift. They would take their daughter to see him the next day. In the next family I visited, I raised the issue of babies being sick with sores in their mouth. The mother immediately invoked lack of hygiene to account for the sickness: "Yeah, these people, many of them bottle-feed their babies, and they don't take care of sterilizing the bottles. That is how their babies get sick," she said. When I remarked that I had heard that some babies were sick the Indian way and needed help, the mother instantly named two babies, whom she knew, who had sores on their faces because their parents had taken them all over the place at night, "getting them exposed to what is going on," a veiled reference to people fighting one another with their power. She then referred to the relatives of the victim of a homicide committed a week earlier: "His sisters and all their babies got sores, but they got help right away. Only [his sister] still has sores on her hands. She works with plastic gloves on her hands." These cases of illness were clearly not the result of poor sanitary practices, so they were not for the doctor or nurse to handle. The help of knowledgeable individuals with the appropriate power was called for. It was for that purpose that one of the Dene Tha dreamers had visited the site of the killing, made offerings on a fire, covered the ground with dirt where the blood of the victim had been, and left a stick with eagle feathers next to that spot. A Dene Tha parent commented: "He is trying to protect the children so that nobody will get sick. It is usually sores that people around get, lots of sores. He didn't want that to happen; he is trying to protect the children."

Sores on the skin may have other causes. When a two-year-old girl broke out with sores all over her body, her parents took her to see a healer in Meander River. The healer sucked a large worm (the mother showed the size of the end of her little finger) from the child's chest, and he blew over her as well as on her mouth. The healer explained that other people were using their power to get at the parents but that their child "had caught it." Following the visit to the healer, the child slept for twenty-four hours, and all the sores, even the ones under her feet, disappeared. As the healer has said, everything was all right now, for the child and for the parents.

A similar diagnosis was found in the case of a woman who had been complaining to her husband of being sick, restless, unable to sleep, and incapable of finding the energy to get out of bed. At the nursing station the doctor told her that he could not find any-

thing wrong with her. The husband took this as a clear indication
that she was sick the Indian way. He immediately said, "Yeah, we
will see." The husband sent his son to get two Dene Tha healers.
The first one sucked a big black thing, the size of thumb, out of
the back of her neck, and the other healer sucked a similar object
out of her throat. They said that Dogribs, who had been visiting
local Elders, had done this to her but that they would not do it
again. They left with the black things to burn at home, and the
woman promptly recovered.

A power to heal extends to psychological as well as physical
conditions. A young Dene Tha healer explained how he used his
power only for good to help others. He gave as an example his
young niece, who had asked him to help her get over a bad cold.
He said, "I helped her with my power; I just put my hand over
her, and she got better." The parents of the girl paid for the cure
by giving the healer a nice belt, which he was proud to show me,
as well as a shirt and a pair of gloves. He knew that he should wait
to be asked before helping someone, but he had not done so in
the case of a friend who was sitting next to him to share her sorrow over the recent death of her father. Without telling her,
when he got up he blew over her. Within minutes he could feel
his power at work flying in circles within his head. A few weeks
later his friend told him that she was not feeling sad and de-
pressed anymore. He told her that he had cured her and that she
had to pay him, which she agreed to do with a beaded bullet
pouch made of moose hide.

In the following case the principle that one's behavior mani-
fests the identity of the animal one knows led healers to identify
the owl as the cause of a young man's insomnia. The young man
consulted three individuals with a power to heal. The first healer
was defeated by one of the patient's powers: "I beat him with my
power. He tried very hard to heal me, but I beat him. The unicorn is my power; it was getting after him with this big pointed
thing in his forehead. He [the healer] even fired at it, because it
would have killed him. So he had to give up." The young man
then consulted another healer, to whom he offered a pair of
gloves as a gift, which she wore before going to sleep. She then reported a dream in which she had seen an owl. She told the young
man that the owl was his power and that it was keeping him

awake at night. The sleeping pattern of the young man followed that of the owl, who hunts at night and sleeps during the day. "That's my power. I just keep them as pets when I was young. I did not know I was related to them," he explained. Although he had failed to recognize an animal helper in his owl pets, he had become related to them and now shared some of their characteristics. The young man approached a third healer, who told him he had had a dream of an owl keeping the young man awake before he came in for help. The owl had wanted to teach the young man how to be a great hunter, but it was too late for that now. The healer thought that in his dream he could overcome the young man's power and thus cure him of his insomnia. In this case, this healer and the preceding one both told the young man that in their dreams they would go after the owl with their own powers to kill it. After they claimed success in their hunt, the young man recovered his sleep, but only for a few weeks, after which the insomnia came back.

The young man then consulted a fourth healer, who explained that other Dene Tha were bothering him with their power. This new interpretation led to more healing rituals that never completely relieved the young man of his insomnia. Still another healer told him that in her dreams she had seen the owl trying to get his hat, which she had prevented by putting a shield before the young man. In the healer's dream the hat represented all the young man's clothes. The healer told him that the owl was taking away his sleep because he had failed to take care of his clothes properly. The healer also told him not to lend his clothes. "My hat, that's all my clothes. It's an invisible hat, even my toque, that's an invisible hat, or my country cowboy hat, I can't lend it or drag it around; I have to hang it up." The healer told the young man that the owl had almost taken his hat and that it if did so one day he would fall asleep and never wake up. She told him to look after his clothes and that, someday, he would sleep again.

Although the young man heeded the woman's advice concerning his clothes, he nevertheless consulted a sixth healer. In this instance, the young man was told that an animal's paw, which he had put in his pillow, were keeping him from sleeping. This animal, which was also one of his powers, was too strong for him to sleep with. The young man therefore stored the paw away in a suitcase in the small log house adjacent to his home. After this he slept very well. A series of consultations with various healers thus focused on different aspects of the patient's life history: his keeping owls as pets as a child, unidentified enemies that he had in the community, his lack of concern for his clothes, and finally, an animal's paw that he was keeping in his pillow. In his search for a cure, offers of help were never denied. Each healing ritual's failure or relative success was explained in terms of powers at work; patient and healers shared the conviction that in due time the definitive cure would materialize.

POWERS TO RESPECT

Health issues are also related to two obvious concerns in Dene Tha domestic life: exposure to menstrual blood and improper care of personal clothing, especially that of young children. In both instances proscriptions apply to prevent illness and, in some cases, even death.

The Power of Menstrual Blood

In many Native North American societies menstrual blood is seen as detrimental to successful hunting. In these societies "menstrual blood is not thought of as polluting but as clashing with a man's power(s)" (Irwin 1994, 177). Joan Ryan (1995, 29) uses the term "endanger" rather than "contamination" to refer to "a woman's power to affect men's ability to hunt, thus endangering the survival of the group." From menarche to menopause, menstrual sequestration was a regular feature of a Dene woman's life. At this time women camped away from the community, never in the company of males, in case men should become incapable of hunting or performing other male tasks.[3] Contemporary Dene women are similarly expected to be mindful when menstruating so as not to endanger the well-being of males.

Guédon, for instance, describes how Nabesna women taught her about the danger of menstrual blood through stories and nonverbal reactions to her behavior. Old women would glance at her to stop her from a certain action and would reward her similarly for the right gesture: "I learned, without ever being told so, to walk while keeping my feet together on the path; to put one foot on the door step; not to step over a stream, over a path, over a tool, never over a man; and to stay in my tent for three days every month" (Guédon 1994a, 41–42). In this important aspect of life, as in all others, the Nabesna women expected Guédon to learn through observation rather than by instruction. Guédon (1994a, 42) writes that she "translated all these experiences into a lapidary saying: 'When a woman, don't step over anything.' But this was not a Dene way of stating this series of prohibitions. No one every told me anything of the kind."

Dene Tha are similarly concerned with this ubiquitous potential source of illness. That is why, behind Dene Tha homes, there are two outhouses, each with its own path, so that males and females never use the same toilet. It is also why, in their kitchens, people keep a separate cup with a red thread attached to its handle, the "danger cup," for the exclusive use of menstruating women. Likewise, when menstruating, women ought to avoid walking all over the house and should forgo washing the clothes of males. Failure to take these elementary precautions puts the health of others at risk.

In every house the danger cup, or "the cup that one is afraid of," expresses this concern to avoid being affected adversely and inadvertently by indirect contact with a menstruating woman. The danger cup usually sits on the kitchen counter or is in the cupboard. Everyone knows not to use it since it is the menstruating woman's cup. Pointing to her three-year-old and six-year-old sons, a young mother said: "They know this and they are not supposed to use it. I tell them it's poison. They call it danger cup. My older one he is six years old. He already knows about menstruation. He knows why he can't use that cup."

In many Dene Tha homes I observed husbands or young bachelors wash their clothes in a tub of their own, that is, one never used by their wives or other menstruating women. Men would do that only when their wives or sisters, who would normally do the washing, were menstruating. A wife explained that she has her own tub to wash her clothes, and one for the girls, and another for the boys and her husband. "I never wash the kids' clothes in my tub, as if it was poison," she said, laughing. "Even the pillow case or bedding has to be washed apart." She added: "My mother told me that in the old days, when they moved from one place to another, even in the winter, the girl who was menstruating had to walk all by herself far behind the sleigh. That's the way it was."

Precautions against contact with the power of menstrual blood are a regular feature of Dene Tha lives. Perhaps because of habitual avoidance, I came across only one case of an illness attributed to the power of menstrual blood. When Peter, a man in his early fifties, became sick with skin rashes and a bleeding nose, a healer identified his three teenage daughters as the cause of his illness. Peter had been sitting on the floor to eat his meals, as men and women of his generation often do. Although the daughters knew about the power of menstrual blood, they had walked all around the house when menstruating. In the words of the eldest of Peter's married daughters: "Like to him, that old man [the healer], it's just like the floor in the house is covered with blood." The eldest daughter added, "When you have your periods, you're not supposed to walk all around the kitchen"; otherwise, others will "get a bleeding nose or some disease." The blame for the man's condition clearly belonged to his younger daughters. Following the healer's diagnosis and healing ritual, the parents set up a table of their own in the dining room and the young girls were admonished for lacking respect toward others.

There are many things that women and men are not supposed to do. One woman said, "Like we are not suppose to use the same tub as the man or lie on the boys' bed, nor may your cousin or your brother hold you by the wrist or the ankle or look you in the eyes." The woman then referred to a story that happened long ago about five brothers who held the wrists of their menstruating sisters. After they did so, their bodies twisted and they died. As she told the story, she dramatically twisted her whole body.

The Power in Personal Clothing
Dene Tha say that "one only puts on his own clothes; one does not put someone else's clothes on." To let someone else have possession of one's clothes, or those of one's children, is to lose control over these clothes and to risk that they be improperly cared for or disposed of, exposed to dogs, or simply thrown around, in which case the clothes' original owner is liable to become sick. The concern for personal clothing is particularly evident in the disposal of children's outgrown clothing or the clothing of a deceased relative or spouse.

It is general knowledge that all old clothing, pillows, and blankets, especially those of children and the deceased, should be carefully disposed of, either buried in the bush away from dogs or passed on to close relatives who may use them for their own children. The Chipewyan think of the dog as a "scavenger and consumer of feces," as well "as exemplars of uncontrolled and unregulated sexuality" (Sharp 1995, 70). This belief is held by many other Dene groups. Dogs are clearly a source of worry to the Dene Tha, who say that if a dog happens to urinate on someone's clothes or picks at them, that person becomes ill.

Used clothes are not to be passed on casually. A mother explained, "If you give it to others, maybe they don't take care of them, they don't look good after it, the kids [whose clothes they were] can get sick." Another mother explained that she either gives her children's clothes to her two sisters or "just puts them in a pile with some moose bones or chicken bones and burns them." Pillows of a dead person may be used by his or her spouse or disposed of in the bush: "You make a hole in it and empty what's in it. Put all the stuff in a hole and cover it with mud. You can keep the cover or put it with everything. It is the same with blankets. You can keep them or give them to someone who keeps it good."

When a young child, whose parents were Cree and Dene Tha, suffered from sores and heavy congestion, a Dene Tha healer attributed her illness to her wearing secondhand clothing. The Cree mother, whose child was registered under her name, had to come to terms with the fact that her child was Dene Tha, not Cree: "Like them Slaveys," she said, "they are not supposed to give old clothes to the babies; if they do, the baby gets sick. I put secondhand clothing on her, and I didn't think it would do anything to her, for it doesn't do anything to Cree, us Cree people. But she got sick." Hence her husband and in-laws knew the child was one of them.

A young Dene Tha healer said he feels it immediately if someone touches his clothes while he is away: "If someone touches it, in my head it moves inside and I know it; when I get home I say, 'Who touched my clothes?' Like my tapes they can touch, but not my clothes." Household members are not to touch his pillow or blanket, or any of his clothes, even if they are messy. This applies also to the mother, who cannot pick them up to wash them unless he puts them together in advance for her to take. For the Dene, there is a close association between one's being and one's clothing, so much so that to touch one is to touch the other.

This conception of the relationship between individuals and their clothing probably informed the petitions that some Dogribs made to Bishop Grandin in 1866. Following his visit to Fort Rae, Grandin wrote: "A chief came urging me to baptize the shirt of one of his hunters who was dying too far for me to be taken to him. Two mothers, whose children had died without being baptized, begged me to baptize their tiny bonnets. Devastated at not being successful on this point, they begged me to take their bonnets and keep them safe" (in Abel 1989, 86; her translation). In Dene Dháh the expression for the verb "to baptize" translates as "pouring water on someone." I imagine that the Dogrib have a corresponding expression that was used to request this action on the part of Bishop Grandin.

The symbolic association between personal clothing and the self is clearly visible in the following account of a dream, which was heard at a store, where it was told for everyone to hear. The woman's dream was preceded by an evening in which her husband had begun to drink at home and had then gone out to look for additional liquor. As he left she told him, "You should not drink!" to which he retorted, "It is not of your business." The woman then went to bed angry with her husband and in her sleep dreamed of her deceased father and mother, whose deaths had both been associated with drinking. In the dream her father was angry at her mother, and in his anger he gathered all her clothes to burn them: "Her dress, her underwear, her blue dress, the one she was buried in, her apron." He threw them in a big hole in the ground in which a woman [the dreamer's cousin] was sitting, smoking. The dreamer asked her what she was doing there and was told, "I got drunk, so I just stayed there." The dreamer extended her index finger for her cousin to grasp and to pull herself out of the hole. The dreamer then gave some matches to her father to light the fire, but the fire would not go into the hole, and as a result he was unable to burn the clothes. All along, the dreamer's mother stood next to the hole without a word. Her father then told the dreamer, "Your mom has been real bad; that is why I want to burn her clothes." To do so would

99

have been to hurt her, not only her feelings at seeing her possessions destroyed but her person, as she would have felt the consequence of this action in her own body.

"Keeping the clothes of children good" is primarily a woman's obligation. The woman is liable to become sick if she fails in this responsibility, as illustrated in the following account. Late one fall a mother suddenly found herself unable to fall asleep. She would lie sleepless in bed feeling all numb. After two bad nights like this, the woman told her sister, who replied, "You're not supposed to hide it," she said, "because sometimes it is too late for help." The woman directed her sister to a local healer, to whom she described her condition. The healer responded with the narration of a dream he had had two nights before. The dream was for a woman who was to visit him for help. In the dream the healer set his snares for beavers. Beavers came up to the snares but did not get caught. In his dream he had seen lots of clothes just scattered around; some were burnt, and others were still smoking. There was also a wolf around that area. When he woke up, he wondered why he had had that dream. He told the sick woman that most people in the community looked after their things well. The woman then told the healer that she had old clothes in the attic, some hers, some belonging to her small girl. Early in the fall they insulated the attic and, while doing so, her son had thrown down into the living room the clothing she had kept up there. She was told to pick up her stuff and look after it but did not bother. Later some children had thrown some of the old clothes on a fire burning out in the yard. The healer said that nothing would happen to the young kids who burned the clothing because they did not know the likely consequence of their actions. But as the healer told her, she fell ill because she knew of these consequences. She had to do what one ought to do and not do just as she pleased.

The clothing was stored in the attic, under the roof, which in Dene Dháh is referred to as "the head of the house." The house is described as a body with its head, back, sides, and face. When I had my first haircut in a Dene Tha home, the man who was my barber took me by surprise when he rapidly retreated against the wall, approximately five feet away from me, as soon as he was done. He was doing so, he told me, to show that he had no intention of keeping any of my hair. It was up to me to take the broom and pick up all my hair and put it in a bag that he handed over. As I did so, I asked where the Dene would put their own hair after a haircut. "Up in the head of the house," was his reply. There, personal things were safe, out of reach of others who might use them to cause harm to their owner. As mentioned earlier, and as is amply illustrated in the following chapter, it is also from one's head or brain that one sends a power to heal, to harm, or to ward off the evil intentions of others.

CONTEXTUAL IDENTITIES AND REALITIES

In their discussion of the cases of illness and healing examined so far Dene Tha sometimes made a contrast between *Dene*, in the sense of Indians who enjoy animal helpers and are susceptible to *ech'int'e*, "a power," and *Egeeyah*, in the sense of Euro-Canadians who do not have animal helpers and, therefore, are not so susceptible to a power to heal or to harm. In the case to follow, however, we see how the Dene Tha, who first categorized a white woman who came to Dene Tha healers for help as someone who could not be helped, later decided that she could be helped. The grounds on which they denied and later granted her access to a power to heal shifted over time. This case shows that it is a vital feature of categorizations that for members of a particular group they "*are revisable as different relevancies unfold themselves*" (Anderson and Lee 1982, 301; emphasis in original). In other words, "in understanding and producing practical actions, members are not concerned to follow determinate sets of rules. Their involvement in a developing and unfolding world requires the capacity to re-learn, and re-constitute, 'events', 'activities' and 'lessons' in a world that is in some sense always changing" (Anderson and Lee 1982, 306). That is, "far from being regulated by rules, people make use of them as tools of interpretation and persuasion" (Watson and Irwin 1996, 88). To invoke a rule to account for one's action is to give the action meaning and to legitimize it in the eyes of others.

Indians and Whites

The Dene Tha use the term *Dene* either to refer exclusively to the people known as Slaveys in English, in opposition to other Indians such as the Beaver (*Tsátien*), the Dogrib (*Tlinchóngé*), the Cree (*Deshine*), and so on, or to refer to the category of Indians generally in opposition to the white man.[4] It is generally true that the Euro-Canadians living in Chateh are never sick the Dene way and, therefore, never call on a Dene Tha with a power to recover their health or ensure their good fortune. In contrast, Dene Tha say they may be sick either the white man's way or the Indian way. Dene are therefore liable to be cured by doctors and nurses, the *yú dené* or "medicine persons," or by individuals who know an animal and have a power to heal.

Categorization of the sort reported here for the Dene Tha can be seen as an instance of a more general phenomenon, that of ethnic reification, or dichotomization between self/us and other(s). Edmund Leach, for instance, remarked, "I identify myself with a collective *we* which is then contrasted with some other" (1967, 34). According to Barth (1969, 15), this dichotomization of "we" and "they," the members of another ethnic group, "implies a recognition of limitations on shared understandings, differences in criteria for judgment of value and performance, and a restriction of interaction to sectors of assumed common understandings and mutual interest." Anthony Cohen writes that one's individual and collective sense of self is "informed by implicit and explicit contrast" (1985, 115). According to Louk Hagendoorn and Roger Henke (1991, 247), when individuals speak of themselves as members of an ethnic group, their "social identity is determined by the position of their in-group relative to other comparison groups." Social identity defines persons by social categories of inclusion and exclusion, giving rise to the "us/them" dichotomy. Relevant to this discussion is the view that ethnic identities are not natural phenomena, "something we are born with whether we like it or not." They are social phenomena and, like age and gender, they are "an emergent property of an ongoing interpersonal bargaining process" (G. Watson 1981, 454). As noted by Slobodin (1975, 285) when he first resided with the Kutchin in 1938, "they were not aware that they were Indians." Kutchins became "'Indianized' in ideology," writes Slobodin (1975, 285), through sustained contact with whites in urban and semiurban environments.[5] Kutchins and Dene from other groups learned to be Indians from Euro-Canadians, who used the term as part of a process of management of ethnic identities. Similarly, "the English term 'culture' did not become part of Tetlin language until the mid 1970's" (Guédon 1994a, 60), and then it was probably as a result of interaction with anthropologists and linguists, as well as with the pursuit of land claims in court. The adoption of new vocabulary goes hand in hand with a complex process of Dene "presentation of themselves to the world and to other Dene" (Guédon 1994a, 64).

The social process of categorization is of great significance, for it is the tool by which one excludes, or tends to exclude, individuals or groups from one's own group. Such management is not always successful. It failed, for instance, in the case of Jack, the Dogrib prophet who promoted an "anti-white, nativistic" interpretation of the Prophet Dance but could not get his followers to agree with his view that whites should be excluded from attending his ceremonies (Helm 1994, 34–35, 70–71, 159–160). Management of identities, or the recognition of someone as a co-villager or not, can also be seen in D. Smith's observation (personal communication, May 1995) that "Dene Nu Kwan did not simply mean the native people of Fort Resolution but all people who were really *of* the village [including whites]. Either a white or an Indian could dwell in the village all his/her life and still be an outsider if, for some reason, they excluded themselves from the prevailing communitas."

D. Smith (1988, in Helm 1994, 88), therefore, warns us not to misinterpret apparent categorical oppositions that are really those of "polarity (extremes of the same dimension) and not of true opposition (as between entities or conditions that exclude or deny one another)," and Sharp (1994, 38) writes that "Chipewyan classification schemes make for greater use of polythetic (nonbinary) categories (Needham 1972, 1975) than do English language classification schemes, often giving a relativistic aspect to categorizations that may confound a binary analysis." The opposition between us and them, between Dene and white man, is best seen as part of situated interactions, an opposition we therefore should not elevate to the status of a feature of Dene Tha thought or an aspect of Dene Tha culture.

Generally speaking, it is not sufficient to recognize that "in contemporary Native American culture 'the Whiteman' is a key social category and cultural symbol of what 'the Indian' is not" (B. Tedlock 1992, 293). It is necessary to identify the social contexts in which social actors will want to invoke this categorical opposition to exclude, or revoke it to include. Exclusion and inclusion are both social actions. To label someone as essentially different from oneself is to rebuff him or her as a person one will not associate with; conversely, "to label someone as essentially like oneself is to activate latent solidarity, to recruit someone as a potential ally, and simultaneously to rebuff others" (G. Watson 1981, 464). The most compelling evidence in support of this view came to me following an unexpected request by a Cree medicine man who was well known to the Dene Tha generally and to the Dene Tha healers in particular. This Cree medicine man directed a young woman, a non-Indian, to seek me in Chateh and ask me to take her to Dene Tha healers who would relieve her from an illness. I was suddenly thrust in the position of intermediary between a white woman and Dene Tha healers.[6]

I began with visits to Dene Tha friends, introducing this woman to them, explaining the circumstances that had brought her to Chateh. I then asked whom we might approach about her condition and what gifts we should bring. The names of two dreamers were suggested and the appropriate gifts specified. In the evening, when we approached the residences of these healers, a son in the first case and a daughter in the second case came to the door to hear our request and convey it to the father, while we remained outdoors. Assistance was denied in both cases. One healer denied assistance on the grounds that he could not call on his power to help others, as this time was too close to the death of a son. The other healer declined assistance on the grounds that he had not received any dream indicating that he would help this woman. We were back to square one. I sought more names and more information about gifts to bring. Again the requests were denied. This continued for five consecutive nights, concluding with an Elder's daughter telling us in Dene Dháh on the doorstep of their house: "The Whiteman have lost their soul; they cannot be helped."

Dispirited, I thought I could not assist this woman and carry out the task the Cree medicine man had given me. Without much sense of direction we walked onto the reserve. We ran into another Dene Tha friend who, on hearing our predicament, told us to go to Meander River. She gave us the name of a Dene Tha medicine man who, she assured us, would help. The gift we should take consisted of five ribbons of different colors and five twenty-five-cent coins. And thus we went. When we arrived in Meander River, we asked the first person we met on the street where we could find the Dene Tha healer we had been referred to. The woman immediately offered to accompany us and serve as an interpreter. To my great surprise, this man said he was expecting us. Through the interpreter he listened to the woman's account of her ailment and then proceeded with a healing ceremony, which I was asked not to write about. Following the healing ritual, the woman reported the end of the symptoms she had suffered from, and from which she has never suffered since.

Back in Chateh we were in for more surprises. People asked how our journey had been and expressed satisfaction at the results. We stopped at the house of the woman who had told us that "the Whiteman have lost their soul; they cannot be helped." There her father told us that this was not the case. Showing us his forearm and pulling the skin up with the other hand, he told us that although the Indian and the white man differed in skin color, this difference was very superficial. He pointed to the veins running beneath the surface of his arm and said that underneath our skin we all shared the same life-sustaining, red blood. In this conversation the speaker categorically denied that there was any essential difference between Indians and Euro-Canadians. In his words and actions the Dene Tha Elder showed that categorizations are not immutable because they are the means by which actors choose to exclude or include those they want to rebuff or those they want to make one of their own. "Categories," or better, "categorizations," "do work within the context of their occasion" (Anderson and Lee 1982, 298).

Dene Tha Reality Self-Validating

A close examination of the accounts in this chapter and the preceding one reveal that Dene Tha reality (like all realities) is self-validating in two related but analytically distinct ways (G. Watson and Goulet 1992). In the first place, elements of Dene Tha reality, like the elements of a gestalt contexture, are mutually constitutive. They elaborate each other in a back-and-forth process. Similarly, the process of constituting an event as an instance of healing with a power is involved in the cases described above. The scene consisting of the woman blowing on a glass of water and giving it to her mother, who then stops bleeding, is constituted by communicative acts: the request that not the nurse but this particular woman with a power to stop bleeding be called to the patient's bed, and the cooperation of the sick woman, who unquestioningly takes the glass of water that now contains her daughter's power. In turn, the scene, as formulated, gives specific meaning to otherwise inherently ambiguous words and gestures. The same occurs in the case of the man who relieved the pain his daughter was having as a result of the steel braces used to reconstruct her jawbone, and who prevented her from bleeding profusely, as is usually the case when the braces are removed. The woman with the broken jaw is well aware that her doctor may not share her view, and she therefore tells him: "Maybe you won't believe it, but my dad helped me." Having heard the woman's account, the doctor, like Western-minded readers of this book, will probably see it as a psychosomatic phenomenon. The pain went away because the woman believed in her father's power. That is not the Dene Tha way of reading the evidence, however. It is not just to any healer that one goes for help, but to a healer with a power to deal with a specific illness or condition. The blood stops or the pain goes away after the patient has drunk the water to which the healer has transferred his healing power by blowing over it. The power is transferred because the patient has given the appropriate gifts. From beginning to end, the sequence of events is immediately seen as a case of healing with *echinte*.

Dene Tha reality is also self-validating in that, like all other realities, it stipulates in advance what shall count as evidence (see Mehan and Wood 1975). According to Dene Tha canons of evidence, parts of plants *do* heal when one gives a gift of tobacco to replace what one has taken, and powers *do* help individuals recover their health or their lives. In all these cases, empirical refutation, as Euro–North Americans understand it, is rendered impossible in two ways. First, alternative accounts are always available, and second, what satisfies any one criterion of evidence is highly flexible, as for instance in the Dene Tha explanation of the young man's insomnia. If he could not sleep, it might be because of the owl. In this case, the young man remembered keeping owls as pets when he was young, and he therefore concluded that he had unknowingly become related to them. This explains his insomnia as well as the healers' decision to go with their own powers, while dreaming, to kill the owl. After the healers reported that their pursuit had been successful, the young man regained his sleep. After a few weeks, when he suffered from insomnia again, other Dene Tha healers attributed his condition to the ill will of other Dene Tha who were using their power to undermine his health. And so a new cycle of interpretation and validation began.

In writing thus of Dene Tha accounts, as in G. Watson and Goulet 1992, I do not intend to leave the impression that they are calculating or in any way dishonest in their search for evidence, for it is not the case that they witness a phenomenon and then characterize it as evidence; rather, the phenomenon is immediately and self-evidently available to them as evidence. All realities are socially generated, and the process of generation involves work. All realities are self-validating, in that their elements, like those of a gestalt contexture, are mutually constitutive, that is, they stipulate in advance what constitutes plausible evidence for their truths. The ever-present possibility of giving alternative accounts of Dene Tha events is no less characteristic of scientific discourse or judicial discourse than it is of Dene discourse (Gilbert and Mulkay 1984; G. Watson 1991, 1994). Whether as scientist or layman, as Dene or Euro–North American, as writer or reader, we are all engaged in similar activities: "We describe and simultaneously constitute reality (not once and for all, but from moment to moment, and not necessarily in agreement with one another) and then orientate to it as if it had an existence independent of the work we perform in constituting it; we reify it" (G. Watson 1994, 411). This orientation to reality characterizes our attitude in our day-to-day lives. All sorts of realities confront us "as if" they existed independently of our role in constituting them. These realities are therefore experienced as a set of constraints. It is in this sense that "reality confronts us and cannot be wished away" (G. Watson 1994, 411).

The analysis of Dene Tha accounts of illness and of healing reveals the complexity of the sociocultural system of management of the self and social relations that the Dene live by. In the field of health both *yú* and *ech'int'e* figure prominently, not as competing but as complementary resources within the domain of Euro-Canadian health care. This is true both of Dene Tha medicine drawn from parts of animals or plants and of Western medicine received from Western health professionals, *yú dené*. This is also true of the highly specialized skills of Western doctors and surgeons, on the one hand, and of the highly developed skills of individuals who know an animal, or steel, on the other. Dene Tha enjoy the best of both worlds as they seek the benefits of both Western and Dene doctors. Although accounts of illness and of healing the Indian way suggest a categorical opposition between Dene or Indian and whites, we have shown that such oppositions are situational, for in some contexts Dene Tha abandon the us/them dichotomy to stress similarities at the expense of differences. The suppression of the categorical opposition between Euro-Canadians and Indians allows the Dene Tha to activate latent solidarities, to state that we are all the same, and to extend the ministration of their power to Euro-Canadian individuals who seek their help in earnest.

5. Visions of Conflict, Conflicts of Vision

You can do crazy things
when you are drinking.
—Dene Tha speaker

In previous chapters I have argued that Dene deeply respect one another's autonomy. This respect is manifest in their pursuit of true knowledge as personal knowledge, as well as in their emphasis on self-reliance. There is, however, another side to Dene lives, namely, the experience of aggression at the hands of fellow Dene who, when drunk, inflict injuries on others, or who, when resentful, secretly use their *ech'int'e*, their power, to bring misfortune and even death to others. It is to these aspects of Dene lives that we now turn.[1]

When I initiated fieldwork in Chateh, I avoided Paul's home because it was the scene of heavy drinking and fighting, including the knifing of a family member. Paul eventually became a friendly teacher of Dene Dháh and of Dene Tha ways of living. Over the years, as Paul quit drinking and healed his body and spirit, he often reminded me in his jovial voice that his rehabilitation was proceeding the "Indian way," with the help of Dene Elders. Similarly, Myrna told me that she gave up a long-standing drinking habit following a severe admonition and warning from dead relatives (see her account in chapter 6). Her change of habit led her to participate more regularly in the Prophet Dance. As documented in chapter 8, young Dene Tha men given to drinking and abusive behavior were also eventually rehabilitated by the community and Elders. These young men became drummers in the Prophet Dance. Other cases reported in this chapter and in following ones substantiate the Dene Tha view that sobriety goes hand in hand with deep experiences of dreams and visions, as well as with interaction with Elders living either in this land or in the other land.

Dene Tha Elders and younger Dene Tha men and women who live productively and soberly suffer at the sight of relatives and loved ones whose lives are devastated by the abuse of alcohol. As reported in chapter 1, the first question I was asked in a Dene Tha home concerned the state of people who drink and destroy their lives. Did I know how to stop this calamity? This is one of the most difficult issues that anyone, Dene or non-Dene, close to someone abusing alcohol has to deal with.

The widespread abuse of alcohol, which is a recent development in the lives of the Dene Tha, is an all-too-common feature of indigenous communities around the world. The pattern of massive social disruption that follows the intrusion of Western economic, political, military, and religious powers in indigenous communities is well documented (Bodley 1988, 1990; Maybury-Lewis 1997). Indigenous people lose access to the land and to the resources that supported their way of life. Population declines dramatically because of new diseases, and the surviving individuals subsist at the margins of the new social order. They lack full citizenship rights but are expected to participate as cheap labor in the frontier wage economy. The social fabric of old is torn along generation and gender lines as young and old, men and women are drawn differently into the new social order. Tensions and frustrations manifest themselves in the lives of individuals, males especially, who take to drinking, vent their anger in family disputes, destroy property, and sometimes take their own lives or those of fellow community members.

Although the concept of violence is a contested one in anthropology (Krohn-Hansen 1994), I take as a violent action an act of aggression carried out with the intention to cause physical and/or emotional harm to another. Violence may lead to conflict. A conflict comprises an initial act of aggression and the subsequent retaliatory act, also aimed at causing physical and/or emotional harm to another. Although violence does not always escalate to the level of conflict, both are rooted in hostility and antagonism. In this chapter I argue that, in the course of the last thirty years, in the midst of dramatic changes in their socioeconomic environment, the Dene Tha have learned to operate within a complex system of management of self and of social relationships; they vigorously check any directly aggressive behavior when sober, but when drunk they vent their hostility and attack individuals they resent. Under the cover of drunkenness, individuals find the socially accepted conditions in which to engage in acts of aggression that allow them to infringe, within limits, on one another's autonomy in a socially expected and permissible way. This argument is based on numerous observations and on an examination of Dene Tha accounts of aggression among fellow band members.

ANTHROPOLOGICAL ACCOUNTS OF DENE AGGRESSION

According to Honigmann (1981, 736), Athapaskan and Algonkian populations in the Canadian subarctic "normally controlled the release of hostility" and vigorously checked any "direct aggressive behavior, verbal or physical, toward other people."[2] The majority of authors attribute this general suppression of hostility and aggression in interpersonal relations to the respect for personal autonomy, a core value of subarctic indigenous populations. In Honigmann's words, "in avoiding domination of others through aggression a person showed that he respected and recognized others' freedom of action" (1981, 737).[3] A few dissenting authors, however, namely Hallowell (1938) and Slobodin (1960), attribute the absence of aggression to fear rather than regard for personal autonomy. This is also the view of Helm (1961, 87), who writes that "the general diffidence and restraint exhibited in interpersonal contacts spring from a fear of conflict or unpleasantness." Helm (1961, 176) further remarks that "the respect for the autonomy of the other is, of course, ultimately for the individual a self-protective device, for to infringe on another's autonomy is to call down hostility upon one's self." According to this view, "pervasive anxiety" and "social distrust" characterize life in subarctic communities, because individuals are constantly "afraid of what might happen should they infringe on the right of somebody else" (Honigmann 1981, 737).

Faced with these conflicting views of Dene life, Honigmann suggests that we simply conclude that fear motivates people to refrain from aggression, whereas "from an outside vantage point, Indians showed regard for one another's feelings" (1981, 737). This conclusion is unsatisfactory. It fails to consider the possibility that both fear of retaliation and regard for personal autonomy motivate Dene not to intervene in one another's lives, and more important, it falls short of considering seriously how Dene construct their accounts of nonaggression and of aggression.

Visions of Conflict

Before turning to such accounts, we must take note of the fact that students of subarctic communities consistently report that after heavy drinking "normal" controls on aggressive behavior rapidly dissolve to give way to "flamboyant emotionality, ready expression of anger, and loss of other inhibitions" (Honigmann 1981, 737). Under these conditions violent behavior frequently leads to serious injury, attempted homicide, and even death, for which individuals consistently disclaim responsibility.

In its own brief to the Alberta Task Force on the Criminal Justice System the Dene Tha Women's Society reports that "wife abuse on the Assumption reserve is very common. It is sometimes very violent. Women get slapped, punched, kicked, raped, beaten at times so badly, they have to be medivaced [sic] to High Level" (1990, 2). Such abuse is suffered consistently at the hands of drunken husbands who would never attack their wives when sober. Similarly, men regularly suffer serious injuries at the hands of other drunken men. I recall the sight one early morning of Peter, with a broken tooth, a bleeding nose, and a swollen black eye, staring out into empty space and sitting on the living room floor of his cousin's house, surrounded by his young (two to five years old) nephews and nieces, or that of Luke rushed to the hospital with a severe abdominal wound following a shooting incident. I also remember conversing with a mother of five children as she wandered aimlessly on the road, her face swollen and her nose bleeding. She told me that her drunken daughters had beaten her up. These are only a few of many other similar recollections.

All across the subarctic, individuals and communities seem to alternate between two conflicting visions of life: one according to which they profess the highest regard for one another's autonomy, the other according to which they become one another's victims or fiercest aggressors. The change involved is so drastic, "the wildness and chaos of uninhibited spree drinking" so "dismaying and terrifying," writes Hugh Brody, that "possibly this is something that has to be seen to be believed" (1981, 110). As noted by Savishinsky (1982, 118), young children "observe all aspects of drunken comportment, and they therefore become accustomed to its characteristics long before they begin to fully participate in drinking as teen-agers."

This cycle of peaceful coexistence and open aggression calls for an explanation. Craig MacAndrew and Robert Edgerton (1969) were the first to suggest that following contact with Euro–North Americans, Native North American populations had learned to structure drunkenness in cultural terms. They noted that "except for a few southwestern tribes, the North American Indians had no alcoholic beverages prior to the coming of the white man" (1969, 100). They argued that, in any society, drunken individuals behave according to that society's knowledge about drunkenness, "losing" those inhibitions that one is allowed to lose while drunk, in socially acceptable contexts. MacAndrew and Edgerton thus reiterated John Honigmann and Irma Honigmann's earlier hypothesis (1945, 577) "that drinking and many of its effects are culturally regulated behavior."

In the same vein, Honigmann (1981, 737) states that Athapaskans and Algonkians give expression to their animosity and behave aggressively when drunk because they have come to "know that, within limits, drunkenness made such behaviour expectable and socially excusable." Under such circumstances it would seem that neither the respect for one another's autonomy nor the fear of others is sufficient to prevent acts of aggression. Why is this so? Who is the likely target of a drunken individual's animosity? To answer these questions one must examine closely the relationship between the circumstances that precede acts of aggression and the environments in which they are played out. As this chapter demonstrates, drunken Dene Tha appear to choose the appropriate moment to direct their aggression against those whom they consider the legitimate objects of their anger. They do so because, although they fear the aggression of others, they also wish to retaliate against those who, they feel, have interfered with their goals.

DENE THA ACCOUNTS OF AGGRESSION

To read generalizations about patterns of behavior of distant others is not the same as coming face to face with individuals whose behavior fully fits the pattern. This was the case in February 1980, when two strongly built Dene Tha men in their early thirties came to visit me and have tea early one afternoon. It was our first meeting, as I was in the initial weeks of my first six-month period of fieldwork. Full of laughter, they introduced

themselves as very best friends and sat next to each other, shoulder
to shoulder, on the living room sofa. I could not help but focus on
one man's bluish, bruised face, the nose covered with a wide ban-
dage. The man immediately and spontaneously explained his recent injuries, telling me first that they had been inflicted by his
friend sitting next to him. At this, both men immediately laughed
and nudged each other with their elbows as they insisted they could
not get angry over this incident because the blow had been unintended. The circumstances were as follows. While at a drinking party
the victim's friend, who had a large piece of lumber in hand, had
waited behind a door to smash it in the face of a foe, who was expected to walk across the threshold. It was the friend and not the
foe, however, who had entered the room. As they told me about
this turn of events, both men broke into laughter. The broken nose
and bruised face were really nothing at all, they said. The victim reiterated that his friend did not know who he was when he delivered
the blow with the piece of wood. Laughing again, both men repeated how much they enjoyed each other's company. When the
two men eventually walked away, I doubted that it was possible not
to feel anger toward someone, albeit a friend, who had inflicted
such serious injury. Although individuals involved in acts of aggression may deny that they knew what they were doing when drunk,
in some cases one cannot help but think like Yngve Georg Lithman
(1979, 119) "that people drink because they want to do what they
can do when they are drunk."[4]

Their account of the event made it clear that this was not a case
of random violence. The aggressor and the intended victim, who
were known to each other, had scores to settle. Although the two
men would never fight it out when sober (Dene never do so), retaliation was due. The appropriate moment presented itself
when the two enemies were drunk in the midst of a large party.
Though the blow did not fall on the anticipated victim, the aggressor knew all along that he would not be held accountable for
his act of aggression. He could always claim, according to the
generally accepted Dene convention, that when drunk, one does
not know what one does.

On the basis of such reports one might rightly conclude that
Dene Tha social life alternates between the more common responsible, peaceful, and often merry demeanor of adults and

teenagers and the sporadic, disturbing, violent outbursts of the same individuals, who, it is said, are not responsible for their actions since they do not know what they are doing when under the influence of alcohol. Among contemporary Dene Tha, as among the Lynx Point Slaveys in the early 1950s, if "the drunk is not held responsible" for his or her actions, "the sober person feels no moral superiority, for in his turn he will behave much the same" (Helm 1961, 105–6). That is because "far from being regulated by rules, people make use of them as tools of interpretation and persuasion" (G. Watson and Irwin 1996, 88).

There are, however, acts of violence that appear to be random. As the following case illustrates, acts that are not directed at anyone in particular cannot be construed as acts of retaliation. Parents of a teenage son came to visit me to discuss their son's appearance in court to face a charge of having shot and seriously injured his brother (mother's sister's son). One of the first things the mother said was: "They say our son shot him; but who would shoot his own brother? No, he was drunk; he did not know what he was doing." The father continued, saying that the boy had shot through a door and thus did not know that he might hit someone. "He is just a little boy; he doesn't know; he was drunk when it happened and he did not know," added the mother. The parents then pointed out further circumstantial evidence that removed the blame from their son. The rifle used by their son was normally disassembled and unloaded under their bed, precisely to prevent any accident in the house. Their son, his brothers, and other friends had gathered in their house to drink. In the course of the night the brother (mother's sister's son) who was to be shot took the rifle from under the bed, reassembled it, and loaded it. The son then took the gun to chase after a friend who was going around the house imitating a duck. In the excitement of the mock hunting expedition a first shot went off in the air. The young man who was imitating the duck sped away. The second shot went through a door and seriously injured the brother (mother's sister's son), who was in the room. But, the father insisted, "he didn't know his brother was there." When the son realized what he had done, he said to his mother, "Mammy, I did not know; I am very afraid; I was drunk." Having informed me of the case, they left for the court hearing. A few hours later they returned elated with the news that their son had been set free, on probation.

According to the Dene Tha, "a good judge is one who listens." Referring to the judge who was hearing the case described above, Dene Tha said that "this judge doesn't get mad, he listens, and even when someone stabs someone else, he listens; he doesn't send him to jail. He gives someone many chances. He is good. Before him there was another one who was tough. He would get mad, not ask questions; you could not talk." The mention of a stabbing referred to a recent case in which a woman had been acquitted of stabbing her husband with a pair of scissors when the two were drunk. According to the Dene Tha, this woman, as well as the young man who had inadvertently shot his brother, had to be released because they had not known what they were doing while drunk. Under such circumstances, as the Dene Tha reminded me again and again, one is not accountable for one's behavior and, therefore, one should not be punished.

At some level, people hold the view that if someone behaves improperly, there is no need for human punishment; life itself will mete out the suitable punishment at the appropriate time. This view is expressed in the following story incorporated by the Dene Tha band in its submission to the Task Force on the Criminal Justice System and Its Impact on the Indian and Metis People of Alberta (1990, 22): "A man was bit by a mosquito and sought revenge by gathering a whole bunch of them which he placed in a bag. In the winter, he released them in the cold, saying: 'Xonte uh sade: eat me now.' The mosquitoes all died. Next summer, the man went hunting and was found dead, without blood, in the bush." The story expresses the Dene Tha concept of justice, rendered by the word *tandi*. According to this concept, "if someone commits a crime, s/he will suffer the consequences. Life itself has a way of establishing justice even for the smallest form of life" (Dene Tha band 1990, 22). This view, as the preceding chapters have shown, also informs the Dene Tha way of socializing children. Children, like adults, are largely expected to learn from the consequences of their actions.

FEAR OF RETALIATION/WISH FOR RETALIATION

Among the Dene, as elsewhere, social factors determine the forms of aggressive behavior, its targets, its frequency, and the contexts in which it is manifested. Conversely, the ways in which likely targets of aggressive behavior respond to a potential threat are also foreordained by social factors. Alcohol in itself does not automatically lead to violent behavior; rather, under the cover of drunkenness, Dene Tha choose the appropriate moment to retaliate against what they see as legitimate targets for violence.

The Appropriate Moment and the Legitimate Target
Over the years numerous observations and conversations with Dene Tha have led me to see that, in many instances, these two contrasting states of affairs, the attentive and joyful climate of sober life on the one hand and the uninhibited outbursts and violence associated with drinking on the other, are phases in a continuous, complex process of social interaction. Individuals who feel belittled or undermined by others live in the knowledge that, come the appropriate moment, they can always join a drinking party, vent their hostility, and attack others without being held accountable for their behavior. Dene Tha women who have been abused by their drunken husbands have told me how they would confide in their brothers, when their brothers were sober. The women went on to explain how their brothers and friends, when drunk, would later appear at their home to beat their husbands up. "When he gets drunk, he just wants to take revenge right away," said a Dene Tha woman of her brother.

Conversely, when Dene Tha refrain from interference in other people's lives, they do so out of fear of eventual retaliation by a drunken party. Dene Tha employees at the local store, for instance, told me that they did not report, to their employer or to the police, theft by fellow employees or customers, for if they did so it would only be a matter of time before they would suffer injury at the hands of the intoxicated person they had reported. A Dene woman who had been threatened by a young man at the store sent her own son to the young man's house to remind him and his family that she had many sons and that if she was molested, something would happen to them. Growing accustomed to this logic, I spontaneously asked a Dene Tha woman who reported that the drunken son of the neighbors had slashed the four tires of her pickup truck, "What have you done?" She immediately replied: "I'm keeping my niece away from him. We might have to move to Edmonton for a while." In typical Dene fashion, withdrawal from Chateh with her niece, rather than confrontation or laying charges with the police officer, was her preferred course of action. And so on. In conflicts many acts of aggression are acts of retaliation.

In many Dene Tha accounts a close association is established between alcohol and violence without the assumption that this association is causal in nature. Dene Tha do not subscribe to the "malevolence assumption," the phrase coined by Claire Hamilton and James Collins Jr. (1982) to refer to the tendency to assume "that alcohol is a cause of violence between family members" when they find "an offender with a drinking problem or the presence of alcohol in an incident of family violence" (Hamilton and Collins 1982, 26; in Gusfield 1992, 125). Rather, in many cases Dene Tha recognize drunkenness as providing themselves and others with a socially legitimate context within which to pursue objectives they cannot seek when sober. If Dene Tha do not take justice in their hands when sober, they are seen to do so in many cases when drunk. Dene Tha recognize that, although drunk and "not knowing" what they are doing, individuals turn against a fellow employee who has denounced them, beat up a brother-in-law who has abused a sister, or destroy the property of those who stand in their way. In the words of one Dene Tha, "You can do crazy things when you are drinking." In and out of drunkenness, Dene Tha operate within a complex system of management of self and of social relationships.

A Welcomed Truce

The cases discussed so far are largely ones in which the "crazy things" one does when drunk are directed at very specific individuals with whom the drunken aggressor has a close relationship. The following case shows how the revelation of the identity of a victim can suddenly change the mood and behavior of the would-be aggressor. I had spent a pleasant evening with a Dene Tha family and at eleven o'clock at night expressed my intention to leave. The walk back home would take me about an hour. As I left, members of the family warned me about drunks who roam around at night. Indeed, within a few minutes of walking I could hear loud voices on the road ahead of me. I soon distinguished the silhouettes of four tall men walking side by side, hardly keeping their balance, obviously drunk. They suddenly turned around when they heard the sound of my footsteps on the snow. From a distance of approximately fifty feet one of them held his fists up, shouting at me and inviting me to a fight. I continued approaching to identify them, confident that I could run for shelter in the bush if need be. I realized that they were the young men I had shared a meal with two days earlier. I felt reassured. We were about six feet apart when the man who was threatening me with his fists also recognized me. He immediately threw his arms around my shoulders and began to cry. Sobbing, he said, "Oh, I am so tired of playing the tough guy." The potential foe had melted into a hurting man crying out his pain. I slowly turned him around and supported him all the way down the path to his cousin's home, where I left him to rest and recover. I wondered how many young men get involved in fights only to prove to others that they are "tough." This case, and other similar ones, show that in and of itself, alcohol does not lead to violence. Alcohol leads to aggression when a legitimate target of violence is in sight.

STRATEGIES OF SOCIAL CONTROL

In the face of drunks who are disturbed and threatening, Dene Tha may avoid confrontation and simply withdraw to a safer place. They may also call on the police to intervene and remove the threatening individual from their midst. Dene Tha parents and Elders may talk to disturbed and disturbing individuals to restore the strength and self-respect expected from an autonomous and responsible member of the community. Such a rehabilitative process may take years to reach its goal. It culminates in the rehabilitated individual's becoming an important player in local ceremonies, as illustrated in chapter 9.

It Is Best to Withdraw

The respect for other people's choices and the responsibility for one's own well-being account for the preferred strategy of Dene Tha, which is simply to withdraw when in the presence of someone drunk who threatens them. Once, at two o'clock in the morning, I met a five-year-old girl walking on the road away from her home. I asked her where she was going. She answered: "To my grandfather's place. My parents are drunk and fighting." She intended to return home to her parents when they had sobered up. On another occasion I met a woman with all her children in the house of their neighbors, where they had spent the night. They explained that, as the father and his friends were drinking in their home, they had preferred to leave until the men sobered up. Similarly, one summer, when a few drunks were disturbing a Prophet Dance performance involving more than one hundred fifty sober Dene Tha, people did not confront them. Rather, they stopped dancing and sat quietly as they looked at the drunks acting up around the ceremonial fire. Half an hour went by. The drunks appeared determined to stay. People decided to pick up their things and return home. People said, "They are bothering us, better go home." As I was leaving the ceremonial grounds, one of the drunks, a strongly built young man over six feet tall, blocked my way out, asking what I had come for. Visibly drunk, he was prepared to fight and had begun to push me around when his cousin stepped right in between us and said to me, "Hi, I hadn't had a chance to say hello yet." Surprised, I stayed there, not knowing what to do. She then said, "Can't you see that I am giving you a chance to get away?" When confronted with a disturbed individual, the preferred course of action is a quick withdrawal.

Fumoleau (1995, 77) observed a similar response in 1970 in Detah, a Dene settlement close to Yellowknife, the capital of the Northwest Territories. The Dene had gathered at Christmastime to inaugurate their new community hall. Three hundred Dene were dancing passionately to the sound of eight drummers when two drunks from Yellowknife walked in. "They tried to dance but could hardly walk. They screamed and yelled as only drunks can do," writes Fumoleau. The drummers and singers kept drumming and singing while the dancing circle dissolved and the Dene quietly retreated to their seats along the walls of the hall. No one intervened to confront the two drunks or evict them from the hall. While the two drunks were left to themselves in the center of the room, a Dene whispered in Fumoleau's ear, "We were having a good time." Fumoleau then volunteered the solution that would occur to any Euro–North American: "Why don't you kick them out?" The Dene answered:

"Why add to their trouble? Don't you think they are pitiful enough as they are?" Everyone sat silently as the drunks kept yelling and acting up. Apparently tired of their act, they suddenly walked out of their own accord. "In ten seconds the dance was on again" (Fumoleau 1995, 77). This is the Dene response to intruding drunks: withdraw, observe, and decide on the course of action to take.

In 1984 I observed a similar event in Meander River, where many Dene Tha from Chateh had come to take part in the Easter Prophet Dance. More than two hundred people had gathered in the community hall to dance enthusiastically to the sound of songs and Dene drums. A drunken man from Chateh entered the hall and stumbled around, shouting at people, struggling to keep his balance. As he did so, the drumming and singing continued as the dancers silently withdrew to their seats. The drunk was left alone in the center of the hall, vacillating around in an apparent attempt to dance. We all sat in silence watching. A few minutes went by. Then an Elder from Meander River walked up to the man, offered him her right arm to lean against, and gently directed their steps in a circle. The two danced to the sound of the drums and the songs. Everyone watched. When the round of dancing came to an end, the woman led the man to a chair to sit, where he remained for the rest of the evening. As soon as the drums began beating again, people resumed dancing. The interruption had been superbly managed in Dene fashion, in a nonjudgmental, nonconfrontational way.

Some Dene Tha have suggested that people might drink to withdraw and "to avoid the real situation." To illustrate their point, they referred to Louis, who had been drunk for the last two weeks. They said: "His wife came back about two weeks ago, and since then he really drinks. He doesn't want to go back with her. When she came back, he got drinking, and doesn't go back to her." It was mentioned that their children had tried to get them back together, but without success. A woman added: "They come to talk to me at [work]; they look up to me to help them. I tell them: 'It's up to them; there is nothing you or I can do about it.'" From this account we can see, once again, how the Dene Tha invoke one's responsibility for one's own life to justify not interfering in another's life.

When I asked for the translation to Dene Dháh of "drinking to avoid the real situation," I was given the following sentence: *dene dahani la guyindi ch'a lint' ónh edon úson*, literally, "some people are probably drinking to totally get away from their mind." Of a drunken individual, Dene Tha say, *mindí xule*, "his/her mind is gone." This statement publicly exonerates the individual from any responsibility for his or her actions. As we have seen, however, Dene Tha clearly recognize that individuals may want to achieve this state of mind precisely to avoid having to do what they would otherwise have to do, or else to be in a position to carry out acts of retaliation that would otherwise be ruled out.

"Call the Police!"
When Dene Tha call on a non-Dene third party to intervene and remove a threatening individual from their midst, this third party is invariably a local, non-Native police officer from the Royal Canadian Mounted Police (R.C.M.P.). The police officer is known as *dene kuelehi*, literally, "the person who puts one inside," a clear reference to one's imprisonment in the local "holding tank" or in regional prisons. It is noteworthy that the person who makes the decision to call the police asks a third party to make the call. In the words of an adult student: "Even my mom tells me: 'Your dad's drunk! Call the cops!'" (in Dene Tha Band of Assumption 1990, 8). Over the years many families asked me to call the R.C.M.P. on their behalf to come and remove a drunk parent or child from their homes. Since I would not do so, parents or grandparents would then ask another household member to place the call.

Failing to find a third party to call the police, one must, of course, do so oneself. This was the case with one Dene Tha woman who told me, "[My husband] said he would kill me. At three in the morning I ran at the cops just in socks. When he drinks, he thinks he is a man; he does all kinds of crazy things." The police officer came to her house and took the husband away before he could hurt anyone. The next day the man returned home sober, and the angry words and threats of the previous night were completely gone. In a sense, his wife had protected him from himself. During the years I spent in Chateh, abused women who had called the police to remove their drunken husbands from their homes refused to press charges against their abusive husbands in case they later retaliated with more violence. Abusive husbands could, nevertheless, be charged and brought before the judge by police officers acting in the name of the Crown. The responsibility for the resulting imprisonment, if any, would then rest with a non-Dene.

In 1984, following a change of policy, the R.C.M.P. for a time stopped going into people's homes to remove drunks. I learned of this change when visiting a Dene Tha Elder who complained that he had had a sleepless night because one of his sons had been drinking with his friend. The Elder explained that he had wanted the police to come and put his son in jail for the night but that they had refused to do so because of the change in policy. The Elder was of course surprised at this unanticipated response. He doubted that the band councillors were responsible for the change, for they had always supported the right of people to call on the R.C.M.P. to come to their houses and charge a household member with drinking and disturbing the peace. The Elder, therefore, asked me to call the R.C.M.P. headquarters in Peace River and Edmonton to find out who had ordered the policy change. When I said I might be willing to do so later, the Elder pointed to the fence around his house. "This," he said, "is the boundary within which I am boss. There is a similar boundary around the reserve, and within that boundary, the chief is boss." He therefore concluded that "what a white judge says shouldn't apply within the reserve where the R.C.M.P. should also keep going into houses to remove drunks from there." When the Elder says he is the boss within his fenced-in home, he does not mean that he has the power to stop his son from drinking with his friends in his own home. He means that he should have power over the R.C.M.P., who should come to his home at his will. That is why, exasperated, the Elder repeated again and again: "Because of whom is it so, because of whom is it so that they [the R.C.M.P.] do not come to people's house?" Pressure from band members soon had the R.C.M.P. revert to its former practice.

Alcoholic beverages are readily available to the Dene Tha, and on any given evening as many as fifty or more people may be drunk, especially on weekends and on days following the arrival of a paycheck or a government check. As in traditional Slavey brew parties (Carterette n.d., 93–94, in Helm 1961, 104–5), in contemporary Dene Tha drinking parties "drinking always occurs in a group; there is no solitary drinking." People with liquor invariably drive up to a friend's house to invite him or her to drink. There are, therefore, numerous occasions on which non-Dene police officers are called to arrest Dene Tha who are drunk and who threaten their spouses or other household members. Since there are many such calls, and since there is a contingent of five R.C.M.P. officers stationed in Chateh prepared to work seventeen to eighteen hours a day (Dene Tha Band of Assumption 1990, 7), the level of incarceration is high. Out of a population of approximately one thousand, the majority being under sixteen years of age, the Dene Tha averaged six cases of incarceration per day in 1989, for a total of 1,392 cases of imprisonment on the reserve, and 803 off the reserve (Dene Tha Band of Assumption 1990, 2). Of the 1,392 short terms spent in prison on the reserve, 935 were alcohol-related. In 1990 the local band reported 518 instances of on-reserve imprisonment, an average of 4.3 per day in the first four months of that year, most of them alcohol-related.

In Chateh, as in many other Indian communities, a number of factors account for this "alarming" rate of alcohol-related arrests (Mail 1980; Heath 1991, 37). Dene Tha indicate that drunks were rare in Chateh before 1965, the year of the construction of a road that connected the reservation to the nearby town of High Level. With year-round travel to and from High Level possible, the High Level bars and liquor store became a regular destination for more and more Dene Tha under the age of fifty, especially on weekends. It is they, not their parents and grandparents, who use the cover of drunkenness to act aggressively against others in the ways discussed in this chapter. This pattern of interaction came about when the sporadic drinking of the past (when people brewed their own liquor) gave way to the regular heavy drinking of contemporary reserve life.

Drinking periods are tied to availability of funds, an economic limitation noted by Medicine (1983), James Leland (1976), and Jack Waddell and Michael Everett (1980). In Chateh higher levels of drinking also varied according to the flow of cash in the community. Such were the days after men returned from firefighting, for instance. Dene Tha men observed that "firefighting money is for fire water." Dene Tha men, however, did not spend all their money on drink. When they returned from firefighting with their paychecks, they would typically buy gifts for their parents and spouse (a piece of furniture, a major appliance, or a television, for instance), give some money to siblings and cousins, and keep some of their money for their own enjoyment for drinking in High Level and in Chateh.

When the drinking problems became more and more serious in the community, the band council passed a bylaw that made Chateh a "dry" reserve. The intention of the bylaw was to prevent people from bringing liquor back to Chateh and drinking it on the reserve. The bylaw created new grounds for arrest by the R.C.M.P. One became liable to arrest for possession of an alcoholic beverage on the reserve, for being drunk on the reserve, or for selling liquor on the reserve. As Dene Tha friends explained, "When they had this wet reserve, the drinking wasn't so bad; but when they started this dry reserve business, that is when the drinking picked up. That's when the challenge began. There's nothing better to do, there's the challenge, you know, trying to evade the R.C.M.P., just the challenge." A Dene Tha woman told me, "There are lot of them around, bootlegger; they buy some booze, keep the money rotating." Her husband immediately added: "Just like stealing. They buy something at five dollars and sell it here at twenty or twenty-five; buy something at ten and sell it at forty or forty-five. They spend some money to drink and keep the rest to buy some more to sell." Even Dene Tha who had given up drinking would sometimes engage in bootlegging to raise quick cash when in need. When I confronted a Dene Tha couple who were doing so, asking them how they could peddle liquor when they themselves had given up drinking because of the pain it had brought to their home, they answered, "But if they choose to drink, that's their decision. It's up to them."

Finally, as noted earlier, Dene Tha often call on the police to remove a drunken spouse or kin from their midst, with the expectation that the individual will be released when sober. Again, these individuals are, in the great majority of cases, males under fifty years of age. It is they who appear predominantly in the daunting criminal statistics generated by the justice system. Again, in the eyes of the Dene, arrest by the police is seen not as a punishment of the intoxicated person but rather as a means to protect others temporarily from one who has lost his or her mind.[5]

That is so because contemporary Dene Tha, young and old, share many of the values and attitudes of their predecessors, as, indeed, do many other Dene from other communities (Rushforth and Chisholm 1991). In the past, as in the present, in their socialization of children as in their own lives, Dene Tha privilege observation over instruction, and individual autonomy over subordination. In this respect, there is great continuity from generation to generation. The consequences of living by these values are, however, quite different today from what they were yesterday, because the physical and social environments have changed so drastically. To live by these Dene values in the context of a hunting and gathering economy, in which extended families or small bands were dispersed over a large territory for most of the year, is one thing. To live by these same values in the context of a reservation, in which close to eight hundred people, the majority under sixteen years old, dwell in constant proximity, is another.

Earlier generations of Dene Tha dealt with their children in the context of a dwelling they had built in the bush in which their children would fall asleep at night as the fire went out, and everything was dark, indoors and outdoors. Nowadays children may keep their parents awake night after night in a single-family dwelling serviced with electricity, which permits light and television after dark. Children play and watch television in the presence of parents who will not turn off the lights, pick them up, and put them to bed, because that is simply not done. To do so would infringe on their autonomy.

In the past men and women had clear and complementary productive domestic roles. Through observation, girls would learn from their mothers, and sons from their fathers. Dene then experienced themselves as largely autonomous and self-governing. They sought gifts and songs from animal helpers and developed a strong mind with which to know how to conduct themselves competently in their environment. Not surprisingly, anthropologists who spent time with the Dene under such circumstances could not see them as victims. As noted by Slobodin (1975, 285), "It would have required more gall than most of us possessed to depict as mere victims the men, women, and children who had hauled us through the broken ice, disentangled dogs, given us dry clothing, and poured hot caribou soup down our throats." In this context Dene could even feel superior to the occasional white man who ventured into their midst and who depended on them for food, shelter, and orientation. Not so in the present, when most men and women are unemployed and are, to a significant degree, dependent on unemployment and welfare checks. The tragedy is that for contemporary adults on the reserve there is a lack of constructive challenges to meet and succeed in.

The dream of full employment was vividly expressed by a young girl nine years old whose father had been drinking with his brothers and friends for four consecutive days. One man in the group was paying for all the liquor since he had received three checks of three hundred forty dollars each. Once the men were drunk, the girl and her mother hid one of the checks away. When the man asked for his last check, the girl told him he would not get it back until he was sober. She added: "I am tired of you drinking. I will buy the band store, you will be the meat cutter, and your brother will be the meat grinder for hamburger, and your mom, she is old, her, she will work on the food side, and Mom will work on clothes, and my sister will be at the Post Office, and Dad will be the manager. I will buy the nursing station, and I will buy the school too, and Dad's brother will be the principal. And I will buy the coffee shop and I will run it." In reality, except for the positions of the school principal and store manager, held by non-Dene hired by the band, all the other positions mentioned by the girl were already held by Dene Tha men and women. On its own, the band simply cannot generate jobs for everyone on the reserve.

For most Dene Tha men and women under fifty, long periods of unemployment are the norm. Some women are employed as clerks by the local store, as teacher's aides or secretaries by the school, and as cleaning ladies by the local police station. Men are typically unemployed except when they engage in seasonal firefighting and occasional work clearing cutlines and assisting seismic crews working in the area. Within this younger generation of Dene Tha one observes a broad spectrum of socially disruptive behavior: truancy and destruction of property, break-ins and thefts, alcohol abuse and family violence, leading at times to suicide and homicide. In Chateh, as in many other indigenous communities, "this wide range of symptoms . . . are in large part interchangeable as expressions of the burden of loss, grief and anger experienced by Aboriginal people in Canadian society" (Royal Commission on Aboriginal Peoples 1994, 2).

TO KNOW WHAT IS GOING ON

The foregoing observations are important for understanding the local dynamics of nonaggression and aggression. Nevertheless, our discussion of whether Dene Tha account for their restrained behavior when sober in terms of fear of one another or in terms of respect for one another's autonomy would remain incomplete if we did not mention another source of fear, *ech'int'e*, "a power." Dene Tha also say they have regard for one another's feelings because to hurt someone else's feelings or to interfere with someone else's behavior may not only trigger the kind of physical aggression under intoxication described above but also cause that person to retaliate through the use of "a power." What is feared most is not overt but covert aggression.

Consider, for instance, Matonabbee's 1778 appeal to Samuel Hearne, the eighteenth-century Hudson's Bay Company officer, to kill one of Matonabbee's enemies with his power (Hearne 1958, 143, in Krech 1981, 98–99). Hearne spent two years traveling extensively in the western Canadian subarctic with a group of Chipewyans led by Matonabbee, who had resided at Fort Prince of Wales and who spoke some English. In the course of their travels Matonabbee told Hearne that he feared for his life because of another man who had become his enemy. Matonabbee pressed Hearne to kill this man, though they were several hundred miles apart. To please Matonabbee, Hearne drew "a rough sketch of two human figures on a piece of paper, in the attitude of wrestling; in the hand of one of them, [he] drew the figure of a bayonet pointing to the breast of the other" (Krech 1981, 98). Pointing to the figure holding the bayonet, Hearne told Matonabbee, "This is me; and the other is your enemy." Hearne instructed Matonabbee to make this picture "as publicly known as possible." This was done, and the following year Matonabbee could report to Hearne that on hearing of his design, the enemy had "immediately afterwards become quite gloomy, and refusing all kind of sustenance, in a very few days died" (Krech 1981, 98). Other leading Indians were soon petitioning Hearne to do the same with their enemies. Hearne writes that he "never thought it proper to comply with their requests; by which means I not only preserved the credit I gained on the first attempt, but always kept them in awe, and in some degree of respect and obedience to me" (Krech 1981, 99).[6]

D. Smith (1990) reports the case of a hunting party in which an elderly Chipewyan was attacked and knocked to the ground by a younger man. As soon as the old man got up, he told his aggressor: "'My marten is going to eat your brain. In one year's time you are going to be dead'" (Smith 1990, 161). The young man received the Elder's declaration in silence and immediately left the hunting party. Within a year the young man had died. Chipewyan understood that "the old man's power animal, a marten . . . ultimately overpowered the younger man's power-animal and then proceeded to 'eat' the latter's brain, causing insanity and death" (D. Smith 1990, 161).

The use of a power to harm others, like witchcraft in Africa, "is conceived as an act of secret hostility between people who ought to be friendly" (Mair 1969, 218).[7] Monica Wilson (1971, 57), who noted that people "dream in the symbols of their society, as they think in the categories of their own language," saw "witch beliefs [such as the belief that fellow Dene can use a power to harm others] as the standardized nightmare of a group" (1969, 313). The Dene nightmare par excellence, then, is to have one's own autonomy and sense of control over events secretly undermined by others. To use a power to harm rather than to heal is to breach the assumption of respect for each person's autonomy which is the cornerstone of Dene social life. Dene Tha would, therefore, readily understand the teaching of Naidzo, the Bear Lake prophet, who told the Dogribs that "the worst thing you can do is to kill somebody, whether it is by ink'on or with a club" (Helm 1994, 29).[8]

This book opened with an account of Dene Tha parents who were anxiously waiting for their son to appear in court, where he would be charged before a Euro-Canadian judge for having seriously injured a fellow Dene with a firearm. The parents suggested that the tragic incident was due to *chinte*, or "power." The account is worth repeating here, so that it can be kept in mind in the discussion to follow:

> There are two ways, *chint'e* [power] and *yú* [medicine]. You do not say bad medicine. It is good; it is to help others. Some person knows something; his power, he has it. He doesn't like what you do to him. He could think of you one night, and your spirit would follow his power. He could take your spirit, and you get into an accident. Like [that woman] wants to kill him [names a neighbor] through medicine or power, but his mother and dad protect him with their power too. It's like he is in a bottle; they can't get into you. If you're Indian, you know what is going on; it is really powerful.

When the speaker says "If you're Indian, you know what is going on," I may take it in two ways, not necessarily exclusive of each other. He may be implicitly commenting on the fact that the Euro-Canadian judge who will pass sentence on his son will not know what is going on, in this case, precisely because he is not an Indian. By implication the speaker may also be telling me, another non-Indian, that I do not know what is really going on. This interpretation is consistent with the Dene view of true knowledge as firsthand, experiential knowledge. When presenting his views, the Dene Tha speaker is minimally expecting that I consider events as Dene Tha themselves see them unfold.

A Power to Harm/A Power to Protect
We are already familiar with the distinction between *echint'e* and *yú* from our discussion of the Dene Tha concept of "powerfulness" inherent in plants, animals, and other inanimate objects, such as steel. We are concerned now with understanding the Dene Tha view that people who have a power may take someone's spirit away to ensure that some misfortune befalls the victim. Although all Dene Tha would agree that to use one's *ech'int'e* to harm others is wrong, all eventually attribute a misfortune, an illness, or a death to such abuse on the part of fellow Dene Tha, who may be assisted at times by the power of faraway Crees or Dogribs. What Mills (1988a, 50) writes about the Beaver applies

equally well to the Dene Tha: "Where a western observer might attribute death to alcohol-related behaviour, as in the case of a house burning down when its occupants were highly inebriated, the Beaver would blame interpersonal hostility, often on psychic levels, rather than inebriation." Conversely, Dene Tha say that people who know what is really going on can use their own power to shelter and protect others who are so threatened.

It is general knowledge that to offend someone is to risk becoming the object of his or her evil thoughts. Speaking of Elders, a Dene Tha man in his forties said: "Old people they are very bad, they know. But they are OK. They don't bother you as long as you don't get them mad. You make them mad, they can hurt you [with their power]. If not, they can help you lots of ways." Another man expressed this view in the following way: "Last night I went to [their] house to sing, but they were drinking. [He] wanted to fight me, but they told him to stop. I have power. He doesn't know, but I could make him ill; I go to sleep, and if I dream of him, I make him sick; it is very easy for me to do that. I would send my power over there; I would sent it with my brain over there." The power would overtake the mind of the intended victim, who would then be very likely to have an accident, most probably a serious, if not a fatal, one. Referring to two "powerful" old people, whom he resented, another individual said, "Just in my dream, if I would want to get rid of them, I could." He insisted that he preferred not to attack his enemies but to use his power to keep their own power and evil intentions at bay.

The Dene Tha speaker quoted earlier says of a fellow Dene Tha that "she wants to kill him through medicine or power." He uses the term "medicine" to refer not to *yú* but to *ech'int'e*.[9] In typical Dene fashion, suspicion and hostility between members of two extended families are depicted as unfolding within a medicine fight. There is no overt aggression, but covert powers are at work. Thus among the Dene Tha as among the Chipewyan, accounts of medicine fights draw on the notion of "a power" "as a ubiquitous explanatory principle" (D. Smith 1990, 170).

The Dene Tha speaker also alludes to the fact that parents intervene with their own power to protect their child from an attack by other powerful people: "It's like he is in a bottle; they can't get in to you." Other adults often reported to me that their parents or grandparents were protecting them with their own power. Thus, a woman mentioned that she did not worry that other Dene Tha were trying to get at her with their power because her mother was helping her from a distance: "When I came back here [to Chateh] in January, my mother [who lives in a distant settlement] did not want me to come back; when I came back, sometimes we have the same dream; [in the dream] my mother called me and told me not to worry the next morning if something would happen. The next morning I heard a knock on the window; I knew it was my mother; she had come to protect me." The same women claimed that her mother had earlier prevented her estranged husband from coming to get her by having him stopped by the police and later sent to jail for impaired driving.

Dene Tha say that they have to use their own power to protect themselves from someone else's malevolent misuse of power. R. Ridington (1981, 357), who reports the same phenomenon among the Beaver of northwestern British Columbia, writes: "No one admitted to using his powers to harm others, but everyone believed that there were those who misused their powers and that it might be necessary to defend oneself from attack. Medicine fights were brought on by secret attacks." What anthropologists are told about are accusations against fellow Dene, not confessions about abusing a power to harm others. Among the Dene Tha, much the same pattern obtains, except that two men talked about having used their powers to harm others, one because others had ridiculed him in public, the other to punish those who had neglected to bring the appropriate gifts they had promised after he had healed their child with his power.

Dene Tha refer to the use of a power for evil purposes in many ways. Conversations about such matters were most often in English with Dene Tha in their thirties or forties, but I always asked them to translate key passages of their accounts into Dene Dháh and then back into English. This process of dual translation was invariably instructive of Dene categorizations of agencies in their social world. Although a few individuals might refer to "bad medicine" when speaking in English, they never used the expression *yú edu újon*, "bad medicine," or *ech'int'e edu újon*, "bad power," when translating their statements into Dene Dháh.

When a Dene Tha man reported that "they placed a curse on him," he translated this phrase as *ede guch'int'e t'ah giyéhchedah*, which he translated back into English as "they bother him with their spiritual beings." *Guch'int'e*, which he and other individuals translated as "their power," is glossed here as "their spiritual beings." The expression "to place a curse on someone" stands for the Dene expression *giyéhchedah*, "they bother him." When a black spot appeared on the drum of a Dene Tha Elder, it was seen as evidence that people were bothering him. As one Dene Tha said, "Almost everyone knows that [names the family] are bad to [names the Elder]. *Guch'int'e t'ah giyéhchedah*, 'they bother him with their spirit beings.'" This is the same verb that parents would use to tell their children not to bother me when I was working on transcripts and translations of conversations in their homes. Similarly, when a mother shared her concern over her children because "someone [was] throwing bad medicine around the school," she translated her statement in Dene Dháh as *edéhtl'éh kóan woteh kindí edu újon wonlin*, which she restated in English as "someone's bad thoughts are around the school." The key concept here is *kindí edu újon*, which is, literally, "someone's mind [or thought] is not good." As in the earlier account, we see here the reference to one's mind as the source of evil thoughts that wander around. Dene Tha accounts of the use and abuse of a power vary in important ways, whether they are told in English or in Dene Dháh. A close examination of the manner in which Dene Tha speak of events in their society, in their language, is essential to grasp their point of view. Lacking such an examination, we will read into their English spoken accounts of events meanings that are simply not there.[10]

When Dene Tha Elders reported that they were seeing "like a thread, a long thread over the townsite," people concluded that "it must be medicine hanging over there." The townsite was, therefore, a place to avoid at night, for "you can get things not meant for you." If someone's bad thoughts are around a certain place, they may end up affecting individuals for whom they were not intended in the first place: "That's why it is not good for kids to go outside at night; they run into something that is not meant for them." In support of this view a Dene Tha speaker gave the example of his teenage cousin, who had almost lost his mind:

"He's always walking around at night, and all of a sudden he could not get to sleep. He got to walk round and round in the house. He could not stay still, could not eat. He forgot everything." He was the victim of someone's "bad thoughts" lying in wait for another person. His mother took him to a powerful Dene Tha dreamer who was able to help him recover his mind and usual composure, but not entirely.

This is also how the death of the young son of a Dene Tha prophet from Assumption, who had been among the Dogribs to teach them the Prophet Dance, was explained. While the young man's parents were in Fort Rae, some Dogribs, it was claimed, had not liked what the parents did. These Dogribs later directed their power against the Dene Tha prophet and his wife, but "it just hang there" over their house, and their son caught it. Soon after, he died in an accident. This interpretation of the young man's death was shared by his parents and many other Dene Tha. Visits to the Dogribs on the part of the Dene Tha prophet and his wife, and to the Dene Tha on the part of the Dogribs, nevertheless continued over the years. The friendliness between the Dene Tha prophet and the Dogribs who sought him as a teacher and healer was not shared by all Dene Tha. On the occasion of such a visit a Dene Tha friend observed, "When Dogribs walked in the store today, nobody talks to them, no one greets them; you could just feel the tension." The tension was due to the attribution of local accidents and/or deaths to Dogribs who had felt wronged by Dene Tha or who had been called by Dene Tha to use their power in local medicine fights.

A Case of Aggression with a Power
Dene Tha invariably commented on serious accidents and deaths as caused by a power directed at the victim or at a close relative of the victim. Accounts of medicine fights can be told from a number of perspectives, from that of the aggressor, that of the victim, or that of the healer. To figure in an account of a medicine fight in any of these capacities is to claim personal knowledge and, therefore, true knowledge about what is going on. Most accounts of medicine fights that came to my attention were carried out by a healer using his or her own power to fight that of the patient's enemies. Dene Tha also accounted for extreme acts of ag-

gression against a spouse carried out while in a state of intoxication by reference to a power sent by others to destroy the lives of their enemies. The intended victim could always seek help from a healer, who would send the power back to the sender. The sender would then suffer the evil that had been wished on someone else, as is seen in the following case.[11]

It was the end of the month of May, and the ground was covered with snow after an unexpected storm. Referring to the unusual snow for this time of the year, a Dene Tha friend commented that the bad weather had been because of Peter, who had been shot dead two days earlier. The friend said, "It is his feelings; he is mad because he had to go. He had to go, he was shot, he had to die. Yesterday it was windy, snowed storm and all. 'That was how he felt,' the old people say. Today it is sunny; maybe he accepts it now."

Peter's death had to do with an attempt by Marcella to avenge the death of Nancy, her young daughter. Nancy had happened to be standing on the bank of the river, where she became the victim of an "unintended" shot from a rifle. Standing right in the path of the bullet, she had been killed instantly. The girl's relatives asked, Why had she been standing there at that very moment? Why had the rifle been accidentally triggered then, and not a minute earlier or later? Someone's power was certainly involved. All that remained was to determine whose power was at work.

In such a case, the Dene Tha reasoning is like that of the Azande, who use their notion of witchcraft to explain why someone was adversely affected at a particular place, at a particular point in time. A Zande potter, whose pots break although he has used the same material and technique as always, wants to know why they break there and then. In fact, writes Edward Evans-Pritchard (1972, 68), "he already knows, for the reason is known in advance, as it were. If the pots break it is due to witchcraft." Similarly, when a granary collapses on people, Zande know that the structure did so because termites eat the supports of the granary and wood simply decays in the course of time. When a granary collapses on people, the question Azande ask is, Why did it collapse "at the particular moment when these particular people were sitting beneath it?" (Evans-Pritchard 1972, 69). The answer resides in witchcraft. It explains why "these two events occurred at a precisely similar moment in time and space" (Evans-Pritchard 1972, 69). Among the Dene Tha it is the notion of *ech'int'e* that explains why Nancy had been standing at that precise location on the riverbank where a stray bullet would strike her down. Among the Azande and the Dene Tha we see at work what Nietzsche (1970, 295, in McGrane 1989, 134) referred to as the "belief that every event is a deed," an expression of "our inability to interpret events otherwise than as events caused by intentions."

Six months after Nancy's death her aunt, who was in an Edmonton bar, met the sister of the boy whose rifle had "accidentally" killed the girl. The two women fought it out and were arrested for disturbing the peace. Undaunted, the aunt of the dead girl reported: "I beat the shit out of her. I chased her out of the city and told her next time I get her, she won't live to bring me to court." In the mind of Nancy's relatives, a couple, Monica and her husband, were the prime suspects in Nancy's death. When Monica and her husband were told so, they decided to leave the reserve and let things cool off.

Another aunt of Nancy's then went on a trip to Hobbema, a Cree reservation in southern Alberta; then to Hay River, a Slavey settlement near the border of the Northwest Territories; and finally to Fort Rae, farther north in Dogrib country. People said that in each locality she had paid people to get at Monica with "medicine." Monica, who was living with her husband at his mother's place, knew what was going on, and so did her grandfather. One day he walked into the house and told Monica, "Someone is trying to kill you." With his power he immediately cut the "medicine" that he could see as a thread hanging over Monica's head and sent it back to those who were doing it. He named an old man in Hay River who had done it. Soon thereafter, when Peter (Marcella's cousin) died, Monica and her kinsmen said that it was Marcella's hired medicine coming back to her and her close ones. Laughing, one Dene Tha compared this practice of sending a curse back to its source as a parcel sent COD (cash on delivery) through the postal service. In the end someone has to pay.

Marcella's hired medicine was also seen at work in the life of

Louis, Monica's brother, who was beating not only his wife but also his mother. Soon thereafter Monica's grandfather went to sit down with Louis and his wife. He took the liquor they were drinking and poured it on the floor, "and those three old men appeared, their faces, they are all Dogribs." The faces of the three Dogribs in the liquor poured on the floor were invisible to all except the grandfather; because of his ability to see these things, he knows what is really going on. His intervention can be seen as an expression of a "pattern of assuming responsibility for preventing the actual or potential harm that might be a consequence of the action (or inaction) of others" (Sharp 1994, 41), a pattern first mentioned by Slobodin (1962, 1969) for the Kutchin.[12]

The grandfather, who knew the Dogribs, named them. He told Louis and his wife that there was "a string going right to their bedroom." He cut it with his power and turned it back to where it had come from. The grandfather said that two old Dene Tha ladies had gone to the Territories to hire these Dogribs. Louis and his wife immediately knew who they were; they were Marcella and the friend she had traveled with to visit the Dogribs. Hence Louis's behavior—beating up his wife and even his mother—is explained, for who would do this, unless one has lost one's own mind to the power of enemies? Following the grandfather's intervention, Louis's behavior changed. His drinking bouts were no longer accompanied by violent attacks on his loved ones. If he drinks and fights now, he does so in a socially tolerable manner, operating according to Dene Tha knowledge about normal drunkenness, "losing his mind" and those inhibitions that Dene Tha are allowed to lose while drunk, in socially acceptable contexts.

In this account, as in others I was told over the years, it can be seen how contemporary Dene Tha are said to have traveled to faraway Dogribs in the Northwest Territories (720 kilometers north of Chateh) or to Cree in southern Alberta (920 kilometers south of Chateh) to enlist other knowledgeable and powerful individuals in what began as a local medicine fight. The regionalized Dene Tha medicine fights contrast with the numerous instances of localized medicine fights that have been mentioned in the literature (Mills 1986; R. Ridington 1968, 1988; Rushforth 1986; Sharp 1986; D. Smith 1973).

These developments may constitute an unexamined dimension of the recent Dogrib prophet movement. This movement brought Dene Tha, Cree, and Dogrib in close contact across vast geographical expanses. These same contacts also give Dene Tha the opportunity to hire Cree or Dogrib "medicine men" to use their power to get back at enemies. Such alliances are sought to bolster one's own power to bring misfortune and even death on one's foe. This is possible because Cree, Dene Tha, Dogrib, and many people around the world share a theory of causation in the light of which misfortune, whatever its form, "is sent by personalized beings, either spirits who have authority to punish you or humans who envy or hate you" (Mair 1969, 10). In the words of a young Dene Tha woman, "Cree people can kill; like they don't kill with their hands, they kill with their medicine. Like if their medicine is an animal, they make their animal kill." It is noteworthy that in the summers of 1994 and of 1995 the Dogribs had invited a Cree medicine man to their community to hold healing rituals and minister among them (David Young, personal communication). Like the Dogribs of thirty years ago, contemporary Dogribs continue to seek individuals with a power to heal well beyond the confines of their community and linguistic family.

SEEKING PROTECTION

Although evil thoughts are sent with an intended victim in mind, they can always fall on other people who happen to be at the wrong place at the wrong time. This notion leads people to take precautionary measures. The boy who was referred to as being "in a bottle," protected by his parents' power from the woman who was paying thousands of dollars "to get rid of him in spirit like," was always seen in public wearing colored ribbons on his jacket sleeve. Many other children could also be seen on the road wearing ribbons, usually one and a half centimeters wide and twelve to fourteen centimeters long, on their sleeves. A red ribbon is the unmistakable sign that the bearer is warding off a power sent with evil thoughts to harm others. Dianne Meili (1991, 188) reports that a Dene Tha healer from Meander River "has in his room a crucifix from which stream four ribbons: white representing God, blue for the Virgin Mary, green for the earth, and red for protection from evil spirits."

As one Dene Tha told me, "To be on the safe side, you should have a mirror and wear ribbons, red ribbons. They say the bad medicine is afraid of its reflection; it will run away from its reflection." For the same reason, when I was told how three Dene Tha dreamers had called on their animal helpers to bring back the soul of a dying girl and restore her to life, the speaker mentioned how the dreamers had been careful to cover the mirrors in the room where the girl was lying down. How could they call on their animal helpers to a place where the sight of their reflection would immediately send them away? Dene Tha also mentioned the rosary, carried in one's pocket in place of a small mirror, as an effective protection against someone else's power. Similarly, holy water received from the priest could also be sprinkled in one's house "against things that bother you in the night."

As seen in chapter 8, Dene Tha have consistently reinterpreted Christian symbols and concepts in the light of their own cosmology and epistemology. Moore and Wheelock (1990, 62) report that a Dene Tha Elder "might place a rosary on the upwind side of a gathering to part and clear away approaching rain clouds." They also write (1990, 77) that Nogha, a Dene Tha prophet active in the first part of this century, was telling people they "should offer tobacco and feed the fire with it, even if they are alone," and should also "hold onto the rosary" and pray with the rosary before they go to sleep; "then danger won't come near," Nogha promised. In the same vein, the Bear Lake prophet Naidzo urged fellow Dene to make the sign of the cross to protect themselves from things in the night: "The first signing of the cross stops a danger at arm's length and the second signing causes that danger to shoot off in an instant" (Helm 1994, 34). In Dene Tha thought, "things in the night" that one needs protection from are the souls of the deceased and the powers of fellow Dene sent to affect an adversary negatively. For this reason, precautionary measures against the many entities inhabiting the invisible world are widespread and common.

People may also protect themselves from attacks by others with their own power, as discussed earlier, or with "medicine bags" received from other powerful men or women. This was the case with Flora, who had a bout of nightmares followed by suicidal thoughts one spring. "I started to feel real bad, like I wanted to kill myself. My body was not sick, but my mind was," she explained. Whenever she went to sleep, she would dream of something fighting her. Terrified, she would try to hide under her child, but it was only a baby. She tried to call her own mother, in whose house she was staying, but her voice was too weak to be heard. Flora told her sister, Lisa, about these recurring nightmares that she had had for nearly a month. Lisa told Flora, "My husband knows what is going on with you; you have to beg him to help you." Flora answered, "How can I go and beg somebody to help me when I don't know what's wrong with me?" Flora nevertheless bought a long knife and boxes of snuff as instructed by her sister as a "gift" to pay the "powers" and went to see Lisa's husband, Albert.

Albert, who knew what was going on with Flora, began to talk about his powers and then proceeded to sing. He said that in the earth, in the middle, there was a great big hole where he fought with his "powers." As he talked, Flora began to feel "real happy inside." Albert then gave her a small feather to keep as protection in a little bag inside her blouse. He said he would send "this bad medicine" back on the person who put it on her. Soon thereafter Flora's former boyfriend was found dead in a remote settlement—a victim of his own medicine sent back to him "COD" A month later, when Flora dreamed of a thing chasing her, "not a human being, but a thing, like a rubber thing," she grabbed her bag with the feather and threw the bag at it, and it disappeared. "I had destroyed it. If I lose that feather, I have no protection," she concluded.

*

Using numerous observations and a close examination of the ways in which Dene themselves account for their behavior and that of fellow Dene, in this chapter I have attempted to understand how and why the Dene vigorously check any direct aggressive behavior when sober, and when drunk vent their hostility and attack people they resent. I have shown how the value of autonomy that pervades Dene Tha social life is consistent with the two strategies they employ when faced with drunks who are out of control: withdrawal from the environment where the drunks are acting out or reliance on non-Dene third parties to incarcerate the threatening individual temporarily. Both strategies acknowledge the Dene commitment to respect as far as possible one another's autonomy, including the right of each individual to give up drinking when he or she wants to make that decision. I thus support Honigmann's view, and that of the majority of students of Dene societies, that respect for one another's autonomy is a major determinant of Dene behavior.

I have also documented, however, how Dene Tha refrain from interfering with someone else's behavior because they fear to become the object of retaliation when the person is drunk. A close examination of the circumstances preceding acts of aggression and the environment in which they are played out revealed that in many cases, under the cover of drunkenness, Dene Tha choose the appropriate moment to direct their aggression against those whom they consider the legitimate object of their anger. Dene Tha do so because although they fear the aggression of others, they also on occasion wish to retaliate against others who, they feel, have interfered with their goals. By being drunk and having "lost their minds," individuals create the socially accepted conditions under which to engage in acts of aggression that would be ruled out in other circumstances. In words and in deeds Dene Tha tell one another and themselves, "You can do crazy things when you are drinking," but it should be in such a way that "there is nothing to worry about." They do so, within limits, in the knowledge that fellow Dene will not publicly hold them accountable for their behavior. Therefore, contrary to what Honigmann says, I conclude that it is not only regard for one another's feelings but also fear that motivates people to refrain from interfering with someone else's goals.

I have focused on the Dene Tha notion of *ech'int'e*, "a power" that can be used by individuals to retaliate secretly against their enemies and cause them misfortune and even death. I argue that although this notion instills deep fear among the Dene, it also provides them with an interpretive tool to account for extreme cases of aggression by a drunken kinsman or a spouse. Dene Tha travel to geographically remote communities (Cree, Slavey, or Dogrib) to recruit others as allies in their efforts to retaliate against fellow Dene Tha. Local conflicts thus escalate into regional ones as Dene Tha proceed in their disputes on the basis of their own notion of accountability and assumptions about human capabilities.

6. Journeys of the Soul

They usually make someone die
who is young, who is free from sin;
they try to follow him or her
to heaven.—Dene Tha speaker

From Dene Tha accounts of experiences in life we can infer that
the mind is the seat of one's will, intellect, and memory. With
one's mind one knows animal helpers who transfer to human
beings a power to heal or to harm. When drunk, one's mind is
gone. From this perspective it follows that after a state of drunkenness one does not remember one's actions and is not accountable for them. The mind is an essential part of one's individuality
that endures beyond one's current incarnation. As we see in this
chapter, individuals may always choose to come back to our land
to be born again in a new body. That is why a reincarnated individual remembers people, places, and events from his or her earlier life. The mind, therefore, resides transiently in "someone's
body," *kezí*, and permanently in "someone's spirit or soul," *key-
uné*.[1]

Dene Tha indeed conceive of dreaming, sickness, and death as
so many journeys of the soul. Dreaming involves the soul's jour-
neying away from the body to explore areas in our land, to engage in a medicine fight with other powers, or momentarily to
spend time in the other land in the company of dead relatives. At
the end of each journey, when one wakes up, one remembers the
events that took place beyond the confines of the body. That is
why, a dreamer told me, when waking someone, one must do so
cautiously, preferably by gently pulling on the sleeper's big toe,
thus giving the person's soul or spirit time to reenter the body.
Sickness may be induced by a prolonged absence of the soul from
the body, in which case Dene Tha healers can be called on to retrieve the soul, bring it back to the body, and restore health.
Death is the definitive separation of the mortal body and the enduring immortal soul.

"Do not cry!" is the most common injunction Dene Tha repeat to one another in the eventuality of a death. Individuals who cry as they grieve the death of a loved one are reminded that to do so is to hold onto the departing relative and, therefore, to hinder his or her progress to the other land. Individuals who are about to die say so to their close ones: "Do not cry, I am going to the other land." Peter, a young man in his early twenties, told me how a friend of his had had a premonition that he would soon die. The friend told Peter: "I got to tell you, Peter, I am going to die. If I don't tell you, you are going to cry. If you hear my singing, you will know that I am alive and happy." This statement expresses the view that "when someone does make it safely to the other side they send a song back to earthly friends or relatives" that is impossible to forget (Meili 1991, 9). In death what is most desired is that "our souls fly to heaven like a [prairie] chicken" (Alexis Seniantha, in Meili 1991, 3).[2]

Despite the injunction not to cry when a loved one dies, Dene Tha nevertheless do so, at times publicly and more often privately. When his brother died in the mid-1980s, Alexis Seniantha was shocked and cried with all his heart. "He had told me before not to cry, but I couldn't help it," said Alexis. Soon thereafter, when Alexis looked into his brother's house, he saw his brother crawling on the floor, unable to get up and start on the path to heaven. "Just like I told you before, I would fly like a grouse to heaven. Why are you holding me back?" his brother told Alexis (in Meili 1991, 8). This vision encouraged Alexis to wipe his tears and let his brother go. A few days later a soft blanket of pure white snow covered the ground, and the people commented that it meant Alexis's brother had made it to heaven and was happy.

Making it safely to the other side is not always possible or easy, even if one's relatives and friends are not crying. It is general knowledge that good deeds, the generous provision of food and gifts to others, and earnest participation in the Prophet Dance shorten the journey to the other land. Conversely, a deficit in good deeds in our land makes the journey to heaven very difficult, if not impossible, on one's own. Consistent with this view, when one prays for a dead person, the wish most often heard is that he or she may make it quickly to the other land. This is the desired fate of the soul, for it is well known that "people who die and who do not go quickly to heaven want someone to go with them." A Dene Tha mother whose daughter had nearly died following a recent encounter with a ghost said: "They keep wandering around, and they could make somebody die and lead them to heaven. They usually make somebody die who is young, who is free from sin; they try to follow him or her to heaven." That is why children are reminded not to answer a voice near a graveyard, "because it is a sure sign of impending death for yourself. If you answer, your soul goes; the spirits take you with them."

A young mother whose grandfather had recently died explained that she stayed home at night with her little girl because his spirit might come and get her daughter if she went outdoors after dark. Another woman told of her boy, who was passing by the graveyard at night: "Someone grabbed his hair, and his head is not right," the mother said. When a young man attempted suicide, he explained that he had done so because he was tired of the ghost of his grandmother bothering him all the time. His parents immediately asked the priest and the Dene Tha dreamers to pray for their son and free him from the disturbing ghost. Another mother spoke about her young son, who was losing his mind after having seen a ghost at night by the graveyard. The boy was taken to his grandfather, who helped him with his power. In the words of one Dene Tha mother: "Lots of people don't want their children to stay out at night because of people who died."

Dene Tha compare a ghost to a shadow. "When the sun is shining, if you move your hand, there is a shadow. When a person is moving in the sunshine, there is a shadow. What looks like the shape of a person as he walks, that is the kind of thing [the spirit] that is told things [in dreams and/or visions]," said a Dene Tha dreamer as he waved his hand underneath a lamp for me to see its shadow on the floor. In the same vein, a Dene Tha instructor said, "If you see something like a person's shadow, it's a ghost."[3] A ghost had once followed him back on a very dark night. All the way home he could clearly hear someone walking behind him, but once home where the porch light was on, he turned back to look at who was following him and couldn't see anything. "When it [the ghost] got to the light, it disappeared," he concluded.

A one-and-a-half-year-old boy kept having bad dreams, waking up screaming almost every other night. His mother would hold him tight and call his name in his ear. "He would come back; it was as if he was far, far away," said the mother. Thinking it was a ghost bothering him, she took ashes from the Tea Dance ceremonial grounds with which to make lines around his head and along his body from the crown of his head to the tip of his toes. When she completed the line on the left foot, the child just fell asleep. The mother commented: "A few days after I made these ash markings on him, I asked him: 'You don't have those dreams anymore?' and he smiled at me. He knew." Her child never had those dreams again; the ghost had left.

Ribbons are worn to ward off the souls of the deceased who bother human beings in our land. Children, and at times adults, wear ribbons twelve to fourteen centimeters long attached with a safety pin to the top of their jacket sleeves. For instance, when I came across a man who was wearing a white ribbon on his left shoulder while riding a horse with a green ribbon hanging from its right ear, I asked him, "Why does this horse have a ribbon?" He answered, "It is probably the same as with people; at night ghosts will not bother them; if you do not have a ribbon, you are bothered."[4]

This was the case with twelve-year-old Jennie. She would not eat and tossed around all night, which convinced her mother, Lucy, that something was wrong. "Jennie, I think there is something wrong with you; this is why I am here. I am your mother; I am here to help you," said Lucy as she went to her daughter one morning. Jennie told her mother that for a long time she had had a bad feeling and kept thinking of a ghost. Lucy got really scared and immediately talked to her own mother, who told Lucy to take Jennie to her grandfather, who could help, provided he was given a piece of moose hide embroidered with yellow, blue, and red thread. Lucy quickly prepared the appropriate gift and in the afternoon, "before it got dark," went with her daughter across the road to her grandfather's place. The grandfather told Jennie that in a dream he had seen a ghost that had nearly touched her. He was worried about her and said that if she had waited a little longer to get help, she would have died. He took a pink ribbon, pulled a few feathers out of his pillow, and tied them to the ribbon, instructing Jennie to carry it around her neck as a protection. Pointing to her daughter, Lucy said, "That is what she has around her neck now, and she is OK."[5]

This was the second time Jennie's grandfather had helped her get rid of a ghost, and it would be the last. At his age, to help her a third time would be to invite death. Jennie's mother explained that this had happened to a man who had tried, in vain, to help a relative get rid of a ghost for a third time: "That relative died, and for seven days he came back to that man who helped him, for seven days in a row. And my dad helped him get rid of it, and that man that my dad helped, he never did that kind of stuff again." Lucy then offered a brief account of her close encounter with a ghost: "*I tell you, even if you don't believe in it, you experience it, you know*. It happened to me. I was always thinking of a ghost, my mind was always going thinking about ghosts, and then I went to see that old man in Meander and he told me, 'Boy, that shadow was almost this close to you; you almost died.' The same with Jennie now; we are really worried" (my emphasis). Lucy's account was meant not for my ears only but also for her daughter, who was listening to our conversation. Jennie's experience is one that her mother shares. Given the Dene Tha view of true knowledge as personal knowledge, Lucy's opening statement makes her account indisputable. Jennie should now trust her own experience and knowledge. Like her mother before her, Jennie can expect to survive a close encounter with a ghost.

The concern for one's life following a visitation from a ghost was also expressed by Gill, who had been visited by her brother a month after his death:

> I was staying at Grandpa's place and I had that dream. I was downstairs in what used to be the residence [the local residential school that was closed in 1969]. There was lots of people, and I was standing next to Grandpa, and we were looking at the coffin. In it was my brother, and I was thinking, "Why is he here in the coffin if he is buried?" And I got scared. Someone touched my shoulder here and I turned around, and it was my brother again. So I ran out of that place and told the taxi to take me home. It tried to leave, but it would only spin in place and could not go. And then I woke up, and so did Grandpa. I told him my dream. He told

me to get up and we will pray. He knelt down by the fire and
put tobacco and tea in the fire.

In this instance, the grandfather, a well-known dreamer, was
able to help his grandson get on the path to heaven, after which
he stopped bothering his surviving sister.

"When dead relatives come back to you, if they come back real
close, it means you are ready to die," explained the daughter of another dreamer. "If they come back, and don't come close to you,
they tell you about things that will happen." Then, referring to an
old man who had recently died, she said, "Him, they came really
close to him; he knew, he wasn't afraid to die, and he died fast." In
this case it was the old man's father and son, who had died the previous summer, who came to get him: "They came to him in his
dreams. He knew they were coming to get him. My dad went with
them to get him." In spirit, her father went with the two ghosts to
the house of the dying friend to help him leave his body and get to
the other land, where his father and son already lived.[6]

A NEAR-DEATH EXPERIENCE

The quotations from Dene Tha speakers offered so far in support of a view of death as a journey of the soul are removed from
their original context. Such an exposition has the advantage of
substantiating a thematic presentation of Dene Tha views. It has
also the disadvantage of ignoring the work involved between ethnographer and Dene Tha speaker, as they jointly elaborate accounts of events. To ignore such work and to insist on presenting
quotations from fieldnotes "as tokens of ethnographic objectivity," writes Fabian (1991, 396), is to risk the danger of lapsing
"into textual fundamentalism."

An ethnography that takes performance seriously recognizes
that information is not neatly stored in the heads of speakers to
be called up at the request of the inquisitive investigator, as
writers of informative ethnography suggest. Rather, ethnographic information, or what comes to pass as such, is always
made present through enactment, or performance. In other
words, says Fabian (1990, 5), "the answers we get to our ethnographic questions can be interpreted as so many cultural performances. . . . The ethnographer's role, then, is no longer that

of questioner; he is but a provider of occasions, a catalyser in the weakest sense, and a producer in the strongest."

To attend to this work is to "alert us to the extent to which field-notes are the product, not so much of the cognitive efforts of an individual, as of a process of social interaction" (G. Watson 1992, 1). The ethnographer is in the business of cooperatively constituting the knowledge he or she is seeking. This process of social constitution can be examined in the following transcript of a conversation between myself (I) and Brenda (H):[7]

1	H:	I do not know what I have.
2		My eyes always hurt at this time of the year.
3		I went to see the doctor last year but he couldn't do nothing.
4	I:	Did something important happen to you around this time of the year
5		a few years back?
6	H:	Yeah, about three years ago my father died.
7	I:	Did you cry when he died?
8	H:	Yes, I was the first one to cry.
9		It really hurt me when he died.
10		It was even more difficult for my younger sister [Lisa].
11		When my father died, she almost died too.
12		The old people from here and some from Meander helped her.
13		We had to go in one room; that was the night before the funeral.
14		My sister could not eat, and we felt her going away.
15		When old people help, they do not like light. They have to be in the dark.
16		We were all in one room; we close the door.
17		I sit next to my sister, and the old people sing.
18		They call their helpers, their animal helpers, to go after my sister's soul.
19		I guess my sister subconsciously wanted to stay here, but she had
20		already started to go to my dad.
21		That is why they had to help her.

148

22   She didn't know what was going on. She was already going.

23   When she woke up after, she asked us what we did to her.

24   She said she had been traveling up to a fence

25   on the other side of which was Dad,

26   and she had almost crossed that fence.

27   That is how my sister is still here. They helped her.

28   I: What about these animal helpers? How does one get them?

29   H: I don't really know.

30   Like my older brother, he never talks to us about it,

31   but my mom told us once that one day Frederick went in the bush

32   with little provisions, and was supposed to come back the same

33   day but stayed two days and two nights.

34   On his way he had met wolves who had come to meet him;

35   and he had been with them all that time.

36   I guess they became his helpers.

37   But that is all I know. We do not talk about these things.

If we approach this conversation thematically, we focus on the Dene Tha healers, their animal helpers, and the dying woman whose soul they rescue on its journey to the other land. We can approach this transcript of a conversation differently, keeping in mind the ethnomethodological notions of indexicality and reflexivity, to examine the social process whereby participants in this conversation go about constituting the Dene Tha world as a recognizable state of affairs for them. The notion of "indexicality refers to the context dependency of meaning; reflexivity, to the way in which accounts and the settings they describe elaborate and modify each other in a back-and-forth process" (G. Watson 1991, 75).

The verbatim record makes available part of the first conversation I had with Brenda, perfectly bilingual, who lives with her husband and children in a large urban center where she works as a professional. We met on the occasion of one of her visits to her family in Chateh. We knew of each other through Brenda's mother, who had mentioned Brenda to me and talked about me to Brenda. This previous knowledge certainly informed the expectations we had of each other. She would have known of my habit of writing down verbatim as much as I could of what people told me. The reader may remember from the first chapter how, before our first meeting, Paul had already learned from his kinsmen how we would proceed in our sessions of instruction in Dene Dháh. When Brenda and I met, we immediately talked about her family, recent events in Chateh, and my purpose for being among the Dene Tha.

The verbatim record begins with Brenda's innocuous remark that her eyes always hurt at this time of the year, a condition that the doctor cannot help (lines 1–3). I ask what might have happened in the past at this time of the year (lines 4–5). This is an open question, based on my presumption that recurring bodily symptoms express reactions to significant past events. When I ask my question, I do not know if Brenda shares my belief. She may or may not be inclined to look to the past for a significant event that happened at that time of year. "Nothing really special, as far as I know"; "I don't remember anything"; "It must be an allergy of some sort": these and any number of other similar statements could have constituted equally good answers to my question. Brenda's answer is that her father died three years earlier (line 6).

Given Brenda's answer, I could of course have asked what her father died of, or at what age, or whether he died suddenly. In lieu of a question, I might have said that I never had the experience of losing a parent, or that this explains her recurring pain in the eyes, or that counseling might help her through her grief. All these possible responses would have oriented the conversation in a particular way. I asked about whether she cried or not at the time (line 7), suggesting a link with her opening remark about her eyes (line 2). Brenda immediately said that she did cry and provided the additional detail that she was the first one to do so (line 8). Retrospectively, this bit of information can be seen as a way of introducing her sister Lisa, for whom their father's death was even more difficult (line 10). That Brenda takes my statement as a question to be answered and that I take her statement as an answer to my question constitutes our statements cooperatively, as sensible questions and pertinent answers. Throughout the conversation we continuously transform "that which is in theory irremediably uncertain into what is, for all practical purposes, transparently obvious" (G. Watson and Irwin 1996, 94).

The exchange between Brenda and myself is obviously highly structured. I ask all the questions, and Brenda answers them. When accepting my questions and answering them with personal information, Brenda constitutes me as someone who will not receive her account with skepticism or ridicule. I support this view by being receptive to her answers, letting her story of Lisa's near-death experience unfold unchallenged, much as a Dene Tha would let it stand. By accepting Brenda's account and following with a question about animal helpers (line 28), I make her an informed individual from whom I might learn much about Dene Tha culture.

The Dene code of conduct gives one the right to speak at considerable length without being interrupted and without ever being directly contradicted. As noted by Scollon and Scollon (1983, 26), in Dene conversation, "something like a monologue is the normal speaking turn." When I respect this flow of speech, I constitute myself as a Dene-like listening counterpart. Brenda also distinguishes among what she knows (lines 11–27), what she witnessed when sitting next to her sister, and what she does not really know (lines 29–36) but heard from her mother about her brother's acquisition of a power. In typical Dene Tha fashion, she answers my query about the acquisition of animal helpers (line 28) with a story (lines 30–35), which she concludes with the well-known Dene injunction concerning these matters: "We do not talk about these things" (line 37). Brenda does all the things a competent Dene Tha is supposed to do in such circumstances. Not to press with further questions or pressure her to reveal more than there is in the story is to interact with her in an appropriately Dene way. In acting thus, we cooperatively constitute each other as competent Dene Tha speaker and listener.

The verbal exchange between Brenda and myself is also structured in other important ways. While telling the story of her sister's near-death experience, Brenda shows that she is well aware that she is not speaking to a Dene Tha. Line 15 is obviously addressed to a non-Dene, who may not know, or who may need reminding of what every Dene Tha knows, namely, that when old people seek to retrieve someone's soul, they do so in the dark. Line 18, "they call their animal helpers," similarly makes explicit what any Dene Tha would have known from the mention that the old people sang (line 17). Line 19, Brenda's comment that her sister's subconscious will to stay here was too weak to overcome her will to join her father in the other land, draws on Euro–North American categories designed to make the account intelligible to a non-Dene listener. As noted in chapter 1, through a process called recipient design (Sacks and Schegloff 1979), Brenda and other Dene Tha speakers, like speakers everywhere, "design their utterances for certain aspects of the context, especially for who the other participants are and what they have just said" (Nofsinger 1991, 9). As a competent speaker, Brenda fills in the background so that I might better grasp the significance of things taken for granted by those who are intimately acquainted with Dene Tha ways.

In her account of Lisa's near-death experience Brenda orientates to the phenomena she reports as objective. She sets about to describe things—old people, a sister who is near death, songs that call animal helpers, and a path to the other land—that exist prior to and independently of her account, as she would expect any other competent Dene Tha to do. It is "facts" that Brenda is reporting. She brings to her account the "thesis of the interchangeability of perspective" characteristic of the natural attitude in which we conduct our daily lives (Schutz 1967). We assume that what is not immediately available to each other is nonetheless so in principle. What I do not perceive from where I stand, I would perceive if I were where you are. What a blind person does not perceive, she would perceive if she were not so. What Alfred Schutz (1967) called "the natural attitude of everyday life" is characterized by its specific epoche, by the bracketing or the suspension of doubt concerning the reality of the shared world of everyday life.

Brenda is reporting events that she was a witness to. I learn this only in line 16, however, when she says, "We were all in one room; we close the door. I sit next to my sister, and the old people sing." Before that statement I do not know if Brenda's account is hearsay or not. With this statement Brenda constitutes herself as a coherent entity enduring over time: she who tells the story is the very same person who saw the old people come to her sister's assistance and who heard her sister when she revived. Without this statement of identity Brenda's account loses its plausibility, for it does not have the stamp of personal experience without which knowledge is not true knowledge. In presenting herself this way, Brenda presumes that in the natural attitude, I share with her a sense of self as an enduring entity in the course of one's life history. I, of course, accept this stance and do not challenge her with the analytical view that since our bodily cells, as well as our mental and emotional states, change continuously, we are literally never the same. To take this stance would obviously destroy the whole exercise, which is possible only within the natural attitude (G. Watson 1992, 13).

The quick succession of details in Brenda's account (lines 13–17) set the near-death experience at a specific time (the night before her father's funeral), a specific place (in one room), in specific circumstances (behind a closed door, in the dark). In this account, as in every good ethnography, it is the abundance of circumstantial details that "attest to the accuracy of, and the very existence of, the 'I' who witnesses" (G. Watson 1992, 14). For this scheme to work, I, as a listener, must use the corresponding interpretive device that Harold Garfinkel (1967b, 178) calls "let it pass." I do not stop Brenda to ask her the exact date on which the funeral was to take place. I do not insist on knowing the names of the old people who were singing. I do not interrupt her to inquire how dark it really was: pitch dark as in a sweat lodge? Or was is not so dark that one could not see what the old people were doing? I do not insist on knowing in which room they were: her sister's room? If not, why another room? And so on. Conversation and constant prodding for more exact information are simply impossible to carry out together. Conversation involves being absorbed in the unfolding story. For the story to unfold as a story, my work as a listener is to let Brenda proceed with her narration and trust that eventually all will be clear, or at least sufficiently so for the conversation to flow meaningfully. To interrupt the flow of talk constantly with questions is to undermine each other's credibility as competent speakers and listeners.

When I move away from an experiential retelling of a near-death experience (or of any other Dene Tha account) to its ethnomethodological analysis, the intent is not to challenge the understanding that one shares with others in the natural attitude but to show how such an agreed-on understanding is achieved. In Brenda's account all details, those referring to our land and those referring to the other land, are given the same minimal descriptive treatment. The animal helpers, the fence halfway between our land and the other land, Lisa's soul traveling away from her body and coming back to it are not treated as anomalous or extraordinary. They are no less real than the phenomena belonging to our land: the body of the deceased father or that of Lisa, the darkness, or the room in which the old people sing. Moreover, in Brenda's account the old people, her mother, and especially her sister share her world. The reality she is describing is a consensual one; the entities she posits are part of everyone's stock of knowledge. We are, therefore, dealing not with a hallucination or a vivid dream but with routine events, taking place "out there," in the real world, in our land and in the other land.

The intervention of the old people presupposes the loss of the soul, which explains Lisa's unconscious state. In turn, Lisa's condition gives the explanation and the old people's actions something to be an explanation of and an objective for. In this fashion, in Brenda's account, Lisa's condition, the explanation for it, and the remedy to it constitute one another as elements of a single meaningful event: a near-death experience. Details pertaining to this world and to the other world are eventually collected in a gestalt contexture, not because of any intrinsic property but because of a particular way of seeing them. In prompting the listener to adopt this reading, Brenda uses the indexical and reflexive properties of talk as an interpretive resource. In the end, this analysis of the transcript shows that it is in the conversation itself that individuals "make available to each other—and, incidentally, to others, including the analyst—continually updated understandings of what is going on in and through talk as the talk unfolds" (G. Watson 1992, 3).

In chapter 4 the analysis of Dene Tha accounts of illness and healing with a power revealed how Dene Tha reality is self-validating in the sense, first, that alternative accounts are always available and, second, that what satisfies any one criterion of evidence is highly flexible. In the case of Lisa's near-death experience, consider the following. She "nearly dies" on the day of her father's funeral. In the Dene Tha view, children are particularly vulnerable following the death of a parent, when their souls may be enticed to the other land by the soul of the dead person. Lisa's family and healers gather round, calling on their animal helpers. Together they work up an account of her rescue. Said Brenda: "She didn't know what was going on. She was already going. When she woke up after, she asked us what we did to her. She said she had been traveling up to a fence on the other side of which was Dad, and she had almost crossed that fence. That is how my sister is still here. They helped her."

As mentioned in G. Watson and Goulet (1992), if a woman survives a serious illness, there are multifarious ways of interpreting the fact. It is common knowledge that if one is healthy, one's soul is united with one's body; if one falls seriously ill or dies, one's soul is wandering. Should Lisa's soul remain in our land, it could be because she successfully sought the aid of her animal helper, or because dreamers called on their animal helpers to bring her soul back to her body before death supervened, or because angels (or Jesus, or Mary) intervened, or, as we see in other cases later in this chapter, because the soul of a dead person intervened. If, on the other hand, her soul eventually goes to the other land, it could be because it was enticed there by the animal helpers of fellow Dene Tha or by the souls of the dead, or because it decided on its own to follow the soul of a dead person. Should the community's healers attempt to save her but fail, it could be because they were too late, or it could be that she succeeded in bringing herself back to enter the womb of a woman, to be born again in this land. These alternative plausible accounts of one and the same phenomenon are available to the Dene Tha partly because accounts are formulated not prospectively but retrospectively—accounts do not predict what will happen; rather, they interpret what has already happened— and partly because the Dene Tha display considerable flexibility about how many criteria must be satisfied before evidence is considered firm.

DREAMING AND KNOWING WHAT IS AHEAD OF US

The belief that dreams are journeys of the soul in which it communicates with inhabitants of the other land and/or sees things unfolding in our land is prevalent among Dene, young and old. A dreamer once contrasted the Dene with the white man, emphasizing the illiteracy of the first, to conclude that, finding the Dene pitiful, God decided to give some Dene the power to know with their minds: "You don't just dream without a purpose. The Dene do not know much, they do not know how to read, but they go with their minds. Because they do not know much, the Dene are pitiful; they get misguided and confused, and therefore some people are made so that they know. God made them that way." The dreamer went on to describe how he had developed as someone who knows and sees many things with his mind:

> Me myself, when I was a kid, I did not know anything. But I took it slow, I wasn't that big, and I was very active. In my forehead I felt like there was something solid poking straight through. Once I turned fifteen, my mind was there. I was sleeping, and I was looking somewhere [in his dream]. It happens sometimes, not too often, not too close to each other most often. Sometimes when I sleep, I look at the land, but it does not seem to be the land that I am sleeping on.
>
> Why is it that sometimes I sleep and I see many things? I do not know. I'll be told what to do. People talk to me, and I watch them [while dreaming]. I really thought it over. I was confused. You know, when you are a young kid, you are confused; that is how I was, confused. When you are a kid, your mind is not very strong.
>
> Why is it like that? It is not very close. Once in a while I dream, I would foresee something. Sometimes I dream, and I see lots. And then when I was twenty years old or so, I got married to my wife.

In a few sentences the dreamer has described how, before he married, his mind progressively opened up to the world of dreams. With his mind he saw and heard people from the other land who addressed him and instructed him. These experiences left him somewhat perplexed. Even as an Elder, he does not really know why he is occasionally shown things to come.

Dreaming in this manner, one knows where to go to kill a moose, discerns if a medicine fight has ended with the destruction of the power of an enemy, or learns that deceased relatives are well and happy in the other land. A young man commented to me: "We Catholics, we believe, we believe, like sometimes we have dreams and they come true. Like my brother and I, we always tell our dreams to one another, and we look ahead. Sometimes what will happen ahead of us we know because of our dreams." Accounts of prophetic or revelationary dream journeys express the Dene equation of some knowledge with power.

Consider the same view expressed by a Dene from the Northwest Territories:

> There are a lot of people—dreamers—who live by dreams. I believe that dreams are very true. When I was about seventeen, I was up at Bear Lake, and there were not many boats there. I used to swim here. There was an old man who was supposed to be some sort of Prophet. I asked him how the boat would make it going across the lake; the crossing takes about two days—around two hundred miles. He said he saw a boat crossing the lake, and catching on fire just before it reached the shore, and one man badly burned. We waited for the word, and sure enough it happened. Before the schooner got into Fort Raven, it caught on fire, and one man was badly burned. Things like that, he could see. (Julian Hardistry, in Waugh and Prithipaul 1979, 67)

Accounts such as these are commonplace among the Dene. Dreaming, seeing with one's mind what is likely to happen in the future, is expected on the part of not only prophets but also Dene individuals generally.

For instance, a Dene Tha wife and husband told me that they had had bad dreams for a couple of nights. In one dream someone was pulling the wife away from her family, pulling her left hand. Even when she woke up she could feel someone pulling her hand. She told her husband, who said that he also had had a dream in which he saw somebody coming for her but he thought it was for somebody else. She explained: "'Cause if you dream bad dreams too close to your family, it is usually meant for somebody else." As supporting evidence for this view she said that two weeks earlier, while in Edmonton, her husband had dreamed of something happening to his two sons. Two days later, two boys, not theirs, were seriously injured in a car accident. As a precaution, she and her husband had burned tobacco and a pack of cigarettes in the fire, asking "not to have anything happen to anybody, especially not our kids."

In another family a dreamer had told the parents not to move close to the river in Habay, early in the summer, as they had intended. "I saw an older boy going; you better not move now," the dreamer told them. Soon thereafter a sixteen-year-old boy drowned in the river at Habay. Only then was it safe to move to Habay, as the drowning would not concern one of their own boys. Similarly, one evening I came across a four-year-old girl who told me in perfectly good English, "I know why you don't play in the schoolyard." I looked back at the schoolyard, where an hour earlier I had seen a dozen kids playing together. Not a single child was in sight. I asked the little girl why this was. She answered, "Because somebody is going to die in the schoolyard; they have dreams; they are having terrible dreams about the playground." I asked her who had had the dreams. She said, "My dad." Then, looking at her slightly older companion, the child said, "Nobody." They quickly walked away. Later in the evening a friend told me that he had seen parents taking their children out of the schoolyard as he was driving by. When parents had heard of the bad dreams concerning the schoolyard, they had quickly come to take the children away.

The following account involves Paul, who nearly died because people he had thrown out of a residence when they were drunk got mad at him and were trying to kill him with medicine power. Paul became sick and was admitted to the hospital, where doctors did not know what was the matter with him. His mother-in-law then called and told his wife that she should take him to his in-laws for help. At the house of his in-laws an old man helped him and told him not to go back to the place where he had worked for four years. Paul and his family, therefore, moved away to a nearby town, and his health recovered. Before four years were over, he agreed to follow his wife and children to his former place of residence, where his wife had found work. He did so with some anxiety, because the old man who had told him not to return there within four years had died in the meantime and Paul could not consult him.

Before moving back with his family, Paul had had dreams of

living anew in his former place of residence. In his dream "a big hole would form," growing bigger and bigger, and he "would sink in the hole to die." He then learned that his father-in-law had a similar dream in which he would see Paul falling into a hole and would try to hold Paul by the arms but could not pull him out. Paul's father-in-law was yelling in his dream when his daughter woke him up. "He said it was a good thing she did, for if not, both of us would have gone down the hole and die." Paul knew that he was in danger. He then remembered that if one is to sleep in a place where one does not want to be, one brings a stone from one's home, or from a clean place, and places it under the pillow where one will sleep. "That way," Paul said, "you are not where you sleep; your spirit is protected." Not being where his body was, he could not be reached by his enemies. As evidence of this Paul remarked that ever since he had been sleeping thus he had not had a dream.

VISITS FROM RELATIVES LIVING IN THE OTHER LAND

Across cultures there is a widespread association between depression and soul loss, particularly following the death of a loved one (Shweder 1985, 193–200). Lisa's near-death experience followed the loss of her father. Many other Dene Tha also reported that they wished to die after the death of a close relative. A young widow who longed to join her husband in the other land declared: "Sometimes, when I go to bed, I think the way he [her husband] was telling me, 'If I die, I'll go right through to heaven; I'll be looking at you, don't worry.' Since he died, three times I dreamed about him. I want to go with him. 'No,' he says, 'it is not time.' Maybe that is why I never get sick." An older woman told me how in a dream she had joined her son in the other land, but he sent her back to our land: "Last month, all month, I was sick, but I kept it to myself. I did not tell anyone. I had dreamt that I was to be sick. I went to the other land and there I was with my son and then he told me to look down here. There was a woman lying down on a bed. He told me: 'Do you know that woman?' I looked at him and told him, 'I don't know who she is.' He told me, 'It is you.'" The son then told her she ought to return to her body, that it was not her time yet to die. After this dream the woman soon recovered her health and resumed her regular activities.

The same woman told me that this was the second time she had visited her son in heaven. In her first visit to the other land she met Mary, the mother of Jesus, who told her to go back to this land, as it was not time for her to die. A young woman reported that twice her daughter had shown her the other land. "It is very nice, that is why I am not afraid to die; I am ready," the woman said. Still another woman admitted that when her brother-in-law died, she wanted to follow him and die too: "I had a dream: I stand there with [names a dead grandfather] at my right, and facing me is my mother [also dead], just there. And I want to take her hand, this one [lifts her left hand], but she doesn't want me to take her hand and go with her." The mother's response is also telling the daughter that it is not time for her to go, despite her grief.

In the early 1980s Dene Tha often told the story of Rose, a Kaska woman who had died and come back from the other land. I had the opportunity to meet her and hear an account of her death from her daughter when I traveled to Fort Simpson in September 1984 to see Pope Paul John II, who was to visit the Dene. His airplane was not allowed to land because of a heavy fog over the Mackenzie River and Fort Simpson area. A large Tea Dance had been organized in the community hall, where a few Dogribs announced that they were four hundred dollars short of the fourteen hundred dollars it would take to charter a plane to fly Rose from her home in the Yukon to Fort Simpson. A hat was passed around, and within half an hour more than seven hundred dollars was collected. The next day Rose was in Fort Simpson, and a steady stream of Dene from all over the Northwest Territories and Alberta came to pay their respects and speak briefly with her. After I did the same, her daughter told me that her mother had died because of someone's bad medicine.

Rose had been hunting on someone else's trapline and had killed two moose when the owner of the trapline came up to her to tell her she was on his territory. She told the man, "Take the meat and everything but give me one hide." But he refused to take anything and told her that she would regret what she had done. "He got to her with bad medicine, and she became sick and died. She did not die from death, like she died because of the bad medicine, so I guess that is why she could come back," explained

160

the daughter. People had been preparing her burial for three days when Rose came back to life. While dead, Rose said, she "saw herself going down the road to the fire and was trying to pull herself from it, but she couldn't. She was going to that fire and in there she saw that uncle of hers who really liked her when she was a young girl. She was really scared and then a voice told her she had to come back to earth and tell the people to pray."[8]

Some Dene Tha distinguish between someone's bad spirit, *ket-suné*, which "is always accompanied by impending [death] or something to do with death or warning," and a good spirit, *key-uné*, which "is easy to tell apart from the bad one because it is accompanied by light color, pink, yellow or white, and always smiles." I asked if someone could be both a good and a bad spirit and was told: "It all depends on the one who is seeing it. It depends on how the viewer feels. I have an example. John, his brother Henry, he says '*sechidla tsuné' sechedah,*' 'my brother's bad spirit is after me.' He says John always bothers him and wants him to be dead with him. John is a bad spirit [to Henry], but it depends on how Henry thinks. He expects something bad to happen to him. It's only his brother trying to have him change his life. It is very plain to see." "It is very plain to see," of course, because the work of interpretation is completed and unaccounted for. The resulting constellation of details is set in a precise gestalt. It is taken for granted. From the perspective of the speaker, if Henry would only change his thinking, he would also clearly see that John's spirit is there not to bother him but to call him to change his life.

In the course of the conversation the speaker assumes that we share what was common knowledge, namely, that John had been found frozen to death, halfway between his home and the house he had been drinking at with friends, and that since his death John had repeatedly come to Henry in his dreams. Whereas Henry saw these visitations as a bad omen, others interpreted them as an invitation to mend his ways and to give up drinking before he ended up like his brother. Indeed, the week before, I was offered this interpretation of John's appearances to his brother after Henry had been found lying unconscious in the snow by the staff at the nursing station. Luke, Henry's brother, visibly drunk, had stopped over to tell me that Henry would probably have to have his foot amputated but that he was all right. Luke then added, "I guess he got a warning but never heeded that warning. He said he was at the turnoff near High Level and a fox ran from him, barked at him, and ran away." Things that know were giving Henry a warning, in addition to the one already offered by his brother.

Dene Tha take it for granted that spirits of individuals who make it to heaven keep visiting their relatives to communicate with them and to encourage them to live well in our land. A flag flying from a post by the house of an Elder or a dreamer usually indicates that the person has been visited by a dead person. When I asked a dreamer about the green flag by his house, he told me he had had a dream the night before in which his father was coming back to him. His father had done this only once before, opening his arms three times and telling him *"edulin sa ahde,"* "nothing happened to me." In the dream of the previous night his father was coming back to him, and the dreamer was hoping he would hear what his father would tell him. Unfortunately, the dream was disturbed when the neighbors knocked on the door. They asked him to call the R.C.M.P. as they feared being beaten up by the young men of the family, who were drunk. He declined to do so but invited them to stay overnight away from the disturbing drunks.

The following story is an example of an instructive and predictive dream that was offered by another dreamer. When he was a young man, the dreamer was sleeping in the bush while on a hunting expedition when he suddenly saw a crowd of people and heard a voice asking him, "Do you know that man?" The dreamer recognized his father's voice but did not know whom to look for. "That man! That you're are going to turn into a song person," he was told. The dreamer recognized a fellow Dene who was known for his predilection for card games and drinking. The voice told the dreamer: "You will talk to him up to three times; up to the first two you talk to him a lot. The first time you say it to him, you are going to be frightened. The second time you tell him, you might not be sounding pleasant to him, but that's all right. Talk to him more. He is going to be scared, he will be afraid to move, he will look after himself. Toward the end, a long ways, if he is still alive, he will foresee a lot." More than forty years after this dream the dreamer comments: "My father said that far back ago. Right now he [the song person] knows a lot. I listen to him speak sometimes. I am happy, very glad. I did not do it myself. My father did. I was told what to tell him. I was sleeping and I saw. After three times I talk to him a lot. He does not play cards that much, he quits drinking." The injunction not to consume alcohol is particularly strong with dreamers and singers. Drinking makes one's mind go away. Dreamers and singers, therefore, ought not to drink, in order to be constantly alert, to know what is happening to them and around them.

Myrna similarly attributed her sobriety to a visit she had had from her deceased aunt and uncle, whose son, Erik, she was raising. Not long before she stopped drinking, she had a dream in which she did not see but clearly heard Erik's parents address her: "If you do not smarten up, someone will punish you, get at those you love most." Myrna said that at the time "even with that dream it did not really sink into me." The significance of the dream became clear when a shotgun accidentally went off while they were on a hunting expedition. Then, said Myrna, "his face [Erik's] was all full of blood, and I really prayed. I held my hand over his face and I promised God I would stop drinking, that I understood, that I was ready to change. And when I took my hand off his face, it had stopped bleeding." Myrna nevertheless forgot about her promise to God, and when she went to the bar the following week with her friend, they each ordered a beer. "I took a first gulp at it," stated Myrna, "and then I remembered everything, the dream, how I prayed, and what I said, and just there I stopped drinking. It's hard sometimes, but I don't really crave for it, not anymore. The first month was especially hard." Another woman attributed her sobriety to a dramatic dream in which she saw herself rapidly sinking waist-deep into sand as she attempted to proceed on the path to heaven. She could hardly move when she heard a voice tell her: "This too you find hard; you must quit what is bad." She understood this to be a reference to the liquor that she regularly accepted from her sister, and henceforth she gave up drinking.

The following account contains all the themes associated with death mentioned so far: the grief and the crying over the death of a loved one, the apparition of the deceased relative in the narrator's dreams, the fear that the visitation would cause harm, and the reassurance on the part of the deceased relative that it would not be so:

> You remember my little niece [Lucy, in her early twenties], she died; she had an accident. About two months after she died I was just crying and then I dreamed about her. Just like a person in person. I could hear that foot, foot, you know [with her hands on the kitchen table she makes the movement and noise of footsteps]. She was carrying a paper like this [she rolls the TV guide in her hands to show me]. When I was dreaming, looking at her, first thing I see her, I say, "She is gone; how come she is back?" First time she says, "Where's Peter?" [her son]. He was sleeping in the next room. "I want to see Peter and Rose [his wife]," she said. I was surprised, scared. She could ask for something if she couldn't go to heaven. She said, "No, I will not do nothing; I just want to see again."

The next morning Rose woke up screaming and shaking. She was terrified by a dream in which she had seen Lucy coming back to her. What would it mean? A month later Rose found out that she was pregnant. Rose then knew that Lucy had come back to her not to take her soul away to journey to heaven but to be made again and raised once more as a child in our land.

The interpretation of dreams and their eventual status as prophetic or revelatory involves all the social skills and processes we have seen at work in the constitution of a conversation as a meaningful flow of talk. Just as various parts of a conversation are given a determinate meaning according to their place in a sequential context, so it is with accounts of dreams and visions. Although these accounts are in principle susceptible of various plausible interpretations, they end up in situated and negotiated circumstances, having a definite signification. A month after seeing Lucy coming back to her, when Rose learned she was pregnant, she knew that Lucy had come back to be made again. Had she not become pregnant, Rose would have known, with her mother-in-law, that Lucy had simply come to see them, as indeed she had said, "I just want to see again." That Lucy actually wanted more, that she wanted to be reincarnated, is discovered later in the light of Rose's pregnancy. Details from the dream account and information concerning the state of the dreamer or of close relatives constitute each other as elements of a single meaningful revelation.

Accounts of dreams are selectively constructed in a number of commonplace but crucial ways. First, they are given in intelligible language rather than in some from-outer-space gibberish incomprehensible to the Dene Tha. When telling a dream, Dene Tha dreamers often describe a voice—most often one of a known dead relative or dead predecessor—addressing them in Dene Dháh, instructing them to look at this or that and to perform certain actions, to walk on a path, to walk into a building, or to eat a substance that is given to them. Such instructions are always in Dene Dháh. Second, Dene Tha dreams and visions are composed of images, themes, and concepts that are familiar to the Dene rather than ones that are unimaginable, inaccessible, or unintelligible to them. Third, the themes they are built of are not random. Accounts of dreams and visions are not just about anything. They are in some degree conventionalized; they constitute a recognizable genre, frequently dealing with traveling to the other land or with encountering the dead, the dying, and the soon to be reborn. Finally, the use of the adverb *enuudli*, meaning "probably," is typical of narration of dreams that appear to predict events to come. Built into the very process of foretelling is a clause indicating that the foreseen may not materialize. Typically, predictions are not about the inevitable but about the probable. They can be read retrospectively in various ways.

*

Dreaming, sickness, and death are so many journeys away from the body undertaken by the individual's spirit, conceived of as the seat of consciousness continuously aware of what it is directly experiencing in our land, in the other land, or in between the two, to and fro. The care not to wake someone suddenly, the injunction not to cry when a loved one dies, the ribbons worn on one's sleeve or the rosary one carries on oneself, the songs of healers calling on their animal helpers to retrieve the soul of their dying patient are all aspects of the relationships that Dene Tha living in our land entertain with other Dene Tha who are beyond our land, in spirit.

Journeys of the Soul

In this analysis of accounts of predictive dreams, of healing rituals, and of near-death experiences we have seen how the notions of indexicality and reflexivity can be used productively to identity the methods social actors (including the anthropologist in conversation with Dene Tha speakers) employ in the natural attitude to constitute the Dene Tha world as a recognizable state of affairs. Dreams are predictive and healing rituals are effective because Dene Tha formulate accounts concerning dreams and healing rituals not prospectively but retrospectively. Dene Tha can continuously interpret what has already happened in terms of previous dreams or ritual actions. They can do so because alternative plausible accounts of one and the same phenomenon are available to the Dene Tha, who display considerable flexibility about how many criteria must be satisfied before evidence is considered firm.

7. Searching for a Womb

*

There is always somebody who knows
who it is going to be. They see the spirit
going into you.—Dene Tha mother

Following death, people seek a woman's womb in which to be born again. This view is central to the Dene apprehension of themselves and of one another, as documented by Frederica De Laguna (1954) for the Tlingit, Goulet (1989, 1994b) for the Dene Tha, Ake Hultkrantz (1973) for the Hare, Mills (1988a and 1988b) for the Beaver and Wetsuweten, and Slobodin (1994a) for the Kutchin. Slobodin (1994b, 145) writes that "despite official Christian opposition," including "three ordained Anglican priests, two Anglican catechists, a Pentecostal lay reader, a dozen of the most devout Roman Catholic and Anglican laity," the Kutchin remain firm in their conviction that reincarnation occurs. This belief is long-standing. In 1876, for instance, Emile Petitot (in Savoie 1971, 79) reported that, while among the Dene, he tried in vain to dispel a young woman's opinion that she had lived an earlier life under another name and other appearances; he failed equally in his attempts to discredit a grandmother's conviction that she should claim as her own the child of a neighbor that she "knew" to be her own son reincarnated. Were Petitot to visit Dene communities today, he would find the same beliefs and his efforts to discredit the Dene conviction that some individuals are born again would be equally fruitless.[1]

Views concerning reincarnation differ considerably from one Dene community to another. Among the Dunne-za of northeast British Columbia "all people are said to be the reincarnation of souls who have been on earth before" (Mills 1988a, 25). This is not so, however, among the Chipewyan, who "believe that new souls are always entering the world" (Sharp 1976, 31), which explains why the majority of Chipewyans do not recall having had a previous life on earth.[2] In Meander River, near Chateh, Adam Salopree told Meili (1991, 130) that it is only those who did bad things in their lives that come back to a woman when she is pregnant to be born again. In Chateh not everyone comes back to be born again, only those who cannot find the path to heaven or those who had not wanted to die in the first place. "Like halfway to heaven there is a door, and they look at heaven on the other side and they look back on this earth. Sometimes they do not want to leave this earth; they come to be reborn," said the daughter of a dreamer. A Dene Tha woman died, having lived a long life in which she had been known for her generosity and assiduous participation in the Prophet Dance. Six months later I was told that she had reincarnated. I asked why, given her exemplary life, she had not simply journeyed to heaven. I was told that she had died before completing all she had wanted to do in our land. Hence, she was coming back.

Ghosts of the deceased are often sighted around the cemetery, the schoolyard, or people's homes. When I would return to Chateh after a six-month absence, people would invariably tell me who had died and who was still going around to be made again.[3] One Dene Tha, who commented that there were many people going around who wanted to be reincarnated, proceeded to give the names of the individuals concerned. Another Dene Tha mentioned that her brother had been to her house: "[He] wants to be a baby again. He came at night and around the school too he was seen." Another speaker said of an old woman that "she is still seen walking among people," because "she could find nobody to bring her back."

ACCOUNTS OF REINCARNATION

In their discussion of individuals dying and being born again, Dene Tha speakers seldom use the expression "reincarnation." When speaking in English, they use phrases such as "he or she was done to us again" or "he or she was done again," a phraseology that is very close to the Dene expression denoting such a person: *Dene andats' ındla*, "a person who was made again by others." Dene Tha recognize five possible indications that someone is being made again, two concerning occurrences prior to a pregnancy and three connected with characteristics of the reincarnated child. Any Dene Tha account of a case of reincarnation is likely to include a combination of indications and accounts of the same reincarnation told in different circumstances and emphasizing different signs.

Annunciatory Dreams

Dene Tha, as we have seen in the previous chapters, report many kinds of encounters with deceased relatives through dreams. Many of these encounters are occasions for the dead person to exhort relatives to amend their ways or simply to remind them that it is not yet their time to die. There are dreams, however, in which it appears to the dreamer that a deceased person communicates his or her search for a womb in which to be made again. Such annunciatory dreams are reported by people in numerous societies across the world. Among the Mission Chipewyan, for instance, "the deceased, usually only those who were young when they died or who felt their death unjust or were unwilling to die, are able to pursue rebirth by seeking out pregnant women. They appear in dreams during pregnancy and request rebirth but must cease to do so if she refuses their request" (Sharp 1986, 259).[4]

This is not so, however, according to the Dene Tha, among whom a dead person sometimes comes to a woman to be reincarnated without her knowing. Moreover, when a dead Dene Tha communicates his or her wish to be made again, he or she does so before the woman becomes pregnant. The annunciatory dream may be experienced by the mother-to-be or the father-to-be or a close relative of either. For example, a woman lost a boy and kept dreaming about him for two consecutive years. When she told Dene Tha Elders about her dreams, they told her, "He wants to come back to you, that's why." After she got pregnant, the woman never dreamed of him again. In another case, a man said: "Like Peter, he really loved Jayne. And like when he [Peter] is in his grave, his ghost, I guess you call it, like when she sleeps it comes into her. She dreams about it and she wakes up screaming. Then she knows her baby will be like him." In another case it was the man, not the woman, who repeatedly saw the ghost of his dead cousin, Doug, come to his place. When his daughter was born, she had a dark spot on her face just as Doug had had before. "When we were kids, we lived at Zama," the man explained, and "[my brother] had a dog, really mean. From up onto a wagon box, he [Doug] fell down and got bitten by the dog. He had a scar here [he points to the area of the face that corresponds to his daughter's birthmark]." From birth everyone knows who she is, and everyone addresses her/him accordingly. Her uncle, for instance, called her "my son," and she called him "my father." Having heard numerous accounts of her reincarnation, she also saw the scar on her face as evidence that in her previous incarnation she had been bitten by a dog. Her life history thus included a typical Dene Tha journey from our land to the other land at death, and back to our land through reincarnation.

Visions of a Deceased Person

Dene Tha distinguish between sightings of a ghost in an annunciatory dream and observations of a ghost's movements in broad daylight in a vision. Following such a vision, everyone in an extended family was eagerly awaiting the birth of a deceased relative. Referring to her cousin's pregnancy, a woman commented: "Grandpa sees that guy around that place [points to her cousin's house across the road] and he [the ghost] doesn't come out; then you know a reincarnation is going to happen. She [names cousin] is bringing him back; we are all just waiting." In another household a man saw his late mother-in-law come in his house and then disappear. A month later, when his daughter announced she was pregnant, he could tell her who was being reincarnated. A similar process of interpretation is at work in the following case reported by a Dene Tha woman: "My dad saw me standing in a field, and my [late uncle] was walking toward me. When he got to me, he disappeared. Then he [my father] knew it was going to be a reincarnation." They knew a man was about to come back to them; nevertheless, a girl was born. As the girl grew, she demonstrated psychological traits, such as stubbornness, that were reminiscent of her grandfather's late brother. When interacting with the girl, the grandfather told her who she was: "You are my brother." Recollections of past activities and past interactions became part of the child's socialization, and she came to know herself, as others knew her, as her grandfather's brother reincarnated. Her relative's use of appropriate kinship terms of address reflected this continuing identity.

Personality Similarities

When a person is made again, people expect his or her personality to manifest itself again in the newborn child. "It is just the spirit that comes back, all the traits," says a woman. These traits include psychological characteristics such as stubbornness or joviality, as well as likes and dislikes of certain people, objects, foods, or activities. A young girl is known to be as stubborn and quick-tempered as her great-uncle. Her grandfather tells her that she used to be his brother and that they were always fighting when drinking. Commenting on her four-year-old daughter, a woman says: "She sits quiet, just like Jose [whom she was in her previous incarnation]. She likes music, and as soon as he hears it, she dances." (In Dene Dháh the third-person singular pronoun is neutral; there is no distinction between "he" and "she." Thus the Dene Tha alternate between the English pronouns "he" and "she" to refer to the same individual, as in the statement above.) In other Dene families children who liked dancing to the music on the radio were seen as the reincarnation of relatives who used to do the same. In the same vein, a father says of his daughter: "My grandmother used to love oranges; my dad would buy her lots. This girl just loves them too." The child grows up hearing not that she is like her grandmother but that she is her grandmother made again, liking oranges in this life just as she liked them in her previous life. And so it is, in some respects, with most Dene Tha children; their likes and dislikes and their dominant personality traits are those that they had in a previous incarnation.

Waking Recollections from Past Lives
Dene Tha expect someone who has died and has come back to be made again to remember events from his or her previous life. Dene Tha compare the soul's journey to the other land and back to our land to a trip I might make to and from the nearby town of High Level. Having made the trip, I would remember having been to High Level and could also reorient myself easily in Chateh, since I would find myself once again in familiar surroundings. So it is with someone who is made again.

Accounts locally constituted as recollections of a previous life enter all kinds of conversations in houses, at the local store, or at the band office. For instance, in the local store I heard Dene Tha men jokingly remind a mature Dene Tha woman of the time she had been a male among them and could join them in all-male drinking bouts in the bush. She was not expected to join them now, as this would not be consistent with her present life as a wife, mother, and grandmother. She, like other children who are identified as cases of cross-sex reincarnation, is not expected to dress and behave like a member of the opposite sex.

A woman who sees her six-year-old daughter as the reincarnation of her late uncle says: "She [the daughter] said, 'I had lots of money and lost it all. Money is really not important.' Her uncle was a rich man. He had lots of money when he died. She says things like that." According to her parents, the girl says such things because she remembers her condition in her past life. Concerning her five-year-old son, a woman says that he is Bob's, her brother's, best friend: "He likes to see Bob; he likes to visit. 'Why you like come to visit me?' Bob asked. 'Because we used to go together,' he said." In another family parents discussed the case of Lucy, a thirty-year-old deceased daughter, recently reincarnated. When Lucy comes to her previous home, she goes directly to her former mother's room. There the girl does as she used to do when living there as an adult with a child of her own: "She takes lipstick and other things to color her eyes and lips." Not only that, the child remembers where her mother used to keep her money. "She takes my purse and takes money out. Whatever she takes, even twenty dollars, I let her go with it. No one told her that. She knows. She is only two years old and she knows," explains the mother. Lucy had had a child in her previous life, a child who is still living with her earlier family. Accordingly, when Lucy visits her former home, she looks at this child and calls him "my baby." Members of Lucy's former household are convinced that since "nobody told her it's her son," it follows that she recognizes him, indeed that she recognizes all of them, from her previous life.

Birthmarks

As evidence of their reincarnation, people would often point to a birthmark that somehow related to their previous incarnation. Individuals could do so because their parents and relatives had constantly pointed out the birthmark as part of the evidence leading them to conclude that a reincarnation had taken place. "When she died, she got burnt; that's her scar on my baby's face. All her hair was burnt, gone away; my baby had no hair," says a

Dene Tha. "She died in a car accident; her face was all cut. When Lucy was born, you can see the scar above her eyes on her forehead and in the back too, a scar," says another. And so, depending on the child's physical characteristics, a red mark across the head or on the back of a newborn baby, lines suggestive of an old scar on a leg or a wrist, a few white hairs on the head are all seen as "the same marks" that the individual had in his or her previous incarnation.[5]

CASES OF REINCARNATION

What Ian Anderson and J. R. E. Lee (1982, 307) write about case studies in the social sciences applies equally well to the Dene Tha presentation of their cases of reincarnation: "Cases do not exist as 'cases' in the world, independently of the ways in which they are displayed and used as cases." Concerning the Dene thinking process at work in making the case that an individual is reincarnated, Moore suggests that "you have to infer the presence of something from seeing parts of its effects, parts of the effects you would expect if 'it' was there" (personal communication, 1982). This thinking process is what Karla Poewe (1994, 234) calls a "metonymic pattern of thought," that is, "the habit of seeing a simple happening as an aspect of a whole that caused it, even when that whole is but tacitly known." Following Leach (1976), Poewe (1994, 244–45) distinguishes three aspects of metonymy: sign (A stands for B as part of a whole), index (A indicates B), and signal (A triggers or causes B). This pattern of thought is at work among the Dene Tha, who see A, a physical or psychological characteristic of a child, as being a signal of, being part of, and being caused by B, a reincarnation. So, for instance, A, gray hair on an infant's head, is a sign, a part of an individual's previous incarnation (B). The tuft of hair also serves as an index (A), since it indicates B, which triggered A in the first place. "In this sense metonymic thought is revelation and metonym a vehicle that makes known personally a reality that is otherwise invisible and independent" (Poewe 1994, 235).

People say that the deceased "come back to girls or women who are ready to have children." Slobodin (1994a, 137) reports the case of a Peel River Kutchin woman, Lucy Martin, who left her body when she was over eighty years old in search of a new mother to be born again. In Lucy Martin's words: "I had to find a new mother, some woman who was going to have a baby. I thought of Rowena, Andrew's wife. . . . But she was not going to have a baby. . . . Nobody in camp was. I could not be born again. . . . I had to go back." Lucy then came back to her body to recover and live another ten years. A Dene Tha woman who dreamed repeatedly of her mother's sister reported the following: "Once she was saying that she wants to come back to me [to be born again] one more time. I was talking to her in my dream, and I told her that I am supposed to go see the doctor again and see what I could do. She was crying and I was crying. And I woke up, and I had my tears."

A woman who had made up her mind not to have more children, under any circumstances, gave the following account of a ghost who was roaming around her in order to be reincarnated: "When I was living in the log house, I was coming home when it was dark; all of a sudden I saw a woman coming toward me; she was wearing a red dress and had black hair; she was coming from the graveyard; she was coming closer and closer to me. I had my rosary in my hand, and I put it around my neck. I knew this woman was [names her]. She kept coming every night. Finally I told [my sister] Anna, I told her I don't feel good, and I asked what is wrong with me. She told me, you better tell our dad. I told him; he gave me water to drink and he blew over me. He told me that woman wanted to be reincarnated. He told me he could see her spirit around the house every evening, trying to get close to me." In this instance both father and daughter saw the ghost who wanted to be reincarnated. To prevent any ghost from coming too close to her at night, the daughter wore a rosary. The father, who supported her decision not to bear more children, used his own power to chase the ghost away, thus freeing his daughter from an unwanted visitor. In this case, there was no consideration of what might be done to assist the ghost in its wish to be reborn.[6]

Ghosts of the dead can come to a woman without her knowing it, as was the case with Myrna's first child. When Myrna became pregnant at nineteen years of age, four months after beginning to live with her husband, she had no indication that her newborn girl was someone reincarnated. Soon after birth, when the daughter became sick, refused to take her mother's breast, and cried endlessly, Myrna went to consult her grandfather. "When they are going to help a person with their power, they know they are going to use their power, they dream about it a day ahead," she said. The grandfather had in effect dreamed of a small baby, and in the morning he had told his wife, "At our old age, why do I dream like that?" The same day the sick baby was brought to his house. "That is what I was dreaming," he told Myrna and her husband. The grandfather began to sing; he took the baby in his hands and kept on singing until she calmed down and went to sleep. He then told the mother and father that "the baby was kind of lost because there was a really old lady that had passed away many years ago, and kept wandering on this earth, and finally she went back to you. This is who the baby is."

The grandfather explained that since Myrna and her husband were in the habit of driving around at night and drinking, with their baby in the car, the baby did not know if it should stay with the parents or leave them. Although the grandfather never identified this old woman, Myrna was satisfied that she now knew what the trouble was with her little girl. In Myrna's words: "For myself, I never knew I had a reincarnated baby before my grandfather told me. We got married, and I guess it just happened that she found us. In 1969 I didn't know birth control existed, I couldn't. I was with [my husband] three months, and he wanted to have a baby right away; the fourth month, I guess that is when the wandering soul found us. I never thought I would have a child so soon."

Dene Tha note that a sexually active couple may remain without a child for a few years, and further that conception often occurs after the wife or husband has seen a deceased relative coming back to them to be born again. Indeed, many Dene Tha couples say they have conceived a child only after having seen a deceased relative coming back to be born again. Dene Tha also recognize that in the past twenty years a significant number of women have been sterilized, in some cases, it is said, without their full informed consent. Other women use contraceptives. These new facts of life have had a profound impact on the lives of Dene Tha males and females, living and dead. In two of the cases described below Dene Tha express the view that sexually active teenagers become pregnant because of all the people wandering around in the hope of being reincarnated and finding that no other female is available.

The first case is that of Luke, who came back to his father's brother's daughter to be born again. The account is told by Luke's aunt: "Andrew's brother, his boy died. Not long after, I went to visit Susan [Andrew's wife]. Andrew started to talk about this little boy [Luke, his brother's dead son], and Andrew was crying like a baby. He said: 'Why nowadays do these women have to use birth control? I've seen Luke standing at a corner of the house. It was raining, and the wind was blowing. He had no place to go. He had no choice but to come to my house; that is how my girl is pregnant.' Beverley [Andrew's daughter] had a boy [Luke, reincarnated]." On a separate occasion I heard a similar account of a man crying as he told of his pregnant teenage daughter. The man stated that the dead relative had no choice but to come to his daughter, as few other women of childbearing age were available to come back to, because they had been sterilized. The cycle of reincarnation can continue only through fertile women, and in the eyes of some Dene Tha, these women are now likely to be young adolescents. Ghosts or souls of the dead are, therefore, of particular concern to young women. When asked why she and her younger siblings were wearing ribbons, a young woman told me: "It's to protect, especially those who go out at night. Because we live close to the cemetery, like us girls could get pregnant; strange how this happens."

When young adolescents are attracted to each other and begin sleeping with each other in the home of either partner, some parents, including the speaker quoted above, do not interfere with their child's preferences and activities. "How could I tell her not to, he looked so pitiful," said a Dene Tha mother of the teenager who had moved in to sleep with her daughter in her house. Whether this permissiveness is new or not is an open question. It takes on an added meaning in the light of the parents' desire to have their deceased relatives "be made again" and the parents' knowledge that fewer and fewer people in their generation can bring someone back to this land. The question remains, What do the tears of fathers represent? Sorrow at the thought that they themselves will not father more children through their wives?

Guilt at seeing their daughters visited by dead relatives who would have preferred to be made again in the wombs of the preceding generation of women? Or some other motive that Dene Tha are aware of and that I have not yet identified in the course of my fieldwork?[7]

A GRADUAL PROCESS OF IDENTIFICATION

Dene Tha accounts of cases of reincarnation indicate that the identification of someone as a reincarnated person is sometimes a gradual process. In some cases, one crucial event is remembered as conclusive evidence that an earlier identification was correct. Consider the following example. Beverley, the woman who gave birth to her father's brother, also gave birth to one of her father's hunting partners. Her father had dreams of his late partner and suspected that this man might soon be born again to his pregnant daughter. The child had reached the stage when she was grasping things and taking them to her mouth; one day she began to cry and could not be consoled by anyone in the household. Many objects were offered to the child, who simply kept crying. The baby's grandfather then said, "Try give her an onion." The mother gave the child an onion, and the child, she said, "grabs it and . . . eats it. She is really happy."

According to the mother of the child, everyone in the family, except the baby's grandfather, was surprised at this ending to an unusual spell of crying. The grandfather had had a dream of his hunting friend wandering around his house but had kept the dream to himself. Soon thereafter his daughter had become pregnant. Following the birth of the child, the grandfather had expected other signs that would confirm his suspicion that his close friend had reincarnated through his daughter, hence his suggestion that the child be given an onion, as the late hunting partner was known for his love of onions. After the child ate the onion, the man told the family that the baby was his hunting partner. The family doubted, as indeed I did myself, that any other child in the community would have grasped an onion and eaten it so eagerly. The fact that this child did precisely that was interpreted as evidence that a hunting partner was back and alive, growing among them as a young girl.

From Dene Tha accounts of reincarnation I understand that

the individual going into a woman to be born comes to her with a clear sexual identity—it is a known male or female who comes back to a kinswoman to be born again. When the child is born in a sex opposite to its previous sex, the previous sex determines what kinship terms of address are used. In turn, these kinship terms of address trigger a wide range of accounts of the child's previous life that progressively enter that child's sense of its own identity. The grandmother who constantly greeted her grandson with the exclamation *Aa, tsido ndadlinhi*, "Aa, the child who is made again," set the stage for others to engage in recollections of events allegedly lived by the child in an earlier life. So also did the man who told his one-year-old reincarnated nephew, "So you decided to leave this place, too much trouble." The child immediately voiced a clear "aan," which the man took to be the child's confirmation of what had been said. In the context of such interactions and recollections, adults teach a child knowledge that is culturally defined as recollections of a past life. The implication of this process of socialization is that one's sense of identity is mediated by others who "know" because they "saw" the spirit come back to be made again. Cumulative knowledge of oneself as a reincarnated individual is, thus, always predicated on someone's true knowledge.

Consider the case of the reincarnation of Nancy, who was accidentally shot in the head by a boy carrying a hunting rifle. Her family and I had seen the young girl leave happily with friends in the morning to go to a nearby river. Her tragic death had led to a very emotional wake and burial. Relatives and friends were torn between an intense grief at the loss of the girl and an equally deep anger at the hunter, who had not emptied the barrel of his rifle at the end of his hunting journey. Such were the circumstances when I left Chateh to return to Ottawa after a six-month period of fieldwork, the third in three consecutive years. Nancy's death was to have a major impact on my involvement in the Dene community, beginning with a vision of Nancy while I was back in Ottawa.

Imagine the setting: a large university auditorium in which more than 150 participants were listening to sociologists, historians, theologians, and a Metis shaman discuss the topic of secularization. As I listened to the shaman tell of experiences of spirits among indigenous people in the Canadian North, my eye was caught suddenly by an apparition to my right, in midair. I couldn't believe my eyes. I saw Nancy, looking at me, smiling, and extending open hands toward me. The life-size figure was radiant with light and smiled as it moved a little closer to me from a distance of approximately fifty feet. I looked at Nancy, then turned my eyes toward the podium. Yes, the speaker was still there. I looked at my hand and at the paper on which I had been taking notes. Yes, I was wide-awake. I looked back up to my right. Yes, Nancy was still there. A few moments later the vision subsided, Nancy disappeared, and everything returned to "normal."[8]

The following January, when I was back among the Dene Tha, I visited Nancy's mother and grandparents to tell them of my vision. They listened attentively and thanked me for reporting it to them. A few days later one of Nancy's relatives came to visit me:

> Is it true that you saw [her] when you were in Ottawa?
>
> Yes.
>
> What was it? Was it in a dream?
>
> No. It was during a meeting. All of a sudden I saw [her]. We were more than one hundred people in a large room, with an Elder talking about Indian religion, when it happened.
>
> Me too. I saw [her]. One night last summer, I was dreaming and woke up. I looked outside and [she] was sitting on a pile of wood, smiling to me. Very peaceful. I told her grandma I saw [her], and to keep praying, that she would see [her] too.

The conversation begins with the question, "Is it true?" The speaker had obviously heard of my report to Nancy's parents and grandparents. The relative asked about my state of consciousness when I saw Nancy: "Was it in a dream?" I answered that I had not been dreaming but was wide awake, at a meeting. The relative then offered her account of a sighting: she too had seen Nancy, not in a dream but in a wide-awake state.

Two weeks later, while I was visiting with another family, the mother asked when I had seen Nancy:

When did this happen? [She appears excited, wants to know.]

It happened in August. I told a few friends over there [in Ottawa], then I told the mother and grandmother. They were happy to hear that.

Yeah. I can just see it. It is very nice. She was coming back to say good-bye to you. Trying to tell someone she was becoming like a little angel, that she was OK. Yes, that's it.

Through conversations such as these I became aware of an emerging process of reciprocity. Dene Tha adults were offering accounts of visions and interpretations of them in response to my own sharing with them of the experience I had had in Ottawa. They were no longer too reticent to talk about their experiences. Each conversation drew me into deeper and deeper participation in the family dynamics associated with the expectation that Nancy was to reincarnate.

At the beginning of February I paid a visit to Lois, Nancy's maternal grandmother. Lois told that me that her brother, Arthur, had had a dream and that on the basis of that dream had announced that his daughter, Roberta, was now pregnant with Nancy. A reincarnation was on the way. Lois asked me to pay a visit to Roberta and "tell her she should refrain from drinking, traveling, and getting beaten up, for the baby she is carrying is not her baby but our baby." During the pregnancy Lois and her daughters continually referred to Roberta's child as "my baby" or "our baby." When I conveyed the message as instructed, Roberta offered additional information concerning other reincarnations that had occurred in her family.

In due time a child was born, but it was a boy, not a girl. After the birth Lois's daughter, Marcella, told me the following:

My girl called me the other night and told me our little girl [Nancy] had come to her. She had dreamed of her. In her dream I was standing by the coffin but the coffin was empty. She saw Nancy running home across the field. She was all OK except for her front teeth; they were a little rusty. Nancy told her that Mom [Lois] should not worry about her, that she is coming back this time as a boy, that she always wanted to be a boy. That is true, she always had her slingshot and didn't want to play with her dolls. They called her tomboy. They say she came back as this little boy of Roberta's. And I would not have believed it if it wasn't for this tuft of black hair, just here [she points to the location where the injury had been inflicted], and the rest is just baby hair.

This account of a dream specifies that Nancy is coming back as a boy of her own free will. The tuft of black hair on the boy's head, in the location where the girl had suffered her fatal injury, is seen as physical evidence that the boy is indeed the girl reincarnated.

On 27 June 1983, when I went with Marcella to see the baby at Roberta's house, Marcella picked the baby up, held it near, kissed it, and then showed me the conspicuous tuft of black hair behind his ear and temple. At least an inch long, it clearly stood out on a head otherwise covered with thinly spaced, light-colored baby hair. To my surprise, Marcella then looked at me and said, "Now you believe!" Marcella appeared convinced that this "evidence" would convince me that the child was Nancy reincarnated, as predicted by her uncle's dream and confirmed by her daughter's dream.

KNOWING ONESELF AS SOMEONE MADE AGAIN

When Europeans and Euro–North Americans think of auto-biography, they include events that have occurred in the world of everyday life. When Dene, and many other Native Americans, think of autobiography, they include events that they or others have perceived in dreams or in visions. Knowledge derived from these sources is of vital importance in determining who one is and in developing a shared sense of personal identity. This is obvious, for instance, in the following account by Paul, in his late twenties, of his death as a girl and reincarnation as a boy (this is not the same individual, also named Paul, referred to in chapter 1). In this account Paul presents knowledge that he shares with other Dene Tha concerning his identity: he was not the man he appeared to be; he was really Denise.

The transcript of Paul's account recorded in March 1984 is presented in four segments:[9]

I was a little girl [Denise] growing up at the residence [the mission residential school] and then one day I got sick. I

went to the hospital and died over there. And one year later
I came back with Rose [his mother's deceased sister] holding
my arm. I came back to the hospital in Edmonton where my
mother Rita is, and I came back to live as Paul.

"I was a little girl." Paul immediately identifies himself as a little
girl and tells of his/her death in the first-person singular. He is
she. She is also he who came back to live as a boy. There is obviously more to a person's identity than meets the eye. Paul's account of his life continues as follow:

My mother was in the hospital [in Edmonton], and while she
went to the hospital her sister Rose died. And she [Rose]
came in [the hospital room] and said, "I am walking to you
with [Denise]." [My mother] said Rose told her, "I arrive
here next to you for her [Denise] to be born again." Then
[my mother] went out. "I fell unconscious," Mom said. [De-
nise] grabbed her from behind. "I fell unconscious," she
said. From there Rose went to the neighbors [back in
Chateh] and was made again. She is Hubert. My mother
calls him "my sister" because of that.

Paul takes for granted that after death Rose and Denise somehow found each other. Rose does not, as Dene Tha often mention, take advantage of a child's death to follow it on its way to
heaven. Rather, Rose has in mind her own reincarnation as well
as that of her niece, Denise. Paul refers to himself/herself in the
third person as the one who grabs his mother from behind to be
reincarnated. In a subsequent commentary on this segment of
his narration Paul emphasized that his mother, Rita, was awake
when she saw her sister and Denise walk into her hospital room.

Paul carried on with his account of his reincarnation with a reference to a birthmark on his abdomen that corresponded to a
similar mark evident in his previous incarnation as Denise:

You want to see the birthmark? [He raises his shirt and
shows me a pale line one inch long on his abdomen.] It is
[Denise's] birthmark. I am a man who came back. That is
why when I was young I looked like a girl. Wilbert's mother,
she knows that I am his sister. They knew I came back. They
always told me who I was.

His kinsmen could tell him who he was because of the cumulative evidence they had that this was so: his mother's vision in the hospital, his grandfather's annunciatory dream in Chateh, and at birth the mark on his abdomen. Because people know this, they use the relevant kinship term of address: Wilbert addresses Paul as his sister, and Wilbert's mother addresses Paul as her daughter.

In the last segment of the account of his cross-sex reincarnation Paul comments on his parents' reaction when he was born as a boy and not a girl:

> I will be a baby girl, they thought. But I [a boy] was. Now they knew that I had come back, and they loved me very much. If I put my hair behind, from a distance I am as a woman, and when they tell me I am a girl, I colour my eyes and my mouth, and sometimes they ask me to put my hair behind like this [pulls his hair back in a ponytail], and they tell me: "Yes, you look like a woman."

It is because they know who is coming back to be made again that Paul's parents and relatives do not question his male sexual identity at birth. Household members, however, asked him for a moment to manifest more clearly his underlying sexual identity. He did so through changes in hairstyle, mannerisms, and use of cosmetics. Paul then appeared before them as the woman he is.

One may view gender identity as the constellation of meanings "associated with being male or female," meanings that guide the behavior of individuals as they "respond to themselves as objects along the male-female dimension of meanings (Burke et al. 1988), that is, as more masculine or feminine, or as a mixture" (Stets 1995, 131). According to this perspective Paul's alternate presentations of self as either man or woman is "grounded in 'shared stereotypes' of masculinity and femininity" (1995, 131). Paul may emphasize one aspect or the other of his dual personal identity; he is a female, Denise reincarnated, and a male, the boy Denise was reincarnated as. His presentation of self always proceeds according to locally recognized markers of gender identity. Others, therefore, readily recognize him as such: now a man, now a woman.

However satisfying analytically, this account falls short of grasping how Paul's identity and behavior were understood by himself and by those with whom he interacted. Paul's behavior can be understood when we take into full consideration the complex set of indigenous ideas that provide the context for the Dene Tha presentation of self as a male in a female body or vice versa, a female in a male body. Seeing Paul as a female in a male body is possible within the context of a knowledge system in which the concept of the soul/spirit is associated with the idea of a person being made again, which gives rise at times to individuals reincarnating in a sex opposite to the one in which they lived their previous lives (Slobodin 1994b). Like other Northern Athapaskans, Dene Tha also expect that those reincarnated in a sex other than the one they had in a previous existence will eventually marry and have children of their own. In other words, regardless of one's antecedent sexual identity, one eventually engages as an adult with an opposite-sex partner in the procreative business of life.

This, however, was not the case with Paul. Among the many instances of cross-sex reincarnation in Chateh, Paul was alone in having identified himself so strongly with his previous gender identity. The other women and men of his age who had experienced cross-sex reincarnation were definitely living their lives as the men or women they had reincarnated as. Among them were successful married local entrepreneurs and industrious individuals, all with spouses and children of their own. Somehow Paul had not evolved as they had. Paul had spent much of his preadolescence in all-girl company and had taken pleasure in not being recognized as a boy. When I first met him, he was in his late twenties and still single. When young men congregated in the bush for all-male beer parties, Paul was not among them. Although invited, Paul did not join the young unmarried men and women in the abandoned house they use for parties and sex. The walls of this house were covered with drawings of male and female figures engaged in sexual intercourse, along with drawings of hearts and genitals. In 1981, among these drawings, I noticed two hearts, one with a cherry within, the other with a penis within. Around these two hearts, one next to the other, was the following inscription: "Paul never broke his cherry. I don't know how to break Paul's cherry, but someday I break his cherry for her."

Although Paul did not take part in the parties held in this house, sex was certainly on his mind, as shown in the following account of a dream he had shortly before his first experience of sex with a young woman. The dream involves John, his very close friend, who has fathered children with a number of young Dene Tha women. In the opening scene of the dream Paul sees John holding a woman lying in thick dry grass: "They were on a big prairie; I am there too, and there is a woman I want. I tell John: 'There are no woman for me, not one of them likes me.' But John says: 'Go for it, that woman is your woman, go play with her over there.' And I woke up. Those women. I knew who they were; but when I woke up I did not remember." Immediately after recounting his dream, Paul asked me, "Is it bad to do witchcraft on somebody?" I asked, "Why would you want to do witchcraft on someone?" He answered, "I want some people to do something I want them to do." He showed me a pocket-size magazine advertising witchcraft spells and love potions for sale. "Like I would make love with them, I would make them turn into lovers, it's for myself," he said. Paul then added that he had recently had a private encounter with a young woman who had kissed him. He attributed her attitude and behavior to someone's power making her interested in him.

The drawing of the two hearts publicly stated the problem as Paul's peers saw it. His body was obviously that of a male, yet he carried within his personal identity that of a female. His cherry, the marker of his female identity, had to be broken; his penis, the sign of his male identity, had to be affirmed. Paul's dream and his secret encounter with a young woman who kissed him reflected his own inclination to change his past. A radical transformation was called for if Paul were to evolve into adulthood in the expected relationship with an opposite sex partner. This was initiated by his peers. In the mid-1980s news circulated around the community that Paul's cherry had finally been broken. Young men and women had finally succeeded in having Paul join them at a drinking party where they had him have sex with a young woman from the group. For a week or so after the event, Paul was constantly teased in public, in the store, at church, on the road, with people asking him in Dene Dháh if he had enjoyed himself. Paul would invariably laugh with them, acknowledging that the experience had, indeed, taken place and that it had given him much pleasure. Following his sexual initiation Paul emerged in the community with a complete personal identity that he did not have before, that of an active heterosexual male who had enjoyed himself with an opposite-sex partner.[10]

Dene Tha knowledge of oneself and of others is, thus, continuously produced and reproduced on the basis of what is taken to be true knowledge. What is locally taken as true knowledge is in many instances private knowledge that cannot be controlled and falsified. Did the parents really see Denise come back to be reincarnated as they report? The fact is that, in Chateh, information presented as derived from dreams and visions is generally accepted as true knowledge. This is shown in the social implications of such knowledge. Someone who knows someone else as a same-sex or an opposite-sex relative reincarnated behaves accordingly, addressing the child with appropriate kinship terms, teasing the child with reminiscences of activities in his or her past life, and so on. The ones who claim knowledge of one's true identity are always adults and parents. The child's construction of his or her social identity is then based on someone else's true knowledge, and the statements the child will eventually make concerning a previous life are based on information he or she has learned from people in his or her environment.

SEEING IS BELIEVING

Time after time, Dene Tha told me that the soul of the person one raises as a reincarnated relative is also present in heaven. Dene Tha prayed to a relative they thought of in heaven when in need of assistance in stressful and difficult situations. They maintained that this relative had returned to them to "be made again" and raised by them as a child. This was the case with the husband and wife whose visit I described in the opening chapter of this book. They mentioned their reincarnated daughter as someone in heaven to whom they could pray for a positive outcome to her brother's trial. "Would you believe the daughter we lost came back to us through some Indian superstition, through three persons we paid. We went to superstition people, his dad [her father-in-law], Brock, and Brian, and they helped us with their power. They had her done to us again. We did not want a boy to come; she was done again as a girl," said the mother. No sooner had she concluded her statement than her husband added the following: "My daughter has become an angel. I pray to my father, I pray to my daughter, and to my sister-in-law [also dead]. 'My daughter, help me, remember your brother; my baby, you have become an angel. Your mother is my wife. Look at your sister, at your brother.' I pray to her with my mind." The man paused and then reiterated that it is with his mind that he prays by himself: "I think about them, and if something happens, she helps me. When I go to sleep, I also pray to my child, my sister-in-law, my father. I don't tell my wife. It's with my mind I pray."

"Superstition people" is an expression that Dene Tha often used to refer to someone who knows an animal, *Dene wonlin edadíhi*. Although the husband agrees with his wife that their daughter has been made again as a girl, he adds that she has become an angel, the word used to refer to *yak'e wodené*, "people of heaven." Listening to them talk, I remained confused. How could they claim to have had her reincarnate and still in heaven as an angel? I asked them, "How is it you pray to her and you say she is in your house, reincarnated?" The husband said, "Every individual has a soul, *mbetsuné andats'edla*, 'they made her soul be made again to us.'" The wife immediately added, "My little girl, she has a birthmark on her leg and also here [she touches her right wrist]. Now this little baby has the same marks. On her leg her marks are still to be seen. That is why she is my daughter, I know."

They were not addressing the issue I had in mind, so I insisted that I could not understand how they could pray to their daughter in heaven while they claimed she was with them at home. The man then grabbed the lid of a coffee jar lying on the table. He placed it next to me, removed his hand, and said, "Take it!" I moved my hand to pick the lid up, but he quickly removed it. He looked at me and said, "See you can't take it; you would have to fight me." He then let go of the lid, and again told me, "Take it!" This second time, he let me do so. He then said: "See, you can take it. I tell you everything. We teach you, we say everything to you. If there is a guy who doesn't know anything, if you don't say the right words, and we don't like it, you are in trouble. We don't like it. Like you write what we tell you, we could walk away, we go away, what do you do? Nothing, you can't write anymore." I suddenly understood that I was not saying the right words, that my questions were rude and insensitive. Their patience was running short. I could easily alienate them, in which case they would leave and I would have nothing to write. Dene Tha speakers clearly expected the uncooperative listener who questions what Dene Tha normally take for granted to change his attitude. As demonstrated again and again in the course of this book, the task of communicating Dene Tha views can proceed only with the tacit acceptance of specific notions of personhood, agency, and powerfulness, which Dene Tha leave unexamined when they adopt the natural attitude, as they must if they are to carry on with their lives responsibly and effectively.[11] As I lifted the lid of the coffee jar, I told him that I understood what he meant. We proceeded quietly again, as I took notes and they offered more information related to animal helpers and their powers.

When the husband and wife left, I still had not understood how or why people could hold such apparently contradictory propositions. I decided to take the matter up with Dene Tha friends whom I was in the habit of consulting when confused about observations I had made or information I had received. I told them that I could not understand how people could say they were praying to a child in heaven and also hold that that child was with them in their house, as someone reincarnated. Without a moment's hesitation, the friend answered: "Yeah, it is possible, it can happen. They die, the parents know they become angels, but the parents, somehow or another, they know when he is reincarnated. There is always a sign to know it is their child that is reincarnated. . . . Yeah, everybody knows that a kid who is clean and has no sins becomes an angel when he dies." I reminded my friend that the parents insisted that the child was not only an angel but also born again. "They know, there are signs," was the answer. I then said one would have to conclude that the child is in two places, to which the friend simply affirmed: "That's the way it is." My friend's response to my puzzlement was similar to the one given by the husband and wife. They, like other Dene Tha I talked to, did not think that everyone has two souls, one going to heaven, the other coming back to be reincarnated. They simply stated that they knew a deceased may be in two places at one time. They presented me with facts of life, normative propositions about themselves and their place in the wider scheme of things.

When I persisted in raising the issue of apparent contradiction with my friends, they said they did not understand how I could see a contradiction in the first place. Taking a cup as an example, I said, "If you tell me it is here on the table and that it is also in the kitchen, then I could say to you, 'It's either on the table or in the kitchen, but it cannot be in two places at the same time.'" My friend immediately answered: "But talking about something we can see, it can create problems. But it is things you can't see but you believe in, it's faith." Clearly, a Dene Tha could be an angel and a reincarnated individual at the same time.

Although I easily accepted their remark that I had erred in thinking of things we cannot see as if they were things we could see, I was puzzled at their statement that this was a matter of "faith." When asked how they would say this in Dene Dháh, they said they could not really say it. The expression they would use was equivalent to "things that I say that are true." In Dene Dháh the question is not, "Do you believe me?" but, "According to you, do I tell the truth?" And how does one answer? One answers negatively or positively, either on the basis of what one truly knows on the grounds of personal experience (including dreams and/or visions) or on the basis of one's confidence in the speaker's claim of things he or she knows firsthand.

Things being so, I asked my Dene Tha friend what would happen if I told someone *Dene andats'edla úh mbeyuné edu yak'e k'eh at'in*, "the person is made again and her soul is not in heaven." Her response was emphatic: "If you say that, the parents will think you laugh at them or don't believe them. . . . They might think you are mocking their faith; it is going to upset them. I would think the parents believe that you believe in the same thing. If you say that, they think you laugh at them." I immediately reassured her that this was certainly not my intention but that I still had difficulty accepting what I was being told. She insisted there were signs that make people believe: "If someone like you has doubts about it, there are signs to show you, signs that people can show you, to make you believe." "What kinds of signs?" I asked. "Like the people that had died had scars, or habits of doing something make people recognize who they were before," she replied.

A birthmark held to resemble a mark on the person in a previous incarnation is a sign—a tuft of hair at the spot on a baby's head equivalent to the place where the person, in an earlier incarnation, had received a mortal injury, or a dark line at a place where the person had been bitten by a dog. The work that goes into making the tuft of hair or the dark line evidence of reincarnation is immense. What constitutes a dark line? How dark does it have to be? How close does it have to be to the site of the injury sustained in the earlier incarnation? How closely must it resemble in shape or size? All the work that interprets the actual mark as "good enough" for the purpose at hand is smoothly achieved and goes unnoticed. That the mark is evidence seems obvious to the Dene Tha: "Now you believe!" exclaims Marcella when she shows me the tuft of hair in the "right place." Had she spoken in Dene Dháh, she would have said: "Now you know that I say the truth!"

When listening to Dene Tha accounts of their beliefs and behavior and looking for logical consistency, I erred, as Hultkrantz had done when he interviewed Harold Cook, a twenty-two-year-old Hare Indian visiting in Stockholm.[12] This interview demonstrated to Hultkrantz "the tenacity with which some youths today cling to the past heritage, and particularly that part of it which contains the life values—religion" (1973, 114). Of interest to Hultkrantz was the belief held by Harold and his family that he was the reincarnation of his mother's father. Indeed, Harold is known among the Hare by the name of his forefather, Little Fox. Harold said "that each year his grandmother walks to her husband's grave on his death day and sings to him" (Hultkrantz 1973, 140). Hultkrantz immediately discounted the information, dismissing it on the grounds that the grandmother's attitude was "incompatible with the belief in reincarnation" (Hultkrantz 1973, 148 n. 47). Hultkrantz assumed, as I did among the Dene Tha, that if the grandmother really believed that her husband had been reincarnated as Harold Cook, she would not engage in the activities reported by her grandson. To see as logically inconsistent the fact that the grandmother believes in reincarnation and prays at the grave of someone reincarnated is an indication of the tenacity with which we hold to the principle of identity (*A* but not its contrary *B* can be true of *x*) when we consider other people's beliefs. We then fail to follow other people into their own experience world and thinking. When we examine the anthropological and historical records, we realize that the Hare and the Dene Tha share "the almost universal conviction that the dead are present both on earth and in a spiritual world," a view that "reveals the secret hope that, in spite of all evidence to the contrary, the dead are able to partake somehow in the world of the living" (Eliade 1977, 19). Who are we then to object to the Dene view that someone is in the other world and in this world reincarnated? Who are we to reject the presentation of someone reincarnated not in one but in two different bodies, one male, the other female, living here as a husband and there as a healer's wife? In such instances, if the philosophical principle of identity appears to be violated, this is a problem for the analyst, not for the Dene (G. Watson and Goulet 1998, 99).

A reviewer of the manuscript of this book suggested that further "questioning" of the Dene Tha and more "plumbing of concepts of the soul, breath, spirit and their vocabulary" might allow me to expand on a discussion of reincarnation and of the presence of a soul in both this land and the other land. The reviewer expressed the hope that in the process of such probing I could "learn more" than I have so far learned "about whether a person is likely to have powers from the same animals reincarnation after reincarnation, or whether there is variance on how that works itself out." The reviewer concluded with the observation that "these questions are not easy for Westerners to fathom, but that is what the book is about."

I think this reviewer is looking for a kind of systematization of knowledge concerning these topics that Dene Tha do not produce even if prompted to do so by a visiting anthropologist. American Indian and Inuit concepts of reincarnation are not easily isolated, not only "because they vary widely between groups, and they are embedded in a whole constellation of complex concepts about the nature of humans, animals, trees, birds, and spirits—guardian and otherwise" (Mills 1994a, 7) but, just as important, because they are transmitted and learned in societies that privilege experiential learning over instruction and that require that one keeps for oneself certain things one learns.

Among the Dene there is no well-articulated body of knowledge that is explicitly handed down from generation to generation in the way seniors initiate their juniors in Western scholastic traditions. The Dene, however, share a consistent body of attitude that leads each and every individual to careful consideration of life experience in the light of a long-standing oral tradition and of other stories offered by relatives and friends. In the process of such listening and experiential learning, one—including the visiting anthropologist—makes up one's mind about a number of issues. Questioning is not the avenue to more knowledge, for Dene see direct questioning on any topic as rude and disrespectful.

*

Social identities, like any other social reality, are created and sustained in and through linguistic and social practices. Among the Dene Tha, personal identities are more complex than among Euro–North Americans. First, one's life history often includes an episode in the other land from which one has chosen to come back to this world to be made again. Second, sexual identity is not an unchangeable attribute of the individual. For many, death involves a journey from our land to the other land and back to our land to be made again. There are many signs that tell other Dene Tha in our land that this is the case: annunciatory dreams, visions, similarities between one's present and past personalities, recollections of a previous life, and birthmarks. Parents and kinsmen, who know who the individual is, address the child with appropriate kinship terms and tease the child with reminiscences of activities in his or her past life. Since those who claim knowledge of one's true identity are always adults and parents, a child's construction of his or her social identity is based on their true knowledge. Thus, an individual may accumulate many lives, as male or as female or both.

8. When the Drum and the Rosary Meet

*

When only two people are left on earth,
one to sing and another to dance for him,
this song will not become old, but will
remain fresh. —Dene Tha dreamer

Dene Tha live their lives according to a distinct indigenous tradition. They do so in a social context that includes numerous Western institutions: the school, the police station, the nursing station, and the church. The schoolteachers, the R.C.M.P. officers, the nurse, and the doctors all expect Dene Tha to accept Euro–North American standards of life. These professionals, however, have not eradicated or rendered obsolete Dene ways of teaching, of avoiding open conflict when sober, and of healing. Rather, Dene Tha draw on Western institutions to complement their own practices in the areas of education, social control, and health. A similar form of adaptation can be seen in the Dene Tha response to the presence of missionaries among them.

Nearly all Dene are Christians of one denomination or another, mostly Roman Catholic or Anglican. The question nevertheless remains: Were the missionaries able to "change Dene moral concepts and abolish Dene spiritual values?" (Abel 1989, 81). According to Kerry Abel (1989, 90), a careful analysis of the historical and anthropological record suggests that "the Christian missions did not make profound changes in the daily lives or cultural outlook of the Dene; . . . Christian labels have been applied to non-Christian concepts; Christian rituals have been interwoven with traditional ceremonies." Helm (1994, 70) similarly writes that among the Dogribs "the world of *inkon* and the Christian cosmos do not merge," the former being the world within which contemporary Dogribs, like their predecessors of old, continue to live their lives. This is certainly the case for the contemporary Dene Tha, despite the long-standing efforts of missionaries and educators of all sorts to convince them otherwise.

In chapter 2 I described how I began to go weekly to Alexis Seniantha's house to learn from him the Dene Tha way of praying.
In the third year of our association he asked me to tape and later
write an account of how he became a dreamer. I had already
heard this account on a number of occasions in his home, in the
presence of a few of his relatives. The following discussion of his
status as a Christian Dene Tha dreamer is based on a transcrip-
tion and translation of the tape recording by Pat Moore and a
Dene Tha assistant. A number precedes each full sentence in the
transcript. As the 214-line transcript is too long to present in its
entirety, I focus on four key sections. In the presentation of this
record I add descriptions of gestures Alexis made, since the narration of his story always involved dramatic reenactments of
many of the scenes he had lived in his vision. In fact, parts of the
transcript depend for their meaning on this nonverbal aspect of
the enacted narration.

1. I was dreaming of a person long ago.
2. I was standing this way looking back.
3. I looked far into the past where there were many people
   gathered.
4. "That person standing before you was a prophet," someone said as I dreamed.
5. The prophet was singing and drumming, but I couldn't really follow it all.
6. Maybe toward the end of my time I will know more about
   that vision.
7. Sometimes I sleep and hear singing, and when I wake up, I
   remember everything.
8. I am able to sing songs that I have dreamed in that way.
9. I have lived through difficult times.
10. I almost died during the first vision I experienced.
11. I was extremely weak, reduced to a pitiful state of skin and
    bones.

Alexis thus begins his account with a reference to a dream he had
that he could not really follow and whose meaning may become
clearer toward the end of his life (lines 1–6). This is in contrast to
other dreams from which he remembers everything (lines 7–9).
Alexis then refers to his first vision (lines 10–11), experienced

during a bout of severe illness during which he was cared for by his wife and his brother, Billy Semansha (lines 12–14). Alexis went fifteen days without food or water, too weak to walk on his own. Lifting the skin from his wrist, he says: "I was just skin and bones" (line 23), "I felt pain in my chest and was short of breath" (line 25), "getting weaker and weaker" (line 28). Alexis then began to wonder why he was suffering, thinking to himself, "I don't need to go through this" (line 39). That is when he decided to make an offering:

40. I told the people who were there,
41. "Get me a clean plate, spread out a clean white cloth
42. and bring some white moose fat, tobacco, and tea."
43. There was a campfire nearby.
44. My wife held me up under the armpits, and I crawled to the fire.
45. I prayed with all my strength and put tobacco in the fire.
46. I said, "If I am to die, I should die, and if I am to live, let me live. I am in great pain."
47. My wife put me back where I was lying.
48. I was covered with mosquitoes where I lay sleeping, so she put a mosquito net over me.
49. I don't know what happened to me from that point [he falls unconscious].

It is then that Alexis saw himself standing near a table and heard someone come toward him. A woman came up to him and told him to look in the middle of "a pure white bowl" standing about the same height as his head (lines 52–54). He looked into the bowl, saw something white in the middle, and heard the woman tell him (line 58): "You have not been called yet." Gently touching his hand, the woman told Alexis (line 60): "Back there you will be told something. Move fast." Rather than move, Alexis simply turned his head in the direction the woman indicated he should go:

61. I looked toward the earth but it was difficult for me [he is standing up to tell the next part of the vision].
62. I stood facing toward the sunrise.

63. "Look over there," I was told, and I looked [he moves his head forward and strains his eyes as if to see something in the distance].

64. I was wondering to myself what was moving in the distance.

65. There was a loud buzzing sound as it [a large cross] approached. [He extends his right arm outward, moving his hand clockwise as if winding an alarm bell; cringing, he then puts his two hands facing outward next to his right ear, to protect himself from the noise coming from the alarm bell.]

66. It [the cross] was right at my feet finally, and I was scared.

67. I looked down, and between my feet was a piece of wood the size of a four-by-four beam. [He makes a sign of the cross at his feet to suggest he is standing at its base.]

68. It was suspended ahead of me.

69. "Try it out," I was told.

70. I stood on top, but it was difficult for me [arms extended, he sways back and forth, left and right, to keep his balance, as he looks down at the distant land].

71. Below was a blue expanse.

72. "Hurry up, jump!" they said.

73. The first time, I was scared and couldn't look [he hides his eyes with his right hand].

74. They told me to jump again, but I was still afraid [he turns his head right and left, refusing to look down where he is told to jump; he has difficulty keeping his balance].

75. "The last time you are told to move, if you continue to stay where you are,

76. something will pass in front of you, and you will have no choice of action," they said.

77. I decided to take a chance and sat on the cross with my fingertips touching it.

78. There was a sound of trumpets and everything was going lower,

79. descending right to the treetops.

80. I was told, "Look over there."

81. I could see my bones, and I looked at my body.

82. My wife was resting her head at my feet.

83. I was told, "If you care for her, let it be good."

84. It was difficult.
85. "Look toward the sunrise and down over your people," I was told.
86. "After a while the sun will be coming up toward the east again.
87. "Look over the people," I was told.
88. I thought to myself, "Why is it some can be seen clearly while some look like shadows?"
89. Then I was told, "You will go back soon."
90. I looked again, and a cow moose was being led toward me.
91. There was a rope hanging down from it, and it was being led.
92. They told me:
93. "You will be drifting back to earth, and when you wake, look this way at noon."
94. As I watched, I thought, "I have returned. This is really my land."
95. As I was watching, a sleeping moose appeared.
96. I was told, "Send people to get it. Eat, and then you will return [to heaven for the second part of his vision]."
97. I still remember. [He takes a small cross from his trousers pocket.]
98. "By this sign you will know," they said.
99. I looked at my body below again where I lay sleeping under a mosquito net.
100. "A white bird is going to be sent with you," they told me.
101. I woke up, and my wife had her head at my feet.
102. I tapped her with my foot.

As soon as his wife was awake, Alexis asked for water and food. She piled moose meat, bannock, and duck meat on a plate, all of which he ate (lines 111–12). His wife then noticed a live bird sitting on his pillow (lines 118–19), as predicted in his vision (line 100). Alexis touched the bird (line 120), which stayed on the pillow for a long time. His wife asked him, "What is that bird doing there?" (line 122). After the bird had flown away, Alexis answered (line 125), "That was the message I was told about. It will not be difficult."

Alexis continues his account with a description of the hunting expedition to get the moose he had been told to kill (lines 95–96).

People took Alexis by canoe "around Ndawohi," the crossing at Second Forks, above Habay (lines 130–31). He was still weak, apparently from the sickness that afflicted him. The hunt itself was then preceded by a dream in which Alexis was told that the animal he was given was really six moose. Present in this account, as in accounts of vision quests examined in chapter 3, is the association between the pitiful state of a human being and the "gifts" one receives as a result:

136. I went to sleep.
137. I looked beyond the place that I saw before.
138. "This animal you were given was really six animals," I was told.
139. "Over here, not far away, the very first moose killed will be a big moose.
140. From there the next one that is going to be killed will be a one-year-old moose."
141. When everybody got up in the morning, they all prepared to go hunting.
142. There was a large number of hunters, and they were very happy to be going hunting.
143. They gathered around across the fire.
144. "Wait, I have to tell you something before you go," I said.
145. Across the fire there were lots of people.
146. They laid down their rifles and packs as I talked to them.
147. "Not far from here there is a beaver dam,
148. beyond the pond there is a lake on the other side.
149. On this side in the direction of the setting sun there will be a big moose killed.
150. From then on, one after another, then another, and then another moose will be killed.
151. Once the big moose is killed, back this way toward camp
152. a dry cow with tender meat will be killed.
153. The first one that is killed on the other side of the trail will be a yearling.
154. That is as much as I will tell you."

Alexis then gives a detailed account of the successful hunt for six moose (lines 164–74), exactly as predicted by his dream. When the hunters returned with the meat from the six moose that were killed, Alexis says that "there was plenty of meat" and that "in the evening everybody ate well" (lines 188 and 189). Alexis and the hunters then returned home to feast and celebrate with all the people, who rejoiced at his recovery and the demonstration of his "power" to see ahead:

203. We returned home on Saturday, and on Sunday everyone gathered at my house.
204. There was a big area by the house where they prepared sun
205. shades with saplings.
     People cooked while everyone feasted.
206. Everyone said, "Thank you! It was difficult for you, but you have survived."
207. From then on I dreamed periodically.
208. If I was instructed to look at something as I slept, then I looked.
209. It was challenging.
210. I have experienced many things.
211. It is not difficult, that other world.
212. If you are destined to live, it's not difficult.
213. My father helped me.
214. Eventually, I recovered from the pain I had endured.

Alexis's journey to heaven and back to "our land," with his dramatic experience standing on the foot of a cross (lines 63–76) and the gift of a moose to kill (lines 95–96), is clearly rooted in the hunting ethos as well as in the missionized world of the Dene. These two themes are recaptured in lines 94–97: "As I watched, I thought, 'I have returned. This is really my land.' As I was watching, a sleeping moose appeared. I was told, 'Send people to get it. Eat, and then you will return.' I still remember. 'By this sign [he takes a small cross from his trousers pocket] you will know,' they said." The sign Alexis refers to (line 97–98) is the small crucifix, which he always carries in his pocket and holds in his hands when addressing people in his role as a dreamer in public meetings or ceremonies. It is this sign that most dramatically reveals the integration of Christian symbols into the Dene Tha way of praying, over which he presides as head dreamer.

Alexis's vision is one particular expression of the interaction between an indigenous way of life and Christian symbols introduced by Euro-Canadian missionaries. Alexis says he has become a good person because of the Tea Dance. He is the leading Dene Tha dreamer. He also says he was transformed because of his vision of standing on the cross in heaven. He is a devout Roman Catholic. He sometimes compares the acute pain he felt in the chest at the time of his vision to the pain suffered by Christ when he was pierced on the cross. Alexis was clearly transformed by this visionary experience. The drum and the crucifix have become personal symbols of his role as a dreamer who travels from our land to the other land to help his people. He has become a Christian Dene Tha shaman who, in the process of his vision, transformed Christian symbols and incorporated them into a distinct Dene world view.[1]

At the end of his involuntary fast and vision Alexis is clearly recognized as a Dene dreamer who, in the footsteps of his predecessors, travels to and from the other land. As a dreamer with a strong mind, he receives premonitions of things to come through dreams and visions. Alexis is also recognized as someone who in a dream/vision has gained direct experience of the cross, the central symbol introduced to the Dene by the missionaries. Thus the traditional distinction between dreamer—the person with direct experience of spiritual realities in dreams and visions—and priest—the person who speaks of spiritual realities from the Bible—has been maintained and reinforced. After his vision Alexis's world view and experience still differ radically from the world view and experience of the priests and other Euro-Canadian Christians who live in Chateh and beyond. Thus Alexis Seniantha lives as a dreamer for whom Christ is real in a sense that missionaries never anticipated.[2]

A HISTORICAL PROPHETIC TRADITION

In her study of the relationships between Dene and missionaries in nineteenth-century northwestern Canada, historian Karen Abel found multiple references to Dene prophets or dreamers, first in the journals of Sir John Franklin and Thomas Simpson, in 1820 and 1836 respectively, and then, from 1849 to 1880, in numerous accounts by Catholic priests and Anglican ministers. These sources show that traditionally for the Dene, "a lifetime was experienced simultaneously in both the physical and spiritual worlds," as men and women developed the skills to "travel at will between these worlds, and communicate with all of it, including animals, other human souls, and unnamed spirits" (Abel 1986, 212). As "all areas of life, from success in the hunt to illness or the weather," could be affected by spiritual entities, maintaining appropriate relationships with these spirits was a constant concern (Abel 1986, 216).

When I first arrived in Chateh, people identified five dreamers, Alexis Seniantha (born 1908, according to church records), Billy Semansha (Alexis Seniantha's older brother),[3] Emile Choncho, Willie Denechoan, and Jean-Marie Talley. Billy Semansha, Emile Choncho, and Jean-Marie Talley have since died, and no one has replaced them. Alexis was referred to as *ndatinti* in Dene Dháh and as "the head prophet" in English. Some Dene Tha compared the relationship of Alexis to the other prophets with the relationship of a bishop, *denadihiti*, to priests, *denadihi*.[4] Although people insisted that these five men were the five Dene Tha prophets or dreamers, I asked if there were also women who were *ndatin*. People readily identified women "who have no drums, but have songs and dreams." These women were also *ndatin*, but they never officiated at the Prophet Dance. In the early 1980s, however, a Dene Tha woman dreamer from Meander was training twelve girls as drummers, setting a clear precedent in Dene communities. Although that woman often came to the Tea Dances in Chateh and spoke to people as a prophet would, she never sang or played the drum. This development is particularly significant in the light of a current prophecy among Dene Tha prophets that they are the last male prophets and that after them there will be female Dene Tha prophets.

In Chateh people could mention the three head dreamers who had officiated at ceremonies before Alexis achieved this status. The first dreamer remembered is Gochee, "Brother," a name given him by his father. Gochee was active as a prophet in the late 1880s and early 1900s, later than similar prophets in other groups across British Columbia (Spier 1935, 25, 62; R. Ridington 1978, 30–31).[5] Moore and Wheelock (1990, 60), therefore, think "it is possible Dene Dhaa had known about prophets from other groups who had gone to heaven even before Gochee received his vision." Whatever the case, there are close ties among Gochee;

his brother's son, Willie Denechoan; and Alexis Seniantha. Alexis, who was raised with Willie, had a firsthand experience of Gochee's songs and activities. Gochee and his father, who was from Fort Nelson, British Columbia, lived near a lake known by the Dene as *Ts'u K'edhe*, "Girl's Place," and as July Lake by the non-Dene (Moore and Wheelock 1990, 72). That is where Gochee died and where he is buried, "across the lake in the bush" (Alexis Seniantha in Moore n.d.b, 5).

Although Gochee's songs were forgotten for a while, they are still sung today in Chateh because they were given back to Alexis Seniantha in a dream he had of an old woman called Yahlinimo. In the dream he heard her singing: "She was holding a lamp on one side, and she was singing for me. I dreamed about her. 'Look over there,' she said to me. 'There is my house, and the woman walking around on the porch is my daughter.' She sang for me, and she said, 'Why don't you pray, singing the song of the Bistcho Lake Prophet? If you pray using his song, maybe it will be good,' she said" (Alexis Seniantha, in Moore n.d.b, 4). Through Alexis and his dreams the songs of Gochee are still a living part of the Dene Tha Prophet Dance tradition.

Alexis Salopree followed Gochee as the Dene Tha prophet. Alexis Seniantha remembers how Alexis Salopree foretold his own death (in Moore n.d.b, 5): "'Far away, near Fort Vermilion, I'm going to see a priest dressed in a blue coat. He will see me, and then I will die,' he said. This happened while Harry Chonkolay [the band's chief] was there. There was a priest there wearing a blue coat. The priest prayed for him and held his hand. It was like he had said it would be when he died. A short time later he stopped breathing." Alexis, who is reporting words he personally heard, has added the name of the chief to add weight to Alexis Salopree's prophecy of his death.

Following Alexis Salopree, the head dreamer was Mbekadhi, "He Is Recovered." According to Alexis Seniantha, Mbekadhi was the only prophet among the Dene Tha at that time. Jean-Marie Talley recalls how "Mbekadhi prayed in the Tea Dance circle, then at dawn put up a pole stripped of its bark beside the circle. He then tied a long ribbon to the pole which fluttered in the breeze. 'With this we buy the land,' he said, 'and in this way we prevent misfortune'" (in Moore 1988, 2). Alexis Seniantha told me that when he was a child he looked at the prophet's body and at his drum lying next to him, wondering who would pray for the people. When I arrived in Chateh, Mbekadhi's drum was in the hands of his grandson, Jean-Marie Tally.

Following the death of Mbekadhi there were two Dene Tha prophets, Harry Dahdona's father and eventually, along with him, Alexis Seniantha's father's brother, Nogha, "Wolverine." Nogha, who may have received his name from his animal helper, is listed under the name Wolverine in the 1891 census of the Fort Vermilion District (Moore and Wheelock 1990, 60–61). Wolverine became the head dreamer and was assisted by Alexis Seniantha and Jean-Marie Talley, who were both to become dreamers in their own right. The North Star and the sun drawn on Nogha's drum "were revealed for his use: they were like a signature. There was also a house drawn on his drum. 'That is my land,' God said [to Nogha]. We are living on this world and Nogha was telling us what will happen in the future," said Alexis Seniantha (in Moore 1988, 2).

Dene Tha still talk about Nogha's visions, his prophecies, and the dances he directed. In the 1930s, when the Dene Tha were still hunters and gatherers living in small groups of families, Nogha foresaw that their land would be overtaken by whites in search of oil, that they would live on a reservation, and that parents and children would become estranged. Referring to Nogha's prophecy, a Dene Tha speaker in his late twenties explained that Nogha meant that people would reach a stage when they would start "looking at their children as numbers and not as children; if I had four more kids, I would get more government money, that sort of mentality." Nogha warned people not to live on the reserve to come, because people would "be roaming around like pack of dogs." He insisted, "Even if you have to live two, even five, families in one house, stay where you are living now. Don't settle there! Don't live there!" (in Moore and Wheelock 1990, 85). Despite Nogha's warnings, his aging mother was one of the first Dene Tha to move to Assumption, because she was no longer able to travel with hunting and trapping parties.

Nogha's teachings express his awareness of Christianity as well as the eschatological themes found in other Northern Athapaskan prophetic traditions (Moore and Wheelock 1990, 74–

76). Nogha said: "This Earth is large but we pray for the whole Earth. When we go to the Tea Dance circle then we pray, just like the priest offers communion. This message is not just for this one place but for the whole world. I hope it will help all" (in Moore 1988, 2). Nogha insisted on the importance of carrying on with the Dene tradition: "You must all place tobacco on the fire and pray at Tea Dance. Don't let go of these traditions. If you are not like that, then there will be nothing left on this great earth—nothing—everything will be destroyed. I carry this heavy burden" (in Moore 1988, 6). As an expression of his faith in the "power" in the Dene song and drum, Nogha taught that "when only two people are left on earth, one to sing and another to dance for him, this song will not become old, but will remain fresh" (in Moore 1988, 9).

Nogha's teachings also integrate traditional and Christian practices in functional complementary terms: "People should offer tobacco and feed the fire with it, even if they are alone. Hold onto the rosary, too," he said, "and pray with the rosary before you go to sleep, and then danger won't come near" (Moore and Wheelock 1990, 77). In the same vein, some young Dene Tha told me that they were encouraged by the Elders to carry a rosary on their person as a protection against other Dene who might attack them with their power. As Moore and Wheelock (1990, 62) also show, Dene Tha "did not always use or interpret the symbols of Christianity in the same way as priests. . . . An elder might place a rosary on the upwind side of a gathering to part and clear away approaching rain clouds." An Elder may also choose to sing to disperse dark clouds that are rapidly moving toward the ceremonial ground. I once saw an Elder do so. The clouds changed direction, and the ceremony proceeded without the anticipated rain.[6] In their contact with missionaries Dene Tha prophets clearly took advantage of what they saw as new sources of power, which complemented, rather than supplanted, their own practices.

Abel (1989, 92–93) reports that in the mid-1880s "an Oblate priest scolded an Indian for reverting to 'magical' practices after being baptized." The priest was referring to the Dene practice of singing and burning tobacco and/or animal parts to ensure success in hunting. The Indian replied that he "could not see his relatives suffer from hunger and do nothing while he knew he could make the caribou come by his incantations." Abel's report is based on a letter from Father Séguin to Bishop Taché dated 1 June 1887; it is also discussed by Martha McCarthy (1981, 305). Contemporary Dene Tha think like the Dene Tha of old. Dene Tha hunters say they commonly burn meat or fat in a fire while asking for success in hunting. Louison Ahkimnatchie, a Dene Tha Elder (in Moore n.d.a, 7), describes the practice as follows: "When people are going out beaver trapping they might pray before they depart. When they kill a beaver they feed some to the fire, and then pray. Because of that they will kill many beavers for furs. They might also place some of the beaver fat, or a small piece of beaver skin on the fire and then pray and eat some of the beaver for success in killing beavers. The same is also true of geese. By feeding some of the goose fat to the fire the geese will become numerous." Offerings of tobacco on the fire are also a common way to entice an animal to give itself to a pitiful hunter. A Dene Tha woman, for instance, told me that they had been hunting moose for many days and were getting nothing. So she prayed to her mother, who had died not long before, and offered tobacco and tea to the fire, and the next morning they killed a moose not far from camp. Like many others, she follows the teachings of Nogha and his predecessors.

Nogha prepared for his succession. He had a drum made for Alexis Seniantha, but without letting him know. One morning Nogha told Alexis to go hunting with two companions, telling him where to go, for in a dream he had seen the moose Alexis was to kill. Alexis went where he was told and killed the moose he found there as his uncle had described. Alexis made the proper offerings and disposed of the animal's gut and head in the prescribed manner. He and his companions then prepared the meat and carried it back to camp. The next morning, when Alexis's wife woke him up, his uncle Nogha walked into the room with a drum in one hand and tobacco in the other. They made a fence for a Tea Dance, chopped wood to build a fire, and shot three times into the air to invite people, while Alexis's wife arrived with the moose fat to feed to the fire. Nogha then took the drum he had prepared for Alexis out of its pouch and told him to walk clockwise around the circle and give people meat and tea. Once this was done, Nogha sang four songs and told the people how Alexis had killed the moose the way Nogha had predicted he would. Nogha sang four more times and then gave Alexis the drum, telling him, "From this day on you will be with it."

When Nogha felt he was nearing death, he sent Jean-Marie Talley and three companions early one morning to go kill a moose and bring him some meat inside the Tea Dance circle. By noon Jean-Marie had already killed a moose, which they butchered, and after making offerings, they quickly returned to Nogha, who "made offerings on the fire at a Tea Dance and although he was exhausted sang for the people" (Moore and Wheelock 1990, 5). Nogha told the people: "The future has already been determined. God wants me. Alexis Seniantha is like my son, and he will be the head prophet in the future. God has told me that my life will soon be finished. I have only five days left before the end. Afterwards, it happened as he said it would" (in Moore and Wheelock 1990, 74).

The oral tradition thus establishes that Alexis Seniantha has close personal ties with the first three Dene Tha prophets, or dreamers. Alexis was adopted by Gochee's family and has an elder sister buried next to Gochee. As a child, impressed by the death of Mbekadhi, Alexis wondered who would pray for the people now that the lead dreamer was dead. As a young adult, Alexis was trained by Nogha, his father's brother. These facts, along with the vivid memories Alexis and other Dene Tha have of Nogha's prophecies, stand in sharp contrast to Abel's generalization to the effect that "once a prophet had died, there was apparently little reference to his/her messages in the community thereafter" (Abel 1986, 222). The apparent lack of reference to the messages of earlier prophets is a feature not of Dene oral tradition but of the written record left by explorers, traders, and missionaries, all foreigners, for historians to analyze. Following interviews with Cree, Chipewyan, Beaver, and Slavey people in six communities across northern Alberta, Moore (1988, 6) notes that "the leaders of the Tea Dance religion in each community as well as their teachings are still well known almost a century after they were actively directing Tea Dances."[7] Similarly, in Fort Franklin, Ayah, who died in September 1940, is remembered as a great teacher and person of strong power who, like Nogha for

the Dene Tha of Chateh, foresaw the changes that would befall
the Dene of Fort Franklin. "People still talk about Ayah's prophecies," and recently, to show respect for their great teacher, the
Dene named the local school after him (Blondin 1990, 241) and
dedicated a house of prayer to his memory (Blondin 1991).

THE PRAYER OF PRIESTS AND PROPHETS

Dene Tha compare and contrast dreamers and priests in many
ways. A Dene Tha dreamer once told of a dream in church in
which he had walked the trail up to heaven, where he saw Nogha
and Father Arbet, a well-respected missionary who had worked
among the Dene Tha at the beginning of the century, standing
side by side. To see the prototypical figures of the two religious
specialists in the community standing side by side in heaven is to
affirm them as distinct yet not antagonistic. That is how Dene
Tha view the two religious traditions to this day. The most important difference between dreamer and priest is that the dreamer
knows through dreams sent him by God whereas the priest
knows through the Bible, referred to as *Ndawotá edéhtl'éhé*, literally "the paper of God." Thus, the mediation of dreams as the
source of knowledge imparted by *yak'e wodené*, "the spirits of the
deceased," or *Ndawotá*, "God," or *Ndawotá chuen*, "God's son"
[Jesus], to the Dene Tha sets the dreamer apart from the literate
priest, who takes the "paper of God" as his source of the knowledge imparted by God to Christians.[8]

Dene Tha identify themselves in terms of their reference
group—people who know through dreams and visions—as opposed to another group—people who know through books. As
rightly stressed by reference-group theoreticians (Merton 1968;
Shweder, Mahapatra, and Miller 1987), self-identification is a
matter of great social significance: "In the course of their lives individuals develop a real or imagined reference group . . . and refer to that reference group when evaluating people, situations,
and life projects" (Hefner 1993, 25).

The sharp distinction between prophet and priest may itself
derive from missionaries, whom the Dene first took to be
prophets, or dreamers. Most missionaries vehemently opposed
this identification, as did Emile Petitot (1865, 382, in Helm 1994,
62), when he used the term *jongleur*, "one who entertains mainly

by song or narration," to refer to Dene prophets: "Everything shown to them through dream is considered as true. It is often through dream that they make what they call medicine, a ridiculous practice to which they attach the cure of diseases, the success of undertakings, the death of a person. For a long time, they thought that the [Catholic] priest, like *jongleurs*, only taught the wild imaginings of his mind." As missionaries corrected the mistaken interpretation of the Dene, the Dene became increasingly aware of a clear distinction between their way of knowing and Euro–North American ways of knowing. In the eyes of the Dene, the teachings of their prophets are anything but the "wild imaginings" of their minds. Dene prophets are recognized as having strong minds. Because of their strong minds prophets know things that remain hidden to less powerful individuals— the missionary among them.

Missionaries presented their teachings as part of God's revelation through the life and teachings of Jesus passed down from one generation of believers to the next, in the one true church. Hence the message that appears at the back of a Roman Catholic catechism written in Dene Dháh and still in use in the 1980s and 1990s: "With only 40 cents, you may get the MOST IMPORTANT BOOK, in which you will learn, day by day, what you must believe and what you must do, if you want to go to HEAVEN." The book contains the commandments of God and of the Roman Catholic Church, the prayers, the devotions, and the catalog of sins and virtues that ought to shape the lives of Catholics wherever they find themselves. The catechism uses Dene vocabulary to refer to European philosophical and religious categories. The book is not an Indian catechism as the missionaries claim; it is a catechism for Indians expected to become Euro-Christians and, therefore, civilized.

At times, prophets of the old days are referred to as priests. In this context speakers do not imply that dreamers of old were literate; they simply mean that they were the sole persons holding a public religious office.[9] Thus, a dreamer explained to me that "Nogha and Mbekadhi were people of prayer before us, who prayed and were priests by themselves." In the words of a Dene Tha dreamer, before the arrival of missionaries, when people

gathered around these prophets to pray, they did so at the Tea
Dance, for the following reasons:

> People would hunt animals and live on meat.
> The one who was a dreamer like Alexis prayed for what
>   they were afraid of, and what they thought was hard.

> They feared sickness, that they feared;
> they also feared not killing moose;
> not to kill any beaver was also hard for them;
> they also feared the cold.

> And we hope it will be warm and not cold, we are people
>   of the bush.
> And they prayed when they left for the bush,
> that they kill moose, kill beaver,
> that they do not suffer much,
> that winter be warm;
> that is what they prayed for, that is how it was long ago,
>   before us.

> People prayed by themselves before us;
> one like Alexis would talk to the people at a big Tea Dance.
> They listened to the dreamer, they listened to the dreamer.
> Girls sat with their mothers, boys sat with their fathers.
> He would tell how it would be in the future.

The seminomadic life referred to in this passage is now only a
memory of the past. The people of the bush have become the
people of the reservation, even if members of most families engage in trapping and hunting and harvest a significant amount
of food from the land. At home and in the bush people continue
to feed tobacco, tea, and animal fat to the fire, a form of prayer
they say contributes to well-being in general and success in hunting in particular. Tea Dances are still performed for the same
reasons, and the dreamer, the one with a strong mind able to see
into the future, still officiates.

Today both the dreamer and the priest officiate at public ceremonies in which they pray. Their prayer is referred to with the
Dene word *eghasulin*, "he/she prays." Public prayer occurs either
in the church or at the Tea Dance circle. Accordingly, Dene Tha
distinguish between *Dene k'íhhín eghasuts'elin*, "prayer in the way

of the Dene," when they refer to the Tea Dance, and *denadihi k'ihhín eghasuts'elin*, "prayer in the way of the priest," when they refer to the Mass. This is in contrast again to *Egeeyah eghasut'selin*, "the prayer in the way of the white man." The term "white man" used here refers to the missionaries from other—non–Roman Catholic—Christian denominations that do not have a church on the reservation and do not conduct public services. The fact that the Dene Tha exclude the priest's prayer from the category of the white man's prayer may reflect the degree to which Roman Catholic ways have become part of Dene lives. Helm (1994, 57) suggests that this is generally the case for the Dene because the Oblate missionaries, who remained many years within a community and spent their lives in daily interaction with Dene, were also the only whites to learn and speak their language. In contrast, writes Helm (1994, 57), "the other whites resident in the North, many of whom are agents of some part of government, are usually Protestant, often transient, and, even if sympathetically inclined, have but superficial interaction with or knowledge of the Dene peoples."

Significantly, the sign of the cross, the crucifix, and the rosary are prominent in both the Tea Dance and the prayer of the Roman Catholic priest. When they perform their Tea Dance ceremony, the Dene Tha place one or two bowls on a long piece of cloth laid on the ground. One by one, participants come, genuflect, and make the sign of the cross as they place their offerings of tobacco in the bowl. When the Elders put these offerings on the fire to burn, they also make the sign of the cross. Elders and other participants often carry rosaries in their hands as they make offerings or, later, dance around the fire. Thus, the Dene Tha have incorporated many Christian elements into their rituals, whereas priests have not incorporated key Dene symbols into Roman Catholic ritual. In Chateh, as in other missions in the subarctic, missionaries often asked the Dene to provide the basic materials—animal pelts, beadwork, wood and stone carvings— which were then shaped into the form of Euro-Christian symbols.[10] In Chateh the most striking example of the incorporation of Dene Tha religious symbols is a large painting of the Prophet Dance on the wall behind the altar. The church's tabernacle, where the hosts are kept for communion, rests precisely in the center of this painting, hiding from view the fire on which dreamers offer tobacco and animal fat. Intentionally or not, it is as if the painting reiterates Nogha's teaching: "When we go to the Tea Dance circle, then we pray, just like the priest offers communion."

Dreamer and priest both pray to God, referred to as *Ndawotá* in Dene. Through conversations with Dene Tha dreamers I have come to understand that the Dene and Christian meanings of these terms differ greatly. Whether Dene Tha and missionaries are actually aware of these different meanings is an open question. In the Dene Tha oral tradition Yamanhdeya or Yamonhdeyi, "He Went around the Edge," is the heroic figure who made human life possible in ancient times by killing the animal monsters who preyed on human beings. As one Dene Tha dreamer explained, Yamanhdeya "is really God. He tricked all the animals that lived on our land; he killed all the giant animals. He put things straight on earth. That is the one we call God" (Moore and Wheelock 1990, 3). The figure of Yamanhdeya probably led to the following Dene Tha interpretation of the rosary: "Each large bead represents a place where the Son of God came to earth. He walked along on earth and then went back to heaven. He did this many times, and each of the small beads represents his tracks on earth" (Moore and Wheelock 1990, 62). The Dene Tha say that the same activity, *eghasut'selin*, "praying," goes on in the Tea Dance circle and in the church. Are they assuming that they and the priest share the same conception of God? Do they pursue similar practical activities in the guise of two quite distinct rituals? The prayer of the priests and the prayer of the prophets may well differ in ways that remain unexamined to this day.

In July 1990 I visited the people of Chateh and attended with them a Tea Dance held on an evening of their annual assembly. People were invited to speak if they so desired. The daughter of one of the prophets stood up, took the microphone, and told of a dream she had had a few months after the pope's failed visit to Fort Simpson in 1984.[11] Having returned home from Fort Simpson, she was pondering in her mind the significance of the fact that the pope had not succeeded in landing as intended among the Dene who had gathered to meet him. In a dream she then saw two people walk up to her, one of them a former prophet. The two visitors told her not to worry, because the Dene have always had, and still have, their way of praying around the fire, with prophets, flags, and tobacco. This dream is consistent with the prediction of Dene Tha prophets that their way of praying will endure in the future. Their view contrasts sharply with that of the Beaver prophet Charlie Yahey, who, at the end of the 1970s, encouraged his people to follow the teaching of the missionaries in the future, as there would be no more Beaver prophets after him (R. Ridington 1978). The Dene Tha, on the other hand, imply that their way of praying might well outlast the priest's way of praying. This is particularly true today when, through attrition, the number of priests in the North is diminishing dramatically, leaving more and more Native communities to live and die—indeed, even to bury their dead—without the presence of a priest. The Dene Tha and other Dene communities in the arctic and subarctic may soon find themselves again with religious leaders who "pray and are priests by themselves," as described earlier by a Dene Tha prophet.[12]

RELIGIOUS DUALISM?

On all continents anthropologists meet indigenous peoples who readily identify themselves as Christians and who have dealt in one way or another with the tension between their indigenous tradition and Christianity. Some, like the Roman Catholic Gapun in the Sepik area in Papua New Guinea (Kulick and Stroud 1990), have relegated their traditional religious practices and even their language to the past as they embrace the language and the religion of the foreign elites whom they strive to emulate. Others, like the Anglican Ojibwe of northern Ontario (Valentine 1995) or the Tlingit of British Columbia, keep their language but rethink their "pre-Christian religion by affirming its validity [in the past] while acknowledging the greater wisdom and power of Christianity" in the present (Kan 1991, 364). Rejection of the past, however, does not come readily to New Guineans poised uneasily between the attraction of a new religion that demands the desecration of temples and ritual objects and the fear of retaliation at the hands of offended local spirits and ancestors (Keesing 1992; Burt 1994). In other places people embrace Christianity but incorporate it into their lives along with their indigenous practices. This is the case among the Catholic Chinese in Taiwan (Jordan 1993) and the Saami, who broad-mindedly adopt Christian figures and symbols but hold them as secondary to their own known powerful beings and ritual objects (Outakoski 1991 in Pentikäinen 1996, 9.) The variety of responses does not end here. People may create new churches or develop novel theologies, postdenominational ones, that are more socially and culturally relevant to their needs (Kao and Kao 1992; Poewe 1994; Hume 1996). Numerous religious developments have thus developed around the world, each claiming to be Christian while rejecting "traditional missionary churches" and attempting to incorporate indigenous beliefs and practices (Hexham and Poewe 1997, 37).

In various localities, and within each locality, a diversity of voices, indigenous and Christian (however foreign or indigenized), compete with one another in a plural world. That in many instances indigenous and Christian elements coexist in the lives of indigenous peoples "is not in itself remarkable unless one first assumes that religions form logically coherent systems that must necessarily displace one another" (Barker 1990, 10). Indeed, for many people, the "profession of new belief belied the fact that other modes of thought and action were never fully laid aside" (Comaroff and Comaroff 1991, 247). Conversion has often meant recasting the message of the missionaries into one's own language and world view. Indigenous peoples who have engaged in this appropriation of Christianity have done so with an awareness of the increasingly explicit distinction between indigenous ways and European ways, each with its own powers and potentialities (Comaroff and Comaroff 1991, 245). As Robert Hefner (1993, 4) correctly remarks, "Not always an exclusivistic change of religious affiliation requiring the repudiation of previously held beliefs (Nock 1933), conversion assumes a variety of forms because it is influenced by a larger interplay of identity, politics, and morality."

From place to place and from time to time Christianity is, therefore, variably experienced, understood, contested, accepted, and recreated. The anthropological challenge is to describe and analyze how the relationship between the two traditions, the indigenous and the Christian, is constituted in the lives of a particular people, in definite places and circumstances, at certain times.[13] In the following discussion I focus on the relationships between indigenous and Christian traditions in the lives of Native North Americans generally and of Dene Tha specifically.

In an earlier publication (Goulet 1982) I argued that two distinct religious traditions, that of the Dene Tha and that of the Roman Catholic Church, were socially available and meaningful to the Dene Tha of Chateh. Following Geertz (1966, 4), I defined a religious tradition as a system of symbols that "establish powerful, pervasive, and long-standing moods and motivations, formulating conceptions of a general order of existence and clothing these conceptions with such an aura of factuality that the moods and motivations seem uniquely realistic." To establish that two religious systems coexisted in the same individuals, I described the alternating moods and motivations of the Dene Tha as being rooted in distinct conceptions of a general order of existence. I showed how Dene Tha, immersed in a conventional act of Roman Catholic worship, suddenly behaved in an entirely unexpected and incomprehensible manner in the eyes of Euro–North Americans. I argued that this was the case when a Dene man ran out of church, rosary in hand, to protect himself from the flash of a camera that resembled the eagle's glaring eye, the eagle being his animal helper. I also put forth for consideration the case of the Dene Tha mother and son praying at the grave of their late son and brother, who had sent his "power" to acknowledge their presence. Both these cases are recounted and analyzed in chapter 3. But how could I account for such observations?

Jacques Rousseau (1953) noted that anthropologists tend to regard Christianity among indigenous populations as a thin veneer covering deeply held native beliefs, whereas missionaries painted their aboriginal converts as true Christians whose faith was still tainted by some old, at times silly, superstitions. Rousseau was not satisfied with either characterization and therefore imagined a "third hypothesis, that of religious dualism: the two religions walk in parallel direction in the same individual, without the one penetrating the other" (1953, 5–6; my translation).

We can imagine here in the religious domain a condition similar to that of the bilingual individual who masters two distinct languages with minimal influence of one over the other. Drawing on Rousseau's concept of religious dualism, I maintained that, like many Native North Americans elsewhere, the Dene Tha saw the two religious traditions as complementary, relying on one or the other according to context and circumstances.[14]

I knew of a number of accounts that support Rousseau's hypothesis. Adrian Tanner (1976) investigated the religious ideology of a Cree population that spent from May to August in the trading post of Mistassini, where part-time wage employment is the main economic activity and the Anglican Church the main focus of religious activities. In Mistassini the Cree held their communal celebrations, rites of marriage, and weekly prayer meetings as Anglicans everywhere generally do. In the fall, when the Cree moved into the bush to hunt and trap from September through April, a decidedly Cree religious outlook established itself "in the context of natural elements, of the environment and of the animals, and in the social context of the hunting group" and informed their hunting rituals, divination ceremonies, commensality, and social intercourse (Tanner 1976, 325). Tanner's description of the coexistence of two religious views in a Cree population paralleled that of Vandersteene, a missionary among the Cree of northern Alberta. Unknown to Vandersteene, the Cree had assembled in the bush to erect a conic lodge for a ceremony to be held for the ancestors. Arriving at the lodge site by accident, he was impressed by the number of Cree present, noting that "all my parishioners were there along with the Protestant Indians" (1960, 182). The opposition of Catholics and Protestants, so important in village life, was altogether irrelevant in the bush. Although unexpected, Vandersteene was invited to participate in the ceremony for the ancestors, including the pipe ceremony, drumming, dancing, and offerings to the dead, which took from dusk until dawn (1960, 182–91). Vandersteene had not even suspected that these beliefs and ceremonies existed in a population he had ministered to for ten years, in their native tongue, in the local church as well as in their homes, where he always felt welcome. He wrote that it took him many months truly to admit that such a thing was possible.[15]

When Drum and Rosary Meet

A similar situation is reported by Carolyn Laird for the natives of California. She tells of her surprise when she heard of a native woman who was a devout Catholic and an equally devout adherent of the Old Religion: In her "youthful absolutism," writes Laird, she was convinced "that a person must either believe or disbelieve and could not possibly accept two different mythologies as equally valid statements of truth" (1977, 107). In her attempt to resolve Laird's dilemma, Doña Marta, a native woman, held her hands in front her, her forefingers extended, moving first one hand and then the other. Each finger represented a religion, existing alongside each other. Doña Marta then quoted her grandmother, saying: "'Los dos corren juntos' (the two run together). When one fails, the other helps" (1977, 107). Verna Johnston, an Ojibwa woman from northern Ontario, reports the same of the old people in her community. Johnston knew that people accepted the two sets of beliefs, the aboriginal and the Christian, "because they acted as if they did. They went to church on Sundays, were married and buried in the church, and kept right on putting out offerings to the Little People and burning tobacco in a thunderstorm" (in Vanderburg 1977, 47). Blackfoot Chief Teddy Yellowknife (in M. Rousseau and J. Rousseau 1967, 125) expresses the same point of view: "I do believe that a large number of [American Indians] sincerely believe in their own religion. That is manifested in the fact that we have layman Indians very high up in church circles; well, they will turn around and join their own societies, the highest societies we have in Indian religion."

In the same vein, Sergei Kan (1991, 366) writes that in the mid-1800s most Tlingit converts to Orthodox Christianity saw it "simply as an additional source of spiritual power and material benefit." Guarantees of success in hunting, fishing, or trade were greater if one used the traditional magic formula and prayed to the Christian God. Similarly, Dominique Morissette (1978, 96, my translation) writes that for the Montagnais of Quebec, "the simultaneous practice of the traditional religion and of Catholic rituals appears contradictory only for the whites; the Montagnais, on their part, see in this the mere broadening of the sacred categories of their thought." It appears that many native populations had adapted to the missionary endeavor, first by organizing their behavior in the context of the village life according to Christian beliefs and practices and then by ordering their actions in the context of the bush life in the light of their aboriginal beliefs. I conclude, like David Mulhall in his study of the Christianization of the Carrier Indians (1986), and Nicole Beaudry in her investigation of Dene prophets (1991), that for the Dene Tha, Roman Catholic symbols and practices were adopted to supplement, not supplant, their own.

Slobodin counters the thesis of religious dualism with the observation that it cannot apply to the Kutchin during the years 1938–66, when he knew them best. According to Slobodin (1994b, 286), the two religions "were decidedly interpenetrant . . . [there being] a great deal of Christianity in the bush and of 'paganism' in town." Thus, we must consider closely Slobodin's claim (1994b, 286) that "as lived and felt by community members, the two kinds of faith, although historically distinct, form a single belief system." This is illustrated in the following account, written down by Slobodin in the field on 3 August 1966, as told by Mrs. Elizabeth Blake, a devout Anglican, of her daughter's reincarnation:

> She had a daughter who died age nine in about 1931. Ruth, born a year later, was clearly natli? [a reincarnation] of her deceased sister. . . . When she was about six, Ruth told her mother that she had died [in 1931], had gone into the sky up a steep and very narrow trail, had been met at a beautiful gate by a man in white who identified himself as St. Peter. She had proceeded along a road and had seen a lot of the old people. Finally she came to a big crowd of people and angels, and there was Jesus. She was frightened, but she was taken up to Jesus, who spoke to her kindly and told her, "This is not the time for you." So she turned away and didn't remember anything else. Ruth was born a year later. (Slobodin 1994a, 151)

To assign different parts of Mrs. Blake's account (the reincarnation of a daughter and the presence of St. Peter and Jesus in heaven) to two different beliefs systems, one indigenous, the other foreign, as Rousseau suggests, would certainly do violence to Mrs. Blake's religious views. All these beliefs now form a single gestalt that defines her religious outlook on life.[16] It is therefore tempting to conclude with Slobodin (1994b, 287) that Mrs. Blake's account of her daughter's reincarnation provides clear evidence that "some aspects of Christian doctrine have had a good deal of time to become established in northern Native belief and practice."

I read Mrs. Blake's account differently. Her account indicates that the Kutchins, like many Native North Americans, have successfully incorporated Christian symbols and figures—including Jesus—into their world. Granted, Mrs. Blake's view of the afterlife is certainly not that of a pre-Christian Kutchin eschatology, according to which "at death most of the people make a long, adventurous journey upriver, southward, to what might be described as a happy hunting ground" (Slobodin 1994a, 146). Nevertheless, this does not mean Mrs. Blake has accepted the Christian doctrine concerning the afterlife. Mrs. Blake's world is obviously one in which souls journey to heaven, where they are greeted by St. Peter and Jesus. This is not, however, the Jesus of European Christians and missionaries, for he sends a soul back to earth to be reincarnated.[17] He is a Kutchin Jesus who reaffirms a Kutchin view of the world and of human life. If, then, Jesus has become a Kutchin, what does it mean to state that the Kutchin are "firm in the conviction that they will go to the Christian heaven" (Slobodin 1994a, 146)?

The same criticism can be leveled at Madeleine Rousseau's and Jacques Rousseau's presentation of evidence in support of their thesis that "the religions—the pagan and the Christian—follow parallel paths in the same person; he adheres really and consciously to the two" (1967, 124; my translation). Rousseau and Rousseau see a clear manifestation of this religious dualism in the burial given Joseph Gunner, an old Cree catechist, in the bush one hundred miles away from the trading post of Mistassini. Gunner's grave was surrounded by a fence bearing a cross. Just outside this enclosure was an old cane and next to it a pole to which was attached a pouch of tobacco. The cane and tobacco were both intended to assist Gunner on his way to heaven. All around the burial site, beaks of ducks and skulls of loons were suspended from trees as offerings that would give Gunner success in the hunt in the other land. And so Rousseau and Rousseau (1967, 124) conclude, "In the enclosure, the Christian burial; outside, the pagan one." This is not necessarily so.

In the absence of a Cree interpretation of Gunner's burial site, we cannot conclude it is a manifestation of religious dualism. In Chateh, for instance, crosses standing at a burial site are there so the dead person can seize their arms and pull himself or herself up, the initial step onto the path to heaven or to a woman through whom to be "made again." To focus on Christian objects and patterns of behavior without consideration of Native interpretations of them is to ignore how Natives have incorporated so-called Christian elements into their world, a process of appropriation crucial to our understanding of the interaction between Native North Americans and the missionaries among them.

If we are to understand the intricate interplay between missionaries and Dene, it is inadequate to state that contemporary Dene individuals live "the two kinds of faith" as "a single belief system" (Slobodin 1994b, 286). We must consider what makes the Kutchin and so many other missionized populations—among them the Dene Tha—impervious to key tenets of Christian doctrine. We must recognize how Dene "indigenize" Jesus and heaven to make them consistent with their own world view. Within each Dene community we must seek to determine what exactly it is that individuals embrace of the Christian doctrine and practices. Abel believes that "the most important reason for the decreasing interest [in missionaries] which followed the initial curiosity among the Dene was the growing realization that at a fundamental level, there were important differences between the teachings of the missionaries and Dene beliefs" (1989, 84). The Dene could never be convinced that they were sinful by nature and that they could be saved only by professing their faith in Christ. They were reluctant, for instance, to learn an Anglican prayer for the forgiveness of sins, because, as an old Dene woman told her minister, "the Indians have no sins, they always walk 'straight', and therefore there was no need for that petition" (Reeve, quoted in Abel 1989, 85). Slobodin (1994a, 146) also notes that the Kutchins "have been remarkably impervious to the concept of hell and of judgment and punishment in the hereafter." "Unable to get the Dene to accept this first step in the chain of missionary thinking," writes Abel (1989, 95), "it is hardly surprising that the missionaries encountered resistance to other ideas."[18]

Consider the Dene Tha dreamer who expressed two views concerning the afterlife, one in which the person, a drunkard, was condemned by God to the fires of hell, the other in which the person came back to "our land" to be made again. The dreamer was clearly acquainted with the views of both the missionaries and his Dene predecessors on the matter. It was, however, the Dene view and not that of the missionary that informed his day-to-day understanding of life and his visions of ghosts wandering around his house leading to the pregnancy of his daughter. Similarly, Mrs. Blake may well be acquainted with the church's teachings on eternal life, but it is not the view that informs her life experience. The missionaries may argue that their teachings are based on the Bible and the church's tradition, but Mrs. Blake can counter that she has it from Jesus himself that her daughter ought to come back to "our land" to be reincarnated.

My earlier discussion of religious dualism among the Dene Tha suggested "an either-or situation with a minimum of syncretism" (Slobodin 1994b, 286) that ignored many aspects of the lives of Native North American Christians. What I failed to appreciate at the time is the degree to which the Dene Tha, and many other native populations, had reinterpreted Christian symbols according to their own distinctive view of the world. For instance, the drum, the dance, and the burnt offering of tobacco on the fire are characteristic of a Dene Tha Prophet Dance, whereas the bell, the collection of monetary offerings from the faithful in their pews, and the offering of the wine and bread are characteristic of a Roman Catholic Mass. In both contexts, and under different guises, Dene Tha say they engage in the same activity, *eghasuídlin*, "we pray." To write of religious dualism among the Dene Tha as I did in earlier publications is wrong, for it misrepresents the ethnographic reality.

The Dene Tha, whom we see alternate between Roman Catholic practices and their own traditional ceremonies, do not, however, change from one world view to another, nor do they subscribe to different eschatological beliefs at different points in time. We cannot conclude, therefore, with Verna Johnston, that native people accept two sets of beliefs because they go to church and give the dead a Christian burial on the one hand and make offerings to Little People and burn tobacco in a thunderstorm on the other. Although they engage in ritual activities originating in two distinct historical traditions, they may do so within a single aboriginal world view, albeit modified by their exposure to Christianity.[19]

Kan (1987, 1) observes, "The role of Christianity in the present-day native cultures of the North has not been a major focus of anthropological research either (for some exceptions, see Savishinsky 1974; Preston 1975; Goulet 1982; Gualtieri 1980a and 1980b)." Antonio Gualtieri, who visited sixteen Catholic, Anglican, and Pentecostal missions in the Canadian Northwest Territories and eastern arctic, reports that there "has been negligible indigenization of Christianity" and that indigenization has not been "especially sought by the missionaries interviewed" (1980b, 55). What Gualtieri fails to consider is that the Natives themselves have indigenized Christianity, often without the knowledge of the missionaries who ministered to them.

This, I argue, is the case among the Dene Tha. The Roman Catholic Church counts them as its faithful members, and they quite willingly identify themselves as such. Yet as the preceding chapters make abundantly clear and the following material substantiates, Dene Tha still consider dreams and visions the privileged mode of experience of the other land and of its inhabitants, within a cosmology that is certainly not of European origin. I therefore now argue that, by and large, the Dene have successfully incorporated key Christian symbols into their ways of knowing and living without changing the essentials of their world view and ethos.

Thus, the challenge is to depict and to comprehend a local/ global historical encounter, one in which local actors and newcomers, Dene and missionaries, seek to engage each other in each other's worlds. I do not seek to grasp and understand a discrete and primordial Dene Tha religion, as, for instance, Boas attempted to do among the Kwakiutl without studying the Kwakiutl Christianity that prevailed at the time of his fieldwork. What I have attempted to do is examine the outcome of "processes of invention and transformation," or the lack thereof, "arising from exogenous cultural transfers and the politico-eco-

nomic contexts" in which they were and are embedded (Brightman 1995, 522).

*

What Abel describes of the Dene religion in the late nineteenth
century I have encountered among contemporary Dene Tha—
despite a century of intense missionary activity among them and
fifty years of Euro-Canadian education. This is not to say that
missionaries and teachers have not had an impact on the Dene
Tha. Dene Tha, like many other Dene in the Canadian subarctic,
readily identify themselves as Roman Catholic. They baptize
their children, pray the rosary, and attend mass, especially on the
occasion of a funeral. Nonetheless, the Dene outlook on the
world and life persists. Christian labels have been applied to
Dene concepts, and Christian symbols have been interwoven into
Dene lives and rituals. In the Dene Tha tradition, prophets or
dreamers are known to have "strong minds" and to travel from
"our land" to the "other land" and back. The vision of Alexis Seniantha is unique in that he came back from the "other land" with
the crucifix as his "sign." The evidence suggests that if Alexis is a
Christian dreamer, he is so in a manner that strengthens his identity as a Dene Tha dreamer, through processes that continue to
distinguish him radically from the priests who pray with him to
Ndawotá. Unbeknown to the missionaries, the Christian teachings and symbols have been incorporated into the Dene Tha
world through traditional processes of knowing with the mind.

9. Dancing Your Way to Heaven

*

Dancing is important, for,
as we dance, God looks at our
feet. He measures our steps.
—Dene Tha dreamer

For more than a century, Euro-Canadians have claimed the land, labor, intellect, and soul of the Dene Tha. The efforts to civilize and to Christianize the Dene Tha have dramatically changed their life experiences. Nevertheless, Dene Tha periodically gather around the fire to make offerings and to pray, recreating a long-standing ritual practice known as the Prophet Dance in the anthropological literature and as a Tea Dance, or *ndahotsethe,* "people dance," among the Dene Tha.[1]

THE PROPHET DANCE

In Chateh the Prophet Dance is usually performed outdoors, around a log fire, inside a fenced corral approximately thirty meters in diameter. If the temperature drops below _30 centigrade, a Prophet Dance may be held in the local community hall without a fire.[2] In 1980 in Chateh there were three permanent ceremonial sites on the reserve. One was in the townsite, by the house of the head prophet, Alexis Seniantha, and it is there that the most-attended ritual of the year, at Easter, was held. A second ceremonial circle was found on the First Prairie in front of the house of another prophet, where most ceremonies were held. A third ceremonial circle could be seen on the Third Prairie. It was no longer used but was in close proximity to the house of two other prophets. Moreover, each summer a temporary ceremonial circle was built in a field adjacent to the airstrip and church to hold the Prophet Dance that is customarily part of the midsummer Treaty Day.

In the summer of 1986 this annual Treaty Day Prophet Dance received its own permanent site, as a fourth ceremonial circle was built for the first Dene Tha general assembly.[3] Significantly, this structure was erected next to a site where new houses were being

built for one of the prophets and his children, who held prominent positions in the band administration and who were major
players in local politics. This new circle was much more elaborate
than the preceding ones. The fence surrounding the fire included a stand that was five benches high with an overhanging
ledge on which to lay poplar branches for shade. When this new
ceremonial circle was established, ashes were taken from the site
at which the Prophet Dance was performed when people lived in
Habay and brought to the new site before its first use. Elders thus
created material and symbolic continuity between the old and
the new, supporting their efforts to recruit and train young men
as drummers at Prophet Dances.

All ceremonial circles had a single top railing, except for the
one by Alexis Seniantha's home, which had two railings about fifteen centimeters apart from the top. The one-meter-high fence
of a ceremonial circle has two four-meter-wide openings, the entrance to the north and the exit to the south, although many enter and leave through either opening. On six poles, two on either
side of the entrance and exit and one each by the fence on the
east and west sides of the circle, the dreamers' flags are put up,
carrying designs they say they have been given in the other land.
Pointing to his flags flying on the poles, Alexis Seniantha once
told me: "I was on the other land, I wasn't far on the other side. I
was on this side [with his hands he suggests that the path to
heaven is divided into two parts]. I was shown flags with the
drawings on them and was told to do the same. I put these flags
up often." Alexis also pointed out a white flag he was shown in a
dream. In the dream he was told to ask the priest to bless the flag
with holy water and then to let the flag fly for three days after the
ceremony before taking it down.[4]

Inside the western segment of the circle, approximately three
meters from the north gate, people place two washbasins on a
cloth two meters long which is laid on hay on the ground. It is
there that one comes to kneel, makes a sign of the cross, and de-
posits one's offerings of tobacco. In the middle of the ceremonial
circle a large fire is lit, signaling that the Prophet Dance is about
to begin. In preparation for the meal to follow, potatoes and
moose meat (when available, or beef when not) cook in a large
metal container next to two pails of water for tea. As part of the

would-be offerings, moose fat, or at times store-bought white lard, melts in a skillet sitting next to the fire. Toward the middle of the western segment of the ceremonial circle, a few meters away from the fire, dreamers and singers hang their drums from a waist-high railing two and a half meters long, supported by two stakes driven into the ground. In front of this railing, facing toward the fire, the prophets and drummers assemble, talk and joke among themselves, smoke or chew tobacco, drink tea or soft drinks, and are generally available for consultation.

An atmosphere of joyful and relaxed sociability pervades the ceremony. Teenagers tend to congregate in groups outside the fence, on their bicycles or next to pickup trucks. There they socialize, tease one another, and engage in gossip as they smoke cigarettes and drink pop. Older members of households, parents and grandparents, gather in their customary place and sit inside the fence, facing toward the fire. In the winter months each extended family builds its own fire to keep warm. Around each fire males and females, old·and young, alternate between lively conversation and joking, and quiet observation of the fire and of other people. This sitting arrangement contrasts with the one seen when people lived in Habay, or in the years when Mbekadhi officiated the Prophet Dance on the Third Prairie. Then men and boys sat on the east side of the ceremonial circle and the women and girls on the west side. Nowadays children between the ages of two and ten continuously dart away from their families to join with other children, running after one another and playing all over and around the ceremonial ground.

The Prophet Dance congregation is therefore a lively one, characterized by the continuous hum of adult conversations and children's bursts of shouts and laughter. The Prophet Dance itself begins to unfold when the head singer sings a song accompanied by his drum. The prophets then take turns to speak to the people, to drum and to sing, in effect inviting people to make their individual offerings of tobacco. One by one, old and young walk to the place of offerings, make the sign of the cross, kneel down, deposit their offerings of tobacco in the designated basins, get up, and make a final sign of the cross. The offerings are to ask for the well-being of loved ones, for the success of a hunt or the safe return of firefighters, for protection on a long journey, or for people to stay around despite their old age to teach the younger generation.[5] Four Elders, usually two prophets and their wives, then pick up the two bowls of tobacco offerings and the two skillets containing melted animal fat. Slowly, to the sound of the drums, they walk to the central fire. As they walk clockwise around the fire, they pour the contents of the skillets and bowls onto the fire. Fueled by the animal fat, flames jump high in the air. Following the offerings, men and women in their late thirties and forties distribute paper plates, Styrofoam cups, and plastic utensils. Potatoes and meat are then passed around, followed by tea and biscuits and, finally, by cigarettes. Once the food is consumed, the ceremony enters its last and longest phase: speeches and songs of Elders loosely alternate with clockwise dancing around the fire to the sound of drums and songs played and sung by the dreamers and other Dene Tha drummers.

The dominant symbols in the Prophet Dance are the circle and the path. The circle represents cosmic and social orderliness. This symbol can be seen in the circular shapes of the fenced corral, the drum, the sun, and the earth itself; in the orientation of all participants toward a single central point, the fire; in the movement of the sun that circles the earth; and in the pattern of the dance around the fire. This form of dancing together, front to back, packed closely in rows three to four deep, is relatively new among Dene Tha and other Native groups in northern Alberta and the Northwest Territories. Early explorers such as Samuel Hearne (1958, 318), who was among the Chipewyan between 1769 and 1772; Alexander Mackenzie (1966, 51–52), along the Mackenzie River in 1789; and David Thompson (1916, 92), among the Cree between 1792 and 1806, recorded "only the interpretive style of dancing" in which dancers "typically dance in place and interpret a specific theme [associated with animals] through movement of their upper body, particularly their arms" (Moore n.d.a, 5, 7). Although such dances were still practiced before 1939 among the Chipewyan and Dene Tha, they were already giving way to the clockwise circle dance associated with the Great Plains (Kurath 1953, 69). Moore (n.d.a, 8) notes that Pliny Goddard, who observed Beaver Tea Dances in Fort Vermillion at the beginning of this century, reports that "the dancers circled the fire clockwise" and that "his informants indicated that the form of dance which he observed had only been practiced . . . for eight or ten years (1916: 230)."

The path is an equally important symbol in the Prophet Dance. It stands for the journey between our land and the other land. In Dene thought there is a direct relationship between the investment an individual makes in dancing and the ease with which he or she will complete his or her eventual journey to the other land. One Dene Tha dreamer told me: "When you dance at the Prophet Dance, dancing is important, for as we dance, God looks at our feet. He measures our steps. The more measurements of our steps God can make, the more we win with him." As he spoke, the dreamer moved his extended hands back and forth, counting and measuring imaginary steps as he repeated the gesture again and again. Other Dene Tha commented that the more steps one takes in the Prophet Dance, the fewer steps one has to take on the road to heaven. The same applies to praying the rosary, each bead being thought of as a step around a circular path. An old woman explained that "every time you pray [one bead] you are getting one step closer to heaven." When she died, she insisted, she was going to heaven and to no place else, emphasizing the fact that she would not be as close to heaven had she been younger and had fewer opportunities to dance and to pray the rosary.[6]

When people dance, they do so before the eyes of Ndawotá, "God," to whom they direct their prayers. In the words of a Dene Tha dreamer: "The Prophet Dance is prayer, and the time to pray is during the day, after noon when the sun is high to the point where it sets. Then the sun goes to sleep, and it is also the time for us to sleep. We pray looking at where the sun comes out, in that direction [indicating toward the east]. During daytime we can see everything. When we pray, God can see us. When the sun sets and it goes, it must dream. And when it comes out, it must know what will happen. And we must follow its way: sleep when it's dark, and get up when it gets up." Sleeping is clearly associated with dreaming, a state in which one acquires knowledge of things to come. Although the dreamer's statement reflects conditions of life in the bush more than those on the reservation, where because of electricity people extend their activities far into the night, people still hope to wake up with dreams that foretell what might happen in the future.

Dene Tha also comment on the orientation to the rising sun as a distinctive feature not only of Dene Tha prayer but of Dene Tha life in general. This is especially true of Elders: "Everything they do, they pray and get their medicine in the bush, they all do it that way, looking at [where] the sun comes out. They say: 'When the sun will come out, it will light it; it will be the first thing it will see, and it will make your prayer strong.' That is why the people always do everything that way." An orientation to the sun also shapes one's life at home: "It's general knowledge. It is supposed to be that way. Like where we put our heads during the night, where we put the kid's hats, and everything face that way." As one healer noted, the sun teaches people a general attitude to life: "The sun is setting an example we should follow. The path is its own, and the way it sleeps and gets up, we should be like the sun, we should pray to God like that. That is why they [the Elders] do everything that way." The speaker went on to say, "Old people say: *Tegeh anet'e*, 'be slow/quiet.' It is best to stop and really think about where you are going. Like the sun is really slow, rising and setting. We should be like that."[7]

To act quietly, without haste, with a clear mind and purpose, is one of the most often repeated injunctions of Elders to fellow Dene. This is the attitude one should have in life generally and in the Prophet Dance specifically. To live like the sun in its daily journey around the earth is to partake in the rhythm of daylight and darkness, wakefulness and dreaming, spending time in our land and in the other land. Thus, as seen in the preceding chapter, at Prophet Dances, as a preface to their accounts of information received from people in the other land, dreamers commonly say, "I dreamed . . . and I heard a voice. . . and I was told," or "I dreamed, and I was shown. . . ."

PROPHETS TALK

To speak of prophets is to suggest that some individuals enjoy special communication with the other world and so are able to predict events to come. Such is the case with Dene Tha dreamers, who, in their speeches to the Prophet Dance congregation, exhort fellow Dene Tha to a good life, warn of impending misfortune, and offer testimony of journeys to the other land. The speeches of dreamers vary in length; the twelve speeches I recorded range from two to sixteen minutes. Dreamers speak in the midst of children's shouts and laughter as they play and run in and out of the ceremonial circle; adults listen to the dreamers while pursuing their own conversations. The insider's undivided attention is not required for the careful consideration of a dreamer's words. Children, who played tag around me, would spontaneously repeat word for word some sentences of a dreamer's speech, while Dene Tha adults, who had talked among themselves while attending to the dreamer's address, would ask me what I had understood in order to complete what I might have missed.

Speeches of Dene Tha dreamers may involve brief descriptions of heaven and performances of songs received while in the other land. In this manner Alexis Seniantha (in Moore n.d.a, 11–12) tells his audience that in heaven someone addressed him as follows: "'Why do you find it difficult? Nothing will happen to you if you are fully assured.' He spoke to me in Beaver language. 'There is a prophet amongst you, although he may not be known,' I was told. I have seen the impossible. In heaven the grass was waist high, and there was a series of bushes of graded sizes." Alexis thus reinforces one of his recurrent themes by suggesting to people that someone among them may already be a prophet who has yet to reveal his status to others. He follows his speech with a song acquired on the occasion of a journey to heaven, one that he often sang in his individual sessions with me and that was transcribed by Moore (n.d.a, 12):

Hée ele, hée ele
Hée it is, hée ele

Ya dígeh ele, dígeh ele.
Heaven land it is, land it is.

Héé hele [sic], dígeh wot'ıne, dígeh ele.
Héé it is, land people, land there is.

Yak'ewot'ine dígeh ele, dígeh ele
Angel land it is, land it is

Ya dígeh ele. Yak'ewot'ine dígeh ele
Heaven land there is. Angel land there is

Dancing Your Way to Heaven

Héé ya dígeh ele.
Héé heaven land it is.

Typical of the songs of Dene Tha prophets, this song is composed of vocables (*Hée ele*) and of a few words referring to heaven, the land of human beings who live in an angelic state. Beaudry, who has analyzed forty-one songs of a Northern Slavey prophet, writes that of these songs, "21 use only vocables, 11 use the term *yake* ('heaven') and vocables; 5 use the term *yak'egoht'ine* ('people from heaven' or 'angels') and vocables; 3 use the term *yak'egonezo* ('heaven very good'); 1 song alternates between *yak'egoht'ine* and *yak'egonezo* between vocables" (1992, 89).

A dreamer may also refer in his speech to soul journeys to places in our land, as in the following case, in which Willy Denechoan (in Simon 1995, 66–67) tells of his first visit, in a dream journey, to Lac Ste-Anne, near Edmonton in southern Alberta: "I got drowsy during the day and fell asleep. In my sleep I can see the lake and it is good, but over there where the sun rises and over there where the sun goes down, these rainbows appeared. I was being called to look at them. I stood up and looked at them. Under these rainbows it almost looked as if the leaves were green and yellow. Under one of the rainbows in a muddy kind of water I see a person but I can't seem to see the person too clearly. I was being told in my dream, 'You will look at it again; the next time you will know more about the situation.'"

When he woke up, the dreamer told his son about his dream. He was surprised to have been shown in a dream a lake that he had not yet examined with his own eyes. He wished he could see more clearly the person he had had merely a glimpse of. His wish was granted as soon as he later went to sleep: "I went to sleep. I had not slept long when I heard a person speaking to me. The person said, 'You will have a look at the people again.' This time nothing obscured my vision, it is right in the open. The person said: 'The first time that you did not have a good look at this body of water was because it was meant for this world. Now you will look upon the place as it really is.'" Then Willy Denechoan not only sees the lake again but watches something coming down from heaven which forms a circle at his eye level. On this platform six individuals appear one after another, and then, in mid-air, a seventh individual above them: "I can see six persons standing upon it. Directly above, in the middle, in the open, stood a person. He held his hands like this [open arms]. He was looking around and he was standing above the level of the other six persons. I thought to myself, 'Is he the one who they call the Son of Our Father? If he is, I am happy to be looking upon him.'" The dreamer notes that the six individuals on the platform are dressed differently, but he thinks to himself: "If they were angels they will all look alike." But then the person who directs his attention to the lake from the beginning of the dream tells him, "No! the three on this side, they are the ones who work with the White people, the other three work with the Indians, that's who they are. The one in the middle above, he is the one they call the Son of Our Father. He is the one who prepared the body of water you look upon for the people before your time. He prepared this when the world was still young. That is why you are seeing it." And so, once again, dreamers and Dene Tha are presented with evidence that the Dene way of praying and the white people's way of praying are equally important and valid in the eyes of the Son of God. Once again, the prophet is seen as the medium between beings in the other land and human beings in our land.

In their speeches dreamers also remind people that their conduct plays an integral part in assuring the continued supply of the fish, game, and fowl that is their traditional source of food. A dreamer tells the congregation, "Let there be more praying than doing bad. Find ways to live as people so maybe in the end the things we depend on, our rabbits and other animals, the grouse, the bucks that are all gone, maybe it might be sent back toward us. It's possible that you might win it. To ask for that, pray regularly." As he goes on, the dreamer explains that animals are there to get only if people give offerings on the fire regularly and pray with their hearts to Our Father. The prophet's message is a traditional Dene one: the animals that people need and want are here in our land; people must pray regularly in order for the animals to manifest themselves again. To emphasize his point, the dreamer says, "It is all your fault that these animals were like being sent away and only you left alone."

Prophets also warn people of impending misfortune, exhorting them to look after themselves and their children to avoid foreseen deaths. For instance, early one spring, at a Prophet

Dance, a dreamer said that soon there would be two deaths: a man and a small girl would die before the grass was knee high. Pointing to her ten-year-old daughter, a mother then commented that the dreamer "makes people afraid. I am afraid for her." Within two months a well-known man from Meander River and a young girl of ten from Chateh had died. People immediately commented, "Just like the dreamer had said." At another Prophet Dance, following the death of a young man, another dreamer announced that there might be an additional death soon, this time that of a woman, possibly in Chateh, possibly in Meander River. He exhorted people to pray hard so it would not happen to any of them. People maintained that the dreamer "was looking ahead in the future" and that he knew who might die but did not reveal all he knew because his purpose was "to let the people understand, to let people know to tell their children not to drink." In their speeches other dreamers also faulted people for the misfortunes in their lives. If there were so many older people dying, one prophet maintained, it was because the younger people lacked respect for them and ill-treated them. This suggestion made many people angry. In the words of one women, who had lost both her elderly parents in the previous year, "They [the dreamers] tell us we should come to pray with them, and here he makes us feel as if we have killed our parents. They talk too much."

SOCIAL ASPECTS OF THE PROPHET DANCE

In March 1981 I arrived at the ceremonial ground at three o'clock in the afternoon, nearly an hour and a half before sunset. Outside the ceremonial grounds approximately thirty teenagers and young adults were leaning against the fence or against parked cars and pickup trucks, smoking and drinking pop, talking and joking among themselves, apparently oblivious to the ritual about to take place. Dressed in their blue jeans, cowboy boots, and denim jackets, they seemed to belong to a different world than the one in which the Prophet Dance was to be held. Within the circle approximately sixty individuals could be seen, including a dozen old men. Among these old men were the five prophets, standing close to the fire. Others, young children, their parents and grandparents, were sitting in small groups along the fence waiting for the moment when they would be called to place their offerings of tobacco in the designated dishes. The sound of drums and songs accompanied the old men and old women who came up first to the place of offering, soon to be followed by the other participants. Rosary in hand, they faced the setting sun, made a sign of the cross; genuflected or knelt down; placed their cigarettes, chewing tobacco, or snuff in the dish; made another sign of the cross; and circled away clockwise. More drumming and singing followed along with speeches by the dreamers. Families sat quietly by the fence talking among themselves while teenagers and young adults remained outside the circle.

An hour and a half had gone by since my arrival. Had I left then I would have taken away the impression that the Prophet Dance was by and large a thing of the past, enacted by old people, attended by few, of no relevance to the younger generation who looked from the outside on the actions of the previous generations. But then, all of a sudden, the young people dropped their soft drinks and cigarettes and entered the circle. They approached the place of offerings, genuflected, signed themselves with the cross, made their offerings of tobacco, and circled away, just as their elders had done before them. The young men were followed by women who were accompanied by their younger children, who also joined in the offering. Then, as is customary, two prophets took the washbasins full of offerings and walked clockwise around the fire as they poured the grease over the fire and then threw the tobacco into the leaping flames. The offering represented the contribution of the whole community, men and women, young and old.[8]

Performances of the Prophet Dance that I observed or participated in involved as few as sixty and as many as four hundred individuals. On two occasions I made an audio recording of the whole ceremony to transcribe parts of the speeches and to note with more precision the pattern of songs, speeches, offerings, and dances. Both times the lead singer opened the ceremony with a solo song accompanied by his drum.

The first recording, on 3 April 1983, was of a ceremony attended by approximately two hundred Dene Tha. The purpose of the ceremony was for the good health of Elders, that they may

TABLE 1

First cycle of activities at a Prophet Dance, 3 April 1983

Actor	Drum & Song	Speech	Feeding the fire
Head singer	3		
Prophet 1		4	
Prophet 1	2		
Prophet 1		2	
Prophet 1	12		
Elder	11		
Prophets			6
Prophets	4		
Prophet 2	·	7	
Total minutes	32	13	6

live long to teach the younger generation the Dene ways (see table 1 for a list of activities and their duration).

In the first hour of the ceremony, songs and speeches preceded and succeeded the act of "feeding the fire" with the people's offerings. In this phase of the ritual performance most people are seated, except for the prophets and drummers, who officiate from near their drum stand.

This phase of the ceremony was followed by a meal and then by a set of vigorous rounds of drumming and singing by a chorus of prophets and drummers who set the pace for people to dance around the fire. The successive rounds of dancing were seven, five, eleven, and fourteen minutes long, respectively, involving more and more people each time. The ceremony would undoubtedly have gone long into the night had it not been for the violent intrusion of a disgruntled young man (described in detail below).

A second ceremony, held for the recovery of Alexis Seniantha, who was operated on in an Edmonton hospital, was recorded on 27 March 1984. The ritual performance began at 2:07 in the afternoon and ended at 9:38 in the evening. I was able to record only a little more than three hours of it because I was asked twice by elderly Dene Tha to give them a ride home. As usual, the cere-

TABLE 2

First cycle of activities at a Prophet Dance, 27 March 1984 (minutes)

Actor	Drum & song	Speech	Feeding the fire
Head singer	4		
Prophet 1		7	
Prophet 1	3		
Prophet 1		2	
Prophet 2	2		
Prophet 2		2	
Elder	2		
Elder		2	
Two prophets & wives			8
Prophet 3		2	
Prophet 3	2		
Prophet 3		2	
Prophet 2		4	
Total minutes	13	21	8

mony opened with a song from the head singer, followed by speeches and singing on the part of the drummers, before and after the offerings (see table 2).

This ceremony involved a minor innovation, following the report by a dreamer that in a dream he had seen himself and three other individuals carrying the basins full of offerings around the fire, genuflecting and making a sign of the cross in each of the four directions before feeding the fire. In the prophet's dream a voice instructed him to do so when they prayed for Alexis. And so it was done exactly as he had described, a slight variation on a basic pattern but one legitimated by communication from the other land.

The ceremony then proceeded with a number of relatively brief rounds of dancing of seven, six, and four minutes each, after which an elderly couple asked me to drive them home. When I returned forty-five minutes later, one of the prophets was addressing the congregation. I recorded the last sixteen minutes of his speech and then, immediately afterward, another fifteen-minute speech by a second prophet, who followed his talk with a nine-minute solo performance of a song that he accompanied with drumming. Immediately thereafter, prophets and singers engaged in drumming and singing, leading people in successive rounds of dance of six, three, six, seven, seven, and seven minutes each. Again I had to absent myself to drive home Elders and their grandchildren.

When I returned for the last hour of the ceremony, it appeared rather unfocused, as small groups quietly engaged in conversation, a dreamer or singer occasionally tapped his drum by the fire, and children ran and played around the ceremonial circle. Then at 8:36 PM the prophets and singers lined up to drum and sing a Cree song to which many people danced merrily. The song was from the Fox Lake people, given to the Dene Tha many years ago as a sign of friendship.[9] After the dance a prophet thanked the people for their prayers, and soon everyone was heading back home.

In Chateh, as elsewhere, ritual performances are not only "the reenactment and thus the reexperiencing of known form" (Geertz 1983, 28), or events that celebrate a social order firmly rooted in a taken-for-granted world view; they are also affairs shaped by local power relations and conflicting values. Ritual performances, then, become the stage on which contests are played out by factions maneuvering among themselves or by groups or individuals who feel deprived (Dirks 1992; Holland and Skinner 1995). Performances of the Prophet Dance were, on occasion, seriously disturbed by inebriated and/or resentful Dene Tha. This was the case on a late summer evening during the Treaty Day celebration. The day had been festive, and by ten o'clock in the evening many individuals were walking around drunk. Soon after midnight some of these drunken individuals intruded on the Prophet Dance, which was being held in the ad hoc ceremonial circle constructed for the occasion. The drunken men stumbled around, talking loudly to dreamers and to people sitting along the fence. These men were quietly told to leave but refused to do so. Dreamers and drummers then simply picked up their drums and left the ceremonial grounds, soon to be followed by the other participants. The next day Alexis Seniantha commented that "people had to quit because bad people were walking around." Once more, when confronted with disturbing individuals, people preferred withdrawal over confrontation.

Premature closure was forced once on another ceremony when a middle-aged woman wielding an ax made her way toward the Elders. People were still assembling, and dreamers and drummers had barely begun to drum and sing. The woman stumbled along, apparently drunk, but clearly angry and threatening an Elder in a loud voice. Once inside the circle she accused the Elder of being responsible for the death of a close relative and told him she would destroy his drum and avenge the death of her loved one. She took a few steps forward. Everyone kept quiet. Silent, the dreamers and singers stood still. Then the woman's old mother entered the circle. Bent over with age, she positioned herself between her daughter and the Elders. In a calm voice she instructed her daughter to get back to the house, a stone's-throw away from the ceremonial circle. The old woman then slowly walked around the fire, signed herself with the cross, and threw tobacco on the fire as an offering. By the time she had completed her round, the daughter was heading back home, though still voicing her angry threats. The mother was soon following on her daughter's footsteps. People sat quietly for a while. Speechless, the Elders just looked at each other. To pursue the ceremony in full view of the women's house would only aggravate a tense situation. The Elders put their drums back in their bags and brought the ceremony to an end. Ten minutes later smoking logs in the middle of the circle were the only evidence left of an intended Prophet Dance.

On another occasion a Prophet Dance performance had to be canceled soon after the ceremony of offerings. It was in the spring, when melting snow and rain turned dirt roads into streams of mud. To reach the slightly higher and relatively dryer ceremonial grounds, pickup trucks had to race through deep puddles of water and stretches of muddy road and field. Many vehicles were parked by the fence, and approximately one hundred and fifty people had made their offerings of tobacco. It was now time for Alexis Seniantha to drum, sing, and speak to the people, which he was doing standing next to the fire, when all eyes suddenly turned toward a large pickup truck, headlights on high beam, speeding toward the ceremonial ground. When it came within two meters of the fence, it swiftly steered to the right and began going around the fence, raising much mud in the process. In his second round the driver moved closer to the fence with the obvious intention of covering participants with mud. The driver looked out his window with apparent satisfaction at the sight of people beginning to move away from the fence. In his third round the driver took his vehicle into the ceremonial ground. Entering by the north gate, he raced across the circle, ran over the edge of the fire, exited by the south gate, and raced away, leaving everyone behind visibly shaken. The vehicle had come within two meters of the leading prophet and had left many people covered with mud. Shocked, people gathered their belongings and headed back home. As I drove people back to their homes, I was told the driver had behaved as he did because he was mad at one of the dreamers, who would not let him have his daughter.

In the next week I stopped at the house of one of the dreamers. In the course of our conversation he and his wife told me not to worry about what had happened at the Prophet Dance. Mentioning the drunk driver and his motive for acting as he did, the woman, who is a reputed dreamer and healer in her own right, said, "It doesn't matter; he is my brother's son; we will look after it our way." In due time the Elders were promoting a revival of drumming among young men, including many who had been known for violent behavior when drunk. In the words of Dominic Habitant (in Moore 1988, 9), a Beaver Indian from Eleske, "Those young drummers used to be the worst ones. Look at them today; they have wives and are doing well."[10] In the summer of 1990, at a Prophet Dance for which at least four hundred people had gathered, I watched nine of these young men sing and drum in perfect harmony. This was part of the response of the Elders and of the whole community to the glaring disrespect that had been shown two years earlier by a member of the community.

KNOWLEDGE REVEALED THROUGH PERSONAL EXPERIENCE

So far we have examined various aspects of the Prophet Dance—its symbolism, its constituting parts, and the way it unfolds or fails to unfold according to expectations. All this the anthropologist, like the Dene themselves, learns largely by observation and participation. In February 1980, when I first observed the Prophet Dance, I stood outside the fenced-in circle within which about one hundred Dene Tha were gathered. I did so as a sign of respect, not knowing if I was welcome in the circle itself. Two months later, on the occasion of the next Prophet Dance, a Dene Tha dreamer waved at me, inviting me to join him and his family within the ceremonial circle, and thus I began a process of greater and greater participation in Dene Tha ritual performances. By 1984, the fourth year in which I was to spend six months in Chateh, I had reached the point at which dreamers gave me advance notice of a Prophet Dance, in effect inviting me to take tobacco to participate in the offerings and prayers, to share in the communal meal, and to take part in the sacred dance. From the Dene Tha point of view, it is only through such an experiential approach that one gradually develops an appreciation for the inner dynamics and many levels of meanings of these ritual performances.

Anthropologists who engage in ritual performances in this fashion tend to move beyond standard interpretivist or functional interpretations of ritual. For instance, Marjorie Halpin (1995, 1), a long-time practitioner of *chanoyu*, the Japanese tea ritual, writes, "Nine years of training to encode or sediment the habit memories of Tea in my body have completely changed my perspective on ritual, which most theorists view as symbolic action. It is not. Rituals are not pointing beyond action to meaning." That is why, Halpin argues, anthropologists often persist in vain to get from a practitioner of a ritual a statement concerning the meaning of his or her actions. Anthropologists simply fail to appreciate the role of habitual action in structuring human lives. "Habit is a knowledge and a remembering in the hands and in the body; and in the cultivation of habit it is our body which 'understands'" (Connerton 1984, 95; cited in Halpin 1995, 2). According to Jackson (1989, 127; cited in Halpin 1995, 20), "it is probably the separateness of the observer from the ritual acts which make him think that the acts refer to or require justification in a domain beyond their actual compass." E. Turner (1996, 231) also maintains, like Jackson (1989), "that ritual experience proves itself to be true and valid in use, not as a preordained system or structure." It is this truth and validity in use that I experienced firsthand in a performance of the Prophet Dance in the summer of 1984, when Dene Tha observed that when dancing, my body was moving just like theirs.

In the spring of 1984 a meeting was organized to bring together Native Elders and non-Native individuals interested in learning experientially about Native ways. The meeting, held in Cree territory near Fox Lake, at Little Red River, northwestern Alberta, involved participants in a number of rituals—Pipe Ceremonies, Sweat Lodges, and Fast—presided over by Cree Elders and medicine men.[11] When preparations for the event were under way, I was asked to offer tobacco to Dene Tha dreamers by way of inviting them to the meeting. I took tobacco to two dreamers and to the head singer. On receiving the tobacco, Alexis Seniantha said he would think about the invitation and respond later. The other dreamer and the singer said they would wait for the first dreamer's response before deciding whether or not they would attend the meeting. Two days passed before I met with the first dreamer again, in the local store, where he gave me the following account: "I will be going there, but I dream. First, two individuals go around me [with his hands he shows them moving left to right, around and behind him]. 'What are they carrying?' I ask. It is probably medicine, I think. I am sleeping, and because I think this, I wake up around four o'clock in the morning. Because of this [dream] I will not go. To you it [the medicine] does not matter, but to me it does. Why did I dream this? It [medicine] does not fit me. There is probably medicine in what they carry. That is why it does not really fit me, that is why I will not go; it would be difficult for me." The dreamer refers to medicine, *yú*, that others may expose him to and that may not fit him. Twice the dreamer uses the word *enudli*, "probably." The use of this adverb is typical of narration of dreams that appear to predict events to come. Built into the very process of foretelling is a clause indicating that the foreseen may not materialize. Typically, a prediction is about not the inevitable but the probable. I was saddened at the news and pondered the significance of his dream.

Despite their decision to stay home, the head dreamer told me that I would attend the meeting and organize a Prophet Dance on their behalf. When I told them I had never done so and did not know how to do so, they retorted that I had participated in and seen them perform the ceremony often enough to set it up myself. This decision came as a total surprise to me. One dreamer sent me to examine the fenced-in circle next to his home. The dreamer told me we were to build a similar circle where the meeting was to take place. When the second dreamer gave me his tobacco to take to the ceremony, he gave me the following instructions:

> Over there you will make offerings on the fire, once. My to-
> bacco, and his [the other dreamer's] tobacco, and your to-
> bacco, and whoever wants to pray may offer tobacco. You
> know our way. You put two plates on a blanket on the
> ground, and after that you genuflect and sign yourself with
> the cross. You put your tobacco in the plates, and everybody
> can do the same. After that you offer the tobacco and some
> fat on the fire. Even if you do not have moose fat, it doesn't
> matter; white lard will do. You still have my songs on tape?
>
> Yes, I do.
>
> You will play my songs. After you all listen to my songs,
> you will offer the tobacco and fat on the fire. You will make
> the offerings soon after noon; the sun will show to remind
> you that God looks at you when you pray.

And so I left for the Little River meeting with these instructions in mind, the tobacco of two prophets, and a tape recording of one of the prophet's songs, to fulfill an unexpected mandate. In-deed, as the following account reveals, the Dene Tha were teach-ing me what the Beaver taught R. Ridington, "that knowledge would reveal itself to me from within personal experience. It might even come to me through myths and dreams" (R. Riding-ton 1988, xi).

One evening early in the meeting I joined the elders and other participants who were sitting around a fire in a teepee discussing the preparation of ceremonies. As we talked, smoke gradually filled the teepee. Annoyed by the smoke, which hurt my eyes, I wondered what could be done about it. I suddenly realized that I was looking at a life-sized image of myself kneeling by the fire. This image was, distinctly, outside myself; it was clearly apart from my actual location in the circle of dreamers and participants. I could see myself in detail by the fire, dressed as I was then dressed, fanning the flames with my hat. Had I been a Cree or a Dene, I would have moved into that image of myself, performed the action projected before me, and obtained the desired result in the appropriate manner, that is, I would have been an informed participant. Being a non-Dene, I was shocked and perplexed at the sight before my eyes. I had no understanding that such an image pertained to an essential dimension of ritual performance. I kept looking at the image, aware all the while of the smoke in the teepee and wondering whether someone would do something about it.

Then someone, a non-Native, got up, knelt down by the fire, and started blowing on it. Immediately, in a loud voice, a Cree medicine man told him not to do so and instructed him to fan the fire with his hat or some other object. The rationale for not blowing on the fire was that such an action would induce a violent windstorm in the camp. I realized that I had actually foreseen the proper way of fanning a fire. Until that moment I had not known either the right or the wrong way of doing this or the rationale behind the prohibition against blowing on a fire. Nor did I know that one could see so vividly, in image form, what the proper action in a given situation might be. From the Dene point of view, I had experienced a form of teaching and communication that occurs not through the medium of words but through the medium of images. To the Native participants, this form of communication is quite common and to be expected in the context of ritual activities. A Dene Tha says *sındíť'ah edahdí,* "with my mind I know."

When I left for the meeting, some Dene Tha dreamers had not yet decided if they would participate. It was agreed that a charter plane would be sent on the following Wednesday to fly them to the meeting place should they so wish. As late as the evening before we were to perform the Prophet Dance, many wondered if Dene Tha dreamers might still come to perform the ceremony themselves. That night, Tuesday, 14 August 1984, I had a dream, which I recorded as follows:

> The dream occurred the night previous to the offering of tobacco on the fire. I saw Alexis Seniantha walking back and forth in the basement of the church on the reservation. He

walked erect, head up, arms swinging back and forth; I had the impression of a healthy, strong, and happy person. As I approached the church, I saw three young people standing at the door. I examined them, dressed in denim jeans and jackets. I was apprehensive because I realized I did not know them. I approached cautiously, wondering who they were, when they told me: "We are Alexis's helpers. We are here, and he sends us all around this land to do work for him. Do not be afraid of us." I stopped being afraid of them and looked again at Alexis walking in the church basement. He was smiling, walking around, looking very well and strong.

When I woke up, I thought the dreamers were staying home. The next morning, when people asked me if they would be coming, I said I didn't think so and told them my dream.

The day we were to perform the ceremony, low, rolling, black clouds filled the sky. A local Cree said, "Look, the clouds are real black. It will rain on you guys." Nevertheless, I told those present that we would soon be praying, following the way of the Dene Tha. Nearly a hundred people gathered within the circle as we proceeded according to the instructions of the dreamers. Two Cree Elders, a man and a woman, were chosen to put the offerings in the fire, and the tape-recorded song of the Dene Tha dreamer was played for all to hear. As the Cree Elders were putting the offerings on the fire, the clouds suddenly broke and the sun shone on all of us, exactly as the Dene Tha dreamer had said it would.

Soon after the ceremony was performed, I was invited into one of the teepees, where a healing ceremony was under way for the benefit of the Cree Elder who had performed the offering of tobacco. The Elder reported that he was becoming ill because of medicine. His report matched the prediction by the Dene Tha dreamer who had chosen not to attend the ceremony, on account of his dream. Two people, a young man and an old man, had come to pray, but when the Cree Elder shook hands with them, he felt they had not come for good. After they left him, walking from left to right, around and behind him, he started to feel ill, so he asked a medicine man for help. The healing ceremony was performed immediately, and he recovered quickly.

Dancing Your Way to Heaven

Late in August, when I was back on the reservation, the two dreamers who had chosen not to attend the ceremony came to visit. I narrated my dream of the dreamer in the church basement and told them that I had thought, on account of that dream, that he would not attend the ceremony. The dreamer smiled and said, "You now know that dreams can tell the truth." I added that the dreamer who made the offerings over the fire was adversely affected by "medicine" that had been carried by two men who walked around him. "I told the truth; I know I dreamt the truth," said the dreamer. To the other dreamer, I described the ceremony and the use we had made of his songs on tape. I mentioned that the sun had shone at the time of the offerings on the fire, as he had said it would. He declared, "You know now that my songs are powerful."

Later in the week, when I told a Dene Tha woman of my dreams and experiences in Little Red River, she immediately commented, "Strange how some things come about." She then proceeded to tell me that while I was away at the meeting in Little Red River, the dreamer had told them "there would be three young people that would be able to show us the way, the old way, how we pray to God; that if we see a young person pray or doing something out of the ordinary, we should not talk about them or bother them, that later they would be the ones to show us the way to God." In her view the three young people that the dreamer had talked about corresponded to the three young men in my dream. An account of a dream on my part thus immediately led to an account of the dreamer's teaching in my absence, each being seen as supporting the other, much as my report to the Elders of events that occurred during the meetings were seen by them as confirming their own dreams and powers.

*

The insights I now have into Dene Tha ritual I attribute to prolonged and intense participation in the Dene Tha world, in coactivity with Dene Tha dreamers who invited me to partake in their ritual performances and their day-to-day life. Participation in the Dene Tha world included not only a sharing of their activities but also direct personal experience of the kind of vivid imagery that appears to the Dene Tha in the midst of ritual activity. These visionary experiences are seen by the Dene and the Cree—and,

244

indeed, by many Native North Americans—as a form of nonverbal instruction that is an integral part of their lives. In the language of the Dene Tha, paying attention to what one knows with one's mind, while awake or while dreaming, is part of competent participation in life generally and in ritual performances specifically.

The circle and the path, the dominant symbols of the Dene Tha ritual complex, speak of harmony and of regularities in the cosmos and in the life cycle of human beings. The Prophet Dance promises a quick journey on the path to the other land to individuals who are generous in life, feed the fire with their offerings, dance at the sound of the drum at the Prophet Dance, or pray the rosary. The tension between this ideal and the realities of collective life are manifest in the open threats that individuals at times make to Elders officiating at a ritual performance. Disturbed and disturbing individuals are met with typical Dene Tha equanimity as people withdraw from the ceremonial site rather than confront those who interfere with their activities. Elders always attempt to reincorporate alienated individuals in the Prophet Dance circle, even if it takes a few years to do so.

10. An Experiential Approach to Knowledge

*

I tell you this, so that you may know a little bit.
—Dene Tha speaker

Ethnographers usually land in strange places, that is, places that are strange to them but, of course, not strange to the people who belong there and live there. For many ethnographers, the ideal was and still is to live without other non-natives, right among others, and there "to grasp the native's point of view, his relation to life, to realize *his* vision of *his* world" (Malinowski 1961, 6, 25; emphasis in original). In this context anthropologists endeavor to meet all the challenges of fieldwork: never to go native, never to become one of them, lest the resulting ethnography become a naive espousal of another people's world view and ethos and thus lose all objective or scientific value; to learn, within a year, or two at the most, enough of the local language to conduct themselves in the native tongue in everyday situations and to work in close association with local interpreters on more specialized topics; to gather through participation and observation data on local social institutions, knowledge, and world view; and finally, to communicate to fellow anthropologists and to a wider public their understanding of and the significance of the data or information so gathered. In the words of Geertz (1973, 30), the result of fieldwork should be "an interpretation of the way a people live which is neither imprisoned within their mental horizon, an ethnography of witchcraft written by a witch, nor systematically deaf to the distinct tonalities of their existence, the ethnography of witchcraft written by a geometer."[1]

In the end, every ethnography claims to represent a distinct way of living in the world at a particular historical moment in the life of a people. Any claim to knowledge, that of the other or that of the anthropologist, is based on an epistemology, however implicit. It is, therefore, to epistemological issues that I now turn to show how Dene Tha views on epistemology are germane to wider anthropological discussions concerning relationships between the investigator and the investigated.

The experience of fieldwork, writes Claude Lévi-Strauss (1963, 373), represents for the anthropologist "not the goal of his profession, or a completion of his schooling, or yet a technical apprenticeship—but a crucial stage of his education, prior to which he may possess miscellaneous knowledge that will never form a whole." To apprehend a social world "as a whole in the form of a personal experience" (Lévi-Strauss 1963, 272) is necessary to depict adequately that world to oneself and to others. That is what this book has attempted to do.

Social competence among the Dene Tha begins with the recognition that learning ought to occur primarily through observation rather than through instruction, a practice that is consistent with the Dene view that true knowledge is personal knowledge. The investigator's willingness to learn experientially is the prerequisite to grasping Dene ways of living and doing things. Investigators who cling to research methods that clearly separate observer and observed stand to lose, because in the eyes of the Dene, they distance themselves too much from what the Dene consider the authoritative source of true knowledge. If the investigator seeks an explanation, he or she is offered one according to the Dene estimation of his or her experiential learning and understanding. This estimation of the ethnographer's knowledge, not the investigator's research agenda, determines the flow of information, which is, preferably, provided in the form of stories between Dene and anthropologist. Given long-standing and deep Dene epistemological views and ethical values, an investigation of Dene Tha social life may be sought, with Dene cooperation, through what Barth, Jackson, Tedlock, V. Turner, and others have referred to as "radical participation" in a people's way of life.

Dene regard true knowledge as personal, firsthand knowledge, and they foster everyone's autonomy as much as possible in all domains of life. This has profound implications for what Dene consider the proper way to teach or inform, not only their children and one another but also the inquisitive ethnographer. The respect for everyone's ability to learn by oneself is the gateway to personal knowledge. In that sense, Dene insist that investigators proceed among them without haste, observing themselves as well as others. Dene expect anthropologists to pay attention to their own lives, including their inner lives. It is through personal experiences of dreams and/or visions experienced while living among the Dene Tha that the ethnographer learns what it means to take part in the rhythm of wakefulness and dreaming, spending time in both our land and the other land.

An analogy with the acquisition of a second language may help convey a sense of this experiential investigative strategy. Learning a people's language, developing the ability to hear and emulate sounds in the native language, is considered good practice in ethnographic work. Having conformed to this practice, the investigator attends to sounds and meanings that would otherwise remain beyond the grasp of his or her auditory and intellectual abilities. In the context of repeated and prolonged exposure to members of a linguistic community, the anthropologist comes to live in an acoustic world different from the one prevailing in his or her home culture. Although the anthropologist rarely, if ever, becomes as fluent as a native, he or she knows enough to get by and to carry on with his or her work, with or without the help of interpreters. Similarly, the anthropologist may come to inhabit, as it were, other domains of the native speaker's society, whether kinship, economic, or ritual, attending to socially constituted realities that otherwise would remain beyond his or her reach. In all cases, writes Katherine Ewing (1994, 571), "the act of participation in a particular mode of life draws us into a common reality. The fieldwork situation provides not only stimuli to respond to but also new models for how to respond to them, as the ethnographer struggles to situate himself or herself in a world of radically changed circumstances."

In reality, few anthropologists would dare lay claim to having absorbed another way of life. One becomes competent in another's world to some degree but always has a sense of having barely scratched the surface. However intense and prolonged one's participation in another's world, one remains, at best, "an outsider who knows something of what it is to be an insider" (Keesing 1992, 77). Tamara Kohn (1994, 21) reminds us, "I can go and spend full days working in the paddy fields with Yahka woman and can experience what their work feels like to me, but will never literally experience what it is to do that work, barefoot, almost every day of one's life." Kirsten Hastrup (1986, 9–10) uses the term "becoming" as "a metaphor for a participation [in the world of others] which can never be complete and which is no natural consequence of physical presence in the 'other culture.'" In this state of becoming, "one gives in to an alien reality and lets oneself change in the process. One is not completely absorbed in the other world, but one is also no longer the same" (Hastrup 1986, 10).[2]

As an ethnographer, I came to the Dene Tha as an adult, having already absorbed a way of life that forever remains in the background of my consciousness. As an incoming fieldworker, I strove "towards what Bourdieu has aptly called 'practical mastery' (1977)," that is, the ability "to read the right signals and arrive at some sort of synchrony of action . . . without sticking out like a sore thumb" (Kohn 1994, 18). I shaped my behavior according to Dene Tha expectations with greater and greater ease, and in the process I became intelligible to them as they did to me: we entered each other's homes without knocking on the door; we carried on with our activities in the presence of an arriving visitor; we avoided eye contact when listening to each other; we pointed to objects or persons with our lips, never with our hands or fingers; we shared information concerning impending activities as a form of invitation to join in them if we so wished; and we offered tobacco and other appropriate gifts to dreamers and healers when in need of assistance.

Doing all this, and much more, I was literally putting myself "in the place of other persons, inhabiting their world" (Jackson 1989, 135). Nonetheless, I never became that other person. Although I often spontaneously behaved as a Dene Tha would have behaved, I remained aware that I would not conduct myself the same way at home. Indeed, there were times when I felt that it was not really right to enter someone's home without knocking or that it would be better to get up and greet a visitor when he or she entered my home. Although I could be seen to behave like a Dene Tha, the affective connotations of my doing so were colored by my own upbringing according to Euro-Canadian ways.

THE FOCUS OF AN EXPERIENTIAL STUDY

The theoretical issue involved in pursuing a largely experiential investigation of Dene Tha social realities is that of defining what is to be the focus of one's anthropological study. The answer to this question varies according to one's theoretical and methodological perspectives. They shape the manner in which one attends to the behavior, beliefs, and environment of a particular population and, consequently, the manner in which one gathers different kinds of data. The "process of choosing what to include and what to exclude" from one's investigation is of great consequence, for "to assume research objectives and directives is to engage in a process of social construction, in effect constituting the object being observed and analyzed" (Gusfield 1992, 119).[3]

In his introduction to the second edition of Malinowski's *Diary in the Strict Sense of the Term*, Raymond Firth (1989, xxviii) remarks that with the publication of this diary anthropologists openly admitted that the ethnographer studying another society "both affects that life and is affected by it." Even if anthropologists had known this for a long time, they nevertheless tried to mitigate their effect on the society and culture they sought to record in their pursuit of scientific knowledge. The modern view of fieldwork assumed that field researchers were "a means to an end with ethnography as the goal" (Barz 1997, 208), hence the efforts to devise fieldwork techniques (unobtrusive observation, census taking, tape recording of naturally occurring conversations) to control for so-called experimenter effects. In the same vein, authors wrote themselves out of their ethnographies, to give the reader as pristine a view as possible of the way of life of others.

This modern vision of fieldwork was predicated on the opposition between an ill-defined We (Westerners) and a residual category encompassing all other peoples, called variously Primitive, non-Western, or Traditional. "One of the central myths of the modern period in the West," writes Shweder (1991, 2) is "the idea that the opposition between religion-superstition-revelation and logic-science-rationality divides the world into then and now, them and us." According to Favret-Saada (1990, 191), the "Great Divide between 'them' and 'us'" was a device used by ethnographers and their audiences to protect themselves "from any contamination" by the object of anthropological study. Of course, "'we' too once believed in witches, but that was three hundred years ago, when 'we' were 'they'" (Favret-Saada 1990, 191). This opposition has been the object of much deserved criticism, by

Johannes Fabian (1983), Edward Said (1978), and Erik Wolf (1982), among many others. It is now generally accepted that others should be seen not "as ontologically given but as historically constituted" (Said 1989, 225). The representation of the other is always, and necessarily so, a derivative of social positions and interpretive assumptions, those of the anthropologist and/or of the other.[4]

Experiential ethnographers accept this. They therefore move away from "the project of classical empiricism . . . to abstract binding and deciding rules from the flux of lived experience" (Jackson 1986, 64), and they promote a view of fieldwork that calls "for the integration of field research experience with the representation or communication of that experience" (Barz 1997, 209). Experientialist ethnographers emphasize over and over again their connectedness in the field to particular individuals, in specific places, at a given point in time, for it is in interaction with other individuals that one gains knowledge of particular forms and processes of social life.

Experientialist ethnographers strive to write accounts of personal experiences in the field without falling victim to the accusation of being narcissistic and thus invite the native's reprimand: "That's enough talking about you, let's talk about me!" (this joke, attributed to Marshall Sahlins, is reported by George Marcus [1994, 569] and included in John Van Maanen 1995, 29). It follows that, as a writer, the anthropologist must train himself or herself "to distinguish between self-indulgence and ethnographically relevant experiences" (Kisliuk 1997, 39). To determine what to include in our ethnography, Michelle Kisliuk (1997, 39) suggests that we "ask ourselves whether an experience changed us in a way that significantly affected how we viewed, reacted to, or interpreted the ethnographic material." It is with this question in mind that I include in this work numerous accounts of personal involvement with Dene Tha that illuminate how I came to move beyond my Euro-Canadian conditioning (but never totally) into a world that is distinctively Dene.

In my earlier work on the Dene Tha I wrote within the tradition of interpretive anthropology. I focused "on the socially available 'systems of significance'—beliefs, rites, meaningful objects—in terms of which subjective life is ordered and outward behavior guided" (Geertz 1971, 95). In this book I focus on the work that people—the Dene Tha and the ethnographer interacting with them—actually engage in to "create their indeterminate realities, and act in them" (Barth 1992, 66). The focus of an interpretive approach differs from that of a generative approach. In the former, one describes and analyzes a public, taken-for-granted system of meaning in terms of which others interpret their world; in the latter, one describes and analyzes the interaction between actors as they engage in the work of constituting a social reality within which to conduct their lives (G. Watson and Goulet 1992).

Interpretive anthropology, like most other schools of anthropology, assumes that the ethnographer's experiences are "instrumental rather than integral to ethnographic description" (R. Ridington 1988, xii). According to the éminence grise of interpretive anthropology, anthropologists "cannot live other people's lives, and it is a piece of bad faith to try" (Geertz 1986, 373). Geertz (1986, 373) argues that whatever sense is made of "how things stand with someone else's inner life, we gain it through their expressions, not through some magical intrusion into their consciousness." It follows, therefore, that as ethnographers "we can but listen to what, in words, in images, in actions, they [others] say about their lives." Hence interpretive anthropology's focus is on the public system of *symbols*—speech, art, actions, artifacts, and the like—in terms of which individuals interact, order their subjective experiences, and speak about them.

Geertz states that what anthropologists say is, or ought to be, "a result of their having actually penetrated (or, if you prefer, been penetrated by) another form of life, of having, one way or another, truly 'been there'" (Geertz 1988, 4–5). Geertz uses a sexual metaphor to suggest that penetrating another form of life, or being penetrated by one, is a matter of preference, of no significance to the process and outcome of fieldwork. This is not the case. Interpretive anthropologists intent on grasping a people's religion, for instance, wait for the propitious moment to interview individuals about their religious beliefs "in a setting about as far removed from the properly religious as it is possible to get. We talk to them in their homes, or the morning after some ceremony, or at best while they are passively watching a ritual"

(Geertz 1971, 108). In his comments Geertz betrays the assumption he shares with most anthropologists in this century, namely, that it is possible "to understand native religion and yet remain outside of it" (D. Tedlock 1995, 269). This is how most anthropologists attempted to grasp any aspect of social life among others. It is an approach that privileges Western canons of investigation and ignores native views on epistemology.

Among the Dene, to seek information in the manner Geertz advocates would be foolish at best. In fact, it would be a clear failure to grasp their view of true knowledge. The Dene insist, not in words but in deeds, that one learn about their rituals experientially, in coactivity with other Dene. Only then will one know or understand "a little bit." An experiential approach to understanding social realities differs considerably from an interpretivist approach and yields qualitatively different results.

The situation among the Dene Tha is comparable to the one Favret-Saada found in her investigation of witchcraft among the peasants of Le Bocage in contemporary France. In Le Bocage, as among the Dene, one "must make up one's mind to engage in another kind of ethnography," since "there is no room for uninvolved observers" (Favret-Saada 1980, 10, 12). Favret-Saada found among French peasants what investigators have found among many other groups: simply "'informing' an ethnographer, that is, someone who claims to know for the sake of knowing, is literally unthinkable" (1980, 9). Similarly, in her work with healers in French Brittany, Ellen Badone (1995, 13) writes that she was wrong in presuming that "cloaked with the immunity of the researcher, thousands of miles from home, one can contemplate the spirituality of Others without being implicated in it." To be involved or implicated is to become an actor in coactivity with others "in the know." In such cases, anthropologists must confront "the fact that the interaction promoted through long-term participation produces not only 'observations' but also conceptualizations and insights that are clearly a *joint* creation of the anthropologists and his/her local partners in interaction" (Barth 1992, 65). Since the ethnographer uses "'participation' much more radically as a method than most interpretivists have imagined" (Barth 1992, 66), his or her experiences become an integral part of the ethnographic description.

An Experiential Approach

I agree with Geertz that we can neither live other people's lives nor magically intrude on their consciousness, whether members of our own culture or of another. But to see the task of the ethnographer as Geertz defines it precludes some of what we can do and learn in the field, not only about others but also about ourselves in our interaction with them. Ethnographic work can—but does not need to—go hand in hand with the anthropologist's experiences of dreams and visions. These often become part of interactions with others, as documented in this book. More than merely listen to what others say about their lives, then, anthropologists pay attention to their own lives, including their inner lives. They observe and listen to other people's responses to their accounts of their own dreams and/or visions experienced while living among these others. To do so is to become an experiential ethnographer.

This experiential perspective is articulated in different terms by various anthropologists. Jackson (1986, 164) refers to it as a form of radical empiricism. Whereas classical British empiricism separated the observer from the observed, radical empiricism takes as its field "experience undergone rather than gone beyond." In other words, to experientialist ethnographers, knowledge is "a form of worldly immanence, a being-with-others, an under-standing" (Jackson 1986, 164). Poewe (1996, 200) notes that "for the production of knowledge and for epistemological reflection, experiential ethnographers depend on how the 'self' of the anthropologist interacts with experiences, people, and the flow of events in the field." E. Turner (1996, xxii) writes that among the Iñupiat of Alaska she became aware of their "own truth, in *process*, in use." She does "not claim that the rest of the world has to abide by what Iñupiat say," but she insists on writing an ethnography derived from living passionately through the shared joys and sorrows, the common anticipations and the recollections, of the people who asked her to tell the whites "that what they say is true" (E. Turner 1996, xxii). In all cases, experiential ethnographers weave themselves, "or are woven by others," into the communities they study, "becoming cultural actors in the very dramas of the society [they] endeavour to understand, and vice versa" (Cooley 1997, 18).

An Experiential Approach

In this respect, reports of waking dreams and visions are consistent with "good ethnography," which "must disturb, shock, or *jolt us* into an awareness we did not have before" (Obeyesekere 1990, 224; emphasis added). The stories that may disturb us do not disturb the Dene. That is so because my accounts of waking dreams and visions are consistent with accounts of similar experiences that Dene constantly produce and share among themselves and, at times, with an ethnographer. Whether these accounts are told by Dene Tha or by the ethnographer is not the issue. To share one's dreams with one's hosts is to communicate with them in a manner that fosters one's inclusion in their society, which then ceases to be simply a subject of one's investigation and becomes a part of one's own life. One could choose simply to ignore such experiences and leave them out of professional discourse, as is most usually done. To do so, however, would be to assume that the ethnographer's experiences are not integral to the ethnographic description, an assumption challenged by more and more anthropologists.

REALITY CONFRONTS US AND CANNOT BE WISHED AWAY

In this book I have described the Dene Tha world and the ethnomethodologically inspired analyses of experiences lived within that world, experiences that were clearly grounded in the social and linguistic practices of the Dene Tha. To achieve such descriptions, I participated, radically, in their world. I made myself vulnerable to their complex human existences, explored new forms of knowledge, became involved in unanticipated local structures of power, engaged in a wide range of Dene practices, and paid close attention to how Dene Tha speak of events in their lives, as well as in ours, in their language. Inevitably, I absorbed some of their way of life, up to a point. By this same measure, I became a competent member in their social environment, that is, someone who could recognize people, other beings, and events for what they obviously were. I have shown how easily we can read into their English spoken accounts of events meanings that are simply not there. The meanings of English words used by Dene Tha become obvious only when they are asked to translate their statements to Dene Dháh and back to English.

An experiential investigation of Dene Tha social realities generates rich contextual accounts of phenomena that the Dene Tha, and the anthropologist among them, cannot wish away: the pursuit of knowledge pertaining to our land and to the other land based on personal, direct experience rather than observation; the encounter with animals, powerful and sentient beings in their own right; the experience of losing one's mind and doing crazy things when drunk; the medicine fights through which individuals oppose each other's will and power; the interaction with the dead through dreams and visions; the birth of children seen as reincarnation; the life histories of those who have had previous incarnations; and the ways of knowing with the mind and of praying that enable the Dene Tha to incorporate and reinterpret Christian ideas, symbols, and rituals according to a distinctively Northern Athapaskan world view.

Narrative ethnography provides the literary form in which the anthropologist and the Dene Tha can be seen for what they are, the coproducers of anthropological knowledge. Ethnomethodologically inspired analyses of accounts of experiences among the Dene Tha allow us to capture the social process whereby participants go about constituting the Dene Tha world as a recognizable state of affairs, without subverting a participant's understandings or replacing them with the understandings of the analyst. The world as it is available to the Dene (and for that matter to any people) "is not available to participants as one among many worlds, but as *the* world" (G. Watson and Irwin 1996, 90).

The world as it is available to the Dene comes to them through socially constituted experiences lived as a particular instance of a more general or typical kind of event. V. Turner (1985, 226) writes that the word "experience" can be traced "right back to the hypothetical Indo-European base *per*, 'to attempt, venture,'" and to the "Latin *experientia*, denoting 'trial, proof, experiment,' . . . which is of course related to *periculum*, 'danger' or 'peril.'" Turner (1986, 35) also notes that these meanings are found in "the Germanic cognates of *per* [that] relate experience to 'fare,' 'fear,' and 'ferry,'" as well as in "the Greek *peraō* [which] relates experience to 'I pass through,' with implications of a rite of passage." Following Wilhelm Dilthey, V. Turner (1986, 36) therefore distinguishes between the mere experience, the passive endurance of events, and "*an* experience," that which "like a rock in a Zen sand garden, stands out of the stream of temporality." In this sense of the word, Dene Tha have an experience when they first demonstrate their successful mastery of a skill learned from the careful observation of others, or when they encounter an animal who becomes an animal helper in life, or when they have a dream that tells them of a reincarnation taking place, or when they dance to the sound of drums in the Prophet Dance. To have an experience, however personal and transformative, one must anchor it in an interpretive community. In other words, to have an experience is to also recognize that what takes place in one's life "is a replaying, in some dimension, of things that happened to others" (Abrahams 1986, 60). What can be shared of the personal is the typical. What can be grasped of the personal is filtered through cultural frames. Through these frames an experience is recognizable as an instance of "this" or "that." Only then can the experience become part of a narrative, to oneself and/or to others.

In interaction and in conversation with Dene Tha, I have used, as far as possible, their socially constituted, taken-for-granted, experience-near concepts, in terms of which they typically understand themselves and the world in which they conduct their lives. To have done anything less would have been to abandon my quest to grasp their point of view, their relationship to life, and their vision of their world. To ensure that I did not stray from my chosen path, Dene Tha astutely reminded me: "If you don't say the right words, and we don't like it, you are in trouble. Like you write what we tell you, we could walk away, what would you do? You can't write anymore." Ethnographic knowledge is, thus, constantly situated, negotiated, a contingent outcome of ongoing processes of interpretation and reinterpretation.

When listening to Dene Tha accounts of their experiences in our land or in the other land, we are paying attention to credible views, ones that work for the purposes at hand of making sense of one's life experiences in terms that are also intelligible to others with whom one lives. Such accounts are immune to the arguments that might be made against them by an outsider to the interpretive community in which they are held to be true. In other words, in any interpretive community, reality is self-validating in that all aspects of it are mutually constitutive and, further, in that it reflexively preserves itself by stipulating in advance what is allowable as evidence.

To refer to a process of continually creating and sustaining social reality is to refer to the human activity of interpretation, of constituting "this" as an instance of "that," of establishing a certain order, as opposed to another one, in human experience. The work involved in producing and reproducing a reality is work that people everywhere perform smoothly, routinely, and unremarkably. It is work they are necessarily inattentive to while performing it. This is true of the work of anthropologists, whatever their persuasion, in producing and reproducing a certain theoretical view of human beings in the world. It is also true of the work of the Dene Tha, of the Kutchin, of the Burmese, or of any other people, in producing and reproducing the world of everyday living in which to conduct rational and moral lives.

Ethnomethodologists teach us that "we describe and simultaneously constitute reality (not once and for all, but from moment to moment, and not necessarily in agreement with one another) and then orientate to it as if it had an existence independent of the work we perform in constituting it; we reify it. Then we feel constrained by it. In this sense reality confronts us and cannot be wished away" (G. Watson 1994, 411). The point to keep in mind is that in the common-sense attitude in which we live our daily lives, we are never aware that "reality is never simply given," that "it is constructed," and that its apprehension "is always an active process involving subject and object" (Bellah 1970, 242). Rather, while living our daily lives, we do so on the basis of *"the general thesis of reciprocal perspective,"* assuming all along that "the world taken for granted by me is also taken for granted by you, my individual fellow-man, even more, that it is taken for granted by . . . everyone who is one of us" (Schutz 1967, 12; emphasis in original). That is to say, for all practical purposes, we inevitably live our lives as if the world existed as it is independently of our role in constituting it as it is. Our work, then, as fieldworkers and ethnographers, is to confront reality as it is confronted by our hosts, to describe all that they cannot wish away and that, therefore, must enter any reasonable and moral account of one's actions and those of others.

An Experiential Approach

Throughout this experiential study of knowledge and power among the Dene Tha I have been concerned with ways of knowing, those of the Dene and those of the anthropologist. In the course of time I have come to grasp the profound implications of the Dene concept of true knowledge as personal knowledge. The acceptance of Dene epistemological assumptions led me to an experiential ethnography that moves beyond the canons of classical anthropological work. I offer the resulting narrative ethnography to the reader to ponder, much as Elders gave extensive narratives to me: "I tell you this, so that you may know a little bit."

Notes

1. I initiated my fieldwork with a week-long visit to Chateh in July 1979, and I pursued my research intensively for six months each year (January through June), from 1980 to 1984 inclusively. Since then I made regular shorter visits up to the summer of 1992.

INTRODUCTION

1. All statements from Dene Tha speakers in this book are verbatim, from my fieldnotes. Although I quote extensively from this verbatim record of our conversations, I have given fictive names to speakers and other individuals to protect their anonymity. Actual names of Dene Tha individuals are used where they appear as such in material borrowed from other sources: Moore n.d.a and b, Moore and Wheelock 1990, Meili 1991, and Robertson 1970. When I quote in Dene Dháh, I follow the orthography proposed by Moore and Wheelock (1990). See Moore and Wheelock 1990, 89–101, for a detailed presentation of vowels and consonants in Dene Dháh. See The Dene Tha' Nation (1997) for numerous photographs of the Dene Tha homeland and of Dene Tha band members who describe in vivid details their living relationship to the land.

2. Asch (1989) and Mills (1994d) discuss the relevance of Dene views in Canadian courts. Asch argues that the Dene ought to base their claim to the aboriginal right to hunt on their own conception of what an animal is, rather than on the Euro-Canadian notion of "wildlife." Mills discusses how Gitksan and Wet'suwet'en chiefs attempted to introduce their evidence before the court of British Columbia. The chiefs were seeking recognition of their aboriginal rights over 55,000 square kilometers (22,000 square miles) of the land considered "Crown Land," that is, property of the province, in north-central British Columbia. The chiefs hoped "that in taking the time to explain themselves and their culture to a judge he would be educable" (Mills 1994d, 150), and that he would recognize their aboriginal rights if he could only grasp "their belief in reincarnation because their sense of self-worth, identity and identification with the land is intimately connected to their perception of themselves as the ancestors . . . who are reborn" (Mills 1994d, 151). Judge McEachern discounted their evidence when he declared that their aboriginal title did not exist. That decision was appealed by the Gitksan and Wet'suwet'en before the Supreme Court of Canada in a case referred to as *Delgammukuu v. British Columbia*. On 11 December 1997 the Supreme

Court ruled in favor of the appellants and ordered a new trial that would give greater weight than Judge McEachern did to aboriginal oral histories, especially of the kind presented by the Gitksan and Wet'suwet'en in the form of song or official litany that stand as proof of the group's internal system of land tenure law. This decision can be found in the University of Montreal Faculty of Law Web site, http://www.droit.umontreal.ca/doc/csc-scc/en/rec/texte/delgamuu.en.txt. See Asch 1997 for an insightful collection of essays concerning the relationships between Canadian law and aboriginal traditions.

3. Since June Helm MacNeish's 1960 article "Kin Terms of Arctic Drainage Déné," published in the *American Anthropologist*, anthropologists use the term "Dene" where their predecessors would have used "Northern Athapaskan." For a history of the use of the terms "Northern Athapaskan" and "Dene" in the anthropological literature, see Goddard 1981 and Abel 1993, xiv-xv.

4. Treaties 1 to 11, signed between 1871 and 1921, are known in Canada as "Numbered Treaties" (Dickason 1992, 273–89). They were political instruments used by the Canadian government, in conformity with the Royal Proclamation of 1763, which is part of the Canadian Constitution, to "purchase" the land occupied by Indians. The federal government and the Indian signatories to these treaties have constantly been at odds as to their significance, the government claiming that the treaties extinguished aboriginal rights to land and to self-government and the Indians insisting that they were a means of establishing friendship and peace between two distinct people who would share their resources. See Fumoleau 1975 and 1994 for a history of Treaties 8 and 11 and G. Watson 1979 for the political significance of a Treaty Day celebration in a Dene community.

5. June Helm MacNeish (1956, 131–32) notes that we have no direct knowledge of Northern Athapaskan aboriginal conditions: "In even the earliest reports it is evident that the contact situation had already wrought changes in the aboriginal way of life. Indeed, if Hearne is correct, a smallpox epidemic, circa 1781, so destroyed the population (90 per cent of the Chipewyan in Hearne's estimate) that northeastern Athabascan society must have been shaken to its foundations. Another indirect effect of the European world upon Déné society that preceded the first explorer was the stimulation given to the gun-bearing Crees to raid and plunder the defenceless Mackenzie River Déné for their furs. Whole populations fled their home territories in consequence. But of the particular movements we have little detail." The Crees, for instance, pushed the ancestors of some of the Dene Tha of Chateh and Meander River northward away from the

Lesser Slave region (see map). For Marxist-inspired analyses of this socioeconomic transformation among the Dene, see Asch 1975, 1979a, 1979b, and 1982.

6. The notion of relative progress in various areas of anthropological investigation among the Dene is an important one. Excellent reviews of Slavey ethnography by Asch (1981) and of the other Northern Athapaskan groups are found in Helm 1981. Lee (1992, 45) notes the work of Ridington and Asch as important contributions to the study of hunter-gatherer societies by anthropologists working within the humanist and political economy paradigms, respectively. Cruikshank's presentation of Dene women's lives "lived like a story" (1990); Helm's study of the contemporary Dogrib Prophet Movement (1994); the study of the Dunne-za view of self and their belief in reincarnation by Mills (1986, 1994a–d); Moore and Wheelock's (1990) presentation of Dene Tha oral literature; Savishinsky's study of mobility, stress, and emotional restraint in small-scale societies (1974, 1982); Sharp's narrative ethnography of the relationship between specific symbolic forms as a means of gender regulation among the Chipewyan (1988a, 1995); Slobodin's (1994a, 1994b) discussion of Northern Athapaskan reincarnation beliefs; and Rushforth and Chisholm's analysis of continuity in values and patterns of behavior among the Bearlake Athapaskans (1991), among others, all mark significant ethnographic and theoretical developments in the study of Dene societies and cultures generally and of Dene so-called religious ideology.

7. Hallowell expressed the same view when he wrote (1976, 400–401), "With respect to the Ojibwa, let me say at once that neither 'natural' nor 'supernatural' are terms appropriate for describing their world outlook. Instead of any fundamental dichotomy, there is, rather, a basic metaphysical unity in the ground of being. In their behavioral environment we cannot say, for example, that the sun is a 'natural object.' It would also involve a distortion of their thinking to say that the sun is a 'personified' object. For this would imply that, at some point in the past, the sun was perceived as an inanimate material thing, and later given animate properties. There is of course, no evidence for this, and all speculation along such lines reflects simply a Western cultural bias, from which we must completely detach ourselves if we are to enter the culturally constituted world of other peoples." See Asad 1993, 27–54, for an insightful discussion entitled "The Construction of Religion as an Anthropological Category."

8. Among the Bear Lake Dene, Rushforth (1986, 253) reports that "through dreams individuals come to 'know a little bit about things.'"

The Dunne-za of Fort St. John "say that a person with power obtained through dream and vision, 'little bit knows something'" (Ridington 1988, 103).

9. In this same vein, members of the Native American Church did not allow Fox to produce a videotape of their ritual performance to "legitimate" it in the eyes of the courts (Bateson and Bateson 1987, 72–76). Fox argued that audiovisual "evidence" would strengthen their claim to entitlement to freedom of religion before the U.S. courts. Indians turned down his offer, saying that it was "nonsense to sacrifice integrity in order to save a religion whose only validity—whose point and purpose—is the cultivation of integrity" (Bateson and Bateson 1987, 75). Halpin (1995) reports a similar attitude among practitioners of Chanoyu, the Japanese tea ritual, who privilege involvement in the ritual and oral tradition as the proper form of learning what it means to be in-the-present.

10. Lett (1991, 307) criticizes Stoller and Olkes (1987) for their deliberate setting aside of the scientific approach to the production of verifiable and replicable knowledge, thus leading themselves to be duped by a standard series of illusionist's tricks that include misdirection, sleight of hand, and after-the-fact interpretation. In the view of Stoller and Olkes, to approach the Songhay with a "scientific" mindset would have produced an anthropology of error, the rationalist showing once again that the "natives" are deluded. The advantage of Stoller and Olkes's experiential approach is its portrayal of the experiential world of Songhay sorcerers and their non-Songhay apprentice as it is lived by them, in the natural attitude.

11. As noted by B. Tedlock (1991b, 165), contemporary anthropologists are more likely to report their dreams than their predecessors. Malinowski (1967, 66–82, 202–8), Nadar (1970, 111–12), and Caesara (1982, 22) limited themselves to publishing accounts of their dreams from their journals. Bruce (1975), Jackson (1978), B. Tedlock (1981), and Stephen (1989) told their dreams to members of the society they were living with, asking for their interpretation. For more recent illustrations of how anthropologists use accounts of their own dreams and/or visions in their ethnographies, see Young and Goulet (1994) and the 1994 issue of *Anthropologie et Sociétés*, "Rêver la Culture/ Dreaming Culture," edited by Sylvie Poirier.

12. Marcus and Cushman (1988, 25) list twenty-two innovative ethnographies that "integrate, within their interpretations, an explicit epistemological concern for how they have constructed such interpretations and how they are representing them textually as objective discourse about subjects among whom research was conducted." In

the same vein, Van Maanen (1988, 69 n. 6) lists a number of works—Bruyn 1966, Denzin 1970, Lofland 1976, Ruby 1982, Douglas 1985, Agar 1986, Adler and Adler 1987a—that "welcome and praise subjectivity, treating it as a central and essential tool of the ethnographic trade rather than as a potential source of error or unwanted variance to be foreclosed." The kind of ethnographic reporting found in this book is therefore not unique. Indeed, B. Tedlock (1991a) lists forty-one authors who published such first-person experiential fieldwork accounts during the 1980s—more than were published during the previous two decades. For reviews of recent narrative ethnographies, see Mills 1995 and Gottlieb 1995; for discussions of theoretical issues involved in the pursuit of "other ways of knowing," see Barth 1995 and Fife 1995.

13. Narrative ethnography should not be confused with narrative anthropology. Narrative ethnography is the work of ethnographers who take an experiential approach to fieldwork. For them, "the self and especially experiences in the field are 'epistemologically productive' (Kulick 1995:20)" (Poewe 1996, 179). The resulting ethnography typically depicts the ethnographer living and learning with specific peoples at a particular place and time. In contrast, narrative anthropology takes the form of ethnographic fiction in which anthropologists employ various rhetorical techniques to blur the distinction between fact and fiction (Richardson 1996, 623; Poewe 1996, 178–79). Jackson 1986, Knab 1995, and Price and Price 1995 are examples of this literary genre.

14. For discussions of concepts of reflexivity and their use in anthropological investigation and writing, see Scholte 1970, Babcock 1980, Myerhoff and Ruby 1982, Sangren 1988, Woolgar 1988, Platt 1989, G. Watson 1991, Hervik 1994, and Hazan 1995. Many papers presented at the 1976 AAA Symposium, "Rituals and Myths of Self: Uses of Occasion for Reflexivity," organized by Barbara Myerhoff and Michelle Rosaldo, were published in Semiotica 30(1980) (1/2): 1–152.

15. Benson and Hughes (1983) provide a good introduction to ethnomethodology. Atkinson (1980) and Maynard and Clayman (1991) offer critical reviews of ethnomethodologists' accomplishments; Sharrock and Watson (1988) discuss current misconceptions about the subject.

16. To combine narrative ethnography and ethnomethodologically inspired analysis is unusual and raises important questions concerning the nature of ethnomethodology and about who counts as an ethnomethodologist. G. Watson (1991, 74) notes that "ethnomethodology is divided into warring camps." In a more recent publication he

remarks that he "cannot vouch for all of them" (1994, 407). He also writes (1994, 407) that in their 1991 survey of the diversity of ethnomethodology, Maynard and Clayman mistakenly identify Melvin Pollner (1987) and Steve Woolgar (1988) with ethnomethodology. However meritorious, Watson (1994, 407) finds that Pollner's and Woolgar's project is not ethnomethodological: "Rather than describe how informants go about constituting *their* world as a recognizable state of affairs for *them*, they [Pollner and Woolgar] have them struggling with analytically imposed problems of epistemology," and as a result, their "informants are unlikely to recognize what purports to be descriptions of their own activities as descriptions of their own activities." It is not my intention to attempt to resolve the intricate issues and complex debates alluded to here. I view ethnomethodology and ethnography as complementary, but I do not claim to practice ethnomethodology's sister discipline, conversation analysis. As noted by G. Watson (1991), some authors argue that ethnomethodology and conversation analysis are "ultimately identical" (Sharrock and Anderson 1986), others see them as "complementary" (Bilmes 1976; Moerman 1988), and still others regard them as "incompatible" (R. Watson 1992). The conversation analyst works from detailed transcriptions of recorded verbal interaction between individuals. My ethnomethodologically inspired analyses of Dene accounts of their experiences are based on a verbatim record. My preference for handwritten verbatim statements over tape-recorded conversations reflects my concern not to alienate Dene Tha, who are very reluctant to have their statements recorded on audiotapes in case others get to hear them. They are not so concerned with handwritten notes. Ethnomethodologically inspired analyses of verbatim records are, however, possible, as demonstrated by G. Watson and Goulet (1992, 1998) and G. Watson (1992, 1996) with some of my Dene Tha material.

17. See Moerman's (1988, 88–100) incisive analysis of the inconsistencies between Geertz's stated interpretive program and his theoretical assumptions concerning the status of linguistic forms that "stand in a one-to-one relationship" to ideas, and the status of culture as an internally coherent "system of ideas."

18. See Stocking Jr.'s (1987, 302–14) and Tedlock and Mannheim's (1995, 9–12) informative survey of the changes in anthropological definitions and understanding of the concept of "culture" over the last century.

1. STORIES FROM THE FIELD

1. B. Tedlock reports a similar experience in the context of a ritual in which Zunis cried as they remembered their dead. She writes (1992,

96) that while the Zunis were doing so, "my own dead were flipping past me like slides in a time carousel."

2. I agree with Price-Williams (1992, 250) that in discussions of such experiences the anthropologist should use the term "waking dream" where the religionist, the student of the paranormal, and the psychiatrist would use the term "vision," "apparition," and "hallucination," respectively. Desjarlais (1992, 20–24) uses the expression "waking dream" to discuss his trance experiences in the course of a shamanic apprenticeship. What Bateson and Bateson (1987, 92) write about ordinary perception applies equally well to waking dreams: "I know which way I aim my eyes and I am conscious of the product of perception but I know nothing of the middle process by which the images are formed."

3. For an excellent narrative account of Dene life, see the recent book by Robert Jarvenpa (1998), in which he presents the intricacies of the Dene way of life from the perspective of an anthropologist turned apprentice to Dene hunters and teachers.

2. TRUE KNOWLEDGE

1. As noted by Rushforth (1992, 483), these features of Dene social life are also described by Brody (1981), Christian and Gardner (1977), Goulet (1989), Hara (1980), Helm (1961, 1965), Honigmann (1946, 1954), MacNeish (1956), Moore and Wheelock (1990), Rushforth (1984, 1985, 1986), Rushforth and Chisholm (1991), Savishinsky (1970, 1971, 1974, 1975), Sharp (1986, 1987, 1988a, 1988b), Slobodin (1970), and D. Smith (1973, 1982, 1985, 1988). Wax and Thomas (1972) see in the ethics of nonintervention a distinctive feature of interaction in all Native North American societies. They write (1972, 34), "The Indian society is unequivocal: interference of any form is forbidden, regardless of the folly, irresponsibility, or ignorance of your brother." As a spectacular example of this ethical stance, Wax and Thomas describe the behavior of Indian passengers who refrain from pointing out to the driver of a car the rock slide or the wandering steer that is likely to cause the car to roll in the ditch. To suggest to the driver that he change course would be "interference." "As the car rolls merrily into the ditch all that may be heard is a quiet exhalation of breath" on the part of the passengers (Wax and Thomas 1972, 35). I thank D. Smith for bringing this work to my attention. Clare Brant, a Mohawk psychiatrist from the Tyendinaga Reserve in southern Ontario, credits Rosalie Wax, "a white woman" and "an anthropologist," for being the person who best explained the Native North American ethics of noninterference, in an article entitled "Indians

and White People" (1952) (Brant 1982 in Ross 1992, 12). See also Brant's (1990) interpretation of Native North American behavior from the perspective of the ethics of noninterference.

2. These students were from the Alberta Vocational College in Grouard, where I had taught a course on Cree history and culture in the spring of 1982.

3. At Lower Post (Yukon), Honigmann's way around the difficulty of engaging Kaska individuals to cooperate in his research agenda was to interview Kaska males who had considerable previous experience working with the formidable Northwest Division of the United States Army when it was building the Alaska Highway through the Kaska homeland. Among these workers, Honigmann found "willing male informants" who were "most cooperative" and possessed "considerable facility in English" (1954, 6). With these individuals Honigmann experienced little of "the reticence, diffidence, and disinterest" so often reported by anthropologists for Northern Athapaskans. See Goulet 1996b for a critique of Honigmann's presentation of information received from these informants, particularly concerning gender roles in Kaska precontact culture.

4. See Kohn (1994, 15–16) for an account of fieldwork experience among the Yahka, a Tibeto-Burman group living in eastern Nepal, which led him to challenge Goodenough's assertion (1981, 50, 63) that one must learn a people's language to learn its culture (that is, a people's local "emic" categories and their meanings), as well as Chomsky's view (1986) "that language is the key to culture—the best mirror of the human mind."

3. POWERFUL BEINGS

1. Notions of power denote various conceptions of agency, not only across cultures but also across theoretical approaches within the social science. Lukes (1978) shows that power is not a concept or a discrete phenomenon but an aspect of sociological discourse: theoreticians advance different concepts of power according to their view of society and political life. For discussions of the lack of consensus on the meaning of the term "power" in the social sciences, see Dahrendorf 1959, 166; Adams 1977, xi; Fogelson and Adams 1977; and Arens and Knapp 1989, xi–xxv. G. Watson and Goulet (1998) compare and contrast the Dene Tha concept and sociological concepts of "power."

2. Students of subarctic populations refer to these experience-near concepts as mental percepts (Preston 1975; Christian and Gardner 1977; Ridington 1988, 1990) or subjective paradigms (Sharp 1986).

To refer to the subjective or perceptual correlate of common-sense reality is not, however, to ignore the fact that "it is a preeminently social phenomenon" (G. Watson and Goulet 1992, 217).

3. For a discussion of the "vision quest" in its various forms among Native North Americans, see Benedict 1964; Dugan 1985; Hallowell 1976, 464–71, and 1992, 80–92; Ridington 1990, 14–21; Brown and Brightman 1988; and Irwin 1994. D. Smith (n.d., 24) argues that the Chipewyan acquisition of power from animal helpers should not be thought of as a form of mysticism or vision quest, as that implies "a separation from the sacred which is transcended through some kind of spiritual discipline or activity." My use of the expression "vision quest" to refer to the Dene Tha practice of seeking power from an animal helper has no such implication. See my discussion in the introduction of the inappropriate use of Eurocentric labels such as religion, mysticism, and supernatural in the description of the Dene Tha world.

4. Hastrup (1996, 153) reports similar experiences in the work of Okely and Díaz de Rada and Cruces. Okely (1984, 5) writes that when working among English-speaking gypsies in Britain, she "had to learn another language in the words of [her] mother tongue." Similarly, Díaz de Rada and Cruces (1994) "uncovered new meanings in their native Spanish once they turned their professional ethnographic gaze towards contemporary compatriots."

5. The reference to the Omaha phrase is from Fletcher and La Flesche 1911, 130.

6. The Dene association of the Eagle with the Thunderbird is also reported for the Plains Indians. "Of all the celestial powers," writes Irwin (1994, 53), "it is the Thunder Being who holds the most prominent place among Plain dreamers as a source of great and fearful power. The manifestations of this mysterious being are the tremendous thunderstorms that roll across the plains, booming and flashing with huge black clouds, shooting fearsome yellow, green, and red lightning. In form, the Thunder Being is frequently associated with the Eagle."

7. This ability to transform oneself into one's animal helper is a common feature of Native North American accounts of vision quest experiences (Hallowell 1934, 399, for the Ojibwa; Irwin 1994, 74, for the Omaha; and Sharp 1986, 258–60, for the Chipewyan).

8. Similar practices are reported by Duchaussois (1923, 218–19) for the Dogrib, by Ridington (1978, 9–17) for the Beaver, and by D. Smith (1973, 8) for the Chipewyan. Petitot reported the practice for the Loucheux when he visited them four times between 1865 and 1877:

"Les indiens se procurent dès qu'ils ont reçu l'initiation, une peau ou quelque partie de l'animal afin d'en fabriquer une amulette, un talisman. Griffes, queues, oiseaux empaillés ou étalés. . . . On portait ces objets sur soi. On en décorait les pirogues, les berceaux et les couches; et les époux prenaient leur repos sous le regard de l'animal tutélaire, suspendu au-dessus de leur lit" (As soon as they have been initiated, the Indians acquire a skin or some other part of the animal to make an amulet or talisman. Claws, tails, stuffed birds . . . were worn. They also adorned boats, cradles, and beds; and spouses would rest under the watchful eye of their animal helper, suspended over their bed) (in Savoie 1971, 90).

9. See Brightman 1993 for a recent account of the Cree view of animals as friends or lovers of human beings, and Feit 1994, 433–36, for a discussion of the Cree view of animals as beings who are "like persons."

10. To perceive childlikeness in a human or nonhuman being is an interpretation based on a tacit understanding of children's qualities. An old Netsilik woman reported to Rasmussen (1931, 328; in Briggs 1972, 328): "It is generally believed that the white men have quite the same minds as children. Therefore one should always give way to them. They are easily angered, and when they cannot get their will, they are moody and, like children, have the strangest ideas and fancies." The white men are seen as children, because in Inuit thought "expressions of ill temper towards human beings (as distinct from dogs) are never considered justified in anyone over the age of three or four" (Briggs 1972, 328). Given this expectation, it is not surprising that in the Utku view the white men "are about as bad-tempered as the dogs from which they are considered to be descended" (Briggs 1972, 329). See also Basso 1979, for a discussion of how the Apache construct the "Whiteman" as childlike.

11. Sharp (1986, 263) notes that this secrecy contrasted "with the openness" concerning sorcery reported by D. M. Smith (1973) at Fort Resolution.

12. The cooperation of anthropologist and indigenous people in "producing" a shared narrative is also true of relationships between missionaries and Native North Americans. In his introduction to *An Annotated Bibliography of American Indian and Eskimo Autobiographies*, David Brumble (1981, 1) writes that "some of the earliest of the American Indian autobiographies, tales of conversion and missionary life . . . were read as evidence of the marvelous ways in which nineteenth-century America's God worked, his wonders to perform. . . .

It is the white society which provided the pen and the letters, the questions and the occasions for written autobiography."

13. See B. Tedlock (1992, 41–45) for an excellent discussion of how contemporary Zuni reconcile their view of the moon as a deity with the news that American astronauts have walked on the moon, and Guédon (1994a, 65–66), who writes that Tetlin Elders were not concerned about "the hole the astronauts had opened in God's sky," for once on the moon the astronauts had been dancing—the Tetlin interpretation of the astronauts' movements. In the eyes of the Tetlin, "the dance made everything all right."

4. POWERS TO HEAL

1. A condensed version of this chapter is to appear as "'A Power' to Heal and 'a Power' to Harm," in a volume to be published in honor of June Helm, edited by David Smith, Henry Stephen Sharp, and Bob Jarvenpa.

2. Borrowing from Williamson (1955), Abel (1993, 28) reports the story of Ehtsontie, the son of a Chipewyan father and Cree mother, who "knew steel" and who distinguished himself in a battle that took place in the earlier part of the eighteenth century: "He was discovered by his people in the heart of the enemy camp, swinging his caribou antler club, breaking the enemy's arms so that they could not shoot their guns. The enemy bullets had merely bounced off his body, so powerful was he even as a child."

3. For a discussion of the "power" of menstrual blood in gender relationships among Native North Americans, see Albers and Medicine 1981, 257; Allen 1992, 152–55; Patterson 1995, 136–41; and Williams 1997, 207.

4. A similar opposition is found in southern Alberta, where "the people of the Blackfoot confederacy often refer to themselves as the Soyitopi, or 'prairie people.' Previously, they referred to themselves as the Nitsi-tapi, or 'real people,' but this term is now used to describe North American Indians in general [including the Blackfoot]. Nonnatives are still known as Napikway, a term which may be translated as 'oldman people' and is roughly the equivalent to the English term sophomore (wise-fool)" (Holyoak 1993, 40).

5. See Krech 1979 for an examination of interethnic relations in the lower Mackenzie River region over the last two centuries.

6. This Cree medicine man once asked me to accompany him to a Dene Tha healer in Meander River, to serve as an interpreter in his request for healing. When we arrived at the healer's residence, I introduced both of us and explained the purpose of our visit. The first question

the Elder asked was, "*Góon ink' onze edanedi?*" "Do you know power?" I answered, "I do not really know power, but I know that Elders do." The Elder then asked questions about the Cree medicine man before proceeding with a healing ceremony that included an identification of the Cree individuals who had used their power to affect him adversely. To my surprise, after I had transmitted all the information I had been asked to and the healing ceremony was concluded, the Cree medicine man and the Dene Tha Elder engaged in a conversation in Cree. The Dene Tha Elder became the interpreter between his Cree visitor and myself as we discussed political developments affecting Dene and Cree regionally and nationally.

5. VISIONS OF CONFLICT

1. A condensed version of this chapter is to appear as "Visions of Conflicts, Conflicts of Visions among Contemporary Dene Tha," in *Hunters and Gatherers in the Modern Context: Social Reproduction, Identity Politics, and Development*, edited by Megan Bisele and Robert K. Hitchcock (Oxford: Berg, forthcoming).

2. Honigmann (1981, 737) supports this characterization, with references to Hallowell 1946, 207–8; Honigmann 1949, 250–58; Helm and De Vos 1963; Helm, De Vos, and Carterette 1963, 127; Slobodin 1960; Helm 1961; Balicki 1963; and Savishinsky 1971; to which we may add Hammer and Steinbring 1980; Brody 1981, 249–53; Ridington 1988, 17; Heath 1991, 27, 38; and this chapter.

3. Consistent with this view, Dene Tha stated that it was wrong to order anyone around. In a review of the manuscript of this book it was suggested that "the Dene and Dene Tha belief in reincarnation plays into the noninterference aspect of their lives, in that it is unthinkable for Dene and many other First Nations/Native peoples to reprimand an Elder, and many babies are seen as Elders returned." I have no evidence that this is the case among the Dene Tha. Although a few Dene Tha babies were seen as Elders made again, the majority of cases of reincarnation concerned children or young adults. I have never heard a Dene Tha suggest that he or she was not ordering a boy or girl around because he or she was an Elder reincarnated, or anyone else reincarnated. The general expectation was that everyone's autonomy would be respected because this is the appropriate way to live.

4. Lithman (1979) notes that the Cree among whom he worked in Saskatchewan did not always say they did not know what they were doing when drunk. They would claim so, and thus were not held accountable for their actions, only after fights with drunken fellow band members. In contrast, drunken Cree who would fight with whites in the bar of the

neighboring town would return home and boast about their exploits to earn the esteem of fellow band members.

5. Sharp (1986, 267) reports a similar pattern among the Fort Mission Chipewyan: "The local R.C.M.P. resented that the local Chipewyan often used them in ways that did not conform to established police procedure. The Chipewyan would report crimes or file charges in order to get the R.C.M.P. to break up fights or contain violence by their presence or an arrest. Once the immediate disruption was resolved by police intervention the complaints were rarely followed. Charges would be dropped or testimony changed to prevent jail sentences or fines. This was frustrating to the R.C.M.P. and frequently made them seem inefficient or inept before the court and their superiors."

6. As noted by Slobodin (1975, 279), Hearne's "two years of living and travelling with Chipewyan, 1969–71, far from any trading post or other European, constitutes an experience unmatched in the recorded contact history of the western American Subarctic."

7. After the publication in 1937 of Evans-Pritchard's classic study of Azande witchcraft (1972) the distinction between witchcraft (the ability to harm others through an innate power) and sorcery (the ability to harm others through medicines or the manipulation of objects) was widely used in the anthropological literature. The Zande distinction, however, is rarely found to match exactly categories of power invoked by members of other societies to explain misfortune. Students of the Dene use both terms to refer to a person's ability to use "a power" to harm others. Honigmann (1979, 221) defines witchcraft as "behavior whereby a person with sufficiently strong shamanistic power would steal, or was believed to steal, the wind or soul of a personal enemy and, thereby, induce illness." D. Smith (1990, 157) writes that "medicine fights are examples of what has ordinarily been referred to as sorcery. They occur between two individuals possessing, or able to access, supernatural power (i.e. medicine-power)."

8. See Krech 1981 for a review of Northern Athapaskan accounts of misfortune suffered at the hands of fellow Northern Athapaskans, in the early historic period, 1789–1860; and Helm (1994, 114–16) for accounts of how, in the same historic period, "powerful" Dogribs overtook the minds of their enemies, including that of a Hudson Bay manager to make him extend credit that he had until then steadfastly withheld.

9. It is in this sense that the term "medicine" is most often used in the anthropological literature. It was Ridington (1968) who first wrote of "medicine fights" as an instrument of local political process among the Beaver Indians, a position reiterated in a more recent publication

(1988, 258–59). D. Smith (1973, 1982, 1985, 1990) examines the concept of *inkonze*, "power," and cases of medicine fights among the westerly Chipewyan of the Great Slave region from an ecological perspective. In a more recent publication Smith (1993) writes a fictive narrative that effectively captures the experiential aspects of dealing with animal helpers and power in Northern Athapaskan lives, as does Ridington (1990, 5–13) for the Beaver. Sharp (1986) draws on Turner's concept of "social drama" to discuss medicine fights in the context of the progressive decline of a Chipewyan prophet, and Helm (1994) explores the concept of *ink'onze* among the Dogribs on the basis of accounts given by her key informant, Vital Thomas. The term "medicine fight" does not appear in the index of the *Handbook of North American Indians*, volume 6, *Subarctic*. In the index, under "Shamans," there are two references to shamanic "contests," the first to the Saulteux of Lake Winnipeg, among whom, following Hallowell, Steinbring (1981, 250) writes about "shamanistic contests in which two rival shamans competing for power and authority would incite each other to the highest pitch of evil-doing sorcery," and the second to the Tutchone, among whom shamans or dream doctors "duelled with the spirit helpers of rival dream doctors from other groups" (McClellan 1981, 502).

10. Helm (1994, 77) reports that "luck and magic were words that some Dogribs fell back on when trying to refer to *ink'on* in English." I have never heard Dene Tha do so in their discussions of *echint'e*. Feit (1994, 434), however, notes that among the Waswanipi Crees, "in hunting, when the things a hunter thinks about actually come to be in the future, he is said to have *miyopayıw*, or 'good luck.' And when they do not come to him, he has *matsiipaio*, or 'bad luck.' Luck or power is thus not a matter of chance, but an ebb and flow of connections between human lives and a personalized universe." Among the Waswanipi Crees "God is said to be all powerful, and the boss, or leader, of all things" (Feit 1994, 434). It is God who gives animals to respectful hunters. "When asked to explain the power of God, the most common statement is that what God thinks, happens. When asked to explain their own power, hunters' most common statement is that they sometimes know what will happen, that what they think sometimes comes true" (Feit 1994, 434).

11. See Goulet forthcoming and n.d. for two similar cases.

12. Sharp demonstrates how Chipewyans who present themselves as "powerless" to others get them to behave in desired ways. Chipewyans get white teachers in the settlement or spouses at home to help them by activating the "sense of responsibility in others" (1994, 48).

6. JOURNEYS OF THE SOUL

1. According to Vital Thomas, June Helm's key Dogrib informant, the Dogribs did not really have a word for soul before the missionaries came (Helm 1994, 78). The same is reported for the Chipewyan of Great Slave Lake, who "sometimes use the expression *inin* to refer to soul or spirit," an expression that Fort Resolution Chipewyan Elders gloss "with the English word 'thinking'" (D. Smith n.d., 27). This word, with its close association to the notions of mind, thinking, willing, and soul or spirit, is equivalent to the Dene Tha word *kindí*, "someone's mind."

2. The image of the flight to heaven contrasts with the more usual one of the path one has to walk to heaven. In our conversations Alexis Seniantha, like other Dene Tha, referred to the path to heaven with a branch forking left. The straight path was the one leading to the other land. In their efforts not to cry when a spouse or kinsman dies, contemporary Dene Tha depart from the traditional pattern of grieving reported for Native North Americans of the subarctic generally, among whom "death produced a sense of loss to which the survivors gave expression by wailing, fasting, destroying their possessions, and abstaining from work" (Honigmann 1981, 727).

3. Dene Tha often compared the body's shadow to someone's ghost or spirit, but they never identified the two. Some anthropologists use the term "shadow" to refer to the Euro–North American concept of "soul." According to Jenness, for instance, the eastern Canadian Indians distinguished between the "corporeal body that decays and disappears after death, a mind or soul that travels after death to the land of souls in the west, and an image or shadow (Latin *imago*) that roams about on earth after death, but generally remains near the grave" (1991, 441). Jenness goes on to write that "the image is slightly more indefinite than the soul and the Indians often confuse them" (1991, 441). I am suspicious of the anthropologist who suddenly becomes the expert on Indian thought, drawing clear distinctions that are often ignored by the Indians themselves. Perhaps it is Jenness who has oversystematized, for a Western audience, his presentation of the Indian view of nature. Concerning the Beaver or Dunne-za, Mills (1982, 26) writes that they "make a threefold distinction between body, shadow, and breath. If I understand their thought correctly, breath is the quality of life coming ultimately from Yagesati [he who created the world from thought], shadow is the equivalent to our concept of soul. . . . As long as the breath stays with the body the shadow can slip back into the body. If the shadow gets lost or frightened and is unable to reenter the body, eventually breath too with-

draws and the body dies." The Dene Tha would say that if the spirit or soul does not reenter the body, the individual eventually ceases to breathe and dies. The Dene Tha simply distinguish between the body and the soul or spirit, which may be in more than one place at the same time, as explained in the following chapter.

4. This answer suggests that a ghost may choose to make a horse die and then follow that horse's spirit on its way to the "other land," a topic I could not pursue with this speaker and did not pick up with other Dene Tha.

5. Individuals may also carry with them "medicine power" that will work against their enemies, as in the following report: "[She] bought a bag from the people in the North; she carries that little bag inside her blouse. Even at the band office, one time she was mad at [him], she took that little bag and swung it around. Boy, people were scared."

6. On another occasion the daughter of this prophet who assisted the old man from Meander River to depart for heaven said the following: "When someone dies, he has to find a path to heaven. My dad and Alexis, if they can't help them find a path, they come back to be reborn. Like the ones who die and do not want to, they come back."

7. In this examination I follow closely G. Watson's analysis (1992, 1996) of the transcript of another conversation from my Dene Tha fieldnotes. The verbatim record differs from the notes of a conversation analysis. As noted by G. Watson (1992, 25), absent from the verbatim record of our conversation are the indications of "pauses, overlaps, cutoffs, alteration of intonation, continuers (uh-huh's) and receipt markers (oh's)", which can be picked up and noted down only from an audiotape of the actual conversation.

8. Other Dene are also "known" to have died and come back to live. Goddard (1916, 227) reports such a case among the Beaver of northern Alberta. According to Dominic Habitant (in Moore 1988, 3–4), "the first Beaver Prophet was called Yahke Ghidíi. He was dead for seven days, but before he died he told the people not to bury him. After seven days he came back to life. Some people still didn't believe it, so there was another sign. While he was gone to Heaven, his drum was hidden away and it reappeared at the top of a tall tree. It had been placed there by angels and on the drum a picture of angels appeared. He told the people to keep the drum tied up outside camp, and when they heard the drum, they should take that as a sign to hold a Tea Dance." Dominic Habitant (in Moore 1988, 3–4) reported another case of resurrection: "Once there was an old woman from here who died and came back. She was just pitiful, you could reach around

her waist with two hands. She came back to tell my mother that there was a place for her in Heaven." Alexis Seniantha (in Moore 1988, 7) also mentions that "somewhere north of Fort Nelson there are people we call Ndahane. There is a woman living there who appeared almost dead for seven days. They had actually put her in a coffin. Finally she got up. She couldn't eat or speak."

7. SEARCHING FOR A WOMB

1. See Matlock and Mills 1994, 299–334, for a comprehensive presentation of trait lists, maps, and bibliography of sources pertaining to reincarnation beliefs among North American Indians and Inuit. Over the years I have recorded forty-one accounts of reincarnation among the Dene Tha, of which eighteen (44 percent) are cases of cross-sex reincarnation. Six cases are discussed in earlier publications: one case in Goulet 1982, 9–10; 1989, 10–11; and 1996b; two other cases in Goulet 1989, 8–9; and three other accounts in Goulet 1994b.

2. According to Mills, the Dunne-za account differently for the fact that some individuals do not remember a previous reincarnation. They say that after reaching heaven "the disincarnate person's soul is washed," making "their memories of their past life, of specific people and places, and of their likes and dislikes" largely unrecoverable when reborn. But some souls "never get past that place where you have to grab hold of the cross" to continue on the path to heaven. These souls are reborn quickly and are known as "special children." They bring with them some of the knowledge, preferences, aversions, and personality they had manifested in previous lives (Mills 1988a, 25).

3. Mills reports the same concerning her return to the Dunne-za in the summer of 1984 after an absence of some years. One of the first things she was told was "who had died and made it to heaven, and who was wandering around as a ghost. Ghosts are seen as being very lonely and sad. . . . Ghosts are also feared because they are said to try to steal the souls of the living, particularly newborn babies, in an attempt to follow the soul to *yage* [heaven]" (Mills 1988a, 50).

4. In her discussion of Beaver, Gitksan, and Wet'suwet'en cases of reincarnation Mills (1988a, 26) uses Stevenson's expression "announcing dream." I. Stevenson (1975, 68) uses the expression "to refer to a dream experienced by a pregnant woman, and sometimes by one of her close relatives or friends, in which, as it seems to the dreamer, a deceased person communicates his wish or intention to be reborn as the baby of the pregnant woman." Among the Dene Tha, however, such a dream is experienced by the woman, or a close relative of hers, before she gets pregnant.

5. See Mills 1994c, 226–32, for photographs of pierced-ear birthmarks that the Gitksan consider signs of the reincarnation of a high chief or warrior.

6. See G. Watson (1992, 1996) for an insightful analysis of this account from an ethnomethodological perspective.

7. Mills (personal communication, July 1991) notes that what has changed among Northern Athapaskan hunters and gatherers "is that nubile girls are no longer married to older men" as was common in the past, when "a young girl might have become the second or third wife of a camp leader (who may have been married to a number of women since his childhood)." On that basis Mills suggests that the men's sorrow may reflect "in part that the marriage pattern is breaking down, and that teenage mothers no longer necessarily settle down with a spouse."

8. My account of seeing Nancy was received as normal by the Dene Tha, as indicated by the lack of astonishment it occasioned and by the spontaneous associations other Dene Tha individuals made with similar experiences of their own. The same account related in the context of an academic work will astonish some members of the profession. In this respect I am in agreement with Fabian (1991, 399) who not only recognizes that "there is an ecstatic side to field work" but insists that it "should not be written off as a quirk but counted among the conditions of knowledge production, hence of objectivity." A growing number of anthropologists agree with this view and therefore pay more attention to ecstasis in their work. One may think of Myerhoff's vision of herself impaled on the Mayan tree of life after having ingested peyote among the Huichol (1972); of Favret-Saada's experience of witching and unwitching among the French peasants of Le Bocage (1980); of Grindal's vision of a corpse dancing in the midst of a funeral among the Sisala (1983); of Laderman's experience of the "Inner Wind" when in trance as an apprentice to a Malay shaman (1988, 1991); and of B. and D. Tedlock's experiences of dreams in the context of apprenticeship to a Quiche Elder (B. Tedlock 1991b; D. Tedlock 1990). As noted by Fabian (1991, 399–400), Goulet and Young (1994, 307), and E. Turner (1996, xxii–xxiv), it is important that anthropologists make their experiences of dreams and/or visions, when awake or when in trance, an integral part of their narrative ethnography. Such reports confirm the expectation that the deeper the penetration by a new culture, the more likely are ethnographers to report changes "at the psychic level in the patterns of cognitive and emotional response and in the unconscious manifestations through dreams and visions" (Kimball 1972, 191). The im-

portant issue from an anthropological perspective is that of the social construction of such experiences and of their social significance in the interaction of individuals in a shared cultural setting.

9. In an article published in the *Journal of the Royal Anthropological Institute* (Goulet 1996b, 696) I used Paul's earlier and slightly different account of his cross-sex reincarnation to discuss the process whereby he was invested with a dual sexual identity. The discussion of that case is used in this chapter in its entirety, along with additional material drawn from my fieldnotes. The article includes an extensive critical analysis of the anthropological construction of Northern Athapaskan gender identities that is not part of this book.

10. This analysis of Paul's transformation from someone with a dual identity is inspired by Strathern's discussion of Melanesian initiation rituals that "replace the child's androgynous body with a single-sex one," allowing the child to emerge "as 'male' or 'female' to encounter its opposite female or male" (1993, 48). Strathern thus argues that initiation rituals gender the individual as "an incomplete being." Paul's transformation was a part of his life and was not a feature of the lives of other girls who had been made again as boys. At no point was Paul expected to occupy the status of "berdache" or of "Two-Spirit," for there is no such status among the Dene Tha, or indeed among any of the other Northern Athapaskan cultures examined in Goulet 1996b.

11. This is also the case with the task of communicating views within other interpretive communities, scientific ones included. See G. Watson 1994 for an insightful analysis of how a judge goes about the task of passing judgment.

12. The Hare Indians are a Northern Athapaskan population living along the shore of the Mackenzie River, in and around Fort Good Hope.

8. WHEN DRUM AND ROSARY MEET

1. Elsewhere (Goulet 1996a) I use Obeyesekere's (1981) analysis of the connections between the private or personal aspects of symbols—their motivational or pragmatic aspects—and the public meaning of symbols (their cultural aspect) to discuss Alexis's status as a Christian shaman. In that publication I make use of another account of Alexis's vision, one recorded by Hernou (1982). The visionary experience of Alexis will undoubtedly bring to mind accounts of other Native North American Indian visions. Irwin (1994) offers an excellent synthesis on the topic. DeMallie (1984), Holler (1995), and Powers (1996) discuss the accounts of the visionary experiences of Black Elk among

the Lakota; Matthews and Roulette (1996) offer a fine case study of Naamiwan Obawajigewin's 1914 vision, which gave him the right to create an innovative dream drum ceremony among the Ojibway.

2. Other Dene prophets also report having had personal encounters with Christ. Alexis Seniantha (in Moore n.d.b, 3) recalls a visit to the Prophet Naidzo at Bear Lake, where he had taken his sick wife to be healed. Naidzo was sleeping on the floor when people appeared to him. He wondered what those people were standing on, when he realized that Christ was looking and smiling at him. Then Christ shook his hand and looked at him. Naidzo wanted to follow after him, but Christ said, "No, stay by my side." Naidzo then walked along next to Christ. At noon Naidzo saw three people eating. Plates, knives, and forks were set to eat. Christ told Naidzo, "This place is for you" (you eat here). Naidzo thought he was being tricked. Christ said, "Let's eat over there." Naidzo went with him over there. After the meal Naidzo came back to earth, saying: "I'm going to live! That was Jesus talking to me."

3. Alexis and his brother Billy go by different family names, as do many other Dene Tha siblings, because these, the Dene Tha say, were the names they were given by the Indian agent following the band's signing of Treaty 8. Elders frequently complained of this government practice, as it means that brothers and their children go by different patronyms when they should be the same.

4. The lexical marker *ti* is used to refer to someone's superior, leader, or parent, as in *keti*. It is also used to distinguish police officers, *dene kuelehi*, from the judge to whom they report, *dene kuelehiti*.

5. The Dunne-za, for instance, say that they have had about sixteen prophets, beginning with Dakwene and ending with Charlie Yahey (Mills 1982, 61). The Northern Slaveys name "Ari, a Dogrib Indian, as the first significant Dene prophet" (Beaudry 1992, 81). Janes and Kelley (1977) identify a number of references to local "prophets" in their compilation of prehistoric crisis cult activities in the Northwest Territories. Helm (1994, 162) notes that their presumption that these prophets invariably rise as a result of a crisis "raises as many evidential questions as it purports to answer." In fact, the "disaster and deprivation" theory is the one drawn on by most authors when they attempt to explain why Canadian Natives accepted Christianity. Abel (1989, 77, 91) notes the following authors who make use of this approach: Conkling (1974) for the Algonkian, Slobodin (1966) for the Métis of the MacKenzie, Trigger (1976) for the Huron, Martin (1978) for the subarctic indigenous populations as a whole, and Grant (1984) for various Indian groups across Canada. This approach is

unwarranted in the case of the Dene (Abel 1989) in general, and for the Dene Tha in particular, who perceived Christian practices as complementary to their own.

6. Dene Tha also mentioned that making a cross of stones and pointing it toward the storm causes it to change course. Similarly, the smell of burnt rubber scares the thunder away. Tlingit shamans are also reported to use crosses and other Christian religious objects (Kan 1991, 371).

7. These communities are Assumption (Slavey), Meander River (Slavey), Eleske (Beaver), Jean D'or Prairie (Cree), Fox Lake (Cree), and Fort Chipewyan (Chipewyan and Cree).

8. The same comparison between dreamer and priest is reported for the Beaver by R. Ridington (1978, 17): "Both [dreamer and priest] teach about heaven, the priest knows about it only from books, while the dreamer knows it from his own experience."

9. Vital, Helm's main informant on Dogrib world view and practices, also says of the Dogrib prophet of old that he "was like a priest" (Helm 1994, 61). That the Dene conceived of dreamers and priests as belonging to the same realm of experience may account for the following observations by Petitot, reported by Helm (1994, 162 n. 6): "Petitot (1893: 98–101) refers to a Slavey, a 'crazy man' at Fort Norman who on the basis of his visions proclaimed himself a 'priest' of God. Petitot (1879: 7–8) also reports that at Fort Good Hope an old Dene who presented himself as the 'Eternal Father' began to confess, baptize, and sing mass, until his wife announced her 'vision from God' that her husband was a liar, while she was the 'Holy Virgin.'"

10. Gualtieri (1980b, 55) notes that the most substantial effort of indigenization was in the area of liturgical decoration, with altar frontals and antependia "made of sealskin or caribou in most cases richly designed albeit mainly with traditional European designs." To become part of the liturgical decoration the piece of art had to "please" the missionaries. For instance, in the mid-1980s a Dene Tha artist had been asked by the local priest to do a painting of the Virgin of Guadalupe for a fellow Roman Catholic priest to set up in a newly built chapel. When this priest saw the Dene Tha artist's depiction of the Virgin, he declared he did not really like it. No sooner had that been said than the local priest turned the painting around, pulled out his own paint and brushes, and drew on the canvas an Orthodox-like Virgin that was to his colleague's liking. This is the Virgin that ended up being seen in public. See Peelman (1995) for a detailed presentation and discussion of recent Native artistic expression of the Christian faith.

11. In preparation for the 1984 visit by the pope to Fort Simpson, where he was to bless a monument consisting of three Dene drums, the Roman Catholic bishops asked the Dene for an explanation of the meaning of the drums so the pope would understand what he was blessing. A Dene from Fort Simpson came to consult with Alexis Seniantha concerning the answer to give the bishops. Alexis told the envoy that all the pope and the bishops needed to know was that the drum is to the Dene as the church organ is to them. When the missionaries introduced the organ to accompany songs and prayers in church, the Dene did not ask for explanations; they accepted the missionaries' statement that the organ was to pray by, and they prayed along with it. According to Alexis, the church should do the same concerning the Dene view of the drum as a means of accompanying their songs and prayers. The priest to whom the envoy reported Alexis's answer was not satisfied, claiming that if dialogue between the Dene and the church was to take place, it had to proceed at a deeper level and to have more to it than what Alexis was asking them to accept. Here again one sees the Dene preference for experiential learning and the Western need for explicit instructions regarding the meaning of actions to perform.

12. This scenario does not exclude the possibility that a wave of Pentecostal missionaries might come to the Dene, as they have indeed come to many other arctic and subarctic populations, among them the Dene Tha neighbors, the Beaver or Dunne-za from the St. John area in northeastern British Columbia. Under such circumstances the reinterpretation of the Pentecostal beliefs in terms of Beaver world view reported by Mills (1986) and R. Ridington (1987) is very likely to occur also among the Dene Tha.

13. There are excellent monographs or collections of essays that do precisely this (e.g., Barker 1990, Badone 1990, Comaroff and Comaroff 1991, Keyes 1991, Hefner 1993, Brett 1996, Hexham and Poewe 1997).

14. The thesis of religious dualism is also employed by Mulhall (1986, 31, 65) and Beaudry (1991, 34) to account for the coexistence of aboriginal and Christian beliefs and practices in the same population. They refer not to Rousseau but to other authors as earlier champions of this thesis, to Nock (1933) and Peel (1968) in the case of Mulhall, and to Powers (1987) in the case of Beaudry. See Peers 1996, I. Stevenson 1996, and Matthews and Roulette 1996 for insightful analyses of the interpretations of Christian beliefs and practices by Native North Americans.

15. See Waugh's (1996) analysis of Vandersteene's career as a missionary and his attempt to integrate Cree religious tradition,and Roman Catholicism. The work of missionaries among the Dene is the topic of several excellent studies: Abel 1984 and 1993, Champagne 1983, Choquette 1995, and McCarthy 1981 and 1995.

16. Spiro, Keyes, and Tambiah are engaged in a similar debate concerning the unity or dualism of South Asian religions. Spiro (1969, 1970) stresses the incompatibility of animist beliefs and Buddhist teachings; he therefore finds religious dualism among the Burmese, who have recourse to "both religions" in different contexts. In contrast, Tambiah (1970) and Keyes (1977) argue that Buddhism and Southeast Asian spirit cults form "a single religious system." See Saler 1993, 36–38, for a discussion of the use of the notion of religious dualism by Spiro for Burmese Buddhists and by myself for Dene Tha Roman Catholics.

17. Similarly, a Gitksan told Mills (1988a, 34) that he heard an evangelist preacher say "that if you're really good, God will send you back to this world" to be reincarnated.

18. In the same vein a Cree medicine man once told me that in a ceremony he performed he had a cross facing down, covered with a cloth, to represent the fact that Christ had come not for the Indians but for the Jews and Europeans, who had "lost their way."

19. Other Native North Americans rethink their "pre-Christian religion by affirming its validity [in the past] while acknowledging the greater wisdom and power of Christianity" (Kan 1991, 364). I once heard an eleven-year-old girl ask her mother: "When they put tobacco on the fire, they are feeding the devil. That's the truth, hé?" The mother answered that she thought the missionary had not told the truth, that the Tea Dance was appropriate for the Dene Tha until the day the priests came to them, but that since then it is best to pray only with the priest on Sunday.

9. DANCING YOUR WAY TO HEAVEN

1. The Dene Tha use of the expression "Tea Dance" differs from the one reported for other Dene populations. Among the Dogribs, as among the Northern Slaveys, one distinguishes between the tea dance, which "has no accompaniment except the human voice" (Helm and Lurie 1966, 10), and the drum dance, which is performed with "the accompaniment of drumming on Indian frame drums" (Asch 1988, 63). In the tea dance, people dance clockwise, shoulder to shoulder, all facing toward the center of the circle. In the drum dance, people also dance clockwise, but front to back, packed closely

283

together in rows three to four deep, "in time with the even beat of the drum" (Beaudry 1992, 83). In Chateh the latter is the form of dancing associated with the Prophet Dance; the former form of dancing I have observed only in the later part of Prophet Dances held at Easter or on Treaty Days. According to Helm and Lurie (1966, 10), the name "Tea Dance" "derives from the fact that traditionally the Hudson's Bay Company provided the chief, in earlier years the trading chief, with tea and bannock to feed the assembled group when people came into the fort with their winter's fur take." Beaudry (1992, 81–83) reports the same distinction for the Northern Slaveys of the Northwest Territories. Northern Slaveys credit Ari, a Dogrib Indian, for the introduction of the drum dance at the turn of the twentieth century. This innovation followed a vision Ari had in which "angels sang to him, holding and playing a drum," after which they told him "that from then on, some of these songs should be used for dancing to the sound of the drums" (Beaudry 1992, 81).

2. The Beaver Prophet Dance is held either in a house or in a "special tipi large enough to hold everyone who is gathering for the dance" (Mills 1982, 78). If the ceremony is held in the house, "the fire is made in a woodstove or if it is impossible to dance around the stove, a wash tub becomes the symbolic fire around which the people dance" (Mills 1982, 78). See Mills 1982, 78–86, for a vivid description of a Beaver Prophet Dance.

3. This is the term Dene Tha organizers gave to what had been until then the traditional gathering of people at Treaty Day. Dene Tha Elders saw the new site and the new name as an important development. In 1986 Alexis Seniantha had his niece write me a letter informing me of the band's first general assembly and inviting me to attend this very special event, which, of course, I did.

4. This flag is also the one Alexis usually puts up on the flagpole behind his house. He once told me: "When I walk to my house, I pray to the white flag there, I pray for my relatives and ask that God helps us. This too I keep here [he took out a small crucifix from his pocket], and I pray with it."

5. Helm (1968, 8 n. 8), who first observed this ceremony among the Dogribs on 30 June 1968, reports that her informants told her it had been introduced at tribal feasts in 1966 "by the present Dogrib Prophet (even before he became the recognized Prophet), who was in turn instructed to do this by the Beaver-Slave Prophet Alexis." Helm (1968, 8) notes that "'feeding the fire' is reported by Goddard (1916, 228) as part of a semi-annual ceremonial gathering of the Bea-

ver Indians (and is to be found elsewhere in the Athapaskan North, e.g., Helm 1961: 101)."

6. In the words of Helm (1994, 59), "the well-lived life is in the service of one's soul, the means to attain heaven." Given what we know from the previous chapters, this is not to say that for the Dene "the lure of and reward for honorable living is that happy next world, the Christian heaven" (Helm 1994, 59).

7. In households where fathers and sons were actively engaged in hunting and trapping, people tended to rise with the sun, if not before, and go to bed early. We have noted this pattern in chapter 1 in the case of Paul and his family. In another family a young man in his late teens told me that he had been up at 5:00 AM, "real early," because otherwise his father would be irritated with him. With his father he had gone to the bush to check their trapline at 6:00 AM Later in the day the young man went duck hunting and brought back five ducks, three of which he gave to his grandmother and two to his mother. He then sat next to me and told me again that he had been getting up very early all week, sometimes before the sun. He was visibly proud of himself. Commenting on his younger brother, who runs around all night and sleeps in the morning, he said, "His way is not good."

8. See Goulet 1982, 11–14, for a discussion of the apparent split between old and young often reported in the literature on Native North Americans.

9. In central Alberta a Cree medicine man and politician showed me pictures taken in the 1970s showing an exchange of flags between himself and Alexis Seniantha as a sign of goodwill and an alliance between the Cree and the Dene.

10. In 1982, when Alexis Seniantha gave a drum to Dominic Habitant, many saw it as an indication that Alexis was choosing him as a potential successor, much as Nogha had done when he gave Alexis a drum.

11. See Peelman's (1991) detailed presentation and discussion of this meeting from the point of view of non-Native participants.

10. AN EXPERIENTIAL APPROACH

1. Stocking Jr. (1991) provides an excellent discussion of the role of Malinowski in the creation of this mystique of fieldwork. B. Tedlock (1991a, 85) lists thirty-six titles of works published between 1959 and 1989 intended to demystify the process of fieldwork. Many works have been published since with the same intent. For illuminating discussions of the process of fieldwork, see also Anderson 1990, Grindal and Salamone 1995, Agar 1996, Brettell 1996, and Colley 1997.

2. Hastrup (1992a, 7), who delves into the theme of puzzlement as the hallmark of anthropology born in the experience of cultural differ-

ence, argues that "although there are no more white patches on the ethnographic map, and no new peoples to discover, there are still untold depths to fathom in the way in which culture and society are shaped by people and vice-versa" (from Rudie 1994, 43; Rudie's translation).

3. Consider, for instance, Geertz's *Islam Observed* (1971), Rappaport's *Ecology, Meaning, and Religion* (1979), Spiro's *Burmese Supernaturalism* (1978), V. Turner's *Drums of Affliction* (1968), or Obeyesekere's *Work of Culture* (1990), each a distinguished contribution in the field of anthropology of religion yet each presenting different data and using distinct terminology according to a chosen theoretical approach.

4. For instance, I once overheard a conversation between two fundamentalist Christians outside the Tyrell Museum of Paleontology in Alberta. Having seen the museum's rich collection of dinosaurs and the many exhibits explaining the evolution of life on earth over more than five hundred million years, one of the men asked his friend, "If the dinosaurs existed, did they exist before or after Noah's ark?" In their eyes the museum exhibits had not established as a "fact" that dinosaurs existed. To accept such a fact, they first had to focus on an intellectual framework within which such "facts" could exist. Similarly, following a tour of the Buffalo-Head-Smashed-In interpretive center in southern Alberta, devoted to the prehistory and history of the Blackfoot in the area, a Blackfoot guide who had just given us the archaeologists' view of the evidence unearthed there said he didn't believe a word of it. Whereas archaeologists claimed that ancestors to the Blackfoot migrated into the area a few thousand years earlier, the Blackfoot hold the view that they were made by the Creator and given this land to live on. In this case of disputing claims, as in any other, "disagreements are not settled by the facts, but are the means by which the facts are settled" (Fish 1980, 338).

References

ABEL, KERRY

1984   The drum and the cross: An ethnohistorical study of mission work among the Dene. Ph.D. diss., Queen's University, Kingston.

1986   Prophets, priests, and preachers: Dene shamans and Christian missions in the nineteenth century. In *Historical papers, communications historiques: A selection from the papers presented at the annual meeting held at Winnipeg,* ed. Dana Avery and Louise Ouellette, 211–24. Ottawa: Tanamac International.

1989   Of two minds: Dene response to the Mackenzie missions, 1858–1902. In *Interpreting Canada's North: Selected readings,* ed. Kenneth S. Coates, 77–93. Toronto: Copp Clark Pitman.

1993   *Drum songs: Glimpses of Dene history.* Montreal: McGill-Queen's University Press.

ABRAHAMS, ROGER D.

1986   Ordinary and extraordinary experience. In *The anthropology of experience,* ed. Victor W. Turner and Edward M. Bruner, 45–72. Urbana: University of Illinois Press.

ABU-LUGHOD, LILA

1991   Writing against culture. In *Recapturing anthropology: Working in the present,* ed. Richard G. Fox, 137–62. Santa Fe NM: School of American Research Press.

1993   *Writing women's worlds: Bedouin stories.* Berkeley: University of California Press.

ADAMS, RICHARD N.

1977   Power in human societies: A synthesis. In *The anthropology of power,* ed. Raymond D. Fogelson and Richard N. Adams, 387–410. New York: Academic Press.

ADLER, PETER S., AND PATRICIA A. ADLER

1987a   *Membership roles in field research.* Newbury Park CA: Sage.

1987b   The past and future of ethnography. *Journal of Contemporary Ethnography* 16(1): 4–24.

AGAR, MICHAEL

1986   *Speaking of ethnography.* Beverly Hills CA: Sage.

1996   *The professional stranger: An informal introduction to ethnography.* 2d ed. London: Academic Press.

ALBERS, PATRICIA, AND BEA MEDICINE

1981   *The hidden half: Studies of Plains Indian women.* Lanham MD: University Press of America.

References

ALLEN, PAULA GUNN

1981   Lesbians in American Indian cultures. *Conditions* 7:76–80.

1992   *The sacred hoop: Recovering the feminine in American Indian traditions.* Boston: Beacon Press.

AMERICAN ANTHROPOLOGICAL ASSOCIATION

1989   General principles of professional responsibility. *Anthropological Newsletter*, November, p. 22.

ANDERSON, BARBARA GALLATIN

1971   Adapative aspects of culture shock. *American Anthropologist* 73:1121–25.

1990   *First fieldwork: The misadventure of an anthropologist.* Prospect Heights IL: Waveland Press.

ANDERSON, IAN G., AND J. R. E. LEE

1982   Taking Professor Gluckman seriously: The case of participant observation. In *Custom and conflict in British society*, ed. Ronald Frankenberg, 286–312. Manchester: Manchester University Press.

ARENS, WILLIAM, AND IVAN KNAPP

1989   Introduction. In *Creativity of power: Cosmology and action in African societies*, ed. William Arens and Ivan Knapp, xi–xxix. Washington DC: Smithsonian Institution Press.

ASAD, TALAL

1993   *Genealogies of religion: Discipline and reasons of power in Christianity and Islam.* Baltimore: Johns Hopkins University Press.

ASCH, MICHAEL I.

1975   The impact of changing trade practices on the economy of the Slavey Indians: Some preliminary conclusions regarding the period 1870–1900. In *Proceedings of the Second Congress, Canadian Ethnology Society*, ed. Jim Freedman and Jerome H. Barkow, 646–57. Ottawa: National Museums of Canada.

1977   The Dene economy. In *Dene nation: The colony within*, ed. Mel Watkins, 47–61. Toronto: University of Toronto Press.

1979a   The ecological-evolutionary model and the concept of mode of production: Two approaches to material reproduction. In *Challenging anthropology*, ed. David Turner and Gavin A. Smith, 81–99. Toronto: McGraw-Hill.

1979b   The economics of Dene self-determination. In *Challenging anthropology*, ed. David H. Turner and Gavin A. Smith, 339–52. Toronto: McGraw-Hill.

288

References

1981   Slavey. In *Subarctic*, ed. June Helm. *Handbook of North American Indians*, vol. 6, 338–49. Washington DC: Smithsonian Institution.

1982   Dene self-determination and the study of hunter-gatherers in the modern world. In *Politics and history in band societies*, ed. Eleanor Leacock and Richard Lee, 347–71. Cambridge: Cambridge University Press.

1986   The Slavey Indians: The relevance of ethnohistory to development. In *Native peoples: The Canadian experience*, ed. R. Bruce Morrison and C. Roderick Wilson, 271–96. Toronto: McClelland & Stewart.

1988   *Kinship and the Drum Dance in a Northern Dene community.* Edmonton: Boreal Institute for Northern Studies.

1989   Wildlife: Defining the animals in the Dene hunt and the settlement of aboriginal rights claims. *Canadian Public Policy—Analyse de Politiques* 15(2): 205–19.

———   ED.

1997   *Aboriginal and treaty rights in Canada: Essays on law, equity, and respect for difference.* Vancouver: University of British Columbia Press.

ATKINSON, PAUL

1980   Ethomethodology: A critical review. *Annual Reviews of Sociology* 14:441–65.

BABCOCK, BARBARA A.

1980   Reflexivity: Definitions and discriminations. *Semiotica* 30(1/2): 1–14.

BADONE, ELLEN

1990   *Religious orthodoxy and popular faith in European society.* Princeton: Princeton University Press.

1995   Suspending disbelief: An encounter with the occult in Brittany. *Anthropology and Humanism* 20(1): 9–14.

BALICKI, ASEN

1963   *Vunta Kutchin social change: A study of the people of Old Crow, Yukon Territory.* NCRC 63–3. Ottawa: Department of Northern Affairs and National Resources, Northern Coordination and Research Centre.

BARKER, JOHN

1990   Introduction: Ethnographic perspectives on Christianity in Oceanic societies. In *Christianity in Oceania: Ethnographic perspectives*, ed. John Barker, 1–24. ASAO Monograph no. 12. Lanham MD: University Press of America.

References

BARTH, FREDERICK

1969   Introduction. In *Ethnic groups and boundaries*, ed. Frederick Barth, 9–38. Boston: Little, Brown.

1987   *Cosmologies in the making: A generative approach to cultural variation in inner Guinea.* Cambridge: Cambridge University Press.

1992   Social/cultural anthropology. In *Wenner-Gren Foundation Report for 1990–1991*, 62–70. Fiftieth anniversary issue. New York: Wenner-Gren Foundation.

1995   Other knowledge and other ways of knowing. *Journal of Anthropological Research* 51(1): 65–69.

BARZ, GREGORY F.

1997   Chasing shadows in the field: An epilogue. In *Shadows in the field: New perspectives for fieldwork in ethnomusicology*, ed. Gregory F. Barz and Timothy J. Cooley, 205–9. New York: Oxford University Press.

BASSO, KEITH H.

1979   *Portraits of "the Whiteman": Linguistic play and cultural symbols among the Western Apache.* Cambridge: Cambridge University Press.

BATESON, GREGORY, AND MARY CATHERINE BATESON

1987   *Angels fear: Toward an epistemology of the sacred.* New York: Macmillan.

BEAUDRY, NICOLE

1991   Rêves, chants et prières Dènès: Une confluence de spiritualités. *Recherches Amérindiennes au Québec* 21(4): 21–36.

1992   The language of dreams: Songs of the Dene Indians (Canada). *World of Music* 34(2): 72–90.

1997   The challenges of human relations in ethnographic enquiry: Examples from arctic and subarctic fieldwork. In *Shadows in the field: New perspectives for fieldwork in ethnomusicology*, ed. Gregory F. Barz and Timothy J. Cooley, 63–83. New York: Oxford University Press.

BELLAH, ROBERT N.

1970   *Beyond belief: Essays on religion in a post-traditional world.* New York: Harper & Row.

BENEDICT, RUTH

1954   *Patterns of culture.* Boston: Houghton Mifflin.

1964   The concept of the guardian spirit in North America. *Memoirs of the American Anthropological Association* 29: 1–97. New York: Kraus Reprint Corp.

References

BENSON, DOUGLAS, AND JOHN A. HUGHES

1983   *The perspective of ethnomethodology.* London: Longman.

BILMES, JACK

1976   Rules and rhetoric. *Journal of Anthropological Research* 32:44–57.

BLACK-ROGERS, MARY

1986   Varieties of "starving": Semantics and survival in the subarctic fur trade, 1750–1850. *Ethnohistory* 33(4): 353–83.

BLONDIN, GEORGE

1990   *When the world was new: Stories of the Sahtu Dene.* Yellowknife NT: Outcrop, the Northern Publishers.

1991   Prayer house opens in the memory of Prophet Ayha. *Press Independent,* 19 July 1991, p. 7.

BLUMER, HERBERT

1969   *Symbolic interactionism: Perspective and method.* Englewood Cliffs NJ: Prentice-Hall.

BODLEY, JOHN H.

1988   *Tribal peoples and development issues: A global overview.* Mountain View CA: Mayfield.

1990   *Victims of progress.* 3d ed. Mountain View CA: Mayfield.

1994   *Cultural anthropology: Tribes, states, and the global system.* Mountain View CA: Mayfield.

BOURDIEU, PIERRE

1977   *Outline of a theory of practice.* Cambridge: Cambridge University Press.

1980   *Le sens pratique.* Paris: Les Editions de Minuit.

1990   *The logic of practice.* Cambridge: Polity Press.

BRADY, IVAN, AND EDITH TURNER

1994   Introduction. *Anthropology and Humanism* 19(1): 3–11.

BRANT, CLARE

1982   Living, loving, hating families in the '80s. Address delivered at the Oshweken Community Hall, 9 January 1982.

1990   Native ethics and rules of behaviour. *Canadian Journal of Psychiatry* 35(6): 534–39.

BRETT, MARK G.

1996   *Ethnicity and the Bible.* Leiden: E. J. Brill.

BRETTELL, CAROLINE B.

1996   *When they read what we write: The politics of ethnography.* Westport CT: Bergin & Garvey.

BRIGGS, JEAN

1972   *Never in anger: Portrait of an Eskimo family.* Cambridge MA: Harvard University Press.

References

BRIGHTMAN, ROBERT A.

1993   *Grateful prey: Rock Cree human-animal relationships.* Berkeley: University of California Press.

1995   Forget culture: Replacement, transcendence, relexification. *Cultural Anthropology* 10(4): 509–46.

BROCH, HAROLD BEYER

1974   Traits of Hare Indian culture: Some remarks on Ake Hultkrantz's article: "The Hare Indians: Notes on their traditional culture and religion, past and present." *Ethnos* 39(1–4): 159–69.

BRODY, HUGH

1981   *Maps and dreams.* Vancouver: Douglas & McIntyre.

BROWN, JENNIFER S. H., AND ROBERT A. BRIGHTMAN, EDS.

1988   *The orders of the dreamed: George Nelson on Cree and Northern Ojibwa religion and myth, 1823.* Winnipeg: University of Manitoba Press.

BROWN, JENNIFER S. H., AND ELIZABETH VIBERT, EDS.

1996   *Reading beyond words: Contexts in native history.* Peterborough ON: Broadview Press.

BRUCE, ROBERT D.

1975   *Lacandon dream symbolism: Dream symbolism and interpretation,* vol. 1. México DF: Ediciones Euroamericanas.

BRUMBLE, DAVID H.

1981   *An annotated bibliography of American Indian and Eskimo autobiographies.* Lincoln: University of Nebraska Press.

BRUNER, EDWARD M.

1986a   Experience and its expression. In *The anthropology of experience,* ed. Victor W. Turner and Edward M. Bruner, 3–30. Urbana: University of Illinois Press.

1986b   Ethnography as narrative. In *The anthropology of experience,* ed. Victor W. Turner and Edward M. Bruner, 139–55. Urbana: University of Illinois Press.

1993   Introduction: The ethnographic self and the personal self. In *Anthropology and literature,* ed. Paul Benson, 1–26. Urbana: University of Illinois Press.

BRUYN, SEVERYN T.

1966   *The human perspective in sociology.* Englewood Cliffs NJ: Prentice-Hall.

BUCKLEY, THOMAS

1979   Doing your thinking. *Parabola* 2(4): 29–37.

BURKE, PETER J., JAN E. STETS, AND MAUREEN PIROG-GOOD

1988   Gender identity, self-esteem, and physical and sexual

References

abuses in dating relationships. *Social Psychology Quarterly* 51:272–85.

BURT, BEN

1994   *Tradition and Christianity: The colonial transformation of Solomon Island society.* London: Harwood.

CAESARA, MANDA

1982   *Reflections of a woman anthropologist: No hiding place.* London: Academic Press.

CARTERETTE, TERESA

n.d.   The relationship of brewing behavior to other behavior in a Slave Indian society. Manuscript.

CHAMPAGNE, CLAUDE

1983   *Les débuts de la mission dans le Nord-Ouest canadien: Mission et église chez Mgr Vital Grandin, o.m.i. (1829–1902).* Ottawa: Les Éditions de l'Université d'Ottawa.

CHOMSKY, NOAM

1986   *Knowledge of language: Its nature, origin, and use.* New York: Praeger.

CHOQUETTE, ROBERT

1995   *The oblate assault on Canada's Northwest.* Religions and Beliefs Series, no. 3. Ottawa: University of Ottawa Press.

CHRISTIAN, JANE, AND PETER M. GARDNER

1977   *The individual in Northern Dene thought and communication: A study in sharing and diversity.* National Museum of Man, Mercury Series, no. 35. Ottawa: National Museums of Canada.

CLIFFORD, JAMES

1988   *The predicament of culture: Twentieth-century ethnography, literature, and art.* Cambridge MA: Harvard University Press.

COHEN, ANTHONY P.

1985   *The symbolic construction of community.* London: Tavistock.

COMAROFF, JEAN, AND JOHN L. COMAROFF

1991   *Of revelation and revolution.* Chicago: University of Chicago Press.

CONGAR, YVES

1953   *L'Eglise Catholique devant la question raciale.* Paris: UNESCO.

CONKLING, ROBERT

1974   Legitimacy and conversion in social change. *Ethnohistory* 21(1): 1–24.

CONNERTON, PAUL

1989   *How societies remember.* Cambridge: Cambridge University Press.

293

References

COOLEY, TIMOTHY J.

1997 Casting shadows in the field: An introduction. In *Shadows in the field: New perspectives for fieldwork in ethnomusicology*, ed. Gregory F. Barz and Timothy J. Cooley, 3–19. New York: Oxford University Press.

CRICK, MALCOLM R.

1982 Anthropology of knowledge. *Annual review of anthropology* 11:287–313. Palo Alto CA: Annual Reviews.

CROW SPREADING WINGS, LYNNE MARIE DUSENBERRY

1987 Whites learning the Indian way. M.A. thesis, University of Calgary.

CRUIKSHANK, JULIE

1990 *Life lived like a story*. Lincoln: University of Nebraska Press.

CSORDAS, THOMAS

1994a Introduction: The body as representation and being-in-the-world. In *Embodiment and experience: The existential ground of culture and self*, ed. Thomas Csordas, 1–24. Cambridge: Cambridge University Press.

1994b Words from the Holy People: A case study in cultural phenomenology. In *Embodiment and experience: The existential ground of culture and self*, ed. Thomas Csordas, 269–90. Cambridge: Cambridge University Press.

DAHRENDORF, RALF

1959 *Class and class conflict in industrial society*. London: Routledge & Kegan Paul.

DE LAGUNA, FREDERICA

1954 Tlingit ideas about the individual. *Southwestern Journal of Anthropology* 8(1): 1–12.

DE LAGUNA, FREDERICA, AND CATHARINE MCCLELLAN

1981 Ahtna. In *Subarctic*, ed. June Helm. *Handbook of North American Indians*, vol. 6, 641–63. Washington DC: Smithsonian Institution.

DEMALLIE, RAYMOND J.

1984 *The sixth grandfather: Black Elk's teachings given to John G. Neihardt*. Lincoln: University of Nebraska Press.

DENE THA BAND OF ASSUMPTION

1990 Submission to the Task Force on the Criminal Justice System and Its Impact on the Indian and Metis People of Alberta. 12 June 1990. Manuscript.

THE DENE THA' NATION

1997 *Dene Tha' traditional land-use and occupancy study*. Calgary: Arctic Institute of North America.

References

DENE THA WOMEN'S SOCIETY

1990   Submission to the Task Force on the Criminal Justice System and Its Impact on the Indian and Metis People of Alberta. 18 April 1990. Manuscript.

DENZIN, NORMAN

1970   *The research act.* Chicago: Aldine.

DEPARTMENT OF INDIAN AND NORTHERN AFFAIRS, CANADA

1987   *Schedule of Indian bands, reserves, and settlements including membership and population, location and area in hectares.* Ottawa.

DESJARLAIS, ROBERT R.

1992   *Body and emotion: The aesthetics of illness and healing in the Nepal Himalayas.* Philadephia: University of Pennsylvania Press.

DESVEAUX, EMMANUEL

1991   Fragments d'une tradition orale. *L'Homme* 31(3): 119–26.

DIAZ DE RADA, ANGEL, AND FRANCISCO CRUCES

1994   The incarnated field: Some problems of analytical language. In *Social experience and anthropological knowledge*, ed. Kirsten Hastrup and Peter Hervik. London: Routledge.

DICKASON, OLIVE PATRICIA

1992   *Canada's first nations: A history of founding peoples from earliest times.* Toronto: McClelland & Stewart.

DIRKS, NICHOLAS B.

1992   Ritual and resistance: Subversion as a social fact. In *Contesting power: Resistance and everyday social relations in South Asia*, ed. Douglas Haynes and Gyan Prakash, 213–38. Berkeley: University of California Press.

DOUGLAS, JACK D.

1985   *Investigative social research.* Beverly Hills CA: Sage.

DUCHAUSSOIS, PIERRE

1923   *Mid snow and ice: The apostles of the North-West.* London: Burns Oates & Washbourne.

DUGAN, KATHLEEN M.

1985   *The vision quest of the Plains Indians.* New York: Edwin Mellen Press.

ELIADE, MIRCEA

1977   Mythologies of death: An introduction. In *Religious encounters with death: Insights from the history and anthropology of religions*, ed. Frank E. Reynolds and Earle H. Waugh, 13–23. University Park: Pennsylvania State University Press.

References

EVANS-PRITCHARD, EDWARD EVAN

1972   *Witchcraft, oracles, and magic among the Azande.* Oxford: Clarendon Press.

EWING, KATHERINE P.

1994   Dreams from a saint: Anthropological atheism and the temptation to believe. *American Anthropologist* 96(3): 571–83.

FABIAN, JOHANNES

1971   History, language, and anthropology. *Philosophy of the Social Sciences* 1:19–47.

1983   *Time and the other: How anthropology makes its object.* New York: Columbia University Press.

1990   *History from below: The "Vocabulary of Elisabethville" by André Yav.* Amsterdam: John Benjamins.

1991   Ethnographic objectivity revisited: From rigor to vigor. In *Rethinking objectivity*, ed. Allan Megill, 381–408. *Annals of Scholarship: International Quarterly in the Humanities and Social Sciences* 8:3–4.

FARELLA, JOHN

1993   *The wind in a jar.* Albuquerque: University of New Mexico Press.

FARIS, JAMES C.

1990   *The Nightway: A history and a history of documentation of a Navajo ceremonial.* Albuquerque: University of New Mexico Press.

FARRER, CLAIRE

1994   *Thunder rides a black horse: Mescalero Apaches and the mythic present.* Prospect Heights IL: Waveland Press.

FAVRET-SAADA, JEANNE

1980   *Deadly words: Witchcraft in the Bocage.* Cambridge: Cambridge University Press.

1990   About participation. *Culture, Medicine, and Psychiatry* 14:189–99.

FEIT, HARVEY

1994   The enduring pursuit: Land, time, and social relationships in anthropological models of hunter-gatherers and in subarctic hunters' images. In *Key issues in hunter-gatherer research*, ed. Ernest S. Burch Jr. and Linda J. Ellanna, 421–39. Oxford: Berg.

FIFE, WAYNE

1995   Along the empirical road: An extended review of Michael Jackson's paths toward a clearing. *Culture* 15(2): 77–85.

References

FIRTH, RAYMOND

1989   Introduction. In *A diary in the strict sense of the term,* by Bronislaw Malinowski. 2d ed. Stanford: Stanford University Press.

FISH, STANLEY

1979   Normal circumstances, literal language, direct speech acts, the ordinary, the everyday, the obvious, what goes without saying, and other special cases. In *Interpretive social science,* ed. Paul Rabinow and William M. Sullivan, 243–66. Berkeley: University of California Press.

1980   *Is there a text in this class? The authority of interpretive communities.* Cambridge MA: Harvard University Press.

FLETCHER, ALICE C., AND FRANCIS LA FLESCHE

1911   *The Omaha tribe.* Bureau of American Ethnology, Twenty-seventh annual report. Washington DC: Smithsonian Institution.

FOGELSON, RAYMOND D., AND RICHARD N. ADAMS

1977   Preface. In *The anthropology of power: Ethnographic studies from Asia, Oceania, and the New World,* ed. Raymond D. Fogelson and Richard N. Adams, xi-xiv. New York: Academic Press.

FOSTER, STEPHEN WILLIAM

1990   Symbolism and the problematics of postmodern representation. In *Victor Turner and the construction of cultural criticism,* ed. Kathleen M. Ashley, 117–37. Bloomington: Indiana University Press.

FRANKLIN, SIR JOHN

1924   *Narrative of a journey to the shores of the Polar Sea.* London: John Murray.

FREEMAN, MINNIE

1978   *Life among the Qallunaat.* Edmonton: Hurtig.

FRYE, NORTHROP

1982   *The great code: The Bible and literature.* Toronto: Academic Press.

FUMOLEAU, RENE

1975   *As long as this land shall last.* Toronto: McClelland & Stewart.

1981   Missionary among the Dene. *Kerygma* 37:139–66.

1994   *Aussi longtemps que le fleuve coulera: La nation Dènèe et le Canada.* Sillery QC: Les Editions du Septentrion.

1995   *Here I sit.* Ottawa: Novalis.

GARFINKEL, HAROLD

1967a   *Studies in ethnomethodology.* Englewood Cliffs NJ: Prentice-Hall.

297

References

1967b   Practical sociological reasoning: Some features in the work of Los Angeles Suicide Prevention Center. In *Essays in self-destruction*, ed. Edwin S. Shneidman, 171–87. New York: Science House.

GEERTZ, CLIFFORD

1966   Religion as a cultural system. In *Anthropological approaches to religion*, ed. Michael Banton, 1–46. New York: Tavistock.

1971   *Islam observed: Religious development in Morocco and Indonesia.* Chicago: University of Chicago Press.

1973   *The interpretation of cultures: Selected essays.* New York: Basic Books.

1983   *Local knowledge: Further essays in interpretive anthropology.* New York: Basic Books.

1986   Making experiences, authoring selves: Epilogue. In *The anthropology of experience*, ed. Victor W. Turner and Edward M. Bruner, 373–80. Urbana: University of Illinois Press.

1988   *Works and lives: The anthropologist as author.* Stanford: Stanford University Press.

GILBERT, NIGEL G., AND MICHAEL MULKAY

1984   *A sociological analysis of scientists' discourse.* Cambridge: Cambridge University Press.

GODDARD, IVES

1981   Synonymy. In *Subarctic*, ed. June Helm. *Handbook of North American Indians*, vol. 6, 168. Washington DC: Smithsonian Institution.

GODDARD, PLINY E.

1916   *The Beaver Indians.* Anthropological Papers of the American Museum of Natural History, vol. 10, part 4.

GOODENOUGH, WARD H.

1981   *Culture, language, and society.* 2d ed. Menlo Park CA: Benjamin/Cummings.

GOODMAN, NELSON

1968   *Languages of art.* New York: Bobbs-Merrill.

1978   *Ways of worldmaking.* New York: Hackett.

GOTTLIEB, ALMA

1995   Possibilities and pitfalls of narrative ethnography. *American Anthropologist* 97(3): 571–73.

GOULET, JEAN-GUY A.

1978   *Guajiro social organization and religion.* 2 vols. Ann Arbor MI: University Microfilms International.

1980   *El universo social y religioso Guajiro.* Caracas: Biblioteca Corpazulia y Universidad Católica Andres Bello.

298

References

1981   The Guajiro kinship system: Its semantic structure and so-
        cial significance. *Anthropological Linguistics*, October: 298–
        325.
1982   Religious dualism among Athapaskan Catholics. *Canadian
        Journal of Anthropology* 3(1): 1–18.
1989   Representation of self and reincarnation among the Dene
        Tha. *Culture* 8:3–18.
1992   Visions et conversions chez les Denes Tha: Expériences
        religieuses chez un peuple autochtone converti. *Reli-
        giologiques* 8:147–82.
1994a   Ways of knowing: Towards a narrative ethnography of ex-
        periences among the Dene Tha. *Journal of Anthropological
        Research* 50:113–39.
1994b   Reincarnation as a fact of life among contemporary De-
        ne Tha. In *Amerindian rebirth: Reincarnation beliefs among
        North American Indians and Inuit*, ed. Antonia Mills and
        Richard Slobodin, 156–76. Toronto: University of
        Toronto Press.
1994c   Dreams and visions in other lifeworlds. In *Being changed by
        cross-cultural encounters: The anthropology of extraordinary ex-
        perience*, ed. David E. Young and Jean-Guy Goulet, 16–38.
        Peterborough ON: Broadview Press.
1996a   A Christian Dene Tha shaman? Aboriginal experiences
        among a missionized aboriginal people. In *Shamanism and
        northern ecology*, ed. Juha Pentikäinen, 345–60. Berlin:
        Mouton de Gruyter.
1996b   The "berdache"/"Two Spirit": A comparison of anthro-
        pological and native constructions of gendered identities
        among the Northern Athapaskans. *Journal of the Royal An-
        thropological Institute*, n.s., 2(4): 683–701.
1997   The Northern Athapaskan "berdache" [*sic*] reconsidered:
        On reading more than there is in the anthropological re-
        cord. In *Two-spirit people: Native American gender identity,
        sexuality, and spirituality*, ed. Sue-Ellen Jacobs, Wesley
        Thomas, and Sabine Lang, 45–68. Urbana: University of
        Illinois Press.
Forthcoming Visions of conflicts, conflicts of visions among con-
        temporary Dene Tha. In *Hunters and gatherers in the modern
        context: Social reproduction, identity politics, and development*,
        ed. Megan Bisele and Robert K. Hitchcock. Oxford: Berg.
n.d.   "A power" to heal and "a power" to harm. Accepted for a

References

volume of papers in honor of June Helm, ed. David Smith, Henry Stephen Sharp, and Bob Jarvenpa.

GOULET, JEAN-GUY A., AND DAVID E. YOUNG

1994   Theoretical and methodological issues. In *Being changed by cross-cultural encounters: The anthropology of extraordinary experience*, ed. David E. Young and Jean-Guy Goulet, 298–335. Peterborough ON: Broadview Press.

GRANT, JOHN WEBSTER

1984   *Moon of wintertime.* Toronto: University of Toronto Press.

GRINDAL, BRUCE T.

1983   Into the heart of Sisala experience: Witnessing death divination. *Journal of Anthropological Research* 39(1): 60–80.

GRINDAL, BRUCE, AND FRANK SALAMONE, EDS.

1995   *Bridges to humanity: Narratives on anthropology and friendship.* Prospect Heights IL: Waveland Press.

GUALTIERI, ANTONIO R.

1980a   Canadian missionary perceptions of Indian and Inuit culture and religious traditions. *Studies in Religion/Sciences Religieuses* 9(2): 299–314.

1980b   Indigenization of Christianity and syncretism among the Indians and Inuit of the western arctic. *Canadian Ethnic Studies* 12(1): 47–57.

GUEDON, MARIE-FRANÇOISE

1988   Du rêve à l'ethnographie: Explorations sur le mode personnel du chamanisme Nabesna. *Recherches Amérindiennes* 18:1–18.

1994a   Dene ways and the ethnographer's culture. In *Being changed by cross-cultural encounters: The anthropology of extraordinary experience*, ed. David E. Young and Jean-Guy Goulet, 39–70. Peterborough ON: Broadview Press.

1994b   Anthropologie et religions amérindiennes au Canada. *Studies in Religion/Sciences Religieuses* 23(3): 265–77.

GUSFIELD, JOSEPH R.

1992   Listening for the silences: The rhetorics of the research field. In *Writing the social text: Poetics and politics in social science discourse*, ed. Richard Harvey Brown, 117–34. New York: Aldine de Gruyter.

HAGENDOORN, LOUK, AND ROGER HENKE

1991   The effect of multiple category membership on intergroup evaluations in a north Indian context: Class, caste, and religion. *British Journal of Social Psychology* 30:247–60.

References

HALLOWELL, A. IRVING

1934   Some empirical aspects of Northern Saulteaux religion. *American Anthropologist* 36:389–404.

1938   Fear and anxiety as cultural and individual variables in a primitive society. *Journal of Social Psychology* 9:25–47.

1946   Some psychological characteristics of the northeastern Indians. In *Man in northeastern North America*, ed. Frederick Johnson, 195–225. Papers of the Robert S. Peabody Foundation for Archaeology 3, Andover MA.

1976   Ojibwa world view and disease. In *Contributions to anthropology: Selected papers of A. Irving Hallowell*, intro. Raymond D. Fogelson, Fred Eggan, Melford E. Spiro, George W. Stocking, Anthony F. C. Wallace, and Wilcomb E. Washburn. Chicago: University of Chicago Press.

1992   The Ojibwa of Berens River, Manitoba: Ethnography into history. In Hallowell, *Case studies in cultural anthropology*, ed. Jennifer S. H. Brown. New York: Harcourt Brace Jovanovich.

HALPIN, MARJORIE M.

1995   Reflections on ritual. Paper presented at Ceramicists Workshop at the Banff Centre for the Arts, 17–18 February 1995.

HAMILTON, CLAIRE, AND JAMES COLLINS JR.

1992   The role of alcohol in wife beating and child abuse. In *Drinking and crime*, ed. James Collins Jr., 253–87. London: Tavistock.

HAMMER, JOHN, AND JACK STEINBRING, EDS.

1980   *Alcohol and native peoples of the North*. Lanham MD: University Press of America.

HARA, HIROKO SUE

1980   *The Hare Indians and their world*. National Museum of Man Series. Canadian Ethnology Service Paper no. 63. Ottawa: National Museums of Canada.

HASTRUP, KIRSTEN

1986   Veracity and visibility: The problem of authenticity in anthropology. *Folk* 28:5–17.

1992a *Det antropologiske projekt—Om forbløffelse*. Copenhagen: Nordisk Forlag AS.

1992b The native voice and the anthrological vision. *Social Anthropology/Anthropologie Sociale* 1(3): 173–76.

1994   Anthropological knowledge incorporated: Discussion. In *Social experience and anthropological knowledge*, ed. Kirsten Hastrup and Peter Hervik, 224–40. London: Routledge.

1995   *A passage to anthropology*. London: Routledge.

References

HASTRUP, KIRSTEN, AND PETER HERVIK

1994　Introduction. In *Social experience and anthropological knowledge*, ed. Kirsten Hastrup and Peter Hervik, 1–12. London: Routledge.

HAZAN, HAIM

1995　The ethnographer's textual presence: On three forms of anthropological authorship. *Cultural Anthropology* 10(3): 395–406.

HEARNE, SAMUEL

1958　*A journey from Prince of Wales's Fort in Hudson's Bay to the Northern Ocean in the years 1769, 1770, 1771, 1772*. Toronto: Macmillan.

HEATH, DWIGHT B.

1991　A decade of development in the anthropological study of alcohol use, 1970–1980. In *Constructive drinking: Perspectives on drink from anthropology*, ed. Mary Douglas, 16–69. Cambridge: Cambridge University Press.

HEFNER, ROBERT W.

1993　Introduction: World building and the rationality of conversion. In *Conversion to Christianity: Historical and anthropological perspectives on a great transformation*, ed. Robert W. Hefner, 3–44. Berkeley: University of California Press.

HELM, JUNE

1961　*The Lynx Point people: The dynamics of a Northern Athapaskan band*. Anthropological Series 53, National Museum of Canada Bulletin 176. Ottawa.

1965　Bilaterality in the socio-territorial organization of the arctic drainage Dene. *Ethnology* 4:361–85.

1968　An annotated description of a Dogrib prophet cult ceremony. Part of the 1968 Final Report to the National Museums of Canada, Ethnographic Advisor. Manuscript.

1989　Manotabbee's map. *Arctic Anthropology* 26:28–47.

1994　*Prophecy and power among the Dogrib Indians*. Lincoln: University of Nebraska Press.

———　ED.

1981　*Subarctic*. Vol. 6, *Handbook of North American Indians*. Washington DC: Smithsonian Institution.

HELM, JUNE, AND GEORGE DEVOS

1963　Dogrib Indian personality: Rorschach, thematic apperception test, and observational data collected in 1959 and 1960, N.W.T., Canada. Manuscript.

References

HELM, JUNE, GEORGE DEVOS, AND TERESA CARTERETTE

1963   Variations in personality and ego identification within a
        Slave Indian kin-community. In *Contributions to anthropol-
        ogy*, ed. Department of Northern Affairs and National Re-
        sources, part 2, 94–138. Anthropological Series 60,
        National Museum of Canada Bulletin 190. Ottawa.

HELM, JUNE, AND ELEANOR BURKE LEACOCK

1971   The hunting tribes of subarctic Canada. In *North American
        Indians in historical perspective*, ed. Eleanor Burke Leacock
        and Nancy Oestreich Lurie, 343–74. New York: Random
        House.

HELM, JUNE, AND NANCY O LURIE

1966   *The Dogrib hand game*. Bulletin of the National Museum of
        Canada 205. Ottawa.

HERNOU, PAUL

1982   Même les oiseaux apportent des messages. *Kerygma*
        16(39): 111–22.

HERVIK, PETER

1994   Shared reasoning in the field: Reflexivity beyond the au-
        thor. In *Social experience and anthropological knowledge*, ed.
        Kirsten Hastrup and Peter Hervik, 78–100. London:
        Routledge.

HEXHAM, IRVING, AND KARLA POEWE

1997   *New religions as global cultures. Making the human sacred.*
        Boulder CO: Westview Press.

HIPPLER, ARTHUR E.

1974   An Alaskan Athabascan technique for overcoming alcohol
        abuse. *Arctic* 27(1): 53–67.

HOLLAND, DOROTHY C., AND DEBRA G. SKINNER

1995   Contested ritual, contested femininities: (Re)forming self
        and society in a Nepali women's festival. *American Ethnolo-
        gist* 22(2): 279–305.

HOLLER, CLYDE

1995   *Black Elk's religion: The Sun Dance and Lakota Catholicism.*
        Syracuse NY: Syracuse University Press.

HOLYOAK, LORNE

1993   The good red road: Relations between Native Elders and
        non-Native seekers. M.A. thesis, University of Calgary.

HONIGMANN, JOHN J.

1946   *Ethnography and acculturation of the Fort Nelson Slave.* Yale
        University Publications in Anthropology, no. 33. New Ha-
        ven: Yale University Press.

References

1949   *Culture and ethos of Kaska society*. Yale University Publications in Anthropology, no. 40. New Haven: Yale University Press.

1954   *The Kaska Indians: An ethnographic reconstruction*. Yale University Publications in Anthropology, no. 51. New Haven: Yale University Press.

1980   Perspectives on alcohol behavior. In *Alcohol and native peoples of the North*, ed. John Hammer and Jack Steinbring, 267–85. Lanham MD: University Press of America.

1981   Expressive aspects of subarctic Indian culture. In *Subarctic*, ed. June Helm. *Handbook of North American Indians*, vol. 6, 718–38. Washington DC: Smithsonian Institution.

HONIGMANN, JOHN J., AND IRMA HONIGMANN

1945   Drinking in an Indian-white community. *Quarterly Journal of Studies on Alcohol* 5(4): 575–619.

HULTKRANTZ, AKE

1973   The Hare Indians: Notes on their traditional culture and religion, past and present. *Ethnos* 38:113–52.

1974   On methods in Hare Indian ethnology—A rejoinder. *Ethnos* 39:170–78.

1990   A decade of progress: Works on North American Indian religions in the 1980s. In *Religion in native North America*, ed. Christopher Vecsey, 167–201. Moscow: University of Idaho Press.

HUME, LYNNE

1996   The rainbow serpent, the cross, and the fax machine: Australian Aboriginal responses to the Bible. In *Ethnicity and the Bible*, ed. Mark G. Brett, 359–79. Leiden: E. J. Brill.

INGOLD, TIM

1988   Introduction. In *What is an animal?* ed. Tim Ingold, 1–16. London: Unwin Hyman.

1993   The art of translation in a continuous world. In *Beyond boundaries: Understanding, translation, and anthropological discourse*, ed. Gisli Pálsson, 210–30. Oxford: Berg.

IRWIN, LEE

1994   *The dream seekers: Native American visionary traditions of the Great Plains*. Norman: University of Oklahoma Press.

JACKSON, MICHAEL

1978   An approach to Kuranko divination. *Human Relations* 31:117–38.

1986   *Barawa and the ways birds fly in the sky*. Washington DC: Smithsonian Institution Press.

References

1989   *Paths toward a clearing: Radical empiricism and ethnographic inquiry.* Bloomington: Indiana University Press.

1995   *At home in the world.* Durham NC: Duke University Press.

1996   Introduction: Phenomenology, radical empiricism, and anthropological critique. In *Things as they are: New directions in phenomenological anthropology*, ed. Michael Jackson, 1–50. Bloomington: Indiana University Press.

JANES, ROBERT R., AND JANE H. KELLEY

1977   Observations on crisis cult activities in the Mackenzie Basin. In *Problems in the prehistory of the North American subarctic: The Athapaskan question*, 153–64. Calgary: Archaeological Association, University of Calgary.

JARVENPA, ROBERT

1998   *Northern passage: Ethnography and apprenticeship among the subarctic Dene.* Prospect Heights IL: Waveland Press.

JENNESS, DIAMOND

1991   The Indian's interpretation of man and nature. In *Sweet promises: A reader on Indian-white relations in Canada*, ed. J. R. Miller, 441–46. Toronto: University of Toronto Press.

JORDAN, DAVID K.

1993   The glyphomancy factor: Observation in Chinese conversion. In *Conversion to Christianity: Historical and anthropological perspectives on a great transformation*, ed. Robert W. Hefner, 285–303. Berkeley: University of California Press.

KAN, SERGEI

1987   Introduction. In *Native cultures and Christianity in northern North America: Selected papers from a symposium*, ed. Sergei Kan, 1–7. *Arctic Anthropology* (special issue) 24(1).

1991   Modern-day Tlingit elders look at the past. *Ethnohistory* 38(4): 363–87.

KAO, KEN TAI, AND DOROTHY KAO

1992   *Malaysia and Brunei church directory, 1992–1994.* Singapore: Everyhome Crusade.

KEESING, ROGER

1992   Not a real fish: The ethnographer as inside outsider. In *The naked anthropologist: Tales from around the world*, ed. Philip R. De Vita, 73–78. Belmont CA: Wadsworth.

KEYES, CHARLES F.

1977   *The golden peninsula: Culture and adaptation in mainland Southeast Asia.* New York: Macmillan.

1991   Christianity as an indigenous religion in Southeast Asia:

References

Report on a conference held in Cebu, the Philippines, 1–5 September 1986. *Social Compass* 38(2): 177–85.

1993 Why the Thai are no Christians. In *Conversion to Christianity: Historical and anthropological perspectives on a great transformation*, ed. Robert W. Hefner, 259–84. Berkeley: University of California Press.

KIMBALL, SOLON T.

1972 Learning a new culture. In *Crossing cultural boundaries: An anthropological experience*, ed. Solon T. Kimball and James B. Watson, 182–92. San Francisco: Chandler.

KISLIUK, MICHELLE

1997 (Un)Doing fieldwork: Sharing songs, sharing lives. In *Shadows in the field: New perspectives for fieldwork in ethnomusicology*, ed. Gregory F. Barz and Timothy J. Cooley, 23–43. New York: Oxford University Press.

KNAB, TIMOTHY J.

1995 *A war of witches: A journey into the underworld of the contemporary Aztecs.* New York: Harper Collins.

KOHN, TAMARA

1994 Incomers and fieldworkers. In *Social experience and anthropological knowledge*, ed. Kirsten Hastrup and Peter Hervik, 13–27. London: Routledge.

KONDO, DORINNE

1986 Dissolution and reconstitution of self: Implications for anthropological epistemology. *Cultural Anthropology* 1:74–96.

1990 *Crafting selves: Power, gender, and discourse of identity in a Japanese workplace.* Chicago: University of Chicago Press.

KOOLAGE JR., WILLIAM W.

1975 Conceptual negativism in Chipewyan ethnology. *Anthropologica* 17(1): 45–60.

KRECH, SHEPARD

1979 Interethnic relations in the Lower Mackenzie River region. *Arctic Anthroplogy* 16(2): 102–23.

1980 Northern Athapaskan ethnology in the 1970s. *Annual Review of Anthropology* 9:83–100. Palo Alto CA: Annual Reviews.

1981 "Throwing bad medicine": Sorcery, disease, and the fur trade among the Kutchin and other Northern Athapaskans. In *Indians, animals, and the fur trade: A critique of keepers of the game*, ed. Shepard Krech III, 73–108. Athens: University of Georgia Press.

References
1985   *Native Canadian anthropology.* Norman: University of Oklahoma Press.

KROHN-HANSEN, CHRISTIAN
1994   The anthropology of violent interaction. *Journal of Anthropological Research* 50:367–81.

KRUPAT, ARNOLD
1989   *The voice in the margin: Native American literature and the canon.* Berkeley: University of California Press.
1992   *Ethnocriticism: Ethnography, history, literature.* Berkeley: University of California Press.

KULICK, DON
1995   Introduction: The sexual life of anthropologists: Erotic subjectivity and ethnographic work. In *Taboo,* ed. Don Kulick and Margaret Wilson, 1–28. London: Routledge.

KULICK, DON, AND CHRISTOPHER STROUD
1990   Christianity, cargo, and ideas of self: Patterns of literacy in a Papua New Guinea village. *Man* 25(2): 286–304.

KURATH, GERTRUDE
1953   Native choreographic areas of North America. *American Anthropologist* 55(1): 60–73.

LADERMAN, CAROL
1988   Wayward winds: Malay archetypes and theory of personality in the context of shamanism. *Social Sciences and Medicine* 27(8): 799–810.
1991   *Taming the wind of desire: Psychology, medicine, and aesthetics in Malay shamanistic performance.* Berkeley: University of California Press.
1994   The embodiment of symbols and the acculturation of anthropologists. In *Embodiment and experience: The existential ground of culture and self,* ed. Thomas Csordas, 183–97. Cambridge: Cambridge University Press.

LAIRD, CAROLYN
1977   *Encounter with an angry God: Recollections of my life with John Peabody Harrington.* New York: Ballantine.

LAVIE, SMADAN
1990   *The poetics of military occupation.* Berkeley: University of California Press.

LEACH, EDMUND R.
1967   *A runaway world?* The BBC Reith Lectures. British Broadcasting Corporation, 1967.
1976   *Culture and communication.* Cambridge: Cambridge University Press.

References

LEE, RICHARD

1992   Art, science, or politics? The crisis in hunter-gatherer
        studies. *American Anthropologist* 94(1): 31–54.

LEITER, KENNETH

1980   *A primer on ethnomethodology.* Oxford: Oxford University
        Press.

LELAND, JAMES

1976   *Firewater myths: North American Indian drinking and alcohol
        addiction.* New Brunswick NJ: Rutgers Center of Alcohol
        Studies.

LETT, JAMES

1991   Interpretive anthropology, metaphysics, and the paranor-
        mal. *Journal of Anthropological Research* 47:305–29.

LÉVI-STRAUSS, CLAUDE

1963   *Structural anthropology.* Trans. Claire Jacobson and Brooke
        Grunfest Schoepf. Garden City NY: Anchor Books.

1976   Jean-Jacques Rousseau, founder of the sciences of man.
        In *Structural anthropology,* vol. 2, 33–43. Trans. Monique
        Layton. New York: Basic Books.

LINDQUIST, GALINA

1995   Travelling by the other's cognitive maps or going native
        and coming back. *Ethnos* 60(1): 5–40.

LITHMAN, YNGVE GEORG

1979   Feeling good and getting smashed: On the symbolism of
        alcohol and drunkenness among Canadian Indians.
        Ethnos 60(1): 119–33.

LOFLAND, JOHN

1976   *Doing social life.* New York: Wiley.

LOWIE, ROBERT

1959   *Robert H. Lowie, ethnologist: A personal record.* Berkeley:
        University of California Press.

1966   Dreams, idle dreams. *Current Anthropology* 7(3): 378–82.

LUKES, STEVEN

1978   Power and authority. In *A history of sociological analysis,* ed.
        Tom Bottomore and Robert Nisbet, 633–76. New York:
        Basic Books.

MACANDREW, CRAIG, AND ROBERT B. EDGERTON

1969   *Drunken comportment: A social explanation.* Chicago: Aldine.

MACAULAY, ALEXANDER JAMES, AND DAVID A. BOAG

1974   Waterfowl harvest by Slave Indians in northern Alberta.
        Arctic 27(1): 15–26.

References

MCCARTHY, MARTHA

1981   The missions of the Oblates of Mary Immaculate to the
        Athapaskans, 1846–1870: Theory, structure, and method.
        Ph.D. diss., University of Manitoba, Winnipeg.

1995   *From the great river to the ends of the earth: Oblate missions to the
        Dene, 1847–1921.* Edmonton: University of Alberta Press/
        Western Canadian Publishers.

MCCLELLAN, CATHARINE

1956   Shamanistic syncretism in southern Yukon Territory.
        Transactions of the New York Academy of Sciences, 2d ser.,
        19(2): 130–37.

1981   Tutchone. In *Subarctic,* ed. June Helm. *Handbook of North
        American Indians,* vol. 6, 493–505. Washington DC:
        Smithsonian Institution.

MCCLELLAN, CATHARINE, AND GLENDA DENNISTON

1981   Environment and culture in the Cordillera. In *Subarctic,*
        ed. June Helm. *Handbook of North American Indians,* vol. 6,
        372–86. Washington DC: Smithsonian Institution.

MCFAYDEN, ANNETTE

1973   Preface. In *Inkonze: Magico-religious beliefs of contact-tradi-
        tional Chipewyan trading at Fort Resolution, NWT, Canada,* by
        D. M. Smith. National Museum of Man, Mercury Series,
        Ethnology Division, no. 6. Ottawa: National Museums of
        Canada.

MCGRANE, BERNARD

1989   *Beyond anthropology: Society and the other.* New York: Colum-
        bia University Press.

MACKENZIE, ALEXANDER

1966   *Exploring the Northwest Territories.* Norman: University of
        Oklahoma Press.

MACNEISH, JUNE HELM

1956   Leadership among the Northern Athapaskans. *Anthro-
        pologica* 2:131–63.

1960   Kin terms of arctic drainage Déné: Hare, Slavey, Chip-
        ewyan. *American Anthropologist* 62(2): 279–95.

MAIL, PATRICIA D.

1980   American Indian drinking behavior: Some possible causes
        and solutions. *Journal of Alcohol and Drug Education* 26:28–
        39.

MAIR, LUCY

1969   *Witchcraft.* World University Library. New York: McGraw-
        Hill.

References

MALINOWSKI, BRONISLAW

1961   *Argonauts of the western Pacific: An account of native enterprise and adventure in the archipelagoes of Melanesian New Guinea.* New York: E. P. Dutton.

1967   *A diary in the strict sense of the term.* New York: Harcourt, Brace and World.

1989   *A diary in the strict sense of the term.* 2d ed. Stanford: Stanford University Press.

MARCUS, GEORGE

1994   What comes (just) after "post"? The case of ethnography. In *The handbook of qualitative research,* ed. Norman Denzin and Y. Lincoln, 565–82. Newbury Park CA: Sage.

MARCUS, GEORGE E., AND DICK CUSHMAN

1982   Ethnographies as texts. *Annual Review of Anthropology* 11:25–69.

MARTIN, CALVIN

1978   *Keepers of the game.* Berkeley: University of California Press.

MASON, J. ALDEN

1946   *Notes on the Indians of the Great Slave Lake area.* Yale University Publications in Anthropology, no. 34. New Haven: Yale University Press.

MATLOCK, JAMES G., AND ANTONIA MILLS

1994   A trait index to North American Indian and Inuit reincarnation. In *Amerindian rebirth: Reincarnation beliefs among North American Indians and Inuit,* ed. Antonia Mills and Richard Slobodin, 300–334. Toronto: University of Toronto Press.

MATTHEWS, MAUREEN, AND ROGER ROULETTE

1996   Fair wind's dream: Naamiwan Obawaajigewin. In *Reading beyond words: Contexts in narrative history,* ed. Jennifer S. H. Brown and Elizabeth Vibert, 330–59. Peterborough ON: Broadview Press.

MAYBURY-LEWIS, DAVID

1997   *Indigenous peoples, ethnic groups, and the state.* Boston: Allyn & Bacon.

MAYNARD, DOUGLAS W., AND STEVEN E. CLAYMAN

1991   The diversity of ethnomethodology. In *Annual Review of Sociology* 17, ed. W. Richard Scott and Judith Blake, 385–418.

MEDICINE, BEATRICE

1983   An ethnography of drinking and sobriety among the Lakota Sioux. Ph.D. diss., University of Wisconsin-Madison.

References

MEHAN, HUGHES, AND HOUSTON WOOD

1975   *The reality of ethnomethodology.* New York: Wiley.

MEILI, DIANNE

1991   *Those who know: Profiles of Alberta's Native elders.* Edmonton: NeWest.

MERTON, ROBERT K.

1968   *Social theory and social structure.* New York: Free Press.

MILLER, CHRISTOPHER L.

1985   *Prophetic worlds: Indians and whites on the Columbia Plateau.* New Brunswick NJ: Rutgers University Press.

MILLS, ANTONIA

1982   The Beaver Indian Prophet Dance and related movements among North American Indians. Ph.D. diss., Harvard University.

1986   The meaningful universe: Intersecting forces in Beaver Indian cosmology. *Culture* 4(2): 81–91.

1988a   A preliminary investigation of cases of reincarnation among the Beaver and Gitksan Indians. *Anthropologica* 30:23–59.

1988b   A comparison of Wetsuweten cases of the reincarnation type with Gitksan and Beaver. *Journal of Anthropological Research* 44:385–415.

1994a   Introduction. In *Amerindian rebirth: Reincarnation belief among North American Indians and Inuit,* ed. Antonia Mills and Richard Slobodin, 3–13. Toronto: University of Toronto Press.

1994b   Making a scientific investigation of ethnographic cases suggestive of reincarnation. In *Being changed by cross-cultural encounters: The anthropology of extraordinary experience,* ed. David E. Young and Jean-Guy Goulet, 237–69. Peterborough ON: Broadview Press.

1994c   Rebirth and identity: Three Gitksan cases of pierced-ear birthmarks. In *Amerindian rebirth: Reincarnation beliefs among North American Indians and Inuit,* ed. Antonia Mills and Richard Slobodin, 211–41. Toronto: University of Toronto Press.

1994d   Cultural contrast: The British Columbia court's evaluation of the Gitksan-Wetsuweten and their own sense of self-worth as revealed in cases of reported reincarnation. *BC Studies* 104:149–72.

1995   Apache mythic present. Review of *Thunder rides a black*

References

horse: Mescalero Apaches and the mythic present, by Claire Farrer. *Anthropological Humanism* 20(2): 11–12.

MOERMAN, MICHAEL

1988   *Talking culture: Ethnography and conversation analysis.* Philadelphia: University of Pennsylvania Press.

MOORE, PATRICK

1988   Tea Dance: The circle of community. Paper presented at
the Ft. Chipewyan Bicentennial Conference, Edmonton,
Alberta, 24 September 1988.

n.d.a   Animals to angels: Native dance in northern Alberta.
Manuscript.

n.d.b   Interview with Alexis Seniantha: History of the prophets.
Recorded and translated by Pat Moore, Yukon Native
Language Centre, Whitehorse YT. Manuscript.

n.d.c   Pliny Earle Goddard. Manuscript.

n.d.d   Kaska ways. Manuscript.

MOORE, PAT, AND ANGELA WHEELOCK, EDS.

1990   *Wolverine myths and visions: Dene traditions from northern Alberta.* Edmonton: University of Alberta Press.

MORICE, RÉVÉREND PÈRE ADRIAN G.

1897   *Au pays de l'ours noir: Chez les sauvages de la Colombie Britan-
nique.* Paris: Delhomme & Briguet.

MORINIS, ALAN

1992   Persistent peregrination: From Sun Dance to Catholic pilgrimage among Canadian Prairie Indians. In *Sacred journeys: The anthropology of pilgrimage,* ed. Alan Morinis, 101–
13. Contributions to the Study of Anthropology, no. 7.
Westport CT: Greenwood Press.

MORISSETTE, DOMINIQUE

1978   Rencontre au centre Monchanin avec Rémi Savard. *Recherches Amérindiennes au Québec* 1:96.

MULHALL, DAVID

1986   *Will to power: The missionary career of Father Morice.* Vancouver: University of British Columbia Press.

MURRAY, DAVID

1992   *Forked tongues: Speech, writing, and representation in North American Indian texts.* Bloomington: Indiana University Press.

MYERHOFF, BARBARA G.

1972   *The peyote hunt: The sacred journey of the Huichol Indians.*
Ithaca NY: Cornell University Press.

1990   The transformation of consciousness in ritual perfor-

References

mances: Some thoughts and questions. In *By means of per-formance: Intercultural studies of theater and ritual*, ed. Richard Schechner and Willa Appel, 245–49. Cambridge: Cambridge University Press.

MYERHOFF, BARBARA, AND JAY RUBY

1982   Introduction. In *A crack in the mirror: Reflexive perspectives in anthropology*, ed. Jay Ruby, 1–35. Philadelphia: University of Pennsylvania Press.

NADAR, LAURA

1970   Research in Mexico. In *Women in the field: Anthropological experiences*, ed. Peggy Golde, 97–116. Chicago: Aldine.

NARAYAN, KIRIN

1989   *Storytellers, saints, and scoundrels: Folk narrative in Hindu religious teaching.* Philadelphia: University of Pennsylvania Press.

NEEDHAM, RODNEY

1972   *Belief, language, and experience.* Chicago: University of Chicago Press.

1975   Polythetic classification. *Man,* n.s., 11:71–88.

NELSON, RICHARD K.

1983   *Make prayers to the raven.* Chicago: University of Chicago Press.

NIETZSCHE, FRIEDRICH

1970   *The will to power.* New York: Vintage.

NOCK, ARTHUR DARBY

1933   *Conversion: The old and new in religion from Alexander the Great to Augustine of Hippo.* London: Oxford University Press.

NOFSINGER, ROBERT E.

1991   *Everyday conversation.* Newbury Park CA: Sage.

OBEYESEKERE, GANATH

1981   *Medusa's hair: An essay on personal symbols and religious experience.* Chicago: University of Chicago Press.

1990   *The work of culture: Symbolic transformation in psychoanalysis and anthropology.* Chicago: University of Chicago Press.

OKELY, JUDITH

1984   Fieldwork in home countries. *Royal Anthropological Institute Newsletter* 61:4–5.

1992   Anthropology and autobiography: Participatory experience and embodied knowledge. In *Anthropology and autobiography*, ed. Judith Okely and Helen Callaway, 1–28. London: Routledge.

References
ONG, WALTER J.
1969   World as view and world as event. *American Anthropologist*
71(4): 634–47.

OSGOOD, CORNELIUS
1936   *Contributions to the ethnography of the Kutchin.* Yale University Publications in Anthropology, no. 14. New Haven: Yale University Press.

1937   *The ethnography of the Tanaina.* Yale University Publications in Anthropology, no. 16. New Haven: Yale University Press.

1953   *Winter.* New York: Norton.

1958   *Ingalik social culture.* Yale University Publications in Anthropology, no. 53. New Haven: Yale University Press.

1959   *Ingalik mental culture.* Yale University Publications in Anthropology, no. 56. New Haven: Yale University Press.

1971   *The Han Indians: A compilation of ethnographic and historical data on the Alaska-Yukon boundary area.* Yale University Publications in Anthropology, no. 74. New Haven: Yale University Press.

1975   An ethnographical map of Great Bear Lake. In *Proceedings: Northern Athapaskan Conference.* Canadian Ethnology Service Paper no. 27, vol. 2, ed. Annette McFayden Clark, 516–44. Ottawa: National Museums of Canada.

OTS, THOMAS
1994   The silenced body—The expressive Lieb: On the dialectic of mind and life in Chinese cathartic healing. In *Embodiment and experience: The existential ground of culture and self,* ed. Thomas Csordas, 116–36. Cambridge: Cambridge University Press.

PÁLSSON, GÍSLI
1993   Introduction: Beyond boundaries. In *Beyond boundaries: Understanding, translation, and anthropological discourse,* ed. Gísli Pálsson, 1–40. Oxford: Berg.

PATTERSON, VICTORIA D.
1995   Evolving gender roles in Pomo society. In *Women and power in native North America,* ed. Laura F. Klein and Lillian A. Ackerman, 126–45. Norman: University of Oklahoma Press.

PEEL, JOHN DAVID Y.
1968   Syncreticism and religious change. *Comparative Studies in Society and History* 10:121–41.

PEELMAN, ACHIEL
1991   Christianisme et cultures amérindiennes: Présentation et

References

analyse d'une démarche théologique interculturelle. *Eglise et Théologie* 22:131–56.

1995   *Christ is a Native American*. Ottawa: Novalis–Saint Paul University.

PEERS, LAURA

1996   "The guardian of all": Jesuit missionary and Salish perceptions of the Virgin Mary. In *Reading beyond words: Contexts for Native history*, ed. Jennifer S. H. Brown and Elizabeth Vibert, 284–303. Peterborough ON: Broadview Press.

PENTIKÄINEN, JUHA Y.

1996   Introduction. In *Shamanism and northern ecology*, ed. Juha Pentikäinen, 1–27. Berlin: Mouton de Gruyter.

PENTLAND, DAVID H.

1975   Cartographic concepts of the Northern Algonquians. *Canadian Cartographer* 12:149–60.

PERRIN, MICHEL

1992   *Les practiciens du rêve: Un exemple de chamanisme*. Paris: Presses Universitaires de France.

PETITOT, EMILE

1876   *Dictionnaire de langue Dene-dinjié, précédé d'une monographie des Déné-dindjié*. Paris: E. Leroux.

PLATT, ROBERT

1989   Reflexivity, recursion, and social life: Elements for a postmodern sociology. *Sociological Review* 37(4): 636–67.

POEWE, KARLA

1994   Rethinking the relationship of anthropology to science and religion. In *Charismatic Christianity as a global culture*, ed. Karla Poewe, 234–58. Columbia: University of South Carolina Press.

1996   Writing culture and writing fieldwork: The proliferation of experimental and experiential ethnographies. *Ethnos* 61(3–4): 177–206.

POIRIER, SYLVIE

1996   *Les jardins du monde: Cosmologie, territoire, et personne dans le désert occidental australien*. Studies in Social and Ritual Morphology/Etudes de Morphologie Sociale et Rituelle/Studien zur Socialen und Rituelle Morphologie. Münster: Lit Verlag.

POLLNER, MELVIN

1987   *Mundane reason: Reality in everyday and sociological discourse*. Cambridge: Cambridge University Press.

References

POOL, ROBERT

1991   "Oh, research, very good!": On fieldwork and representation. In *Constructing knowledge: Authority and critique in social science*, ed. Lorraine Nencel and Peter Pels, 58–77. London: Sage.

POWERS, WILLIAM K.

1987   *Beyond the vision: Essays on American Indian culture.* Norman: University of Oklahoma Press.

1996   Review of *Black Elk's religion: The Sun Dance and Lakota Catholicism,* by Clyde Holler. *American Anthropologist* 98(3): 651–53.

PRATT, MARY LOUISE

1986   Fieldwork in common places. In *Writing culture: The poetics and politics of ethnography,* ed. James Clifford and George E. Marcus, 27–50. Berkeley: University of California Press.

PRESTON, RICHARD J.

1975   *Cree narrative: Expressing the personal meanings of events.* National Museum of Man, Mercury Series, Canadian Ethnology Service, no. 30. Ottawa: National Museums of Canada.

PRICE, RICHARD, AND SALLY PRICE

1995   *Enigma variations.* Cambridge MA: Harvard University Press.

PRICE-WILLIAMS, DOUGLASS

1992   The waking dream in ethnographic perspective. In *Dreaming: Anthropological and psychological interpretations,* ed. Barbara Tedlock, 246–62. New York: Cambridge University Press.

RAPPAPORT, ROY

1979   *Ecology, meaning, and religion.* Richmond VA: North Atlantic Books.

RASMUSSEN, KNUD

1931   *The Netsilik Eskimos: Social life and spiritual culture.* Report of the Fifth Thule Expedition, 1921–1924, vol. 8, nos. 1–2. Copenhagen: Gyldendal.

RICHARDSON, MILES

1996   Blurring the line between fact and fiction. *American Anthropologist* 98(3): 623–24.

RIDINGTON, JILLIAN

1994   Making bannock: Memories of Daeda. Paper presented at Canadian Anthropology Society CASCA Société Canadienne d'Anthropologie 21st Annual Conference: The production and reproduction of culture and society, 5–8

References

May 1994, Department of Anthropology and Sociology,
University of British Columbia, Vancouver.

RIDINGTON, ROBIN

1968   The medicine fight: An instrument of political process
among the Beaver Indians. *American Anthropologist*
70:1152–60.

1971   Beaver dreaming and singing. In *Pilot not commander: Essays in memory of Diamond Jenness*, ed. Pat Lotz and Jim
Lotz. *Anthropologica*, n.s., 13(1–2): 115–18.

1976   Wechuge and Windigo: A comparison of cannibal belief
among Boreal Forest Athapaskans and Algonkians. *Anthropologica*, n.s., 18(2): 107–29.

1978   *Swan people: A study of the Dunne-za Prophet Dance.* National
Museum of Man, Mercury Series, Canadian Ethnology
Service, no. 38. Ottawa: National Museums of Canada.

1981   Beaver. In *Subarctic*, ed. June Helm. *Handbook of North
American Indians*, vol. 6, 350–60. Washington DC: Smithsonian Institution.

1987   From hunt chief to prophet: Beaver Indians and Christianity. *Arctic Anthropology* 24(1): 8–18.

1988   *Trail to heaven: Knowledge and narrative in a northern native
community.* Iowa City: University of Iowa Press.

1990   *Little bit know something: Stories in a language of anthropology.*
Iowa City: University of Iowa Press.

RIDINGTON, ROBIN, AND TONIA RIDINGTON

1975   The inner eye of shamanism and totemism. In *Teachings
from the American earth*, ed. Dennis Tedlock and Barbara
Tedlock, 190–204. New York: Liveright.

ROBERTSON, HEATHER

1970   *Reservations are for Indians.* Toronto: James Lewis & Samuel.

ROGERS, EDWARD S.

1981   History of ethnological research in the subarctic shield
and Mackenzie borderlands. In *Subarctic*, ed. June Helm.
Handbook of North American Indians, vol. 6, 19–29. Washington DC: Smithsonian Institution.

ROGERS, MARY F.

1983   *Sociology, ethnomethodology, and experience: A phenomenological critique.* Cambridge: Cambridge University Press.

ROSS, RUPERT

1992   *Dancing with a ghost: Exploring Indian reality.* Markham ON:
Octopus.

References

ROUSSEAU, JACQUES

1953   *Persistances Paiennes chez les Indiens de la Forêt Boréale.* Montréal: Les Editions des Dix.

ROUSSEAU, JÉRÔME

1978   Quel est l'objet de l'anthropologie religieuse? *Recherches amérindiennes au Québec* 8(2): 105–6.

ROUSSEAU, MADELEINE, AND JACQUES ROUSSEAU

1967   Le dualisme religieux des peuplades de la Forêt Boréale. In *Acculturation in the Americas: Proceedings of the 29th International Congress of Americanists*, ed. Sol Tax, 118–26. New York: Cooper Square.

ROYAL COMMISSION ON ABORIGINAL PEOPLES

1994   *Choosing life: Special report on suicide among aboriginal people.* Minister of Supply and Services, Canada. Ottawa: Canada Communication Group—Publishing.

RUBY, JAY, ED.

1982   *A crack in the mirror: Reflexive perspectives in anthropology.* Philadelphia: University of Pennsylvania Press.

RUDIE, INGRID

1994   Making sense of new experience. In *Social experience and anthropological knowledge*, ed. Kirsten Hastrup and Peter Hervik, 28–44. London: Routledge.

RUSHFORTH, SCOTT

1984   *Bear Lake Athapaskan kinship and task-group formation.* Ottawa: National Museum of Man.

1985   Some directive illocutionary acts among the Bear Lake Athapaskans. *Anthropological Linguistics* 27(4): 387–411.

1986   The Bear Lake Indians. In *Native peoples: The Canadian experience*, ed. Bruce Morrison and Roderick Wilson, 243–71. Toronto: McClelland & Stewart.

1992   The legitimation of beliefs in a hunter-gatherer society: Bearlake Athapaskan knowledge and authority. *American Ethnologist* 19(3): 483–500.

RUSHFORTH, SCOTT, AND JAMES S. CHISHOLM

1991   *Cultural persistence: Continuity in meaning and moral responsibility among the Bearlake Athapaskans.* Tucson: University of Arizona Press.

RYAN, JOAN

1995   *Doing things the right way: Dene traditional justice in Lac La Martre, NWT.* Final report. Calgary: University of Calgary Press and the Arctic Institute of North America.

References

SACKS, HARVEY, AND E. MANUEL SCHEGLOFF

1979   Two preferences in the organization of reference to persons in conversation and their interaction. In *Everyday language: Studies in ethnomethodology*, ed. George Psathas, 15–21. New York: Irvington.

SAID, EDWARD

1978   *Orientalism*. New York: Vintage.

1989   Representing the colonized: Anthropology's interlocutors. *Critical Inquiry* 15:205–25.

SALER, BENSON

1993   *Conceptualizing religion: Immanent anthropologists, transcendent natives, and unbounded categories*. Leiden: E. J. Brill.

SANGREN, STEVEN

1988   Rhetoric and the authority of ethnography: "Postmodernism" and the social reproduction of texts. *Current Anthropology* 29(3): 405–35.

SAVARD, RÉMI

1973–74 Nature, culture, et religion: Réflexions d'un anthropologue. *Studies in Religion/Sciences Religieuses* 3(3): 260–70.

SAVISHINSKY, JOEL S.

1970   Kinship and the expression of values in an Athapaskan bush community. *Western Canadian Journal of Anthropology* 2(2): 31–54.

1971   Mobility as an aspect of stress in an arctic community. *American Anthropologist* 73(3): 604–18.

1974   *The trail of the hare: Life and stress in an arctic community*. New York: Gordon & Breach.

1975   The dog and the hare: Canine culture in an Athapaskan band. In *Proceedings: Northern Athapaskan Conference, 1971*, vol. 2, ed. Annette M. Clark, 462–515. Ottawa: National Museum of Man.

1977   A thematic analysis of drinking behavior in a Hare Indian community. *Papers in Anthropology* 18(2): 43–59.

1982   Vicarious emotions and cultural restraint. *Journal of Psychoanalytical Anthropology* 5(2): 115–35.

SAVISHINSKY, JOEL S., AND HIROKO SUE HARA

1980   Hare. In *Subarctic*, ed. June Helm. *Handbook of North American Indians*, vol. 6, 314–25. Washington DC: Smithsonian Institution.

SAVOIE, DONAT, ED.

1971   *Les Amérindiens du Nord-Ouest Canadien au 19e siècle selon Emi-*

References

le Petitot. Vol. 2: Les Indiens Loucheux. Mackenzie Delta Research Project 10. Ottawa: Department of Indian Afairs and Northern Development.

SCHOLTE, BOB

1970   Toward a self-reflective anthropology: An introduction with some examples. *Critical Anthropology* 1(2): 3–33.

SCHUTZ, ALFRED

1967   *Collected papers 1: The problem of social reality.* The Hague: Martinus Nijhoff.

SCOLLON, RONALD, AND SUSAN B. K. SCOLLON

1979   *Linguistic convergence: An ethnography of speaking at Fort Chipewyan, Alberta.* London: Academic Press.

1983   *Narrative, literacy, and face in interethnic communication.* Norwood NJ: Ablex.

SHARP, HENRY STEPHEN

1976   Man: Wolf: Woman: Dog. *Arctic Anthropology* 13(1): 25–31.

1986   Shared experience and magical death: Chipewyan explanations of a prophet's decline. *Ethnology* 24:257–70.

1987   Giant fish, giant otters, and dinosaurs: "Apparently irrational beliefs" in a Chipewyan community. *American Ethnologist* 14:226–35.

1988a   *The transformation of Bigfoot: Maleness, power, and belief among the Chipewyan.* Smithsonian Series in Ethnographic Inquiry, no. 9. Washington DC: Smithsonian Institution.

1988b   Dry meat and gender: The absence of Chipewyan ritual for the regulation of hunting and animal numbers. In *Hunters and gatherers 2: Property, power, and ideology,* ed. Tim Ingold, David Riches, and James Woodburn, 183–91. Oxford: Berg.

1994   The power of weakness. In *Key issues in hunter-gatherer research,* ed. Ernest S. Burch Jr. and Linda J. Ellanna, 35–58. Oxford: Berg.

1995   Asymmetric equals: Women and men among the Chipewyan. In *Women and power in native North America,* ed. Laura F. Klein and Lillian A. Ackerman, 46–74. Norman: University of Oklahoma Press.

SHARROCK, WES, AND BOB ANDERSON

1986   *The ethnomethodologists.* London: Tavistock.

SHARROCK, WES, AND RODNEY WATSON

1988   Anatomy among social theories: The incarnation of social structures. In *Actions and structure: Research methods and social theory,* ed. Nigel G. Fielding, 56–72. London: Sage.

References

SHWEDER, RICHARD A.

1985 Menstrual pollution, soul loss, and the comparative study of emotions. In *Culture and depression: Studies in the anthropology of cross-cultural psychiatry of affect and disorder*, ed. Arthur Kleinman and Byron Good, 182–215. Berkeley: University of California Press.

1991 *Thinking through cultures: Expeditions in cultural psychology.* Cambridge MA: Harvard University Press.

SHWEDER, RICHARD A., MANAMOHAN MAHAPATRA, AND JOAN G. MILLER

1987 Culture and moral development. In *The emergence of morality in young children*, ed. Jerome Klagan and Sharon Lamb, 1–83. Chicago: University of Chicago Press.

SIMON, STEVE

1995 *Healing waters: The pilgrimage to Lac Ste. Anne.* Edmonton: University of Alberta Press.

SLOBODIN, RICHARD

1960 Some social functions of Kutchin anxiety. *American Anthropologist* 62(1): 122–33.

1962 *Band organization of the Peel River Kutchin.* Bulletin 179. Ottawa: National Museum of Canada.

1966 *Métis of the Mackenzie District.* Ottawa: Centre Canadien de Recherches en Anthropologie/Canadian Research Centre for Anthropology; Université Saint-Paul/Saint Paul University.

1969 Leadership and participation in a Kutchin trapping party. In *Contributions to anthropology: Band societies: Proceedings of the Conference on Band Organization, Ottawa, 30 August to 2 September 1965*, ed. David J. Damas, 56–92. Bulletin 228. Ottawa: National Museums of Canada.

1970 Kutchin concepts of reincarnation. *Western Canadian Journal of Anthropology* 2:67–79.

1975 Canadian subarctic Athapaskans in the literature to 1965. *Canadian Review of Sociology and Anthropology* 12:278–89.

1994a Kutchin concepts of reincarnation. In *Amerindian rebirth: Reincarnation beliefs among North American Indians and Inuit*, ed. Antonia Mills and Richard Slobodin, 136–55. Toronto: University of Toronto Press.

1994b The study of reincarnation in indigenous American cultures: Some comments. In *Amerindian rebirth: Reincarnation beliefs among North American Indians and Inuit*, ed.

References

Antonia Mills and Richard Slobodin, 284–97. Toronto:
University of Toronto Press.

SLUKA, JEFFREY A.

1990   Participant observation in violent social contexts. *Human
Organization* 49(2): 114–26.

SMITH, CAROLYN D., AND WILLIAM KORNBLUM, EDS.

1996   *In the field: Readings on the field research experience.* 2d ed.
New York: Praeger.

SMITH, DAVID M.

1973   *Inkonze: Magico-religious beliefs of contact-traditional Chipewyan trading at Fort Resolution, NWT, Canada.* National Museum of Man, Mercury Series, Ethnology Division, no. 6.
Ottawa: National Museums of Canada.

1982   *Moose-Deer Island House people: A history of the Native people
of Fort Resolution.* National Museum of Man, Mercury Series, Canadian Ethnology Service, no. 81. Ottawa: National Museums of Canada.

1985   Big stone foundations: Manifest meaning in Chipewyan
myths. *Journal of American Culture* 8:73–77.

1988   The concept of medicine-power in Chipewyan thought.
Manuscript.

1990   The Chipewyan medicine fight in cultural and ecological
perspective. In *Culture and the anthropological tradition: Essays in honor of Robert F. Spencer,* ed. Gretchen Chesley
Lang, 153–75. New York: University Press of America.

1992   The dynamics of a Dene struggle for self-detetermination.
Anthropologica 34:21–49.

1993   Albert's power: A fiction narrative. *Anthropology and Humanism* 18(2): 67–73.

n.d.   An Athapaskan way of knowing: Chipewyan ontology.
Manuscript.

SMITH, JAMES G. E.

1987   The Western Woods Cree: Anthropological myth and historical reality. *American Ethnologist* 14:434–48.

SPIER, LESLIE

1935   The Prophet Dance of the Northwest and its derivatives:
The source of the Ghost Dance. *American Anthropologist,*
General Series in Anthropology 1.

SPIRO, MELFORD E.

1969   The psychological function of witchcraft belief: The Burmese case. In *Mental health research in Asia and the Pacific,* ed.

References

William Caudill and Tsung-yi Lin. Honolulu: East-West
Center Press.

1970 *Buddhism and society.* New York: Harper & Row.

1978 *Burmese supernaturalism.* Expanded ed. Philadelphia: Institute for the Study of Human Issues.

1987 Some reflections on cultural determinism and relativism
with special reference to emotion and reason. In *Culture
and nature: Theoretical papers of Melford Spiro,* ed. Benjamin
Kilborne and L. L. Langness, 32–58. Chicago: University
of Chicago Press.

STEINBRING, JACK H.

1981 Saulteux of Lake Winnipeg. In *Subarctic,* ed. June Helm.
Handbook of North American Indians, vol. 6, 244–55. Washington DC: Smithsonian Institution.

STEPHEN, MICHELE

1989 Dreaming and the hidden self: Mekeo definitions of con-
sciousness. In *The religious imagination in New Guinea,* ed.
Gilbert Herdt and Michele Stephen, 160–86. New
Brunswick NJ: Rutgers University Press.

STETS, JAN E.

1995 Role identities and person identities: Gender identity,
mastery identity, and controlling one's partner. *Sociological
Perspectives* 38(2): 129–50.

STEVENSON, IAN

1975 *Cases of the reincarnation type. Vol. 1: Ten cases from India.*
Charlottesville: University Press of Virginia.

STEVENSON, WINONÁ

1996 The journals and voices of a Church of England Native
catechist: Askenootow (Charles Pratt), 1851–1884. In
Reading beyond words: Contexts in narrative history, ed. Jennifer S. H. Brown and Elizabeth Vibert, 304–29. Peterborough ON: Broadview Press.

STOCKING, GEORGE W. JR.

1987 *Victorian anthropology.* New York: Free Press.

1991 Maclay, Kubary, Malinowski: Archetypes from the dreamtime of anthropology. In *Colonial situations: Essays on the
contextualization of ethnographic knowledge,* ed. George W.
Stocking Jr., 9–74. Madison: University of Wisconsin
Press.

STOLLER, PAUL

1995 Ethnographies as texts—Ethnographers as griots. *American Ethnologist* 21(2): 353–66.

323

References

STOLLER, PAUL, AND CHERYL OLKES

1987   *In sorcery's shadow: A memoir of apprenticeship among the Songhay of Niger.* Chicago: University of Chicago Press.

STRATHERN, MARILYN

1993   Making incomplete. In *Carved flesh/cast selves: Gendered symbols and social practices*, ed. Vigdis Broch-Due, Ingrid Rudie, and Tone Bleie, 41–52. Cross-Cultural Perspectives on Women, vol. 8. Oxford: Berg.

STRAUSS, CLAUDIA, AND NAOMI QUINN

1993   A cognitive/cultural anthropology. In *Assessing developments in anthropology*, ed. Robert Borofsky. New York: McGraw-Hill.

TAMBIAH, STANLEY J.

1970   *Buddhism in translations.* Cambridge MA: Harvard University Press.

1990   *Magic, science, religion, and the scope of rationality.* Cambridge: Cambridge University Press.

TANNER, ADRIAN

1976   *Bringing home animals: Religious ideology and mode of production of the Mistassini Cree hunters.* New York: St. Martin's.

TAPPER, RICHARD

1988   Animality, humanity, morality, society. In *What is an animal?* ed. Tim Ingold, 44–62. London: Unwin Hyman.

TEDLOCK, BARBARA

1981   Quiché Maya dream interpretation. *Ethos* 9:313–30.

1991a   From participant observation to the observation of participation. *Journal of Anthropological Research* 47:69–94.

1991b   The new anthropology of dreaming. *Dreaming* 1(2): 161–78.

1992   *The beautiful and the dangerous: Dialogues with the Zuni Indians.* New York: Penguin.

TEDLOCK, DENNIS

1990   *Days from a dream almanac.* Urbana: University of Illinois Press.

1995   Interpretation, participation, and the role of narrative in dialogical anthropology. In *The dialogic emergence of culture*, ed. Dennis Tedlock and Bruce Mannheim, 253–87. Urbana: University of Illinois Press.

TEDLOCK, DENNIS, AND BRUCE MANNHEIM

1995   Introduction. In *The dialogic emergence of culture*, ed. Dennis Tedlock and Bruce Mannheim, 1–33. Urbana: University of Illinois Press.

References

TEDLOCK, DENNIS, AND BARBARA TEDLOCK, EDS.

1975   *Teachings of the American earth: Indian religion and philosophy.*
New York: Liveright.

THOMPSON, DAVID

1916   *David Thompson's narrative of his explorations in western North
America, 1784–1812.* Toronto: Champlain Society.

TRIGGER, BRUCE

1976   *Children of the Aataentsic.* Montreal: McGill University Press.

TURNER, EDITH

1996   *The hands feel it: Healing and spirit presence among a northern
Alaskan people.* DeKalb: Northern Illinois University Press.

TURNER, EDITH, WITH WILLIAM BLODGETT, SINGLETON
KAHONA, AND FIDELI BENWA

1992   *Experiencing ritual: A new interpretation of African healing.*
Philadelphia: University of Pennsylvania Press.

TURNER, VICTOR W.

1968   *The drums of affliction.* Oxford: Clarendon Press.

1975   *Revelation and divination in Ndembu ritual.* Ithaca NY: Cornell University Press.

1985   *On the edge of the bush: Anthropology as experience.* Ed. Edith
L. B. Turner. Tucson: University of Arizona Press.

1986   Dewey, Dilthey, and drama: An essay in the anthropology of
experience. In *The anthropology of experience,* ed. Victor W.
Turner and Edward M. Bruner, 33–44. Urbana: University
of Illinois Press.

VALENTINE, LISA PHILIPS

1995   *Making it their own: Severn Ojibwe communicative practices.*
Toronto: University of Toronto Press.

VANDERBURG, ROSAMUND M.

1977   *I am Nokomis too: The biography of Patronella Johnston.* Don
Mills ON: General.

VANDERSTEENE, ROGER

1960   *Wabasca: Dix ans de vie indienne.* Gemmenich, Belgium:
Editions O.M.I.

VAN MAANEN, JOHN

1988   *Tales of the field: On writing ethnography.* Chicago: University
of Chicago Press.

1995   An end to innocence: The ethnography of ethnography.
In *Representation in ethnography,* ed. John Van Maanen, 1–
35. London: Sage.

VAN STONE, JAMES W.

1963   *The Snowdrift Chipewyan.* Ottawa: Northern Coordination

References

and Research Centre, Department of Northern Affairs
and National Resources.

1974 *Athapaskan adaptations: Hunters and fishermen of the subarctic
forests.* Chicago: Aldine.

WADDELL, JACK, AND MICHAEL EVERETT

1980 *Drinking behavior among southwestern Indians.* Tucson: University of Arizona Press.

WATSON, GRAHAM

1979 On getting nothing back: Managing the meaning of ethnicity in Canada's Northwest Territories. *Ethnos* 1–2:99–118.

1981 The reification of ethnicity and its political consequences in the North. *Canadian Review of Sociology and Anthropology/Revue Canadienne de Sociologie et d'Anthropologie* 8(4): 453–69.

1991 Rewriting culture. In *Recapturing anthropology: Working in the present,* ed. Richard G. Fox, 73–92. Santa Fe NM: School of American Research Press.

1992 *Twenty-nine lines of fieldnotes.* Manchester Occasional Papers, no. 34. Manchester: University of Manchester.

1994 A comparison of social constructionist and ethnomethodological descriptions of how a judge distinguished between the erotic and the obscene. *Philosophy of the Social Sciences* 24(4): 405–25.

1996 Listening to the Native: The non-ironic alternative to "dialogic" ethnography (as well as to functionalism, Marxism, and structuralism). *Canadian Review of Sociology and Anthropology/Revue Canadienne de Sociologie et d'Anthropologie* 33(1): 73–88.

WATSON, GRAHAM, AND JEAN-GUY A. GOULET

1992 Gold in, gold out: The objectivation of Dene Tha dreams and visions. *Journal of Anthropological Research* 48(3): 215–30.

1998 What can ethnomethodology say about power? *Qualitative Inquiry* 4(1): 96–113.

WATSON, GRAHAM, AND ANN IRWIN

1996 The mundane miracle of social order. *Ethnos* 61(1–2): 85–102.

WATSON, RODNEY

1992 The understanding of language use in everyday life: Is there a common ground? In *Text in context: Contributions to ethnomethodology,* ed. Graham Watson and Robert M. Seiler, 1–19. Newbury Park CA: Sage.

326

References

WATSON-FRANKE, MARIA BARBARA

1981   Dreaming as world view and action in Guajiro culture. *Journal of Latin American Lore* 7(2): 239–54.

WAUGH, EARLE H.

1996   *Dissonant worlds: Roger Vandersteene among the Cree.* Waterloo ON: Wilfrid Laurier University Press.

WAUGH, EARLE H., AND K. DAD PRITHIPAUL, EDS.

1979   *Native religious traditions: Proceedings of the Joint International Symposium of Elders and Scholars, Edmonton, Alberta, 1977.* Waterloo ON: Wilfrid Laurier University Press.

WAX, ROSALIE H., AND ROBERT K. THOMAS

1972   American Indians and white people. In *Native Americans today: Sociological perspectives,* ed. Howard M. Bahr, Bruce Chadwick, and Robert D. Day, 31–42. New York: Harper & Row.

WHITE, BRUCE

1982   Give us a little milk: The social and cultural meanings of gift giving in the Lake Superior fur trade. *Minnesota History* 48(2): 60–71.

1994   Encounters with spirits: Ojibwa and Dakota theories about the French and their merchandise. *Ethnohistory* 41(3): 369–405.

WIERZBICKA, ANNA

1989   Soul and mind: Linguistic evidence for ethnopsychology and cultural history. *American Anthropologist* 91(1): 41–58.

WIKAN, UNNI

1991   Toward an experience-near anthropology. *Cultural Anthropology* 6(3): 285–305.

WILLIAMS, WALTER L.

1997   Amazons of America: Female gender variance. In *Gender in cross-cultural perspective,* ed. Caroline B. Brettell and Carolyn F. Sargent, 202–13. Englewood Cliffs NJ: Prentice-Hall.

WILLIAMSON, R. G.

1955   Slave Indian legends. *Anthropologica* 1:119–43.

1956   Slave Indian legends. *Anthropologica* 2:61–92.

WILSON, MONICA

1951   Witch beliefs and social structure. *American Journal of Sociology* 56:307–13.

1971   *Religion and the transformation of society.* Cambridge: Cambridge University Press.

References

WOLF, ERIK

1982   *Europe and the people without history*. Berkeley: University of California Press.

WOOLGAR, STEVE

1988   Reflexivity is the ethnographer of the text. In *Knowledge and reflexivity: New frontiers in the sociology of knowledge*, ed. Steve Woolgar, 14–34. London: Sage.

YOUNG, DAVID, AND JEAN-GUY A. GOULET, EDS.

1994   *Being changed by cross-cultural encounters: The anthropology of extraordinary experience*. Peterborough ON: Broadview Press.

YOUNG, DAVID, GRANT INGRAM, AND LISE SWARTZ

1989   *Cry of the eagle: Encounters with a Cree healer*. Toronto: University of Toronto Press.

Index

Abel, Kerry, 193, 204–5, 271 n.2,
280 n.5
adoption, xxiii
aggression: as accounted for by anthropologists, 111–13, 272 n.4,
273 n.5; as accounted for by
Dene Tha, 14, 113–15, 117–18,
131, 134–35, 137
alcohol in relation to: deaths, 13;
drinking parties, 124; drunkenness, 121, 142; fighting, 13, 79,
118–21; flow of cash, 124–25; intrusion of Western powers, 110,
128; rates of criminal arrests, 124,
violent behavior, 13, 79, 112, 115,
117, 127–28. See also bootlegging
Algonkian band, 84
angel, 187–89, 229
Anglican, 167, 193
animal helper, 65–66, 73, 78, 148–
49; Canada goose as, 77; deer as,
75–77; eagle as, 74, 269 n.6; fox
as, 81; marten as, 129; owl as, 93–
94; ptarmigan as, 72; spider as,
74; unicorn as, 67; wolf as, 70, 81,
149. See also gift; transformation
into animal
animals as game, 231; as object of
respect, 63–64. See also hunting;
trapping
animals as other-than-human-per-
sons, xxix, 62, 73, 270 n.9. See also
animal helper
anthropological task, xiv, 249–50,
258; autobiographical aspects of,
xxxvii; ethical concerns of, xxxvi,
267 n.1; theoretical orientations
of, 258, 265 n.16, 268 n.1, 286
n.4. See also fieldwork; methods
Arbet, xx, 207
Asch, Michael I., 261 n.2, 263 n.6
Assumption, xviii
Athapaskans. See Dene
atmospheric conditions: as expression of emotions, xxvii–xxviii,
135, 143
autonomy: as goal of education,
37–39, 47, 58; as value in adult

social interaction, 27, 36–37, 42,
54, 109, 111, 121, 126, 129, 247,
267 n.1, 272 n.3
Azande, 135–36, 273 n.7

Barth, Frederick, ix, xxi, 1, 25, 102,
252–53
Beaudry, Nicole, 56, 217, 230, 282
n.14, 284 n.1
Beaver, 83–84, 102, 130, 212, 226,
275 n.3, 284 n.2 n.5; See also
Dunne-za
Benedict, Ruth, 65–66
Bible, 207
bilingualism, xxiv, 8, 248
Blondin, George, 207
blood, 91, 92, 106. See also menstrual
blood
Boas, 221
body, 142
bootlegging, 125
bossiness. See autonomy
Breynat, 10
Briggs, Jean, 270 n.10
Bruner, Edward M., xxvi, xxxviii,
83–84

carnival, 47–49, 81
categorization: function of, 101,
105; of white man as childlike,
270 n.10. See also membershipping; us/them dichotomy
cemetery, 75
Chateh, xviii. See also Habay
Chipewyan, 64, 85, 131, 173, 275 n.1
Christ. See Jesus
Christianity, xxvi, 203. See also conversion to Christianity
clothing: association with self, 94,
99; care of, 96–97, 100; disposal
of, 98; use in baptism, 99
communication: non-verbal, xxx,
xxxi, 1–2, 95–96; verbal, xxx, 25,
33–34, 54. See also instruction;
learning by observation
competency, xli, 247–48, 255
confidentiality, xxxv
conflict, defined, 110

Index

Printed in the United States
122193LV00003B/25-42/A

9 780803 270749